■ DIRECTORY MANAGEMENT

Function Number	DOS Version	Description
39h	2.0	Create subdirectory.
3Ah	2.0	Remove subdirectory.
47h	2.0	Get current default directory.
3Bh	2.0	Set default directory.

■ FILE AND DEVICE MANAGEMENT

TRADITIONAL FCB FUNCTIONS

Function Number	DOS Version	Description
0Fh	1.0	Open file.
16h	1.0	Create file.
10h	1.0	Close file.
11h	1.0	Find first matching file.
12h	1.0	Find next matching file.
13h	1.0	Delete file.
17h	1.0	Rename file.
23h	1.0	Get file size.
29h	1.0	Parse file name.

HANDLE FUNCTIONS

Function Number	DOS Version	Description
3Ch	2.0	Create a file.
5Bh	3.0	Create a new file (fails if file exists).
5Ah	3.0	Create a unique file.
3Dh	2.0	Open file.
6Ch	4.0	Extended open/create (combines services of functions 3Dh, 3Ch, and 5Bh).
3Eh	2.0	Close file.
41h	2.0	Delete a file from a specified directory.
43h	2.0	Change file mode.
45h	2.0	Get new duplicate file handle.
46h	2.0	Force duplication of existing file handle.
4Eh	2.0	Find first matching file.
4Fh	2.0	Find next matching file.
56h	2.0	Rename a file.
57h	2.0	Get/set a file's date and time.
67h	3.3	Set file handle count.
68h	3.3	Flush file data and update directory entry.

Inside DOS:
A Programmer's
Guide

INSIDE DOS®:
A PROGRAMMER'S
GUIDE

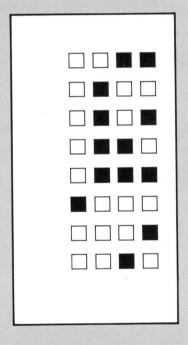

Michael J. Young

SYBEX® San Francisco • Paris • Düsseldorf • Soest

Acquisitions Editor: Dianne King
Editors: Bonnie Gruen, Joanne Cuthbertson, Jon Strickland
Technical Editor: Steve Cavender
Word Processor: Bob Myren
Book Designer: Nancy Webb
Typesetters: Olivia Shinomoto, Elizabeth Newman
Proofreaders: Ed Lin, Rhonda Holmes
Cover Designer: Thomas Ingalls + Associates
Cover Photographer: David Bishop

Library of Congress Card Number: 90-70346
ISBN: 0-89588-710-X

Manufactured in the United States of America
10 9 8 7 6 5 4 3 2 1

ACKNOWLEDGMENTS

It was a pleasure writing this book for SYBEX. First, I would like to thank Dianne King for recruiting me into the project and for her great support. I would like to thank Rudolph Langer for his ideas, enthusiasm, and for providing me the perfect balance of guidance and freedom during the project. I would also like to thank Bonnie Gruen for patiently editing many pages of complex information, and Joanne Cuthbertson and Jon Strickland for their attention to detail throughout the manuscript. Finally, I would like to thank all the other people who contributed to the book: Steve Cavender, technical reviewer; Bob Myren, word processor; Olivia Shinomoto, typesetter; Ed Lin, proofreader; Nancy Webb, designer; and Helen Bruno, production artist. I am also grateful to Microsoft for providing software for developing the programs.

CONTENTS AT A GLANCE

TABLE OF CONTENTS

CHAPTER 6: Other Resources in MS-DOS Machines   125

CHAPTER 7: Compatibility vs. Performance   165

■□ PART 3: Devices

□■ CHAPTER 8: Fast Video Display 195

□■ CHAPTER 9: The Anatomy of a Device Driver 255

▪▫ Part 4: Memory Management

▫▪ Chapter 10: Expanded Memory: A C Interface   295

▫▪ Chapter 11: Memory Residency   321

⬛ PART 5: OS/2 Compatibility

INTRODUCTION

This is a book about achieving optimal performance for programs written to run under the MS-DOS operating system. It is neither a broad survey nor a general MS-DOS programmer's reference manual, but rather an in-depth treatment of selected advanced topics, together with many complete source listings in both C and assembly language. The collection of topics is quite diverse. However, there is a common unifying theme: all of the subject areas treated have a direct and significant impact on software performance. The book emphasizes practical techniques and concrete examples rather than theoretical issues or general information. This is a book written for the experienced programmer who is developing a new application, enhancing an existing program, or porting code to an MS-DOS machine from another system, and who wants to attain optimal software performance by taking full advantage of the rich set of resources available under MS-DOS.

A good computer program performs its functions reliably and accurately. A high-performance program, however, is one that goes beyond basic competence and correctness, and offers another dimension of features. The concept of high performance includes not only fast execution speed, but also compact code size, an attractive and easily used console interface, large data capacity, flexibility, robustness, and compatibility with a wide variety of software and hardware environments.

Achieving high performance is especially critical for today's software developer. The early microcomputer user was easily impressed; almost any competent application could achieve a level of success. In the 1980s, however, expectations for software performance have become much higher, and the challenge to software developers has become much greater. There are several reasons for this trend. First, microcomputers are being used for much more complex and demanding tasks such as financial analysis, retrieval of information from large databases, computer-aided design, desktop publishing, and artificial intelligence. Also, the software market has become fiercely competitive due to the proliferation of sophisticated and finely tuned applications available commercially as well as in the public domain. Favorable software reviews and wide market exposure are both quite difficult to obtain. Finally, a wide variety of new software operating environments and peripheral equipment can permit a greater level of performance, but they can also place added demands on the programmer to develop new interfaces and to follow new rules necessary for maintaining compatibility.

Two general ingredients are needed to develop high-performance software. The first ingredient consists of sound basic programming techniques: structuring the program design, writing efficient algorithms, and implementing effective data structures. These are the general theoretical issues at the heart of computer science, and are important abstract elements for writing high-performance software in any computer language, and for any machine. The second ingredient concerns the specific target machine and operating system: making optimal use of the development tools available for that target machine, and making optimal use of the hardware and software resources present in that computer system. This book deals with the second ingredient, and assumes that the reader is already familiar with the first.

▪ Overview of the Book

This book addresses two primary aspects of writing high-performance software under MS-DOS. The first aspect is selecting the best development tools available and learning to make optimal use of these tools (Part 1). The second aspect is using these development tools to fully exploit the resources of the MS-DOS environment (Parts 2, 3, and 4).

▪ Part 1: The Tools

Part 1 discusses the selection and use of software development tools, including compilers, assemblers, commercial software libraries, profilers, and debuggers. The emphasis is on advanced techniques to enhance software performance.

Chapter 1: Systems Programming in C and Assembler

Chapter 1 begins by describing the unique advantages of C and assembler as the primary development languages, and justifies the selection of these languages for the examples in this book. It then discusses where to use C, where to use assembler, and techniques for making optimal use of each language.

Chapter 2: Interfacing C and Assembler

This chapter focuses on the methods for using C and assembler in concert—how a C program can call an assembler procedure and how an assembler program can call a C function. It also presents source code templates that can facilitate the development of programs that combine C and assembly language.

Chapter 3: Debugging

Chapter 3 discusses the tools and techniques for dealing with the software bugs that inevitably arise when writing high-performance programs.

Part 2: The Resources

Part 2 is a comprehensive treatment of the vast array of hardware and software resources that are present in an MS-DOS machine. The emphasis is on the practical use of these resources to enhance software performance.

Chapter 4: Interrupts and the DOS Functions

Chapter 4 begins with a discussion of the important interrupt mechanism, and then focuses specifically on the MS-DOS function calls that are accessed through software interrupts. This chapter, as well as Chapter 5, emphasizes selection strategies and concrete coding examples.

Chapter 5: The BIOS Functions

Chapter 5 continues the discussion of functions that are available in an MS-DOS machine with a treatment of the low-level services provided by the BIOS (Basic Input Output System).

Chapter 6: Other Resources in MS-DOS Machines

This chapter completes the basic discussion of the resources present in an MS-DOS machine by presenting a diverse but practical collection of techniques.

Chapter 7: Compatibility vs. Performance

Because optimal software performance often requires directly accessing machine specific features, the question of compatibility naturally arises. This chapter argues that high performance and compatibility are not mutually exclusive, and presents methods for a program to determine the resources that are present in the machine at runtime.

Part 3: Devices

Once an overview of the resources of an MS-DOS machine has been presented, Part 3 begins a series of in-depth treatments of selected important resources. Both chapters in Part 3 deal with external devices.

Chapter 8: Fast Video Display

The efficiency and appearance of the video display is of paramount importance to a high-performance application. This chapter compares the different methods for generating controlled screen output, presents the complete assembly language source code for an interactive screen designer, and provides a comprehensive set of video display and window management functions that can be called from a C program.

Chapter 9: The Anatomy of a Device Driver

One of the most unique and valuable resources in an MS-DOS system is the installable device driver. Chapter 9 describes the structure and use of device drivers, and presents the source code for a generic device driver that can be used to quickly generate a functional device interface.

Part 4: Memory Management

Previous sections deal with making optimal use of the standard services offered by MS-DOS. This section, however, presents strategies for stretching MS-DOS beyond two of its primary limitations: the 640K upper limit on memory and the lack of multitasking. Part 3 explores the use of external devices; Part 4 deals with the primary internal milieu of the computer system: random access memory.

Chapter 10: Expanded Memory: A C Interface

One of the most successful strategies for overcoming the inherent memory limitation of MS-DOS is the expanded memory specification. This chapter describes this important resource, and presents a complete set of functions that can be called from a C program to manage expanded memory.

Chapter 11: Memory Residency

Although graphics-based multitasking environments are the microcomputer interface of the future, text-based memory-resident utilities are still the highest performing and most practical method for extending the computing power of MS-DOS. This chapter describes in detail the low-level tactics necessary to develop a memory-resident utility; it also presents a complete set of assembler functions that allow a normal C program to be converted to a memory-resident utility through a single function call.

Part 5: OS/2 Compatibility

Chapter 12: Writing Programs for the OS/2 DOS-Compatibility Environment

Although MS-DOS promises to have a long lifetime, the OS/2 operating system is now on the horizon. This chapter shows you how to write MS-DOS programs so that they will successfully run within the DOS-compatibility environment provided by OS/2.

Appendices

This final section presents important information relevant to the topics treated in the book. This information is collected in the appendices and presented in tabular form to provide a convenient reference source. It should help obviate the need to thumb through the text when developing programs. The appendices include an interrupt vector table, a brief summary of the MS-DOS interrupt services, a relatively complete survey of the BIOS interrupt functions, the structure of the program segment prefix, a memory map, a table of port addresses, a synopsis of the functions presented in this book that may be called from a C program, and, finally, a bibliography.

Suggested Background and Required Materials

The presentations in this book assume a basic understanding of C and 8086/88 assembly language programming, and a familiarity with the use of MS-DOS. For readers who are a little shaky in any of these areas, several good background books are recommended in Appendix H. The only essential reference book is the *DOS Technical Reference* (from IBM, or a version from another OEM), which is also cited in the bibliography. This is a well organized and essential reference source, and contains important information necessary to use the DOS functions that is not duplicated in this book. The bibliography also includes other reference books that are less vital, but yet quite valuable.

All of the programs in this book were developed using either the Microsoft Macro Assembler, version 5.1, or the Microsoft C compiler, version 5.1 (the regular compiler version, not QuickC).

They were tested under PC-DOS versions 2.1, 3.2, 3.3, and 4.0. For programmers using other compilers or assemblers, the general principles remain unchanged, but details of the implementations will need to be modified.

Companion Disk Set

For readers who are not great enthusiasts of typing, and who would like enhanced versions of some of the utilities presented in the book as well as a number of additional programs, a *Performance Programming Toolkit* companion disk set is available. Details for ordering these disks are given at the end of the book. The following files are included:

- All source code listings as they are presented in this book, in ASCII format and ready to compile or assemble

- The executable versions of all programs in the book

- A significantly enhanced version of the screen designer presented in Chapter 8, written entirely in C

- An enhanced set of screen and window management functions, callable from C

- Additional utilities and functions that are not included in the book

Feedback

I always welcome your feedback, ideas, and questions. I may be reached through Compuserve (ID 75156.2572), or at the following address:

Michael J. Young

Software Engineering

P.O. Box 5068

Mill Valley, CA 94942

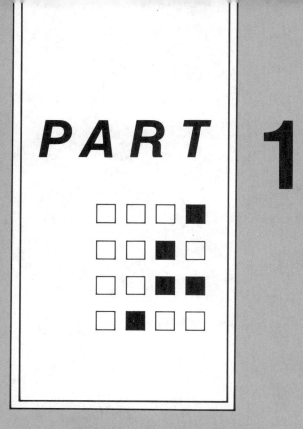

PART 1

THE TOOLS

CHAPTER 1

Systems Programming in C and Assembler

The first steps in achieving high-performance software are selecting the most powerful development tools available, and then making optimal use of these tools. The computer language is the most important development tool, and in order to make full use of the resources available under MS-DOS, a language must be capable of efficient systems level programming. This chapter discusses the reasons for choosing both C and assembler as the primary development languages, and presents techniques for optimizing their use.

Why C and Assembler?

Although C and assembler are rapidly becoming the standard among software developers, the question of which computer language is the best development tool is still open to debate. C is a relatively modern high-level language, but certainly not the most advanced in terms of contemporary software engineering theory. Assembler was supposedly supplanted by high level languages long ago, and is considered by some to be a vestige from the dark ages of computer programming. Why, then, have these two languages been chosen for this book?

Before answering this question and discussing the unique advantages of C and assembler, a good starting point is to examine three of the alternative languages currently available.

Alternative Languages

Pascal

Pascal is a reliable and well structured general purpose language. However, it also has many constraints that greatly limit its use in developing high-performance software. First, Pascal's standard definition severely limits access to low level resources such as individual bits, specific memory locations, and ports. Also, the standard language has very primitive file handling capabilities, and enforces severe type restrictions. Most versions of Pascal for MS-DOS have many enhancements, but since the added features are not part of the standard definition of the language, they vary greatly among implementations. Specific versions of Pascal have a proprietary cast, and software using the enhancements tends to be nonportable.

In addition, some popular versions of Pascal do not support the development of large applications, do not allow separate compilation of individual files, and are not easily interfaced with assembly language modules. Finally, there are not nearly as many compilers, support libraries, and programming tools available for Pascal as for C.

Modula-2 and Ada

Modula-2 and Ada are two of the most sophisticated contemporary languages; they embody many advanced concepts of software engineering such as data abstraction, code encapsulation, concurrency, and exception handling. However, these languages tend to be bulky and complex (especially Ada). They are designed primarily to optimize the development and maintenance of large applications by teams of programmers, and to support the correctness and reliability of the program.

Few Modula-2 or Ada implementations are currently available for MS-DOS. In addition, these languages have a limited supply of third-party libraries and other tools, and it is difficult, if not impossible, to link program modules with Microsoft assembler files.

The Advantages of C and Assembler

The chief advantage of C and assembler is performance. If Ada and Modula-2 are the Rolls Royces of software development, then C and assembler are the Maseratis.

Advantages of C

C is a small and sleek language, and there are currently many excellent optimizing compilers for the MS-DOS environment that produce efficient and compact code. C is also highly suited to directly accessing operating system and machine resources. Furthermore, low-level operations such as manipulating bits and accessing specific memory locations are intrinsic to the language definition, and therefore tend to be standard among different implementations. Thus, C, which was designed as a systems language, is ideal for enhancing software performance through accessing systems-level resources.

In addition to the intrinsic low-level operations included in the C language definition, most compilers for MS-DOS machines have a large and relatively uniform set of system-specific library functions for such purposes as accessing interrupt routines, dealing with segmented memory, obtaining system error codes, determining the operating system version, accessing the environment and program segment prefix (see Chapter 6), locking records for multiuser systems, and accessing ports.

Whereas languages such as Pascal have tended to become less standard as vendors add necessary enhancements, C implementations are becoming more uniform. The ANSI (American National Standards Institute) standardization committee is currently developing a standard for C to resolve some of the ambiguities found in the original Kernighan and Ritchie definition, as well as to sanction certain common language enhancements. The defined core of operations and reserved words in C is quite small; however, a significant part of the ANSI standard is an enumeration of a standard library that will effectively expand the language in a uniform manner.

Standardization of a language translates to portability for the developer, a significant asset for the programmer targeting an application for more than one machine. In addition to the intrinsic portability of C, some vendors (such as Manx Software Systems) offer an entire line of C compilers and cross-compilers for a wide variety of machines.

Another distinct advantage of C is that there are more development tools available for it than for any other language under MS-DOS. These include:

- Third-party libraries (for example, graphics, screen design, file management, and communications)
- Interpreters
- Precompilers
- Code beautifiers
- Lint utilities
- Translators from other languages
- Overlay linkers
- Library utilities
- Structured editors
- Profilers

□□■□

- Source debuggers
- Books, video tutorials, seminars, and classes

C also supports the linking of separately compiled source files, and interfaces easily with Microsoft assembly language modules. Also, C is generally the first language to become available for new programming environments, such as Microsoft Windows and OS/2.

Users and programmers often ask whether C, which is rather spare and low-level, is a good application language, especially for business systems. Given the flexibility of the language and the current availability of third party support libraries, the answer is a strong yes. The very spare nature of the language prevents the developer from being locked into a fixed set of functions for file I/O, screen handling, and other purposes. Rather, the programmer can choose from a great variety of sophisticated and highly specialized function libraries, or better yet, can write his own.

After choosing C, the next step is selecting a particular compiler. Fortunately, much information on this topic is available. In fact, comparative articles on C compilers may be the single most popular topic found in programmer's magazines. The two that I have used most extensively are Microsoft and Aztec:

Microsoft (version 5.1)   I have chosen the Microsoft C compiler (version 5.1) for this book and for most of my general development work because of the speed and compactness of the code it produces, its thorough documentation, and its compatibility with the Microsoft Macro Assembler (and other high level languages such as Microsoft FORTRAN). It also compiles efficiently, and comes with an excellent source level debugger, CodeView. (See Chapter 3.)

QuickC   This compiler is included with Microsoft C version 5.1 and is also available as a separate product. It compiles very efficiently and provides an integrated development environment with a built-in editor and compiler. Although useful for developing application prototypes quickly, it performs only limited optimizations and therefore the regular version of the compiler should be used to prepare the final versions of high-performance applications.

Aztec   I have found that this compiler, sold by Manx Software Systems, also produces fast and compact code, and that it likewise compiles very efficiently. Aztec is an especially good choice for developers targeting their code for several different machines, because an entire family of compilers and cross compilers is available from Manx, supporting a wide range of systems. The main drawback of the Aztec compiler for developers already locked into using the Microsoft Macro Assembler or other Microsoft-compatible languages is its lack of object file compatibility with the Microsoft standard, and the need to deal with yet another assembler syntax.

Turbo C   This is a low-cost yet comprehensive compiler from Borland International, which produces compact and efficient code and is easy to use. It includes both a standard command line compiler and linker, and also an integrated, menu-driven development environment with a built-in editor, compiler, and linker. Turbo C programs can be linked directly with Microsoft Macro Assembler object modules, and many C language extensions are provided that facilitate efficient systems level programming. For further information, see the book *Systems Programming in Turbo C*, cited in the Bibliography.

Advantages of Assembler

Assembly language might be considered the ultimate performance tool because it offers the following important advantages:

- It can optimize the speed of a routine down to a single clock cycle.
- It can generate compact code, containing not a single unnecessary byte.
- It allows direct and simple access to any software, firmware, or hardware resource in the system.
- It allows total flexibility in the placement of code and data.

It would be difficult and generally pointless to write a large, general-purpose application entirely in assembler. However, this language is a very valuable adjunct to C. It is also useful for writing certain types of complete programs; in fact, some tasks that need to be performed by a high-performance program virtually require assembly language. The optimal uses for assembler are discussed later in this chapter.

Using C

Given that C and assembly language have been chosen because of their unique advantages, the next consideration is deciding when to use C, when to use assembler, and how each language can be applied to greatest advantage.

My approach is to use C for the large majority of application programming, and to use assembler only for those specific areas of code where it offers a distinct advantage (discussed below).

Commercial C Libraries

One of the primary decisions to be made before embarking on a large C development project is whether to use a commercial library or write custom routines for such functions as ISAM (Indexed Sequential Access Method) file management, screen I/O, and communications.

The advantages of commercial packages are programming speed and economy. For example, writing a set of ISAM file utilities could require months of dedicated programmer time and necessitate extensive study of complex data structures and algorithms.

The best resources for choosing a commercial library are programmer's magazines such as *PC Tech Journal, Dr. Dobb's Journal, Computer Language,* or *Byte.* These magazines not only review these products, but also contain advertisements of suppliers who are quite willing to supply descriptive literature. In terms of flexibility and control, commercial libraries can be divided into three categories:

1. Packages that are supplied in the form of well-documented source code. These allow the programmer to enhance the routines and adapt them to specific environments.

2. Libraries distributed as binary object modules. Although these cannot be modified, they can be linked into the application selectively, offering a degree of control.

3. Memory-resident runtime libraries. These are the least flexible and the most problematic.

Memory-resident runtime library routines are typically supplied in the form of binary code, must be loaded into memory prior to running the application (an inconvenience for the user), and consume a fixed block of memory regardless of which functions are actually called. Needless memory-resident code should be avoided because of potential conflicts with other resident utilities, and also because of the possible need to reboot the system in order to free the memory (especially if another resident module has been loaded on top of it). Memory-resident utilities are popular with vendors because it is easy for them to interface a single set of routines with many different languages, thus widening their market.

However, it is better to use a library written specifically for the development language, that is linked into the executable code, and is preferably provided in source code form.

The advantages of writing custom routines are greater flexibility and enhanced software performance. Programmers who write all supporting functions can attain the ultimate degree of software control. Although some commercial libraries are supplied in the form of source code and can therefore be modified, the prospect of analyzing the highly complex code of another programmer is daunting, and the probability of creating unwanted side effects is high. Also, commercial packages often emphasize generality and portability at the cost of performance, and it should almost always be possible to write higher performance custom routines using the techniques discussed in this book.

The best way to combine the advantages of a commercial product with custom routines might be to concentrate first on the main thread of program logic, using a commercial package to get the application up and running. Then, once the basic program is functioning and the needs for supporting functions clearly defined, the commercial package can be gradually replaced with custom routines. A good starting point for writing your own code would be supporting functions, such as those for screen output, which are relatively easy to implement and offer a significant return in performance (see Chapter 8). Other types of functions, such as ISAM file managers, which are quite complex and difficult to enhance, might best be permanently relegated to commercial packages.

▫▪ Optimizing C Programs
▫▫

General comments on C programming will be brief; much has already been written about C, and a lengthy discussion of high-level language programming is beyond the scope of this book. However, there are a few specific pointers that are important to efficient C programming under MS-DOS and the 8086 family of processors. Several of the following comments apply specifically to Microsoft C, but it should be possible to translate the general ideas into similar features of other compilers.

Analyze the code produced by the compiler   Microsoft C provides two command line options to generate an assembler file when compiling a program. The first option is:

/Fa[filename]

This command line produces an assembly listing, in Microsoft Macro Assembler format. Unlike some compilers, such as Aztec, Microsoft C directly generates an object file, and does not use an intermediate assembly language file. The assembler output is thus only an optional byproduct, and may require hand modification in order to assemble and link without error. (It also does not contain all the information that the compiler places directly in the object file.)

The following, which causes the compiler to include each original source code statement along with the resulting assembler instructions, is an even more useful option:

/Fc[filename]

A third method of examining assembler output is to load the program into the CodeView debugger. The assembler mode shows both source statements and the resultant assembler code. (Of course the pseudo-op instructions to the assembler are not included.) See Chapter 3 for a description of this debugger.

Declare register variables for frequently used counters and pointers in critical areas of code   Note, however, that only two register variables may be allocated within a single function (registers SI and DI are used for this purpose). Therefore, optimize this resource by selecting the most intensively used variables. For example, in the following nested loops, **j** and **k** are the two best choices for register variables:

```
int i;
register int j,k;

for (i = 1; i < = 10;  + + i)
        for (j = 1; j < = 1000;  + + j)
                for (k = 1; k < = 1000;  + + k)
```

If all three variables were indiscriminately declared as register types,

```
register i,j,k;
```

the compiler would ignore the last request, and thus fail to allocate register space to the most heavily used variable.

Use pointers to objects rather than more indirect addressing modes   For example, consider the following array of structures:

```
struct
        {
        int       field1;
        float     field2;
        char      field3 [16];
```

```
        }
    sample [64];
```

If the individual characters of **field3** are frequently accessed, the most efficient method would be to use a pointer, as follows:

```
    char *chptr;

    chptr = sample[8].field3;   /* Once this assignment is made   /*
                                /* subsequent references to       */
                                /* characters of field3 are */ /* very
                                   efficient.                    */

    *chptr++  =  'a';
    *chptr++  =  'b';
    *chptr++  =  'c';
    /* etc. */
```

The following method involves more address calculation and is less efficient:

```
    sample[8].field3[0]  =  'a';   /* Each reference involves        */
    sample[8].field3[1]  =  'b';   /* extensive address calculation.  */
    sample[8].field3[2]  =  'c';
    /* etc. */
```

Use the smallest memory model possible to maximize the compactness and efficiency of the code   One factor is that data pointers in the small and medium models are 16 bits long, but in the compact, large, and huge models they are 32 bits long. Also, in the small and compact models, function calls are intrasegment (within a segment), are 3 bytes long, and require 23 clock cycles. In the medium, large, and huge models, intersegment call instructions (a call to code in another segment) are 5 bytes long and require 36 clock cycles.

Make an astute choice of C library functions   You should always experiment with different library functions to find the smallest and fastest one that can perform the necessary function. For example, the following two lines both read a floating point value and assign it to the variable **my_float**:

```
    my_float = atof (gets (buff));
    scanf ("%f", &my_float);
```

The first line reads numeric input as string data and then converts it to a floating-point value, while the second line simply calls the multipurpose C library function **scanf**. The first method, however, produces code that is approximately 2K smaller, is more robust, and affords the programmer greater control.

Choose the optimal floating point library   The Microsoft C compiler offers a choice of several floating-point libraries, differing largely in the manner in which they use a numeric coprocessor, and whether they generate function calls or inline code. The options are fairly complex and are thoroughly documented in the manual; however, from the standpoint of optimization, they may be summarized as follows:

- If the target machine has a math coprocessor, the smallest and fastest code is produced by using the **/FPi87** command line option, which generates inline code specifically for the 8087/80287 (which must be installed).

- If the target machine does *not* have a math coprocessor, the smallest and fastest code is produced using the **/FPa** option, which generates calls to the alternate math library (resulting in slightly less accuracy than the standard Microsoft library).

- If you do not know whether the target machine will have a math coprocessor, the best compromise is the **/FPi** option (which need not be specified on the command line since it is the default). The code generated by this option will use a coprocessor if present, and if no coprocessor is present, will emulate its instructions in software.

Use low level operations whenever possible   In addition to the standard arithmetic operators, such as % and +, the C language includes low-level operators that directly correspond to primitive machine language instructions, for example, & (AND) and ++ (increment). In a few cases it is possible to generate considerably more efficient code by substituting low level operators for standard arithmetic expressions.

For example, consider two unsigned integers **i** and **j**,

unsigned int i, j;

where **i** is to be assigned the modulus 8 of **j**. Using Microsoft C version 4.0, the standard arithmetic expression

i = j % 8;

produced the following code:

Instructions	Clock Cycles
mov ax,[bp-4]	21

sub	**dx,dx**	3
mov	**cx,8**	4
div	**cx**	144–162
mov	**[bp-2],dx**	21
Total clocks:		193–211

Alternatively, the equivalent low-level expression

i = j & 07;

produced the code

Instructions		**Clock Cycles**
mov	**ax,[bp-4]**	21
and	**ax,7**	4
mov	**[bp-2],ax**	21
Total clocks:		46

In this example, substituting a low-level operation dramatically increased efficiency. Note, however, that Microsoft C version 5.1 produced the same sequence of instructions in both cases. In general, a compiler designed to generate efficient code will almost always recognize a potential optimization and perform it automatically. For example, the expression

i = i + 1;

would presumably generate an **add** instruction (requiring four clock cycles), while

++i;

should generate an **inc** instruction (two clocks), resulting in a 100% increase in efficiency. While this assumption may be valid for some compilers, Microsoft C (versions 4.0 and 5.1) recognizes that the constant is a 1 and generates an **inc** instruction in both cases.

Another example is integer multiplication. The standard high-level expression

i = j * 3;

would supposedly generate an **imul** (integer multiply) machine instruction (approximately 160 clock cycles), while the equivalent low-level expression

i = (j << 1) + j;

should generate **shl** and **add** instructions, requiring only five clock cycles. Again, however, the ever vigilant Microsoft compiler (4.0 and 5.1) recognizes the possible optimization and generates an **shl** instruction for both expressions. This optimization is more subtle than multiplication by a power of 2, and is not recognized by all compilers (for example, Microsoft C 3.0 used **shl** for i = j * 2, but the costly **imul** for i = j * 3).

In conclusion, substitute low-level operations for high-level arithmetic expressions whenever possible, and monitor the assembler output file for costly instructions such as **imul** and **idiv**. Although a good optimizing compiler will automatically perform many of the substitutions, it cannot always be relied upon to catch the more subtle optimizations, and is not a replacement for the watchful eye of an astute programmer.

Use the compiler's optimization control   Your compiler may have command line switches that affect the type or degree of optimization it performs. The Microsoft C compiler has two such command options, **/O** and **/Gs**. **/O** may be followed by one or more of the following letters, each of which gives specific instructions to the compiler:

s   Minimize code size. When there is a choice between generating faster code, or minimizing code size, the compiler will minimize code size. This is the default for version 3.0 of the compiler, and is not the best choice for a high-performance program, unless memory size is critical.

t   Maximize execution speed. This is the default for versions 4.0 through 5.1.

d   Disable optimization. This option is useful to speed compilation during development and for debugging, but should not be used when generating the final program.

a   Relax alias checking. An *alias* is an expression that refers to the same memory location as another expression. If your code does not contain aliases, you can use the **/Oa** option to allow the compiler to perform certain optimizations that would not be possible if aliases were present.

i   Enable intrinsic functions. If this option is selected, the compiler will replace calls to certain functions with direct inline code, eliminating the overhead associated with the call mechanism. A disadvantage of this flag is that the overall code size will be larger since the code for replaced functions is duplicated for each call contained in the C program.

l   Enable loop optimization. This option causes the compiler to perform optimizations associated with program loops, and is most effective in combination with the **/Oa** option.

x   Maximize optimization. This flag produces the fastest possible code, and is equivalent to **/Otail** plus **/Gs**.

/Gs eliminates the calls at the beginning of each function to **__chkstk**, which tests for stack overflow. Selecting this option will result in smaller and faster code, but is safe only for well-tested programs that have a stack sufficiently large so that there can be no overflow under any run-time conditions (beware of programs containing recursive functions such as quicksorts, which rapidly deplete the stack as the data size increases). The default condition is to include stack checking.

Unless code size is critical or there is danger of stack overflow, the best choice for generating a high-performance program would be:

/Ox

⊞ A Batch File for Generating C Programs

The following batch file, C2E.BAT, is a convenient way of compiling and linking C programs that do not involve multiple object files and illustrates the use of some of the C command line options that have been discussed in this section.

```
if exist %1 goto end
cl  /Ox  /DLINT_ARGS  /W2 %1.C
del %1.obj
:end
```

When you use this batch file, do not include the .C extension. For example, to prepare the program TEST.C, type:

C2E TEST

The first line of the batch file causes the process to terminate if you inadvertently include the file extension. (Otherwise, the third line would delete your source file!) The **/DLINT_ARGS** flag forces the compiler to include full function prototypes for all C library functions, allowing the compiler to check the number and types of parameters passed to these functions by your program. (Note that you must include the appropriate header files. Also, this flag applies only to Microsoft C versions through 4.0; later versions automatically include full prototypes). The **/W2** flag causes the compiler to issue a number of warnings in addition to those generated by default (such as the use of functions with no declared return type, or data conversions that can result in a loss of precision).

▪ Using Assembler

Although C may be the primary language, used for the bulk of application programming, there are situations when a program's performance can be significantly enhanced by using assembly language. This section describes when to use assembler and how to optimize assembly language code.

▪ When to Use Assembler

There are three primary situations when assembly language should be used: for optimizing critical areas of code, for accessing low-level resources, and for writing certain complete programs.

Optimizing Critical Areas of Code

The amount of time the processor spends in various parts of the code tends to be unevenly distributed. Those areas in which the processor concentrates its time are good candidates for optimization. By replacing such critical areas or hot spots of a C program with hand optimized assembly language, it should be possible to approach the performance of a program coded entirely in assembler.

There are two ways of identifying the heavily trafficked areas of a program. First, a little analysis will go a long way. Highly iterative sections of code, such as nested loops, are obvious critical areas. The running time of these areas is often proportional to the square (or higher power) of the size of the input data, and therefore the proportion of time they consume increases dramatically with increasing data. Other prime candidates for optimization are frequently called functions, which can be plucked out and replaced in their entirety with assembler modules.

A more empirical approach, especially valuable with larger and more complex applications, is to use a *profiler,* a utility that analyzes a program and produces a histogram of the relative amounts of time spent in various parts of the code. A profiler performs the following steps:

1. It first sets up an interrupt routine that is invoked with each tick of the system clock (normally 18.2 times per second, but this rate can be increased).

2. It then loads and runs the application to be tested as a child process.

3. Each time the interrupt routine is invoked, it stores the current instruction pointer address of the application (obtained from the stack).

4. When the application terminates, the profiler analyzes and prints out a distribution of the addresses it has stored.

You can typically specify the range of addresses and amount of detail, and thus it is possible to start with a general overview of the entire program, and then zoom in for a detailed analysis of specific critical areas.

It is not difficult to write a custom profiler, and there are also a number of commercial packages available; for example, Code Sifter from David Smith Software, PFinish from Phoenix, The Profiler by DWB (includes source code), and The Watcher by Stony Brook.

In addition to heavily trafficked regions of the program, other types of critical areas are segments of code where response time is very important. One example is a section of a realtime system that must react to an external event within a specified time. Other examples are those areas of a program that support the user interface, such as a program loop that reads and tests characters entered from the keyboard and echoes them to the screen. Such code must be efficient enough to keep pace with the fastest typist (or a keyboard macro program, or a cut-and-paste utility!). Another example is the code that updates the screen display—fast video output is so vital for a responsive, high performance program that Chapter 8 is devoted entirely to this topic.

Once the critical area or areas are defined, replace the block of code with a single function call, exchanging parameters using one of the methods described in Chapter 2. Then, write the actual function in assembly language in a separate file, assemble it, and link it to the C program.

Accessing Low-Level Resources

Code that deals extensively with low-level resources is often more easily written in assembler. A C compiler well-tailored to the MS-DOS environment will generally provide mechanisms, either as built-in operations of the language or as library routines, for addressing specific memory locations, reading and writing ports, generating software interrupts to access DOS and BIOS functions, and other systems level procedures. These facilities are ideal for an occasional quick poke into the system and can sometimes obviate the need to link a separate assembler module to the program. However, when a routine deals extensively with low-level resources, assembly language can be simpler, easier to debug, and more efficient. The advantages can justify writing and linking a separate module. Furthermore, there are certain functions that would be virtually impossible to write in C. A few examples are:

- Functions that need to manipulate specific registers. One example is an interrupt handler that must save the current registers and initialize segment registers in order to be able to access its data. Another example is the context switching module of a multitasking application, which must save and restore all registers.

- Accessing far data. Some C compilers use only 16-bit pointers in the small-memory model (i.e., a program layout in which all code is contained in a single 64K code segment, and all data is in another 64K data segment). These pointers cannot address memory in other segments, and would prevent programs from accessing important areas such as the video buffer in high memory and the BIOS data areas in low memory. (An exception to this limitation is the Microsoft C compiler, which has **far** pointers that allow access to any memory location in the system, even when using a small memory model. **Far** pointers are discussed in Chapter 10.)

- New data types. C has a limited number of data types. If, for example, integer calculations were required for numbers larger than could be accommodated by long integers (32 bits in MS-DOS versions of C), such routines could not be written in the C language. It would be possible, however, to write assembler routines to perform multidigit arithmetic to any desired accuracy.

Complete Applications

Sometimes complete applications, as well as modules called from the framework of a C program, are best written in assembler (or at least the major portion—it is also possible for an assembler program to call a C function). Some examples are:

- Programs in which low-level access pervades the entire body of code; for example, a device driver, or a memory-resident interrupt handler (both of these applications are dealt with in later chapters)

- Simple utilities that can be made extremely small and fast loading if written in assembler. For example, the following assembler utility, which changes the size of the cursor, forms an executable file (.COM format) exactly nine bytes long and loads instantly:

```
mov ah,1
mov ch,0
mov cl,7
int 10
ret
```

The same routine coded in C compiles to an executable file (.EXE format) 2156 bytes long and loads perceptibly more slowly:

```
#include <dos.h>

main ()
    {
    union REGS reg;
    reg.h.ah = 1;    reg.h.ch = 0;
    reg.h.cl = 7;    int86 (0x10, &reg, &reg);
    }
```

The problem with using C for very small utilities is that the compiler generates a fixed amount of overhead code regardless of program size. Also, Microsoft C produces only .EXE files; these files contain a standard header record that must be read and processed (the difference between .EXE and .COM files is discussed below). C is obviously an overpowered tool for such a limited utility.

The DEBUG program or SYMDEB (included with the Microsoft macro assembler) provide a means for rapidly producing small utilities such as the one listed above without having to go through the process of assembling, linking, and converting. These debuggers both have an **a** command that accepts assembler instruction and immediately converts them to machine language. The resulting code can then be written out to an executable .COM file with the following commands:

```
– N filename.COM

– RCX
:number of bytes of code to be written

– W
```

The major problem with DEBUG is its extremely limited editing capability. Once a series of instructions have been entered, it is impossible to insert an additional one in the middle of the code. Also, the source instructions cannot be saved in a file.

A good solution to these limitations is to use a memory-resident editing utility, such as SideKick's notepad, to create, edit, and save a listing of assembler instructions, and then paste them directly into DEBUG after entering the **a** command. Using this technique, small utilities can be written and modified with amazing speed.

Optimizing Assembler Routines

Since one of the primary functions of assembly language is to achieve optimal efficiency for critical program segments, it would be rather self-defeating to write inefficient assembler code (and it might require very careful coding to improve on the output of a modern optimizing compiler).

Assembly language offers one paramount advantage over high-level languages for generating efficient code: there is an almost one-to-one mapping from assembly language mnemonics in the source code to machine language instructions in the final executable file. Assembly language is thus a much finer grained medium than a high level language for the precise construction of algorithms; there are no constraints to the formation of control structures, and while the efficiency of high-level languages is measured by the number of gross operations such as data comparisons, assembler routines can be optimized down to a single clock cycle.

Several important considerations for producing optimal assembly language routines for MS-DOS machines are discussed below.

Use Efficient Algorithms

The literature of computer science abounds with general techniques for designing efficient algorithms. *The Art of Computer Programming, Volume One,* by Donald Knuth, is a highly recommended source, not only because it is one of the most authoritative works on the topic, but also because it uses assembly language. The analysis of algorithms tends to be quite theoretical; there are, however, two very practical results that can be important for the software developer.

First, there is a large class of problems known as *NP-complete,* for which no known efficient algorithms exist. If a programmer could find an efficient algorithm to solve any one of these problems, then the entire set could be solved efficiently, and a very major breakthrough would have been made. The practical implication is that if you are aware that a problem belongs to this class, you should not waste time trying to solve it efficiently unless you are attempting to make a significant theoretical advance.

The other practical result concerns problems that can be solved efficiently, and is a set of algorithms known to perform well, even as the size of the input grows large. For example, there are sort routines that may not seem intuitively to be optimal, but yet can be proven to be highly efficient when sorting a large number of items. The designer of high-performance software for any machine would do well to consult some of the basic computer science references.

Count Clock Cycles

The discussion on low-level operators in C revealed that logically equivalent algorithms can vary greatly in the number of clock cycles they require. On an 8088 system running at 4.77 MHz, a clock cycle is equivalent to approximately 200 nsec of execution time. A handbook on 8086/88 assembly language (such as the *iAPX 88 Book* from Intel) lists the number of clock cycles required to execute each variation of each instruction. The number of cycles for instructions that reference memory sometimes include an *EA* factor, the amount of time required to calculate an effective address. The guide book should also include a chart listing the specific EA values.

The total number of clock cycles is a good indication of the overall efficiency of an algorithm. Also, looking up clock cycles reveals that certain instructions are inherently costly, such as **mul** (from 70 to over 150 cycles) and **div** (from 80 to over 175 cycles). In many situations these costly instructions can be replaced with efficient ones. For instance, as in the C example above, the **mul** operator can often be replaced with **shl**, even when the multiplier is not a power of 2. Therefore, to multiply register AX by 20, avoid using the **mul** instruction (113-118 cycles):

```
mov    bx,20
mul    bx
```

You can instead use **shl** instructions (only two clock cycles each):

```
shl    ax,1
shl    ax,1
mov    bx,ax
shl    ax,1
shl    ax,1
add    ax,bx
```

The second method is significantly more efficient; however, the savings are not as great as would be indicated by simply adding the clock cycles listed in the handbook. The 8086/88 processor contains an internal queue that holds the next four instruction bytes to be processed. The values in the handbook assume that this queue contains all the required bytes when an instruction begins execution. A sequence of short instructions, however, tends to deplete this queue and results in longer execution times. As a consequence, for a sequence of four or more **shl <reg>,1** instructions, it is actually more efficient to use the **shl <reg>,cl** form of the instruction (although simply counting the reported clock cycles would indicate the reverse).

In addition to the depletion of the prefetch queue by short instructions, there can also be an occasional competition for memory between the execution unit and the mechanism that fills the prefetch queue. The net result is that the overall execution time will usually be between 5% to 10% greater than indicated by adding clock cycles.

Use the Repeat Prefix

Take advantage of the repeat prefix (**rep**) whenever possible. When this instruction is placed before any of the primitive string operations, such as **movs** (move a string element) and **cmps** (compare a string element), it causes that operation to be repeated at a high rate until some terminating condition is met. The advantage of this prefix is that a single instruction fetch will result in an entire sequence of operations under the internal control of the processor, so that a string can be processed with maximum efficiency. A conventional loop construction requires repeated instruction fetches and is much less efficient. (This instruction is used for moving large blocks of data in the screen handling routines of Chapter 8.)

Use Register Variables

Place as many stored values as possible in registers, giving preference to heavily used variables. Most operations are much more efficient when performed on registers than when performed on memory locations. For example, adding an immediate value to a register requires only four clock cycles, while the same operation performed on a memory address can consume up to 37 cycles, depending on the addressing mode.

Since there are a limited number of registers available in the 8086/8, using register variables can induce two complications. First, registers are constantly subject to modification. Many instructions use registers to receive and return values, and almost all subroutine and interrupt function calls result in their modification. The consequence is that registers must frequently be saved and restored. Each **push** instruction to save a value on the stack costs 15 clock cycles, and each **pop** instruction to retrieve a value costs 12 cycles. Therefore, store variables in the least used registers, generally SI, DI, DX, BX, and CX. Avoid using other registers than these for variable storage.

Second, memory variables each have a private, permanent location, conveniently associated with a descriptive name. Register variables, however, are difficult to organize. Remembering which variable is stored in which register at a given time is a sizable task, and the temptation to abandon registers in favor of memory is strong. Before giving up register variables, however, consider using a register chart, such as the one reproduced in Figure 1.1.

This chart has a box for each register and each flag, as well as an area for recording the contents of the stack. Using a pencil, enter the contents of every register that is currently in use. After each line of code is written, update the chart to reflect any changes in register contents. Used in this way, a register chart can not only simplify tracking register variables, but will also reveal exactly which registers must be saved when a destructive instruction or procedure is invoked.

There are two different approaches to saving registers for a procedure call. One method is to have the procedure always save and restore all registers. This approach is quite costly but safer for the programmer who has lost track of register usage. The **pusha** and **popa** instructions available on the 80186 and newer processors save all registers with a single instruction and encourage this method. The second method is to have the

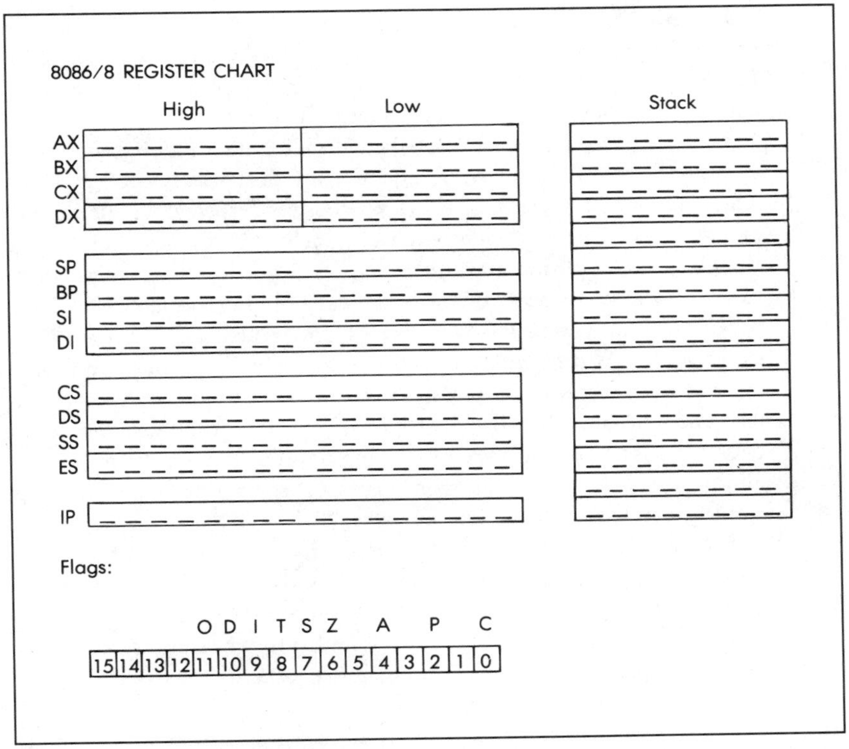

Figure 1.1: *A chart for tracking register use*

calling program save and restore only those registers that must be preserved for the particular call. This approach is considerably more economical and may be easily accomplished as follows:

- At the beginning of each procedure, include a comment that lists every register that is modified by the procedure.

- At the point in the calling program where the procedure is called, consult the register chart and note which registers are currently in use.

- Save only those registers that are modified by the procedure *and* are currently being used by the calling program.

The same mechanism would apply to interrupt function calls and macro invocations.

Use Procedures Judiciously

Procedures are wonderful constructs for implementing top-down program designs, and can help produce compact and well-structured code. However, in terms of raw performance, the procedure call mechanism can result in less than optimal code for two reasons.

First, a procedure call is costly. The **call** instruction requires from 23 to more than 50 clock cycles, and the **ret** instruction between 20 and 33. The frequent invocation of short procedures (especially calls nested within loops) is much less efficient than the inclusion of equivalent inline code. Furthermore, passing parameters to a procedure typically involves the time-consuming process of pushing and popping values from the stack.

Second, the primary advantage of procedures is that a single body of code can be used in many situations. However, the more general-purpose a procedure becomes, the less efficient it becomes as well, because it must test and correctly handle a variety of special situations. Therefore, it is better to write several carefully tailored procedures than to code a single all-purpose behemoth, although writing a special procedure for every call would obviously defeat their purpose.

For producing efficient code, macros are an excellent alternative to procedure calls. When the assembler expands a macro, it places the code directly inline, thus avoiding the runtime overhead of a procedure call. Also, parameters are conveniently passed through a list, quite analogous to the mechanism of high level languages, except that the job is done by the assembler and not at runtime.

The obvious disadvantage of macros is that they use more memory than procedures because the code is duplicated with each occurrence and not shared. However, for small routines called from performance critical areas of a program, they offer the structure and convenience of procedures, combined with significantly greater performance.

Use the .COM Format

An .EXE file contains a header record that must be read and processed when the file is loaded. A .COM file, however, contains only executable code and is an exact image of the program in memory. Consequently, a .COM file is slightly smaller, loads faster, and is somewhat simpler to program. Although Microsoft is phasing out the .COM file, in the meantime it is the optimal format for small, fast, freestanding utilities written in assembler (Microsoft C produces only .EXE files). A .COM file can also be used as a prologue to a large application. The user types the name of a small .COM file, which runs instantaneously and initiates the process of loading the main program; during this relatively long process, the .COM file produces a graphic display that reassures and entertains the user.

It is important to realize, however, that .COM files have two significant limitations:

- The total size of code and initialized data cannot exceed approximately 64K. If this limit is exceeded, the EXE2BIN utility will not be able to convert the .EXE file to a .COM file.

- The DOS loader will not perform segment relocations for a .COM file. With an .EXE file, the loader will patch the actual runtime segment values into requested locations within the code. This feature allows the programmer to load values into segment registers, for example,

    mov ds,dataseg

    even though the value of **dataseg** is unknown until runtime.

There are also several common myths regarding .COM files. One is that a .COM file cannot have more than one segment, and another is that it cannot contain a stack segment. The listing in Figure 1.2 dispels these myths and provides a basic shell for generating a multisegment .COM file. Maintaining separate segments is a good way of organizing code and data, and this particular structure has some additional advantages described later. (The shell is designed for producing a freestanding application; a different format, to be discussed, must be used to interface assembler and C).

The shell begins by declaring three segments: **stackseg**, **codeseg**, and **dataseg**. The **stackseg** segment is declared merely to appease the linker

```
page 50,130

;File:    COMFMT.ASM

;Format for a multisegment .COM File
;
;    To generate .COM file from TEST.ASM:
;        MASM TEST;
;        LINK TEST;
;        EXE2BIN TEST.EXE TEST.COM


                                      ;Declare segments to force
                                      ;loading order.

stackseg    segment stack             ;Placate linker.  This segment must
stackseg    ends                      ;remain empty.

codeseg     segment
codeseg     ends

dataseg     segment                   ;Place all data in this segment.
num_var     db        ?
message     db        'hello from the data segment',10,13,'$'
buffer      label     byte
dataseg     ends

groupseg    group     codeseg,dataseg
            assume    cs:groupseg
            assume    ds:groupseg
            assume    es:groupseg


codeseg     segment

            org       5ch             ;Template for Program Segment Prefix.
parm1       db        12 dup (?)      ;Parameters from command line.
            org       6ch
parm2       db        12 dup (?)
            org       80h
parmlen     db        ?               ;Length of command line.
parmline    db        127 dup (?)     ;Full command line.

            org       100h
main        proc      near
                                      ;Main code.
            mov       ah, 09h         ;Access data segment.
            mov       dx, offset groupseg:message
            int       21h             ;Print message with DOS.

            mov       ah, 4ch         ;Exit w/ errorlevel 0.
            mov       al, 0
            int       21h

main        endp

subr1       proc      near
                                      ;Subroutine code.
            ret
subr1       endp

codeseg     ends

            end       main
```

Figure 1.2: *A format for producing a multisegment .COM file*

and avoid the warning message it normally displays when it cannot find
a stack segment; this segment must remain empty and must not be further referenced.

The code and data segments are then declared to force the linker to place the code segment before the data segment; the loading order is established by the order in which segments are first referenced, and in a .COM file the code must come at the very beginning of the file. (The stack segment is actually first, but it is empty.)

Next, the code segment and data segment are assigned to a group segment called **groupseg**. Consider the following data reference instruction:

mov ah, num_var

Normally, when a data item such as **num_var** is referenced in this type of instruction, the assembler generates the offset of the variable from the beginning of the segment in which it is contained, which in this case would be 0. However, since this is a .COM file, the data segment register points to the beginning of the code segment (as do all segment registers), *not* to the beginning of the data segment. Therefore, the offset of **num_var** from the beginning of the code segment is required. By assigning the data segment to a group, offsets for this type of instruction are automatically generated from the beginning of the first segment in the group, which in this case is, appropriately, the code segment.

Although data reference instructions are automatically handled correctly, the **offset** operator must use a group segment override; thus, the line:

mov dx,offset groupseg:message

Without the override, the offset generated would have been from the beginning of the data segment (= 1) instead of from the beginning of the group.

The next item in the file is the actual data segment **dataseg**. Note that since the data segment appears before the code segment in the source file, all data items are conveniently listed together at the top of the file, and there need be no forward references.

Remember, however, that in the final executable file, the data segment will come after the code segment. This arrangement has an advantage over the usual technique of placing data at the beginning of the code segment and then jumping over it: if a large uninitialized buffer is needed (for example, to read in a file), it can be placed at the end of the data segment as a label (such as **buffer** in the listing), *without* reserving space (note that all user memory beyond the end of a .COM file is automatically allocated to the program when it is loaded). If such a buffer were declared at the beginning of the code segment, space would have to be reserved, which would increase the size of the .COM file on disk by the size of the buffer. (Remember that the stack pointer is initialized to the top of the 64K program segment; be sure to relocate the stack if there is any chance that it will collide with the buffer.)

The final part of the listing is the code segment. The labels that occur before **org 100h** are used to access the program segment prefix (see Chapter 6). When the .EXE file is converted to a .COM file, the initial **100h** bytes are removed (all code or data before the entry point specified by the **end** statement is eliminated), so that the first byte appearing in the executable file will be the first instruction of the main procedure.

The following batch file, A2C.BAT, automates the process of generating a .COM file:

```
if exist %1 goto end
masm %1.asm;
if not errorlevel 1 link %1;
if not errorlevel 1 exe2bin %1.exe %1.com
del %1.obj
del %1.exe
:end
```

To process TEST.ASM, type

A2C TEST

The operation of this file is very similar to the one given above for C programs.

A Template for Generating .EXE Files

The .EXE format is more flexible than a .COM file, is suitable for programs that exceed 64K, and is more likely to be compatible with future operating environments. Also, only .EXE files can be symbolically debugged using the Microsoft CodeView debugger (described in Chapter 3). The listing in Figure 1.3 provides a basic template that can be used to generate .EXE files from assembly language, and is suitable for symbolic debugging. The listing declares the same three segments as the .COM format; however, there are some important differences:

- Unlike a .COM file, the stack segment is functional, and reserves space for the stack. The loader will automatically initialize the stack segment register to the base of this segment, and the stack pointer to its top.

- In a .COM file, all segment registers point to the same segment. In this .EXE template, however, the data segment and extra segment registers are initialized to point to an entirely separate segment (**dataseg**). The assignment of **dataseg** to these registers is possible because of the relocation performed by the loader for

```
page 50,130

;File:    EXEFMT.ASM

;Format for generating an .EXE File
;
;     To generate .EXE file from EXEFMT.ASM:
;          MASM EXEFMT;
;          LINK EXEFMT;

public     message                       ;Declare all symbols 'public'
public     main                          ;for CodeView debugger.

codeseg    segment 'CODE'                ;Declare code segment to force it
codeseg    ends                          ;to load first.

dataseg    segment 'DATA'                ;Place all data in this segment.
message    db      'hello from an .EXE file',10,13,'$'
dataseg    ends

stackseg   segment stack 'STACK'         ;Set up 1K stack.
           db      128 dup ('stack    ')
stackseg   ends

           assume  cs:codeseg
           assume  ds:dataseg
           assume  es:dataseg
           assume  ss:stackseg

codeseg    segment 'CODE'

main       proc    far

           mov     ax, dataseg           ;Set up segment registers.
           mov     ds, ax
           mov     es, ax

           mov     ah, 09h               ;Access data segment.
           mov     dx, offset message
           int     21h                   ;Print message with DOS.

           mov     ah, 4ch               ;Exit w/ errorlevel 0.
           mov     al, 0
           int     21h

main       endp

codeseg    ends

           end     main
```

Figure 1.3: *A format for producing an .EXE file*

.EXE files, as explained above. Furthermore, since the data segment register points to a separate segment, it is unnecessary to declare a segment group, and it is possible to have a full 64K of data as well as a full 64K of code (plus more, if additional segments are declared.)

- Note that data instructions are the same as in a .COM file, but the offset operator does not use a group override.

- The program can expand in size arbitrarily. If the code segment exceeds its capacity of 64K, simply create an additional code segment (and use far calls to branch between segments). Likewise, additional data segments can be declared; however, the data segment register must always contain the base address of the segment that is currently being accessed.

CHAPTER

2

INTERFACING C AND ASSEMBLER

The techniques discussed in Chapter 1 focus on the optimal use of C and assembler as distinct programming tools. A high-performance program, however, often depends on the careful integration of both of these languages. This chapter demonstrates how C and assembler can form a very compatible team: a C program can call an assembler procedure, and an assembler program can call a C function.

■□ Calling an Assembler
■□ Procedure from a C Program

Chapter 1 describes the situations when it can be beneficial to call an assembler routine from a C program. This section presents the actual methods—how to structure an assembler routine so that it can be linked with a C program, and how data may be freely exchanged between the C program and the assembler module.

Figure 2.1 lists a C program that calls an assembler procedure, and Figure 2.2 lists the assembler procedure that is called. These listings illustrate several of the methods for exchanging data between a C program and an assembler procedure, and can be used as a basic model for generating assembler interfaces. The C program passes two parameters to the assembler routine, **asm_ proc**. The assembler procedure calculates the sum of the two parameters, plus the external C variable **ext_int**, and prints the result. Finally, it returns a value of 4 to the calling program.

□■ Declaring Segments

The segments of an assembler module must be declared exactly as they are declared by the C compiler. The Microsoft C compiler sets up many segments; however, an assembler routine typically needs to declare only two of these, **_data** and **_text**, as shown in the listing.

_data is the segment C uses to store initialized external and static data. The assembler routine can use this segment to store permanent private data (e.g., **message** in the listing), which is analogous to local static data in a C program. **_data** belongs to the **dgroup** of segments, and

```
/*
      file:    MAIN.C

   A C Program that Calls an Assembler Routine.

   This program must be linked with the assembler module PROC.ASM
   (Figure 2.2).  You can use the following commands to generate
      the executable file from MAIN.C and PROC.ASM:

          cl /c MAIN.C
          masm PROC;
          link MAIN+PROC;
*/
#include <stdio.h>

int asm_proc (int,int);
int ext_int = 1;

void main ()
     {
     int parm1 = 2;
     int parm2 = 3;
     int ret_val;


     printf ("hello from main\n");

     ret_val = asm_proc (parm1, parm2);

     printf ("\nvalue returned from asm_proc = %d\n", ret_val);
     printf ("goodbye from main\n");

     } /* end main */
```

Figure 2.1: *A C program that calls an assembler procedure*

when an assembler routine is entered, the data segment (DS) register already points to this group. Therefore, data placed in **_data** is easily accessed, for example:

mov dl, message[5]

or

mov dx, offset dgroup:message

Note that the offset operator requires a group override. The **_data** segment can also be used to list **extrn** declarations for accessing external C data of the **near** variety, as explained later.

The **_text** segment contains all of the code belonging to a small- or compact-memory model C program. If you are using one of these models, place all procedures in this segment.

```
 1:    page 50,130
 2:
 3:    ;Figure:   2.2
 4:    ;File:     PROC.ASM
 5:
 6:    ;Format for an Assembler Routine Callable from a Microsoft C Program.
 7:    ;
 8:    ;     to generate .EXE file from MAIN.C and PROC.ASM:
 9:    ;         cl /c MAIN.C
10:    ;         masm PROC;
11:    ;         link MAIN+PROC;
12:
13:
14:    _data      segment word public 'DATA'
15:
16:    extrn      _ext_int : word                ;External data from C.
17:
18:    message    db       'parm1 + parm2 + ext_int = $'
19:                                               ;Private initialized data.
20:    _data      ends
21:
22:
23:    dgroup     group    _data
24:    assume     cs:_text, ds:dgroup            ;For medium/large/huge models, place
25:                                              ;module name before '_text'.
26:    public     _asm_proc                      ;Make procedure accessible from C.
27:
28:
29:    _text      segment byte public 'CODE'     ;For medium/large/huge models, place
30:                                              ;module name before '_text'.
31:    _asm_proc  proc     near                  ;For medium/large/huge models, change
32:                                              ;'near' to 'far'.
33:
34:    sframe     struc                          ;Template to access stack frame.
35:    local_1    dw       ?                     ;List local 'automatic' variables here.
36:    local_2    db       ?
37:    bptr       dw       ?                     ;Position of saved BP register.
38:    ret_ad     dw       ?                     ;For medium+ models change to 'dd'.
39:    parm1      dw       ?                     ;List all parameters here in the order
40:    parm2      dw       ?                     ;listed in the C function call.
41:    sframe     ends
42:
43:    frame      equ      [bp - bptr]           ;Base for accessing stack frame.
44:
45:               push     bp                    ;Set up base pointer to access frame.
46:               mov      bp, sp
47:               sub      sp, bptr              ;Adjust stack pointer for local data.
48:               push     di                    ;Must save di & si if altered.
49:               push     si
50:
51:               mov      ah, 09h               ;Access private initialized data.
52:               mov      dx, offset dgroup:message
53:               int      21h                   ;Call DOS write string function.
```

Figure 2.2: *An assembler procedure that can be called by a C program*

```
54:
55:            mov     ah, 02h
56:            mov     dx, frame.parm1         ;Access parameters.
57:            add     dx, frame.parm2
58:            add     dx, _ext_int            ;Access external data from C.
59:            add     dx, 30h                 ;Convert number to character.
60:            int     21h                     ;Call DOS write character function.
61:
62:            mov     ax, 4                   ;Place return value in AX.
63:
64:            pop     si                      ;Restore registers.
65:            pop     di
66:            mov     sp, bp
67:            pop     bp
68:            ret                             ;Return to C program.
69:
70: _asm_proc  endp
71:                                            ;Place additional procedures here.
72:
73: _text      ends                           ;End of code segment.
74:            end
```

Figure 2.2: *An assembler procedure that can be called by a C program (continued)*

Using Memory Models

The listing in Figure 2.2 is designed for small- or compact-memory models. If you are using the medium, large, or huge models, make the following changes:

- In the larger code models, each module has its own code segment. To follow the compiler's naming conventions, place the name of the assembler module immediately before the identifier **_text** on lines 24, 29, and 73. For example, if the file is named MOD1.ASM, all occurrences of **_text** should be replaced with **mod1_text**.

- On line 31, change **near** to **far**, because the C compiler will be using far calls.

- On line 38, change **dw** to **dd** so that the template used to access the stack will allow for the 4 byte return address of a far call.

Note that all assembler procedures must be declared as public symbols in order to be callable from the C program. An example is the following line from the listing:

public _asm_proc

⊞ Exchanging Data

A well-integrated assembler module must be able to exchange data freely with the calling C program. The three primary channels for data exchange are direct access to external C variables, parameter passing, and returned values.

Accessing External C Data

C data belonging to the **extern** storage class (i.e., declared outside the scope of a function and not static) are global, and can be directly accessed by an assembler module. Each C variable that is to be accessed must be declared with an **extrn** statement within the assembler file as follows:

extrn _dataname : type

For example, the assembler routine in Figure 2.2 gains access to the external integer **ext_int** from the C program through the declaration:

extrn _ext_int : word

Note that the data name from the C program must be preceded with an underscore in the assembler routine. The type field depends on the size of the C data item:

Size of C data	Type
1	byte
2	word
4	dword
8	qword
10	tbyte

How are complex C data structures accessed? You can access C arrays by declaring the type according to the size of the constituent element of the array (e.g., for an array of integers, use type **word**). Assign the starting address of the array to a base register (e.g., BX), and then increment the base register appropriately to access individual array members.

Accessing C structures, however, is a little trickier. For example, consider the following external C structure:

```
struct
    {
    char field1;
    int field2;
```

□□■□

```
long field3
}
ext_str;
```

To access its fields, you must first declare the structure as a byte, and then define an assembler **struc** with fields corresponding to those of the C structure:

```
extrn          _ext_str:byte
template       struc
field1         db        ?
field2         dw        ?
field3         dd        ?
template       ends
```

Then use standard field notation to access individual elements. For example,

```
mov _ext_str.field2, 0fh
```

Note that the **.field2** expression tells the assembler both the offset of the field and its data type, in a compact notation reminiscent of high-level languages.

There is a final important consideration for accessing a C structure. The fields of an assembler **struc** are always contiguous. However, the C compiler performs insidious address alignments by default, often leaving gaps between the individual elements of a **struct** (a great source of incompatibility between different C compilers, and a headache in general, but done in the interest of efficiency for machines that access words on even address boundaries). Fortunately, the Microsoft C command line option **/Zp** will pack structure fields so that they are contiguous, and must be invoked in order to employ the above method (unless the assembler routine uses an alignment scheme identical to that used by the C compiler).

Although an **extrn** declaration is always required to read or write an external C data item, the exact method depends on whether the data item is **near** or **far**.

Near data   **Near** *data* are those data items located within a segment belonging to the **dgroup**. All external variables in a small- or medium-memory model program, which are not explicitly declared as **far**, will automatically be **near**. In the compact-, large-, and huge-memory models, whether a data item is **near** or **far** is not easily predictable (unless it has been declared using the **near** or **far** keywords). In order to determine the type of an external data item in the larger models, link the C program by itself using the /MAP linker option—if the data item has been linked *below* the group of segments in **dgroup** (**null** is the lowest one), then it is a **far** data item; however, if it is linked *above* the beginning of **dgroup**, then it is a **near** data item.

Near data are treated as shown in the listing—the **extrn** declarations are placed within **_data**, and segment registers do not need to be modified in order to address the data.

Far data **Far** *data* items are those placed in segments below the **dgroup**. If you have determined by the above criteria that any of your external variables are **far**, then you must place the **extrn** declaration at the beginning of the program, *outside* of any segment; for example,

> **extrn _far_int : word**

You must also use the ES register to access the variable, for example:

```
mov   ax, seg _far_int          ;Get segment value into
mov   ex, ax                    ;ES register.
mov   ax, es:_far_int           ;Read data using ES
                                ;segment override.
```

Passing Parameters

The C language, largely due to its support for variable length parameter lists, is unique in its parameter-passing mechanism. The salient features are:

- Parameters are pushed on the stack from last to first.
- The calling program is responsible for removing the parameters from the stack after the function returns (therefore C functions do not use **ret n** to restore the stack).
- C data types have the following lengths when pushed on the stack as parameters:

Type	Length in bytes
char, short, int, unsigned	2
near pointer	2
long, unsigned long	4
far pointer	4
float, double	8

The task of maintaining the correct stack offsets for each parameter or local variable is tedious and prone to error. Therefore, **_asm_proc** begins with the structure definition **sframe** on line 34, which represents the exact layout of the stack frame after the stack has been initialized. Simply list each parameter and its type in the order it appears in the parameter list. Also list any local variables as shown in the program; this structure makes it convenient to set up local data storage on the stack (analogous to the C automatic storage class).

Frame is set equal to the bottom of the structure, the base pointer is saved and set to point to the top of the stack, and then the stack is adjusted for local data. Once this structure has been defined and initialized, access to parameters and local variables becomes virtually foolproof; for example,

    mov ax, frame.parm1

or

    mov frame.local_2, 0ffh

Remember that the **ret_ad** must be declared using **dd** for the medium-, large-, and huge-memory models in order to allow room for the 4 byte return address. Also, with large data models (compact, large, and huge) address parameters will be **far** pointers (4 bytes long) by default.

Returning Values

Use the following rules to return values from an assembler module to the calling C program:

- Place values of 2 bytes or less (**char**, **int**, and **near pointer**) in register AX.

- Return the 4-byte types **long** and **far pointer** in registers DX:AX—high-order word in DX (segment for **far** pointer), and low-order word in AX (offset for **far** pointer).

- For **struct**, **union**, **float**, and **double**, place the *address* of the variable in AX.

Preserving Registers

An assembler routine that is called from a C program is responsible for preserving the contents of the following registers: SP, BP, SI, DI, CS, DS, and SS. Also, if the direction flag is set by the routine (**std**), it must be cleared before the program exits (**cld**).

Using Inline Assembler

Another method of interfacing assembler and C is the direct inline inser-tion of assembly code into the C program. Inline assembler is not sup-ported by Microsoft C, but is a feature of some C compilers, such as Aztec, DeSmet, and Turbo C. For the Aztec and DeSmet compilers, all text between the directives **#asm** and **#endasm** is inserted literally into the output assembler file so that the programmer can spontaneously break into fluent assembly language whenever inspired. For example, the following inline assembly language uses the BIOS to position the cursor:

```
printf ("Printed at current cursor position.");
#asm
        mov       ah, 2              ;BIOS set cursor function.
        mov       dh, 5              ;Row 5.
        mov       dl, 10             ;Column 10.
        mov       bh, 0              ;Page 0.
        int       10h                ;BIOS video service interrupt.
#endasm
printf ("Printed at row 5, column 10.");
```

This technique is useful for occasionally accessing a low-level resource. However, as a means of optimizing code it can be self-defeating because it limits the amount of optimization that the compiler can perform. The compiler maintains assumptions regarding register contents so that it can, for example, eliminate the redundant reloading of registers. However, when it encounters an inline directive, it must abandon its assumptions because the enclosed assembly code is not analyzed.

Using A Make Utility

A make utility can be much more convenient than a simple batch file when developing a program that has more than one object file, such as a C program that calls an assembler routine. Both Microsoft C and MASM provide a basic make program. The advantage is that when one or more source files are modified, the make utility automatically performs only those steps required to generate an updated version of the final exe-cutable file. Make operates by reading a make file, which consists of a series of dependency specifications, each of which is followed by one or more commands. If the first file in the dependency statement is older than any of the files following the colon, then the command(s) are exe-cuted. For example, the following is a make file that could be used to maintain the C program CTEST.C, which is linked with an assembler module, ATEST.ASM:

```
CTEST.OBJ : CTEST.C
    cl /c /Ox /DLINT_ARGS /W2 CTEST.C

ATEST.OBJ : ATEST.ASM
    masm ATEST;

CTEST.EXE : CTEST.OBJ ATEST.OBJ
    link CTEST + ATEST;
```

The first two lines specify that if CTEST.C has been modified since CTEST.OBJ was created (or CTEST.OBJ does not exist), then CL must be run to generate an updated version of the object file. Likewise, the second two lines cause ATEST.ASM to be assembled only if it has been modified since ATEST.OBJ was created. Finally, the last two lines run the linker only if either CTEST.OBJ or ATEST.OBJ have been generated since CTEST.EXE was created. Note that the relative modification times are derived from the file dates recorded in the directory; therefore, it is important to maintain the correct system time when saving files.

◼ Calling a C Function from an Assembler Program

Although assembly language may be the optimal tool for certain applications, it lacks one of the most important assets of a high-level language: an extensive library of supporting routines. It is certainly possible to develop or purchase such a library, but it would be a great convenience if the assembly program could simply call functions from the vast and familiar C library.

Unfortunately, even if the proper parameter pushing and segment-naming conventions are followed, most assembler programs cannot directly call a Microsoft C library function. The reason for this limitation is that the compiler does a lot of talking to the linker behind the programmer's back. In order to call a C library function, one or more of the Microsoft object modules from the .LIB file must be linked into the final .EXE program. These object files, however, are not the innocent ones an assembly programmer would be likely to create with the macro assembler; rather, they are full of special instructions to the linker that completely alter the structure of the final program.

For example, these instructions set up a large number of segments (15 or more), instruct the linker to bind in the C startup module CRT0.OBJ, and cause execution to begin with the startup module rather than at the beginning of the assembler program. At runtime, the startup module sets up the entire operating environment, including initializing the segment registers, and then calls **_main** (the programmer's starting routine). In order to peacefully coexist with such an object file, it is necessary to play by a very restrictive set of rules.

The listing in Figure 2.3 plays by these rules and can therefore call C library functions (in fact, it *must* call at least one library function because it relies on the startup module to perform initializations). The basic rules are as follows:

- Use the standard C segment-naming and parameter passing conventions discussed above. Remember that parameters are pushed in the opposite order that they are listed in the call statement, and that the calling program must remove all parameters from the stack after the function returns.

- Declare all outside functions that are called by the program with an **extrn** statement.

- Name the beginning procedure **_main**, and declare it public so that it may be called by the startup module.

- Place a **ret** instruction at the end of **_main** to return control to the startup module, which then terminates the program.

The listing is designed to call small- or compact-memory model C functions. In order to call medium or large model functions, simply replace all occurrences of **near** with **far**, and then link with the appropriate library.

Whether this model can be considered an assembler program that calls C functions, or whether it is actually a C program that calls a single large assembler module, is an open question. In either case, some of the inherent benefits of assembler programming are lost: tight control (the program doesn't get to perform its own initialization) and compact size (linking in just the **printf** module adds about 5K of code). However, the ability to access the C library from a program that must be written in assembler is a significant benefit.

Note that the preceding procedure for declaring and calling a C library function can also be performed from the assembler subroutine of Figure 2.2. Thus, a C program can call an assembly language module, which in turn can call a C library routine. Understanding the various permutations of these two languages increases the probability of arriving at an optimal solution to a given programming problem.

```
page 50,130

;Figure:  2.3
;File:    ASMC.ASM

;Format for an Assembler Program which can Call Microsoft C Library Functions.
;
;    Note: This format is not suitable for a freestanding program; it MUST
;    call a Microsoft C library function.
;
;    To generate .EXE file from ASMC.ASM:
;        masm ASMC;
;        link ASMC,,,SLIBCE;
;
;        (Replace SLIBCE, if necessary, with the appropriate library(ies) for
;        the memory model you are using.)


_data      segment word public 'DATA'
                                        ;Define all data here.
message    db      'enter a line to echo: ',0
buffer     db      128 dup (?)

_data      ends

dgroup     group   _data
assume     cs:_text, ds:dgroup

_text      segment byte public 'CODE'       ;Start of code segment.

extrn      _gets: near                      ;Declare all C functions here.
extrn      _printf:near                     ;For medium/large models change
                                            ;'near' to 'far'.
public     _main
_main      proc    near                     ;For medium/large models change
                                            ;'near' to 'far'.

           mov     ax, offset dgroup:message
           push    ax
           call    _printf                  ;Use C 'printf'.
           pop     ax

           mov     ax, offset dgroup:buffer
           push    ax
           call    _gets                    ;Use C 'gets'.

           call    _printf
           pop     ax

           ret                              ;Return to CRT0.

_main      endp
                                            ;Place additional procedures here.

_text      ends                             ;End of code segment.
           end
```

Figure 2.3: *A format for an assembler program that can call Microsoft C library functions*

CHAPTER 3

DEBUGGING

The techniques used to generate high-performance applications, which push the limits of existing software tools and go beyond the certain ground of well-documented features, inevitably lead to program bugs. Many of the procedures described in this book, as they are implemented and fine tuned for a specific environment, will involve an element of trial and error. Debugging is the art of analyzing the errors and modifying the trials. This chapter explores a wide spectrum of approaches to debugging, ranging from simple, preventive techniques to powerful hardware-assisted methods. No debugging tool, however, can replace careful reasoning. Blindly tracing through an entire program is highly inefficient. Successful debugging requires that the programmer first arrive at a theory regarding the cause of the bug, and then intelligently use a debugger as an analytic tool to either confirm or refute this theory, and to gather more evidence. The techniques are discussed in an order that encourages you to begin with the simplest methods, and then proceed to the more elaborate approaches only as necessary.

Preventive Debugging

In software development, just as in medicine, the best cure for a disease is its prevention. The following basic guidelines are recommended for avoiding software bugs. Most of these guidelines refer to programming in C. An assembler offers fewer safeguards against bugs than a C compiler, but the workings of an assembly language program are often more obvious than those of a C program.

Developing in Layers

Build software in small stages, thoroughly testing each stage before moving on to the next. As obvious as this dictum may seem, it is very tempting to assume that simple modules are working correctly and to start combining them into complex applications before they are individually tested. However, the difficulty of finding software bugs grows immensely with program complexity. This approach is especially vital for developing device drivers, interrupt handlers, and other types of complex systems software.

Using Argument Type-Checking

One of the most common sources of bugs in C programs is the argument passing mechanism, which normally performs no type-checking. The Microsoft C compiler, however, allows forward declarations of functions that include a list of argument types, and will perform argument type-checking for any subsequent function calls.

In order to take advantage of this feature for C library functions, include all of the suggested header files listed in the description of each function, because these files contain function declarations with argument-type lists. The command line option **/DLINT_ARGS** will force the conditional compilation directives in the header files to include the declarations (applies only to Microsoft C versions through 4.0).

To have the compiler perform type-checking on your own functions, include a list of function declarations, with argument types, at the beginning of each source file. To facilitate this process, the **/Zg** option will cause the compiler to generate a file containing complete declarations for all functions defined in a given source file. The resulting output (which is written to standard output and can therefore be redirected to a file) can then be included in any source file that calls one or more of these functions. For example, if the file PROG.C contains a number of function definitions, the command

```
cl prog.c /Zg > prog.h
```

will generate the file PROG.H, which can then be included with any source code that calls one of the functions.

Note that simply having the function definition (i.e., the actual function code, with its formal parameter list) within the same file as the function call is not sufficient to generate parameter type-checking; a forward declaration must also be present. Also, the forward declaration must occur both before the function call *and* before the function definition (if it is in the same file) in order for parameter type-checking to work properly.

The style of type-checking performed is no more stringent than that performed for assignment statements. For example, the following code will *not* generate a warning, and will automatically convert the **long** parameter to a **double**, just like an assignment operation:

```
int flint (double);
```

```
main ()
    {
    long john;
    flint (john);
    }

int flint (bubble)
double bubble;
    {
    return;
    }
```

However, the following code attempts to pass a character pointer as an argument that is declared to be a **double:**

```
int flint (double);

main ()
    {
    char *john;
    flint (john);
    }

int flint (bubble)
double bubble;
    {
    return;
    }
```

This code results in the messages

ctest.C(7) : error 115: 'parameter' : incompatible types
ctest.C(7) : warning 24: different types : parameter 1

because a pointer is not automatically converted to a **double**. Note that declaring a function with an argument-type list not only causes the compiler to flag an argument having an incompatible data type (as in the second example), but also forces the correct type conversion if the data types are dissimilar but compatible (as in the first example). If the type declaration were not supplied, the argument **john** would have be pushed on the stack as a long integer rather than first being converted to a **double**.

Using C Lint Utilities

Another way to help prevent bugs in C programs is to use a commercial lint utility. These programs not only perform argument type-checking, but also flag many other possible sources of problems. If you have the patience to set one up and run it regularly, and if you can avoid taking its many picky criticisms personally, it can enforce a more consistent programming style and help you avoid runtime problems. Among the packages available are PC-Lint by Gimpel Software, and Pre-C from Phoenix.

Setting Compiler Warning Levels

Microsoft C provides an option to control the level of warnings supplied by the compiler. The warning level is specified with the **/Wn** command line flag, where **n** is the desired level and has one of the following values:

Warning level	Compiler warnings
0	Suppresses all warning messages
1	Supplies the default warning messages
2	Supplies additional warning messages
3	Highest warning level; supplies all level 2 warnings *and* flags non-ANSI features and extended keywords.

/W2 is a useful option during the initial development stage, and can help prevent problems and locate program bugs. In addition to the normal warnings provided by the default level, warning level 2 flags additional errors such as the use of functions that do not have a declared return type; functions that have a return type other than **void**, but fail to return a value; and automatic data conversions.

Avoiding Common Bugs in C

The C language is full of subtleties and almost devoid of safeguards. The possible pitfalls are far too numerous to list; however, there are a few notorious ones that you should look out for.

Remember to declare the return type of functions that do not return integers. For example, consider a function that is defined in FILEA and returns a float. If this function is called in FILEB but is not declared in

FILEB, the compiler will *not* generate an error message, but will incorrectly interpret the returned value as an integer (**/W2**, described above, will trigger a warning in this case). Using a function without declaring it constitutes an implicit integer declaration.

Avoid string copy functions that move a variable number of bytes. **strcpy** and **strcat** are especially notorious because they keep writing into the target location until a null character is encountered in the source string, which may be absent in the case of bad input data. It is better to use **strncat** or **strncpy**, which specify the maximum number of bytes to transfer.

Another common bug is the result of uninitialized pointers. There are few C programs that do not at some stage of their development have something similar to

char *string;

strcpy (string, "this will end up at address 0000");

Microsoft C includes a runtime test for this type of blunder, and prints the following error message:

error 2001: Null pointer assignment

Be careful not to use an assignment operator (=) where a boolean comparison (= =) is desired. Also don't forget to force the correct order of evaluation; for example, don't mistakenly use

while (c = getchar() != EOF)

instead of

while ((c = getchar)) != EOF)

The last expression is a well-known C idiom and demonstrates the value of relying on standard usage whenever possible.

■□ Placing Print Statements Judiciously

There are few bugs that do not ultimately succumb to well chosen and carefully placed print statements. For C programming, the usual technique is to use **printf** to display information at strategic locations. However, a **printf** statement, or an MS-DOS function call from assembler, involves lengthy code and uses the DOS interrupt dispatcher. For writing interrupt handlers and other low-level routines, a more direct display technique will be much less likely to cause interference. (Many memory-resident utilities, for example, involve trapping interrupt 21h, and if there is currently a bug in this mechanism, DOS function calls may not operate properly.)

Figure 3.1 lists two assembler macros that are used primarily for tracing program execution. The **showchar** macro places characters at subsequent locations on the screen by writing directly to video memory (Chapter 8 will deal with techniques for writing to video memory). The **printc** macro sends the specified character directly to the printer, using the BIOS printer service interrupt (17h), and is useful for separating tracing output from the program's video display. Similar routines could be written in C.

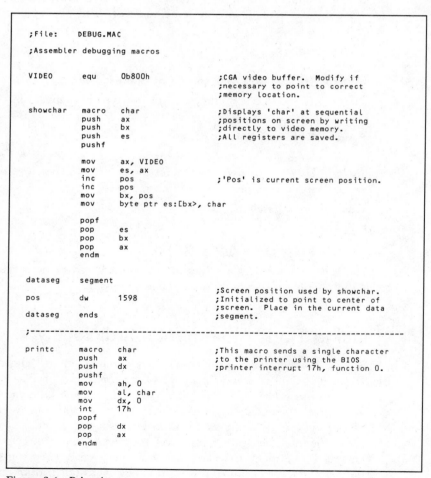

```
;File:     DEBUG.MAC

;Assembler debugging macros


VIDEO      equ      0b800h              ;CGA video buffer.  Modify if
                                        ;necessary to point to correct
                                        ;memory location.

showchar   macro    char                ;Displays 'char' at sequential
           push     ax                  ;positions on screen by writing
           push     bx                  ;directly to video memory.
           push     es                  ;All registers are saved.
           pushf

           mov      ax, VIDEO
           mov      es, ax
           inc      pos                 ;'Pos' is current screen position.
           inc      pos
           mov      bx, pos
           mov      byte ptr es:[bx>, char

           popf
           pop      es
           pop      bx
           pop      ax
           endm


dataseg    segment
                                        ;Screen position used by showchar.
pos        dw       1598                ;Initialized to point to center of
                                        ;screen.  Place in the current data
dataseg    ends                         ;segment.

;--------------------------------------------------------------------------

printc     macro    char                ;This macro sends a single character
           push     ax                  ;to the printer using the BIOS
           push     dx                  ;printer interrupt 17h, function 0.
           pushf
           mov      ah, 0
           mov      al, char
           mov      dx, 0
           int      17h
           popf
           pop      dx
           pop      ax
           endm
```

Figure 3.1: *Debugging macros*

It is a good idea to nest all debugging print statements within a conditional compile/assemble statement. For example, the following lines might be included in an assembler program:

ifdef debug
      showchar 'a'
endif

The following lines are an example of a conditional compilation in a C program:

#if defined (debug)
      printf ("entering proc1, var1 = %d\n", var1);
#endif

Both of these languages accept the **/D** command line directive, which causes the specified identifier to be defined (= 1) for that particular compilation. Therefore, a complex set of debug statements can be left in the file. Whenever trouble arises, they can be called to life with the command line option

    /Ddebug

Software Debuggers

The next layer of defense against program bugs is provided by commercial software debuggers. Some of the available debuggers are discussed below, beginning with the simplest and proceeding to the more sophisticated.

DEBUG

The simplest commercial program is DEBUG from Microsoft, which provides the basic functions of tracing program execution, running a program with breakpoints, assembling and disassembling machine instructions, displaying or altering the contents of memory and registers, reading or writing binary files, and performing pattern searches.

SYMDEB

SYMDEB is a more sophisticated version of DEBUG. Its primary enhancement is the ability to refer to data and instructions by name rather than by address. SYMDEB instructions can reference any externally declared symbols from a Microsoft C or MASM program. Additionally, for a C program, locations can be accessed by the original source code line numbers, and source code statements are displayed along with the corresponding unassembled machine instructions.

CodeView

The next major step in the evolution of Microsoft software debuggers is CodeView, which comes with the C compiler (versions 4.0 and 5.1) and the Macro Assembler (version 5.1). Among the many features of this debugger are the following:

- Multiple windows allow the simultaneous viewing of code, registers, current variable values, and command dialog.

- Commands can be issued through the dialog window (similar to DEBUG), through function keys or pull-down menus, or with a mouse.

- The programmer can toggle between the debugging screen and an intact program output screen.

- Extensive online help is available.

- The value of variables or memory ranges can be evaluated or changed at any time, or constantly monitored through a watch window. Normal C expressions and **printf** formats are supported.

- *Conventional* breakpoints are easily set by a variety of means. Also, *conditional* breakpoints can be defined to be activated when a specified number of repetitions has occurred, a specified expression becomes true, or a specified expression or memory location changes value.

Debugging C with CodeView

With CodeView you can debug C programs in source mode, in which the original source code is displayed and all commands are given in terms of source line numbers and identifiers. Unlike SYMDEB, CodeView can access local automatic variables. In order to debug in source mode, you must include symbolic information in the .EXE file. It is also advisable to disable optimization, so that the assembler code will correspond more closely to the source code. The following batch file prepares a C program for symbolic debugging and fires up the debugger:

```
if exist %1 goto end
cl /Zi /Od /DLINT_ARGS /W2 %1.C
if errorlevel 1 goto end
```

```
del %1.obj
cv %1
:end
```

The **/Zi** compiler option forces inclusion of full symbol and line number information, and **/Od** disables optimization. The **/CO** link option places symbolic and line information in the final .EXE file.

Debugging Assembler with CodeView

To debug assembly language programs in source mode, you must use version 5.0 or later of the Microsoft Macro Assembler. (With earlier versions of the assembler, you can debug in assembler mode, and view the source file in a separate window.) Prepare the program according to the following rules:

- The program must be in .EXE format.
- The code segment must be given the class name **CODE**.

To prepare such a file, you can use the .EXE format shown in Figure 1.3. The following batch file will generate an appropriate executable file for a program consisting of a single assembler module, and will initiate a debugging session:

```
if exist %1 goto end
masm /Zi %1;
if errorlevel 1 goto end
link /CO %1;
if errorlevel 1 goto end
del %1.obj
cv %1
:end
```

Other Software Debuggers

Among the many other software debuggers currently available are Codesmith-86 from Visual Age, DSD86/7 from Soft Advances, and Trace-86 and Advanced Trace-86 from Morgan Computing.

Hardware-Assisted Debugging

If you create powerful bugs, you will need powerful tools to find them. Hardware assisted debuggers provide the ultimate tool. There are two major types of hardware debuggers: those that use hardware assistance to maintain debugger control, and those that directly monitor the CPU.

Hardware Assistance for Maintaining Debugger Control

The following two debuggers use hardware assistance primarily to allow the debugger to maintain control regardless of the actions of the program being tested.

Resident Debug Tool from IBM

IBM's utility is memory-resident and therefore provides globally accessible debugging facilities. It is supplied with a card and switch that generate a nonmaskable interrupt (vector 02h) to allow the debugger to regain control even when a program is stuck with interrupts disabled (a condition that normally requires a cold boot). Thus, the debugger can maintain command unless the memory it occupies becomes corrupted, or the nonmaskable interrupt itself becomes disabled. (Writing 00h to port address A0h masks the "nonmaskable" interrupt. The name of this interrupt is not a misnomer, however, but derives from the fact that it cannot be disabled through the software **cli** machine instruction.)

Periscope

The heart of this highly rated system is a powerful debugger that is also memory resident. A nonmaskable interrupt switch is optional, and does not require a card slot. (It has a simple wire connector that is slipped alongside one of the pins on an existing card. When the switch is pressed, it grounds the channel check bus line, which generates a nonmaskable interrupt. This line is normally used to report parity errors.) An additional hardware option is an expansion card with protected memory, which stores the program code and keeps it safe from corruption by a miscreant application. Thus, using both hardware options, the debugger can almost always regain control and help analyze what went wrong.

Hardware Assistance for Monitoring the CPU

The ultimate degree of hardware assistance is provided by systems that monitor the CPU directly, and can therefore allow code to be traced at full running speed and support breakpoints that do not affect the rate of program execution. Although excellent for analyzing large and complex applications and for revealing timing-related bugs, these systems are quite expensive. Examples are PDT-PC and PDT-AT from Answer Software Corporation, and PC Probe and AT Probe from Atron.

PART 2

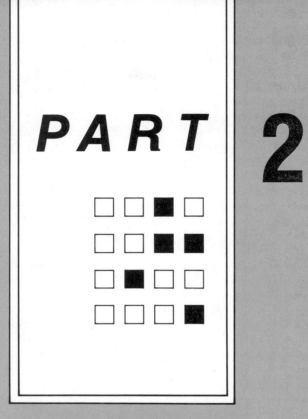

THE RESOURCES

CHAPTER 4

INTERRUPTS AND THE DOS FUNCTIONS

After selecting the set of programming tools, the next task is to start using these tools to tap into the resources of the computer system. A high-level language like C, together with its library of functions, is an important tool for developing reliable and portable computer programs. However, high-level languages, which are designed as generic, abstract development environments, and are purposely not dependent upon machine details, never fully exploit the capabilities of any specific computer. Therefore, to generate a high-performance program, it is often necessary to go beyond the confines of a high-level language and its function library, and directly access the system's underlying resources.

For example, there are many methods for producing video output. You can always use **printf**, accepting the underlying mechanism chosen by the compiler writer, but this may or may not be the best choice for the particular application and computer system. Instead, if you are familiar with the software and hardware resources available in the system, you can make an informed decision and choose the most efficient alternative.

The most easily accessed and important resources in an MS-DOS machine are the basic routines that are provided by the operating system and the BIOS (the Basic Input/Output System that is contained in the read-only memory supplied with the hardware). All of these functions have one feature in common: they are accessed through the mechanism of interrupts. This chapter begins with a general explanation of the interrupt process. It then describes methods for accessing the interrupt routines from assembly language and C programs. The final section is a descriptive overview of the MS-DOS functions—a programmer's field guide that explains how the functions are organized, discusses strategies for selecting the optimal routine, and provides some interesting examples. Chapter 5 will continue this discussion with a description of the BIOS services.

The Interrupt Mechanism

An interrupt is an event that causes the processor to temporarily suspend its current activity and branch to a service routine somewhere in memory.

After the service routine performs its required task, control returns to the suspended process. Interrupts on MS-DOS machines may be divided into three categories based on the manner in which they are generated: internal hardware interrupts, external hardware interrupts, and software interrupts.

Internal hardware interrupts   The processor itself can generate an interrupt. The 8086/88 processor produces an internal interrupt immediately after it finishes executing an instruction if one of the following conditions exists:

- The preceding instruction was a division (**div** or **idiv**) and the resulting quotient was larger than the specified destination (also known as a divide by 0 error).

- The *trap flag* (TF) is set. This flag is typically set by a debugger that is in a single-step tracing mode, and results in an interrupt after each instruction (except those that modify segment registers).

- The preceding instruction was **into** (interrupt on overflow) and the *overflow flag* (OF) is set.

In each of these cases, the interrupt results in the processor branching to an appropriate routine to handle the error or exceptional condition. The 80286 processor has a variety of additional internal interrupts.

External hardware interrupts   A hardware device outside of the processor can trigger an interrupt by placing a signal on either the INTR or NMI processor pins. For example, pressing a key on the keyboard creates a hardware interrupt, which causes branching to a BIOS service routine that reads the character and places it in a buffer. This variety of interrupt is discussed in Chapter 6.

Software interrupts   The **int** machine instruction also causes an interrupt. This kind of interrupt, employed by the operating system and user programs to access the system utilities, is the primary topic of this chapter.

How does the processor know where to branch when it receives a particular interrupt? Whichever of these three mechanisms (internal, external, or software) triggers the interrupt, it must also supply a one-byte number called the *interrupt type*. This number is *not* the physical address of the service routine (which would be a very inflexible mechanism), but rather an index into a table maintained in low memory that contains the actual routine addresses. These addresses are known as *interrupt vectors* because they point to interrupt service routines.

To understand the exact sequence of events that constitute an interrupt, consider the following software interrupt instruction:

int 21h

The number 21h is the interrupt type, and tells the processor that the address of the target routine is located in entry number 21h of the interrupt table. Each entry of this table contains the double word (four-byte) address of the service routine in segment:offset format. A single entry in the interrupt vector table has the structure shown in Figure 4.1. The table begins at offset 0, and therefore the actual memory offset of an entry is obtained by multiplying the interrupt type by 4. The offset for interrupt 21h is thus 4 × 21h, which equals 84h. The address stored at this location could be found by entering DEBUG and issuing the following command:

– D 0:84 L4

If the response happens to be

0000:0080   0B E4 8D 23

then the address of the service routine, expressed in segment:offset form, is currently 238D:E40B. Upon receiving the **int 21h** instruction, the processor would proceed to

- Push the flag register on the stack
- Disable the hardware interrupts by clearing the interrupt flag (IF) and the trap flag (TF)
- Push the current code segment register
- Push the current instruction pointer
- Branch to memory location 238D:E40B

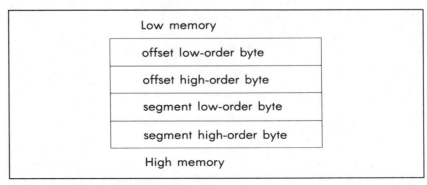

Figure 4.1: *Entry in the interrupt vector table*

The service routine then returns control to the interrupted program through the **iret** instruction, which causes the processor to

- Pop the instruction pointer off the stack
- Pop the code segment
- Pop the flags

Because the interrupt type is a single byte, it can specify only 256 possible entries, and therefore the total size of the table is 1024 bytes. A number of table entries are initialized at system startup by the BIOS and by MS-DOS. Other entries can be initialized at any subsequent time by memory-resident routines and other interrupt handlers loaded at the request of the user. Some interrupt types are reserved for internal hardware interrupts, some for external hardware interrupts, and others for software interrupts. Those used for software interrupts point to routines located within: the system read-only memory (ROM), belonging either to the BIOS or to adapter cards that have been added to the hardware; the MS-DOS kernel; or user-loaded device drivers, memory-resident utilities, and other interrupt service routines.

The interrupt instruction is a very flexible and broad-purpose mechanism for accessing globally available services. When invoking an interrupt service, all programs, including the operating system itself, must use an address at a known location; therefore, it is very easy to modify the global behavior of a given interrupt by replacing that address with one pointing to an alternate routine. For example, virtually all programs read the keyboard through interrupt type 16h, which normally points to a service routine within the BIOS. It is a simple matter, therefore, for a utility either to monitor all keyboard activity, or to change the response of the system to keyboard read requests by rerouting this vector through an alternate procedure.

A chart of the interrupt table, showing the current uses for specific vectors, is contained in Appendix A. Writing hardware and software interrupt handlers is discussed in Chapter 6. Also, Chapter 11 describes methods for intercepting the keyboard hardware interrupt (type 09h).

Accessing Software Interrupt Routines from Assembler

It is very simple to invoke one of the standard DOS or BIOS interrupt routines from assembly language. Information is typically exchanged between the calling program and the interrupt service through registers (and occasionally through control blocks in memory). For each of the DOS and BIOS functions, the documentation explicitly states which values must be loaded into registers before the interrupt instruction, and which values are returned through registers by the routine. As an example, consider the DOS function for obtaining the amount of free space available on a given disk device. This function is accessed through interrupt 21h, and the documentation specifies the following register use:

Entry:

AH   36h (DOS function number)

DL   Drive specification (0 = default, 1 = A)

Return:

AX   Sectors/cluster or FFFFh if drive specification invalid

BX   Available clusters

CX   Bytes/sector

DX   Clusters/drive

The following assembler code illustrates how to use this function to obtain the free space on drive A.

```
mov ah, 36h            ;DOS function number.
mov dl, 1              ;Want free space on drive A.
int 21h               ;Invoke interrupt.
cmp ax, 0ffffh        ;Test for error.
je err_rtn            ;Specified drive is invalid.
mov sec_clu, ax       ;Save sectors per cluster.
mov avl_clu, bx       ;Save available clusters.
mov byt_sec, cx       ;Save bytes per sector.
```

This example illustrates the typical steps required to invoke an interrupt routine from an assembler program:

1. Load the specified values into registers.

2. Invoke the interrupt (**int n**).

3. Test the return code (**cmp ax,0ffffn**), and if an error is indicated, branch to an error handler (**je err_rtn**). Otherwise, save the returned values and continue the program.

Accessing Software Interrupt Routines from C

The C library provides a number of functions for accessing software interrupts: **bdos**, **int86**, **int86x**, **intdos**, and **intdosx**. The functions **bdos**, **intdos**, and **intdosx** are limited to interrupt 21h (the principal entry point for MS-DOS function calls), and there is no advantage to using them; **int86** and **int86x**, however, can be used to invoke any interrupt. If values must be passed or returned through registers ES or DS, then **int86x** must be used; otherwise, **int86** may be used. Of all of these options, **int86x** is the most general and can be used in any situation.

The C program in Figure 4.2 illustrates the use of **int86** to access interrupt 21h, function 36h (the same DOS function employed in the preceding assembler example). After calling DOS, the C function **free_space** uses the returned values to calculate the total number of bytes of free space, which is the product of available clusters (in BX) times the sectors per cluster (in AX) times the bytes per sector (in CX). The function **free_space** then casts each value to a long integer to prevent an overflow, and returns the product.

The function **int86** takes three arguments:

- The interrupt number (an integer)

```
#include <stdio.h>
#include <dos.h>

long free_space (int);

void main ()
    {
    printf ("The free space on drive A is: %ld bytes.\n", free_space (1));
    }

long free_space (drive)
int drive;
    {
    union REGS inreg, outreg;   /* Variables for passing register values. */

    inreg.h.ah = (unsigned char)0x36;              /* DOS function number. */
    inreg.h.dl = (unsigned char)drive;                    /* Disk drive. */
    int86 (0x21, &inreg, &outreg);                        /* Call DOS. */
                  /* Calculate number of free bytes, and return results. */
    return (long)outreg.x.ax * (long)outreg.x.bx * (long)outreg.x.cx;
    }
```

Figure 4.2: *A C program that accesses an interrupt service*

- The address of a union containing the values to be loaded into the registers on function entry (type **union REGS**)
- The address of a union to receive the register values returned from the function (also type **union REGS**)

Because it is generally not necessary to save the values that are passed to the interrupt function, it is often possible to use only one **union REGS** variable; for example,

union REGS reg;

int86 (0x21, &reg, &reg);

The required union type (**REGS**) is defined in the include file DOS.H. **REGS** allows access to 8-bit registers through the **.h** union member (AH, AL, BH, BL, CH, CL, DH, and DL), and to 16-bit registers through the **.x** member (AX, BX, CX, DX, SI, DI, and the carry flag).

Some interrupt services require the exchange of values through segment registers, which are not included in **union REGS**. For these interrupts, **int86x** must be used. The first three parameters required by this function are the same as those passed to **int86**, but there is an additional fourth parameter that is a pointer to a variable of type **struct SREGS**. **Struct SREGS** is also defined in DOS.H, and although it contains integer fields for the ES, CS, SS, and DS segment registers, **int86x** uses only ES and DS. Immediately before invoking the interrupt, **int86x** copies the appropriate values from the **SREGS** variable into the ES and DS registers. Upon return from the interrupt, it copies the values of registers ES and DS back into the **SREGS** variable, and restores the original contents of DS.

MS-DOS function 35h, which returns the current value of a specified interrupt vector, is an example of a service that uses segment registers; the manual specifies the following protocol:

Entry:

AH   35h (DOS function number)

AL   Interrupt type

Return:

ES   Segment address of interrupt vector

BX   Offset address of interrupt vector

The C program in Figure 4.3 illustrates the use of the function **int86x**. The function **getvec** gets the current value of the interrupt vector specified by the first parameter, and assigns the address it obtains to the structure pointed to by the second argument.

```
#include <stdio.h>

struct vector            /* Structure for holding interrupt vector address. */
    {
    unsigned int segment;
    unsigned int offset;
    };

void getvec (int, struct vector *);

void main ()
    {
    struct vector v;            /* Declare variable for containing results. */

    getvec (0x21, &v);              /* Get contents of interrupt type 21h. */
                                    /* Print results stored in structure.  */
    printf ("Segment:Offset of int 21h is %x:%x\n", v.segment, v.offset);
    }

#include <dos.h>                    /* Contains structure definitions. */

void getvec (type, vecptr)
int type;
struct vector *vecptr;
    {
    union REGS regs;                                /* Defined in DOS.H */
    struct SREGS segregs;

    regs.h.ah = 0x35;                           /* DOS function number. */
    regs.h.al = (unsigned char)type;                /* Interrupt type. */
    int86x (0x21, &regs, &regs, &segregs);          /* Call DOS service. */
    vecptr->offset = regs.x.bx;                     /* Store results. */
    vecptr->segment = segregs.es;
    }
```

Figure 4.3: *A C program that uses* **int86x**

Both **int86** and **int86x** load the **cflag** field of **REGS** with the value of the carry flag after return from the interrupt. Many DOS interrupt functions set the carry flag to indicate an error, and return the error code through register AX. If the carry flag is set, this error code can be accessed in one of three ways:

1. The C functions **int86** and **int86x** both return the value of AX, which gives immediate access to the error code.

2. AX can be accessed through the field **outregs.x.ax**.

3. The global variable **_doserrno** is assigned the DOS error code and can be tested immediately after return from the function.

For example, an error condition can be tested as follows:

```
int86x (0x21, &inregs, &outregs, &segregs);
if (outregs.x.cflag)        /* Test for occurrence of an error. */
    switch (_doserrno)      /* Branch depending on error code. */
        {
        ...
        }
```

Selecting an Interrupt Function

The examples in the preceding sections demonstrate how easy it is to access the interrupt functions available in MS-DOS machines from both assembly language and C. Except for the need to use registers, it is not much more difficult to access interrupt functions than to call library routines. However, it can be difficult to select the appropriate routine from the maze of currently available functions. Since this selection can greatly affect software performance, this chapter, as well as Chapter 5, focuses on strategies for choosing the optimal routine.

Why is it often difficult to select the optimal interrupt function? One reason is that the current set of functions in an MS-DOS machine was not designed according to some master plan; rather, it evolved organically into a hierarchical and often redundant array of related routines. Many functions available at the BIOS level are quite similar to functions provided by MS-DOS, and many within the collection of MS-DOS services perform essentially duplicate functions. However, among the duplicated functions there are often subtle differences in features, performance, and compatibility.

Another source of difficulty in selecting an optimal routine is the documentation. First, the basic reference material is contained in two separate manuals. The BIOS functions are documented in the *IBM Personal System/2 and Personal Computer BIOS Interface Technical Reference* and in the technical reference manuals for the IBM-PC and IBM PC-AT. The MS-DOS functions are described in the *DOS Technical Reference* (these manuals are listed in the Bibliography). Also the DOS functions are presented in simple numerical order rather than according to the functions they perform (and there is little logic to this numerical ordering).

The primary purpose of the following section, as well as Chapter 5, is to aid in the selection of the optimal interrupt routine. This part of the book, therefore, organizes the routines by the functions they serve, emphasizes the differences among them, and discusses strategies for making the best selection. The next section also contains listings that illustrate practical uses for certain interrupt functions, and offers tips for getting the most out of this resource.

Additionally, the DOS functions are summarized in Appendix B, and the BIOS functions in Appendix C. Because the DOS technical manual is an essential reference work and is easy to use, the reader is assumed to have access to a copy, and Appendix B only briefly summarizes the DOS functions. Appendix C, however, provides a fairly complete synopsis of the BIOS services. A good approach would be to use the following guidelines to select the optimal routine, and then consult the DOS technical manual for implementation details on the MS-DOS functions, and Appendix C for details on the BIOS functions. The issue of compatibility with the operating system version when selecting an interrupt routine is discussed in Chapter 7.

The MS-DOS Functions

The DOS interrupt utilities, although not the ultimate in high-performance software, are a comprehensive, reliable, and portable set of functions, especially useful for disk file operations. The DOS routines are the old workhorse of MS-DOS compatible computers—the default method and the starting point for most software. Also, the C compiler generally uses DOS functions whenever possible.

When is it best to use the DOS services, and when is it best to choose lower-level methods? Disk and file management is one area where it is best to use DOS. Like any good operating system, DOS has taken an inherently intractable hardware resource, the disk drive, and created a consistent and easily managed logical resource, the file system. Not only does DOS do a good job of file management, but if you bypass the operating system, you must create your own file system, a nontrivial task with a dubious payoff. Alternatively, DOS video display routines are a resource ripe for vast improvement. Chapter 8 compares the DOS video services with other methods, and demonstrates how simple it is to achieve a significant enhancement with lower-level techniques.

The DOS services are divided into what IBM labels *function calls* and *interrupts*. The function calls are an entire battery of routines accessed through a single interrupt number (21h); the individual functions are selected according to the value placed in the AH register. The interrupts are a series of DOS functions accessed through individual interrupt numbers (i.e., 20h, 22h, 23h, 24h, 25h, 26h, 27h, and 2Fh). There is some duplication between these two categories, as well as subtle differences, but in general, IBM recommends using the function calls whenever possible.

(Most new routines have been added as interrupt 21h function calls; using a single interrupt number to dispatch a large number of service requests is a more flexible and expandable mechanism than using separate interrupts.)

The list of DOS services is greatly cluttered because as new versions of the operating system introduce new functions, the old ones must remain in order to maintain upward compatibility. Therefore, there are often two or more functionally similar services. The decision of which one to use must be tempered by considerations of compatibility versus maximum utility.

The DOS technical reference labels the functions available with DOS 1.*x* (ranging from 0 to 2Eh, except 1Ch) as *traditional*. File management functions in this category use a structure known as a *file control block* (FCB). Functions that were introduced with DOS 2.*x* are generally referred to as *extended* (ranging from 2Fh to 57h, plus 1Ch); the extended file services use *file handles*. Versions 3.0 through 4.0 also brought a further set of functions (ranging from 58h to 6Ch), which are marked in the following descriptions with a superscript 3 or 4. The exact version required for each function is given in Appendix B.

⊞ General Use of MS-DOS Functions

Before describing the individual MS-DOS functions, this section reviews some general guidelines for handling errors, preserving registers, and setting up an adequate stack.

Error Handling

Handling errors with MS-DOS functions can be rather confusing because different versions use different methods. MS-DOS uses four basic strategies to report error conditions.

First, many of the DOS 1.*x* traditional functions (in the range from 0 to 2Eh), especially those that manage files, use the AL register for error reporting. If AL equals 0, no error occurred. If AL is not equal to 0, then it contains an error code. There are no standard meanings for these codes; the meanings are documented individually for each function. Most functions use the value FFh to report a single error condition; other functions will return a 01h, 02h, 03h, and so on to indicate one of a small number of possible errors.

A second strategy for handling errors is used by a group of functions introduced with DOS versions 2.0 through 4.0. These functions report errors by setting the carry flag and placing an error code in the AX register. The list of functions is:

38h to 4Bh

4Eh and 4Fh

56h and 57h

5Ah to 5Ch[3]

5Eh and 5Fh[3]

66h[3], 67h[3], and 68h[3]

6Ch[4]

The values returned in AX are known as *extended error codes*. Unlike the codes reported by the traditional functions, these error codes are standard and are listed in a single chart in the technical reference (see Chapter 6 of the March 1987 *DOS Technical Reference* or Appendix B of the July 1988 *DOS Version 4.0 Technical Reference*). There are a total of 88 error codes, but DOS version 2.*x* functions use only the first 18. These 18 codes represent the most common errors and are listed in Table 4.1, together with the version 2.*x* functions that return them; all function numbers are in hexadecimal. The macro **printn** (print the content of a register in decimal) listed in Figure 4.4 is useful for displaying these error messages.

DOS uses a third error handling method to respond to *critical errors* (such as trying to write to a disk with the door open) by invoking interrupt 24h and passing an error code to the interrupt handler. The technique for writing a critical-error handler is discussed in Chapter 6.

DOS 3.0 introduced a fourth mechanism for dealing with error conditions: function 59h, which returns extended error information. This function reports the following data:

- The extended error code (one of the 88 values mentioned above)

- The *error class,* which is the general type of error involved, such as *out of resource, temporary situation, internal error,* and *hardware failure*

- The suggested action, such as *retry, abort,* and *ignore*

- The *locus,* which describes the area involved in the error, such as *block device, serial device,* and *memory*

The DOS technical reference recommends calling function 59h after every DOS 21h function call and at the beginning of an interrupt 24h critical-error handler. This function can be called even after a traditional FCB call, and will report the extended error number having a description closest to the error as described in the technical reference for the specific function. See the DOS technical reference for details.

Code	Meaning	Functions that use the code
1	Invalid function	All
2	File not found	38,3D,41,43,4B,4E,56
3	Path not found	39,3A,3B,3C,3D,41,43,44,4B, 4E,56
4	No more handles	3C,3D,45,46
5	Access denied	39,3A,3C,3D,3F,40,41,43,44, 4B,56
6	Invalid handle	3E,3F,40,42,44,45,46,57
7	Corrupted memory control blocks	48,49,4A
8	Insufficient memory	48,4A,4B
9	Invalid memory block	49,4A
10	Invalid environment	4B
11	Invalid format	4B
12	Invalid access code	3D
13	Invalid data	
14	Reserved	
15	Invalid drive spec	3A
16	Attempt to remove current directory	3A
17	Not same device	56
18	No more files	4E,4F

Table 4.1: *Error codes for DOS version 2.x*

Note that in addition to these four basic methods of error handling, special error codes used by interrupts 25h, 26h, and 2Fh are described in the technical reference.

Register Preservation

As a general rule, you can assume that all registers will be preserved during an interrupt function *except* register AX and any other registers that are explicitly stated to return values. There are a few exceptions to this rule:

- Interrupts 25h and 26h destroy *all* registers except segment registers.

- Interrupt 59h destroys registers AX, BX, CX, DX, SI, DI, ES, and DS.

- Interrupt 4Bh destroys all registers in sight, including SP and SS. SP and SS must be stored within the code segment (where they are addressable from the CS register) so that they may be restored on function return (obviously, the stack can't be used to store them!).

User Stack Requirement

The DOS interrupt services use their own internal stack; however, the technical reference recommends that user programs have a minimum of 200h bytes of free stack space in order to accommodate the interrupt mechanism.

Summary of the DOS Services by Category

In the following functional summary of DOS services, those routines that are accessed by individual interrupt numbers (e.g., interrupt 20h) are prefaced with **int**, and those invoked through interrupt 21h are represented by a single function number.

Traditional Character Device I/O

The traditional character device I/O functions are now considered somewhat obsolete and Microsoft discourages their use. Instead, the handle file functions described later on can be used to read and write these character devices in a manner that is more consistent with standard file I/O, and more likely to be compatible with future versions of the operating system. Note, however, that when writing a critical-error handler or a device driver, these functions are the only ones allowed for performing I/O. (See Chapter 6 for critical-error handlers and Chapter 9 for device drivers.)

The functions in this group that read from the keyboard or write to the console are routed through *standard input* and *standard output,* and are thus subject to redirection by the user (see the description of standard input and output that follows). Although these functions seem to involve much duplication, they vary in details such as whether Ctrl-C is checked, whether input characters are echoed to the screen, and whether input is buffered. Keyboard input functions may return a value of 0, indicating that the key does not have an ASCII value (for example, a function key). The next character read will then be an *extended ASCII code,* which specifies the actual key or key combination pressed. See the list of extended ASCII codes in the DOS technical reference (Chapter 6), and the discussion of extended keyboard codes in Chapter 5 of this book (under "The Keyboard Services").

Routines in this category can be used as quick and dirty methods for dumping the contents of a register or displaying a short message (without having to count the length of the string, which is necessary with the handle functions). Figure 4.4 lists three macros that are especially useful for error handling; for example, first use **prints** to display a short error message, and then print out the contents of any register using **printn** (decimal format, useful for error numbers) or **printh** (hexadecimal format, good for addresses).

The macro **prints** prints a string by placing it directly in the code segment, jumping over it, and then calling the print string function, 0Ah. The macro **printn** converts the contents of the specified register to decimal format and prints each character using function 02h. The macro **printh** also uses function 02h, but simply dumps the contents of the register in hexadecimal format. Various other methods of video output will be compared in Chapter 8.

The following functions read data from the standard input.

Function	Service performed
01h	Keyboard input, echoes, checks Ctrl-C.
06h	Direct console I/O, no Ctrl-C check. Note that since this function returns whether or not a character is ready, it can be used to test the keyboard status, without a Ctrl-C check.
07h	Console input, no echo or Ctrl-C check.
08h	Console input, echoes, no Ctrl-C check.
0Ah	Buffered keyboard input.
0Ch	Clear keyboard buffer and invoke input function.
0Bh	Check standard input status.

```
;File:     DISPLAY.MAC

;Assembler Display Macros:
;
;     PRINTS s         Sends string s to standard output.
;
;     PRINTN r         Prints contents of register r in decimal.
;
;     PRINTH r         Hex dump of register r.

;------------------------------------------------------------------------

prints    macro    s                    ;;Displays string 's' at
          local    a01, str             ;;current cursor position.
          jmp      a01                  ;;Sample usage:
str       db       s                    ;;    prints "hello world"
          db       '$'                  ;;Saves all registers.
a01:      push     ax
          push     dx
          push     ds
          mov      ax, cs               ;;DS:DX must contain address
          mov      ds, ax               ;;of '$' terminated string.
          mov      ah, 09h              ;;DOS print string function.
          mov      dx, offset str
          int      21h
          pop      ds
          pop      dx
          pop      ax
          endm

;------------------------------------------------------------------------

printn    macro    reg                  ;;Prints contents of register 'reg'
          local    a01                  ;;in unsigned decimal format.
                                        ;;Sample usage:
                                        ;;    printn si
          push     ax                   ;;Saves all register.
          push     bx
          push     cx
          push     dx
          push     si

          mov      ax, reg              ;;Place register value in AX.
          mov      cx, 5                ;;Will print 5 digits.
          mov      bx, 10000            ;;= 2710h.
a01:      xor      dx, dx               ;;Zero out upper word of dividend.
          div      bx                   ;;Obtain highest decimal digit.
          mov      si, dx               ;;Save remainder in SI.
          mov      dl, al               ;;Move digit to DL.
          add      dl, 30h              ;;Convert binary to decimal.
          mov      ah, 02h              ;;DOS display character function.
          int      21h                  ;;Print it.
          mov      ax, bx               ;;Divide divisor (BX) by 10.

          mov      bx, 10
          xor      dx, dx               ;;Zero out upper word of dividend.
          div      bx
          mov      bx, ax
          mov      ax, si               ;;Restore remainder.
          loop     a01                  ;;Divide remainder to get next digit.

          pop      si
          pop      dx
          pop      cx
```

Figure 4.4: *Assembler display macros*

```
                pop     bx
                pop     ax

                endm

;--------------------------------------------------------------------

printh  macro   reg                     ;;Prints contents of register 'reg'
local   a01, a02                        ;;in hexadecimal.
                                        ;;Sample usage:
                push   ax               ;;       printh si
                push   bx               ;;Saves all registers.
                push   cx
                push   dx

                mov    bx, reg
                mov    ch, 4            ;;Number of digits.
a01:            mov    cl, 4            ;;Set count to 4 digits.
                rol    bx, cl           ;;Left digit to right.
                mov    al, bl           ;;Move to AL.
                and    al, 0fh          ;;Mask off left digit.
                add    al, 30h          ;;Convert hex to ASCII.
                cmp    al, 3ah          ;;Is it > 9?
                jl     a02              ;;Jump if digit = 0 to 9.
                add    al, 7h           ;;Digit is a to f.
a02:            mov    dl, al           ;;Put ASCII char in DL.
                mov    ah, 2            ;;Display output function.
                int    21h              ;;Call DOS.
                dec    ch               ;;Done 4 digits?
                jnz    a01              ;;Not yet.
                pop    dx
                pop    cx
                pop    bx
                pop    ax

                endm

;--------------------------------------------------------------------
```

Figure 4.4: *Assembler display macros (continued)*

The following set of functions writes to the standard output.

Function	Service performed
02h	Display output, checks Ctrl-C.
06h	Direct console I/O, no Ctrl-C check.
09h	Print string.

The following function manages printer output.

Function	Service performed
05h	Send character to printer.

The following functions manage serial port I/O.

Function	Service performed
03h	Auxiliary input.
04h	Auxiliary output.

Disk-Level Management

Disk-level functions deal with a disk device as a whole, and not with specific files. As an example, the C function **curr_drv** in Figure 4.5 uses function 19h to return a string containing the current drive.

The following are disk-level management functions. The first two functions are useful for such tasks as reading the disk boot sector or file allocation table. See the above for information on register preservation and error codes for these two functions.

Function	Service performed
int 25h	Absolute disk read.
int 26h	Absolute disk write.
0Dh	Disk reset. Flushes all buffers; this function should be called by Ctrl-C handlers, but does not update directory entries (it is necessary to close files to update directory entries).
19h	Get current drive.
0Eh	Set current drive.
1Bh	Get file allocation table (FAT) information for the current drive.
1Ch	Get FAT information for a specific device. This function is identical to 1Bh but can specify any drive.
2Fh	Get disk transfer address (DTA).
1Ah	Set disk transfer address (DTA).
54h	Get verify switch.
2Eh	Set/reset verify switch.
36h	Get disk free space.

Directory-Level Management

Directory-level functions, introduced with DOS 2.*x*, deal with the hierarchical directory structure. For example, the following assembler code

```
/*
      File:    CURDRV.C

      A C Function that uses DOS Function Call 19h to Obtain the Current Drive.
*/
#include <stdio.h>


void main ()
      {
      char *curr_drv (void);

      printf ("The current drive is %s.\n", curr_drv());
      }


#include <dos.h>

char *curr_drv ()                         /* Returns a string containing the */
      {                                   /* current drive designation.      */
      static char *diskname [] = {"A:","B:","C:","D:","E:"};
      union REGS intregs;

      intregs.h.ah = 0x19;                /* Note that 'int86' returns the */
                                          /* value of the AX register.     */
      return (diskname [int86(0x21,&intregs,&intregs) & 0xff]);
      }
```

Figure 4.5: *A C function that uses DOS function 19h to return the current drive*

uses function 47h to load the current directory path into the global variable **cur_dir**. (*Note:* this code assumes that **cur_dir** is located in a segment that is a member of **groupseg**, and that DS already contains the base address of this group.) See Figure 4.8 for an example of this code used in the context of a simple program.

```
mov   ah, 47h                  ;Get current directory.
mov   si, offset groupseg:cur_dir
mov   dl, 0                     ;Specifies default drive.
int   21h
```

The following DOS functions manage directories.

Function	Service performed
39h	Create directory.
3Ah	Remove directory.
47h	Get current directory.
3Bh	Set current directory.

File-Level Management

DOS currently provides two independent sets of functions for managing individual files: the traditional file control block (FCB) functions, and the file handle functions.

Traditional FCB functions   File control block functions, which were introduced with DOS 1.*x*, have been largely replaced by file handle functions. Their primary disadvantage is that they do not support directory paths. They are useful, however, in several special cases:

- When strict downward compatibility with DOS 1.*x* is required.

- When more than 20 files need to be open simultaneously (20 is the normal limit for handle functions, even if the configuration file **files =** line specifies more). See Chapter 6, however, for a way of getting around the 20 file handle limit.

- For file truncation: FCB function 28h can be used to truncate a file to a given length by placing the desired length in the *random record field* of the FCB, and placing 0 in CX. This function has no simple handle function counterpart. (See the DOS technical reference for an explanation of this function and the FCB layout.)

- For renaming a volume label or directory: Use FCB function 17h, with an *extended file control block* (see below). This function also has no simple handle function counterpart.

Figure 4.6 lists a program that uses DOS function 17h to rename a subdirectory (which may be on any drive, but must be in the current directory of the selected drive; remember that FCB functions do not support path names). Function 17h must be passed the address of an *extended* and *modified* file control block. An extended FCB contains a seven-byte header, and is used for files that have special attributes (such as a hidden file or, in this case, a subdirectory). The first byte of the FCB contains 0FFh, to indicate that it is an extended FCB. Offset 6 should contain the attribute value 10h, which indicates that the file is actually a subdirectory. The old drive and directory name is placed at offset 7. The FCB must also be modified to contain the new directory name at offset 24 (the old name is prefaced with a drive designation; the name at offset 24 must *not* begin with a drive).

When running the program, enter the old name (including an optional drive) followed by the new name on the command line. DOS places both values in the program segment prefix. The program transfers these names to the file control block and invokes function 17h.

```
page 50,130

;File:     RENDIR.ASM

;.COM format for a program that renames a directory
;
;     Usage:
;           RENDIR [drive:]oldname newname
;
;     To generate .COM file from RENDIR.ASM:
;           MASM RENDIR;
;           LINK RENDIR;
;           EXE2BIN RENDIR.EXE RENDIR.COM

      include \masm\display.mac               ;Contains macro 'prints', Figure 4.1.

stackseg    segment stack
stackseg    ends

codeseg     segment
codeseg     ends

dataseg     segment

fcb         db        0ffh                    ;Extended file control block.
            db        5 dup (0)               ;Reserved.
            db        10h                     ;10h is code for directory.
d_old       db        12 dup (?)              ;Old drive and directory name.
            db        5 dup (?)               ;Reserved.
n_new       db        20 dup (?)              ;New name (not including drive) &
                                              ;remainder of FCB.

dataseg     ends

groupseg    group     codeseg,dataseg
            assume    cs:groupseg
            assume    ds:groupseg
            assume    es:groupseg

codeseg     segment
                                              ;PSP values entered by user.
            org       5ch
dir1        db        12 dup (?)              ;Old drive and directory name.
            org       6dh
name2       db        11 dup (?)              ;New name only (skips drive at 6Ch).

            org       100h
main        proc      near

            mov       cx, 12                  ;Move old drive and directory into FCB.
            mov       si, offset dir1
            mov       di, offset groupseg:d_old
            cld
            rep       movsb

            mov       cx, 11                  ;Move new name into FCB.
            mov       si, offset name2
            mov       di, offset groupseg:n_new
            cld
            rep       movsb

            mov       ah, 17h                 ;FCB function 17h renames files,
            mov       dx, offset groupseg:fcb ;directories, or volume labels.
            int       21h
            or        al, al
            jz        m01                     ;AL = FFh => error.
            prints    "no such directory or duplicate name"
            mov       ax, 4c01h               ;Exit w/ errorlevel 1.
            int       21h
```

Figure 4.6: *A .COM format for a program that uses DOS function 17h to rename a directory*

```
m01:        mov     ax, 4c00h              ;Exit w/ errorlevel 0.
            int     21h

main        endp

codeseg     ends

            end     main
```

Figure 4.6: *A .COM format for a program that uses DOS function 17h to rename a directory (continued)*

The following are FCB functions for managing files.

Function	Service performed
0Fh	Open file.
16h	Create file.
10h	Close file.
11h	Find first matching file.
12h	Find next matching file.
13h	Delete file.
17h	Rename file.
23h	Get file size.
29h	Parse file name.

Handle functions   The file handle functions should be selected whenever possible. Among their many advantages over the FCB functions are:

- Support for directory paths.

- General simplicity. Files are referenced by a simple two-byte handle, and all control information is maintained internally by DOS; the programmer does not have to keep a control block within the program.

- Speed, and more economical use of system resources.

- More complete error reporting.

- Unlike FCB functions, all file positions and quantities of data to be transferred are specified in bytes, offering greater simplicity and more support for variable length records.

- Greater likelihood of being compatible with future versions of the operating system.

- Support for record-locking and file-sharing on networks.

When a file is opened or created using one of these functions, a 16-bit handle is returned, and is used to reference the file for all subsequent operations. In addition to the handles that are returned by the open functions, there are also five predefined *standard* handles. These handles refer by default to the basic character devices (the console, auxiliary device, and printer), and are always available for use without having to open the device. The following table lists the standard handles, their names, and the devices they reference by default.

Handle	Name	Default device
0000	Standard input	CON
0001	Standard output	CON
0002	Standard error	CON
0003	Standard auxiliary device	AUX
0004	Standard printer device	PRN

Note that the first two standard handles can be redirected by the user. For example, if the program UNWS were run using the command line

UNWS <FILE.DOC >FILE.TXT

all reads from the standard input handle (0000) would come from the file FILE.DOC, and all writes to the standard output handle (0001) would be directed to the file FILE.TXT. It may not always be desirable, however, to allow the user to redirect console I/O; a program may need to communicate explicitly with the console. To generate output to the screen that is not subject to redirection, standard error (0002) can be used instead of standard output (standard error is typically used for sending important messages to the user and is therefore not redirectable).

Another way of avoiding the redirection of console input and output is to open the CON device under a separate handle. For example, the following assembler code opens the console device and saves the returned handle. Subsequent reads and writes with this handle cannot be redirected.

```
dataseg    segment
fname      db 'CON',0        ;ASCIIZ name of console device.
console    dw ?              ;Handle for console.
dataseg    ends

.
.
.
```

```
mov   ah, 3dh                    ;Handle file open.
mov   dx, offset groupseg:fname
mov   al, 2                      ;Open for reading and
                                 ;writing.
int   21h
jc    error                      ;Jump on error to error
                                 ;handler.
mov   console, ax                ;Otherwise save handle.
```

Note that when using the **stream** file functions in C (for example, **fprintf** and **fread**), the standard handles may be directly accessed by using one of the following predefined **streams** (i.e., **FILE** pointers):

DOS standard handle	C predefined stream
Standard input	stdin
Standard output	stdout
Standard error	stderr
Standard auxiliary	stdaux
Standard printer	stdprn

Some C functions, such as **getchar** and **putchar**, automatically use standard input and standard output.

To illustrate the use of some of the other functions in this group, Figure 4.7 lists an assembler program that employs functions 4Eh, 4Fh, and 43h. This program uses functions 4Eh (find first matching file) and 4Fh (find next matching file) to find files matching the specification the user enters on the command line. Function 43h (change file mode) is then used to switch off the *archive* bit in the directory entry for each file. Whenever a file is modified, DOS turns on its archive bit. DOS BACKUP and other utilities will back up a file if this bit is turned on, and then switch the bit off. The program in this listing is useful for preventing a group of files from being backed up, and the user may specify file names using the standard global characters * and ?. Note that the code assumes that there is only one blank space between the program name and its parameter; a more robust implementation would remove all leading blanks from the parameter. The attribute 07h is chosen for the function 4Eh search, which includes all normal, read-only, hidden, and system files (see the DOS technical reference, Chapter 5). See Figure 4.10 for examples of the use of functions 3Ch, 3Eh, and 46h.

```
page 50,130

;File:    NOBAK.ASM

;.COM format for a program that switches off the file archive bit
;
;    Usage:
;          NOBAK filespec                  (filespec can include wildcards)
;
;    To generate .COM file from NOBAK.ASM:
;          MASM NOBAK;
;          LINK NOBAK;
;          EXE2BIN NOBAK.EXE NOBAK.COM

include     \masm\display.mac              ;Contains 'printn' and 'prints' macros
                                           ;(Figure 4.1).

stackseg    segment stack
stackseg    ends

            assume  cs:codeseg
            assume  ds:codeseg

codeseg     segment

            org     80h
dta         label   byte                   ;The default disk transfer area (DTA).
parmlen     db      ?                      ;Length of parameter line.
parmline    db      127 dup (?)            ;Parameter line starts here (includes
                                           ;leading blank).
            org     100h
main        proc    near

            xor     bh, bh                 ;Make parameter ASCIIZ (i.e.
            mov     bl, parmlen            ;place 0 after last byte).
            mov     parmline[bx], 0

            mov     ah, 4eh                ;Find first matching file.
            mov     dx, offset parmline+1  ;NB: assumes single blank!
            mov     cx, 0007h              ;File attribute for search.
            int     21h
            jnc     m01
            prints  'no files found'       ;Error: print message &
            mov     ax, 4c01h              ;bail out w/ errorlevel 1.
            int     21h

m01:        mov     ah, 43h                ;Chmod function.
            mov     dx, offset dta + 30    ;Position of found file name.
            mov     cl, dta[21]            ;Place existing attribute in cl.
            and     cx, 00dfh              ;Mask off archive bit.
            mov     al,1                   ;'Set' subfunction.
            int     21h
            jnc     m02
            printn  ax                     ;Error: print error code &
            prints  ' chmod error'         ;quit w/ errorlevel 1.
            mov     ax, 4c01h
            int     21h

m02:        mov     ah,4fh                 ;Find next file.
            int     21h
            jc      m03                    ;Not an error, just no more files.
            jmp     m01

m03:        mov     ax,4c00h               ;Exit w/ errorlevel 0.
            int     21h

main        endp

codeseg     ends

            end     main
```

Figure 4.7: *A .COM format program that switches off file archive bits*

The following are the handle functions for managing files.

Function	Service performed
3Ch	Create file.
5Bh[3]	Create new file.
5Ah[3]	Create unique file.
3Dh	Open file.
6Ch[4]	Extend open/create. This function combines the services currently provided by function 3Dh (open), 3Ch (create file), and 5Bh (create new file).
3Eh	Close file.
41h	Delete file.
43h	Change file mode.
45h	Get new duplicate file handle. This function can be used to periodically update the directory entry for a file without the need to close and reopen the original handle (a slow process). Simply request and close an additional handle to the same file. Note that under DOS 3.3 you can efficiently flush buffers and update the directory entry through function 68h.
46h	Force duplication of existing handle. This function is handy for redirecting the standard device handles. For an example, see Figure 4.10.
4Eh	Find first matching file.
4Fh	Find next matching file.
56h	Rename a file.
57h	Get/set file date and time.
67h[3]	Set maximum number of file handles.
68h[3]	Commit file (flush buffers, update directory entry).

Record/Byte Level Management of Files

Once a file has been opened (through one of the open or create functions, or by using one of the five predefined device handles), these functions provide a way of transferring either individual bytes or entire blocks of data.

Traditional FCB functions   See the File-Level Management section for the use of FCB functions. The following are the traditional FCB functions for performing file I/O.

Function	Service performed
14h	Sequential read.
15h	Sequential write.
24h	Set relative record field.
21h	Random read, single record.
22h	Random write, single record.
27h	Random block read, multiple records.
28h	Random block write, multiple records. See comment in the File-Level Management section on using this function for truncating a file.

Handle functions   See the File-Level Management section for the many advantages of this set of services.

As mentioned before, the use of handle functions for reading and writing to basic character devices can be optimized by employing function 44h (I/O control for devices) to change the mode of the device from *cooked* to *raw.* Changing modes is also a way to control such features as whether or not input is echoed. In the cooked I/O mode (the default for devices and not available for disk files),

- Characters are checked for Ctrl-S, Ctrl-P, and Ctrl-C.

- Input characters are echoed to standard output.

- Tabs are expanded into spaces.

- Standard input data may be edited using the usual DOS function keys.

In the raw mode, all of these features are disabled, resulting in improved performance (and performance is woefully lacking for standard input/output). Note that when the mode of either standard input, standard output, or standard error is changed, the mode of all three handles automatically changes because they refer to the same actual device. In the more refined language of the IBM technical reference, the *cooked* mode is known as *ASCII,* and the *raw* mode as *binary.* General techniques for optimal video output are discussed in Chapter 8, including a benchmark that demonstrates that the performance advantage of the raw mode for video output can be significant.

See Figure 4.8 for examples of functions 40h, 44h, and 47h. This program first loads the current directory into the variable **cur_dir** (using function 47h, which automatically appends a 0 to the end of the string), and then calls **rawmode**, which uses function 44h to change standard output to the raw mode. The purpose of changing to the raw mode is to demonstrate a method for improving performance; however, in a real application it would obviously not be beneficial to change modes unless a considerable quantity of data were being displayed. Once the mode has been changed, **printz** is called to write the contents of **cur_dir** to standard output via function 40h. The function **printz** is useful for writing zero terminated strings, since it automatically calculates their length. Finally, **cookmode** is called to restore the mode to the default cooked condition. (Otherwise subsequent programs may behave strangely, since in the raw mode tab characters, for example, are no longer expanded into spaces but rather display as little circles.)

Figure 4.9 lists the function **readc**, which uses the handle function 3Fh to read a single character into register AL. This function demonstrates how the traditional character device functions in the range 01h–0Ch can be emulated using the more standard handle functions. If this function is called when standard input is in the raw mode, it behaves very much like function 07, not echoing or checking the character, and returning immediately without waiting for a carriage return.

The following are the DOS handle functions for performing file I/O.

Function	Service performed
44h	I/O control for devices. This function is discussed further in Chapter 9 on device drivers.
3Fh	Read from file/device.
40h	Write to file/device.
42h	Move read/write pointer.

Network Management Functions

DOS version 3.0 was the first to provide functions supporting networks. Note that functions 5Eh and 5Fh are available only with DOS version 3.1 or later, and require that the IBM-PC Network Program be loaded. See the DOS technical reference and the documentation supplied with the network system for more information.

The following is a list of the network management functions.

```
page 50,130

;File:    CURDIR.ASM

;.COM file format for a program that obtains the current directory,  and
;writes it to the standard output, after changing device mode to "raw"
;
;      To generate .COM file from CURDIR.ASM:
;          MASM CURDIR;
;          LINK CURDIR;
;          EXE2BIN CURDIR.EXE CURDIR.COM

stackseg    segment stack
stackseg    ends

codeseg     segment
codeseg     ends

dataseg     segment

cur_dir     db       64 dup (?)              ;Buffer for holding current directory.

dataseg     ends

groupseg    group    codeseg,dataseg
            assume   cs:groupseg
            assume   ds:groupseg
            assume   es:groupseg

codeseg     segment

            org      100h
main        proc     near

            mov      ah, 47h                 ;Use DOS function 47h to load
                                             ;current directory into 'cur_dir'.
            mov      si, offset groupseg:cur_dir
            mov      dl, 0                    ;Specifies the default drive.
            int      21h

            call     rawmode                 ;Change stdin/out/err to "raw"
                                             ;mode to improve performance.

                                             ;Print 0-terminated contents
                                             ;of 'cur_dir'.
            mov      dx, offset groupseg:cur_dir
            call     printz

            call     cookmode                ;Restore stdin/out/err to default
                                             ;"cooked" mode.

            mov      ah, 4ch                 ;Exit w/ errorlevel 0.
            mov      al, 0
            int      21h

main        endp

rawmode     proc     near                    ;Places standard input/output/error
                                             ;in "raw" mode.
                                             ;Alters registers: AX,BX,DX.

            mov      ax, 4400h               ;Read "device information" using
                                             ;function 44h, subfunction 00h.
            xor      bx, bx                  ;Handle for standard input.
            int      21h                     ;Places device information in DX.

            xor      dh, dh                  ;Zero out upper byte of DX.
            or       dl, 20h                 ;Turn on "raw" bit, #5.
            mov      ax, 4401h               ;Write back "device information" using
                                             ;function 44h, subfunction 01h.
```

Figure 4.8: *An assembler program demonstrating the DOS functions 40h, 44h, and 47h*

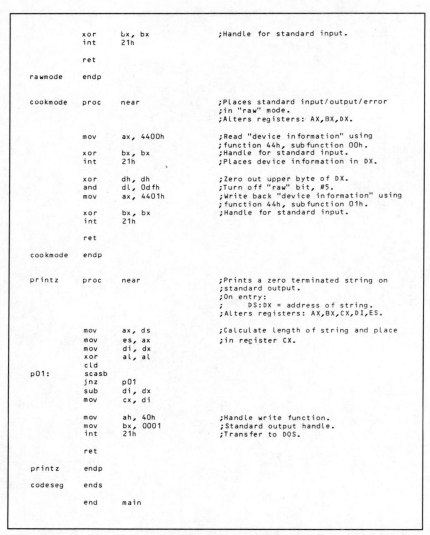

```
            xor     bx, bx              ;Handle for standard input.
            int     21h

            ret

rawmode     endp


cookmode    proc    near                ;Places standard input/output/error
                                        ;in "raw" mode.
                                        ;Alters registers: AX,BX,DX.

            mov     ax, 4400h           ;Read "device information" using
                                        ;function 44h, subfunction 00h.
            xor     bx, bx              ;Handle for standard input.
            int     21h                 ;Places device information in DX.

            xor     dh, dh              ;Zero out upper byte of DX.
            and     dl, 0dfh            ;Turn off "raw" bit, #5.
            mov     ax, 4401h           ;Write back "device information" using
                                        ;function 44h, subfunction 01h.
            xor     bx, bx              ;Handle for standard input.
            int     21h

            ret

cookmode    endp


printz      proc    near                ;Prints a zero terminated string on
                                        ;standard output.
                                        ;On entry:
                                        ;    DS:DX = address of string.
                                        ;Alters registers: AX,BX,CX,DI,ES.

            mov     ax, ds              ;Calculate length of string and place
            mov     es, ax              ;in register CX.
            mov     di, dx
            xor     al, al
            cld
p01:        scasb
            jnz     p01
            sub     di, dx
            mov     cx, di

            mov     ah, 40h             ;Handle write function.
            mov     bx, 0001            ;Standard output handle.
            int     21h                 ;Transfer to DOS.

            ret

printz      endp

codeseg     ends

            end     main
```

Figure 4.8: *An assembler proogram demonstrating the DOS functions 40h, 44h, and 47h (continued)*

Function   Service performed

5Ch[3]   Lock/unlock file access.

5Eh[3]   AH = 00h: Get machine name.

             AH = 02h: Set printer setup.

             AH = 03h: Get printer setup.

```
page 50,130

;File:      READC.ASM

include     DISPLAY.MAC                     ;Contains macros 'prints' & 'printn',
                                            ;Figure 4.4.

readc       proc    near                    ;Reads a single character from stdin
                                            ;into register AL, using function 3Fh.
                                            ;Alters registers:  AX, BX, CX, DX.
                                            ;Returns -1 in AL for end of file.
            jmp     r01

charbuf     db      ?                       ;Function 3Fh requires a buffer.

r01:        push    ds
            mov     ax, cs                  ;Set DS to segment of 'charbuf' (in CS).
            mov     ds, ax
            mov     ah, 3fh                 ;Read from file or device function.
            mov     bx, 00h                 ;Handle for standard input.
            mov     dx, offset charbuf      ;Address of buffer.
            mov     cx, 1                   ;Read single character.
            int     21h
            jnc     r02                     ;Test for error.
            prints  "dos function 3f error "
            printn  ax
            mov     ax, 4c01h               ;Quit with errorlevel 1.
            int     21h

r02:        or      ax, ax                  ;Test for end of file.
            jnz     r03
            mov     al, 0ffh                ;Return -1 (FFh) in AL for eof.
            pop     ds
            ret

r03:        mov     al, charbuf             ;Not end of file.
            pop     ds
            ret

readc       endp
```

Figure 4.9: *A procedure for reading a character from standard input using function 3Fh*

5Fh[3]   AH = 02h: Get redirection list entry.

       AH = 03h: Redirect device.

       AH = 04h: Cancel redirection.

Memory and Process Management

DOS 2.0 introduced an interesting set of functions to allocate and deallocate blocks of system memory, and another function to run a secondary program (a *child process*) from within a parent application. It is thus possible for a program to run a freestanding .EXE or .COM file (including COMMAND.COM) and then return to whatever it was doing. Memory and process management functions are grouped together since a primary use for the memory management services is to free sufficient memory to run a child process. The series of steps required to load and run another process is somewhat tricky, and the best way to explain them is through an example program.

The assembler program in Figure 4.10 demonstrates the use of DOS functions 4Ah (modify allocated memory block) and 4Bh (execute program) to load and run a child process. It also uses function 46h (force duplicate handle), described earlier, to redirect both *standard output* and *standard error*. As mentioned before, standard error cannot be redirected from the command line; this program, however, shows how it can be redirected for a child process from within the parent program. This utility loads and runs MASM.EXE, passing it the command line entered by the user. All output from MASM is redirected to a file having the same name as the source file specified in the command line, but with the extension .ERR. This is a handy utility for users of Microsoft MASM version 4.0, which for some reason does not allow the redirection of error output to a file with the > command line symbol. The basic steps are as follows:

1. Relocate stack. The stack pointer is set to point to 1024 bytes beyond the last defined label in the data segment. The 1K stack space is thus at the very end of the program, and is *not* reserved using **db** since this would unnecessarily lengthen the .COM file on disk.

2. Release allocated memory above program. Since all free memory is initially allocated to a .COM file, function 4Ah is used to release memory above the end of the stack, providing the maximum amount of free memory for the child process. Note that releasing unused memory is a generally good practice, even for programs not executing a child process, and will increase the chances that the program will be compatible with multitasking environments.

3. Build **fname** (the name of the error file) by appending .ERR to the source file name from the command line.

4. Open the error file **fname**, and place the file handle in **fhandle**.

5. Use function 46h (force duplicate handle) to force the handles for standard output (0001) and standard error (0002) to refer to the same file as **fhandle**. Thus, any subsequent output to standard output or error will be redirected to the error file. Furthermore, a child process inherits all open handles from the parent process, and therefore the redirection remains effective during the execution of the child process.

6. Save registers SS and SP in memory addressable from the code segment, and restore them immediately on function return. As mentioned earlier, function 4Bh trashes *all* registers.

7. Use function 4Bh to run the child process. Note from the listing how the parameter block must be set up for this function.

8. Upon return from function 4Bh, close the error file and terminate the parent process.

The following DOS functions manage memory and processes.

Function	Service performed
26h	Create new program segment prefix. *Note:* this method is obsolete; use function 4Bh.
48h	Allocate memory.
49h	Free allocated memory.
4Ah	Modify allocated memory block.
4Bh	Load or execute a program.
4Dh	Get return code of a subprocess. In order to use this function, the subprocess must have terminated through DOS function 4Ch (which is the preferred method, as explained later).

Program Termination

MS-DOS provides two basic methods for terminating a program: simple termination of a transient application that releases the occupied memory, and termination that leaves the code resident in memory.

Simple termination   You can terminate a program by simply issuing a **ret** instruction, but the stack (and also the CS register for a near return) must contain precisely the correct values. (The instruction **ret** causes branching to the first byte of the program segment prefix, which contains an **int 20h** instruction.) A safer method is to use one of the DOS terminate functions. The preferred function is 4Ch, since it returns an error code (which can be tested from a batch file through **errorlevel**, or from a parent process through function 4Dh). Also, function 4Ch is the only terminate function that does *not* require that the CS register contain the segment address of the program segment prefix (see Chapter 6 for an explanation of the program segment prefix). Note that although these functions perform some final housekeeping and close all open file handles, files that have changed in length must be properly closed by the application in order for their directory entries to be correctly updated.

```
page 50,130

;File:    RMASM.ASM

;.COM format for program to run MASM.EXE as a child process after redirecting
;all output to an error file
;
;    Usage:
;         RMASM sourcefile, ...          (same command line as used with MASM)
;
;    To generate .COM file from RMASM.ASM:
;         MASM RMASM;
;         LINK RMASM;
;         EXE2BIN RMASM.EXE RMASM.COM

include    DISPLAY.MAC                  ;Contains 'printn' and 'prints',
                                        ;Figure 4.1.

STD        equ     1                    ;1 => redirect standard output.
ERR        equ     1                    ;1 => redirect standard error.

stackseg   segment stack                ;Fake stack segment to appease linker.
stackseg   ends

codeseg    segment
codeseg    ends

dataseg    segment

fname      db      64 dup (?)           ;Build up error file name here.
fext       db      '.err', '$'          ;File extension for error file.
fhandle    dw      ?                    ;File handle for error file.
                                        ;Name of program to run:
masm       db      'c:\masm\masm.exe',0

parmblk    label   word                 ;Parameter block for function 4Bh.
environ    dw      0                    ;0 => inherit parent's environment.
comm_off   dw      80h                  ;Offset of command line.
comm_seg   dw      ?                    ;Com. line segment: fill in at runtime.
fcb1       dd      -1                   ;File control blocks to copy.
fcb2       dd      -1                   ;-1 => don't copy FCB.

s_seg      dw      ?                    ;Save area for SS and SP.
s_ptr      dw      ?

stackstart label   byte                 ;1024 k stack begins here, but is not
                                        ;"db'ed" to save disk space.
dataseg    ends

groupseg   group   codeseg, dataseg
           assume  cs:groupseg
           assume  ds:groupseg
           assume  es:groupseg

codeseg    segment

           org     80h
parmlen    db      ?                    ;Length of command line.
parm       db      127 dup (?)          ;Full command line.

           org     100h
main       proc    near
                                        ;Lower the stack.
           mov     sp, offset groupseg:stackstart + 1024

           mov     ah, 4ah              ;Reduce memory allocation to make room
                                        ; for child process.
                                        ;Load new memory size into bx, add 15
                                        ;and shr by 4 to convert to paragraphs.
           mov     bx, offset groupseg:stackstart + 1024 + 15
```

Figure 4.10: *An assembler program demonstrating standard device redirection and running a child process*

```
                mov     cl, 4
                shr     bx, cl
                int     21h                     ;Reduce memory block.
                jnc     m01
                printn  ax                      ;Error: print message and quit.
                prints  ' error on function 4Ah'
                mov     ax, 4c01h
                int     21h

m01:                                            ;Build up error file 'fname'.
                xor     bh, bh                  ;Mark end of parameters w/ FFh.
                mov     bl, parmlen
                mov     parm[bx], 0ffh
                                                ;Initialize SI, DI, & DF for transfer.
                mov     si, offset groupseg:parm
                mov     di, offset groupseg:fname
                cld
m02:            cmp     byte ptr[si], ' '       ;Scan past leading blanks in parm.
                jne     m03
                inc     si
                jmp     m02
m03:            cmp     byte ptr[si], '.'       ;End of source file name is
                je      m04                     ;indicated by one of these
                cmp     byte ptr[si], ';'       ;characters, therefore STOP
                je      m04                     ;copying from 'parm' to 'fname'.
                cmp     byte ptr[si], ' '
                je      m04
                cmp     byte ptr[si], '/'
                je      m04
                cmp     byte ptr[si], ','
                je      m04
                cmp     byte ptr[si], 0ffh
                je      m04
                movsb                           ;Copy a character from parm to fname.
                jmp     m03                     ;Go back for another character.

m04:            mov     cx, 5                   ;Copy 5 byte 'fext' onto end of 'fname'.
                mov     si, offset groupseg:fext
                rep     movsb

                mov     ah, 3ch                 ;Open error file.
                mov     dx, offset groupseg:fname
                mov     cx, 0                   ;Normal file attribute.
                int     21h
                jnc     m05
                printn  ax                      ;Error: print message and quit.
                prints  ' error on function 3Ch'
                mov     ax, 4c01h
                int     21h

m05:
if STD
                mov     fhandle, ax             ;Redirect standard out -- i.e. force
                mov     ah, 46h                 ;standard output file handle to refer
                mov     bx, fhandle             ;to the error file.
                mov     cx, 0001
                int     21h
                jnc     m06
                printn  ax
                prints  ' error on function 46h'
                mov     ax, 4c01h
                int     21h
endif

m06:
if ERR
                mov     ah, 46h                 ;Redirect standard error.
                mov     bx, fhandle
                mov     cx, 0002
```

Figure 4.10: *An assembler program demonstrating standard device redirection and running a child process (continued)*

```
              int       21h
              jnc       m07
              printn    ax
              prints    ' error on function 46h'
              mov       ax, 4c01h
              int       21h
      endif

      m07:    mov       ah, 4bh                  ;Execute program function.
              mov       dx, offset groupseg:masm ;Pointer to program name.
              mov       comm_seg, cs             ;Fill in segment of command line.
                                                 ;Point BX to parameter block.
              mov       bx, offset groupseg:parmblk
              mov       al, 00                   ;0 => EXEC subfunction.

              push      ds                       ;Save any registers here.
              mov       s_seg, ss                ;Save SS & SP in memory addressible
              mov       s_ptr, sp                ;from CS.
              int       21h                      ;Branch to child process here.
              mov       ss, cs:s_seg             ;Restore SS & SP FIRST.

              mov       sp, cs:s_ptr
              pop       ds                       ;Restore any other registers here.

              mov       ah, 3eh                  ;Close the error file.
              mov       bx, fhandle
              int       21h
              jnc       m08
              printn    ax
              prints    ' error on function 3eh'
              mov       ax, 4c01h
              int       21h

      m08:    mov       ax, 4c00h                ;Exit w/ errorlevel 0.
              int       21h

      main    endp

      codeseg ends

              end       main
```

Figure 4.10: *An assembler program demonstrating standard device redirection and running a child process (continued)*

The following are the simple termination functions.

Function	Service performed
int 20h	Program terminate.
00h	Program terminate.

The above two methods are identical, although the better route is to use interrupt 21h function 0. Note that CS must contain the segment address of the program segment prefix.

4Ch	Terminate a process. This function is used in the example programs in this chapter, and is the preferred method.

Terminate and stay resident   Function 31h is the preferred method for terminating a memory-resident program because it returns an error code (as does function 4Ch) and allows the program to retain more than 64K in memory. The use of this function is illustrated in Chapter 11.

The following are the terminate and stay-resident functions.

Function   Service performed

int 27h   Terminate and remain resident. Note that this function does not allow the program to return an error code, and limits the resident program size to 64K.

31h   Terminate and remain resident. This is the preferred method.

Miscellaneous Functions

The following are the remaining MS-DOS functions that do not fit into any of the previous categories.

Function   Service performed

int 2Fh[3]   Print spooler access and multiplex interrupt.

35h   Get interrupt vector. This function is demonstrated above in the section Accessing the Interrupt Functions from C.

25h   Set interrupt vector. The use of the above two functions is illustrated in Chapters 6 and 11.

2Ah   Get date.

2Bh   Set date.

2Ch   Get time.

2Dh   Set time.

30h   Get DOS version number. This function is used in Chapter 7.

33h   Get/set Ctrl-Break check status.

38h   Get/set country-dependent information.

44h   I/O control for devices. The listing in Figure 4.8 demonstrates one of the many uses for this function, which will be discussed further in Chapter 9 on device drivers.

59h[3]   Get extended error information. This function is discussed in the section on error handling.

62h[3]   Get program segment prefix address.

65h[3]   Get extended country information.

66h[3]   Get/set global code page.

CHAPTER 5

The BIOS Functions

The IBM-PC BIOS (Basic Input-Output System), which is contained in the read-only memory supplied with the hardware, provides another set of useful functions for the MS-DOS programmer. These functions are at a lower level than the DOS functions, in two senses.

First, following the classical design of operating systems, MS-DOS is built in layers: higher level layers are implemented using the resources provided by the lower layers. Accordingly, application programs typically call DOS functions, and DOS functions ultimately call BIOS functions. However, also according to the classical design, a higher level may generally bypass the next lower level and directly access the lowest layers. Consequently, the programmer may circumvent DOS and directly call the BIOS, potentially achieving greater program performance by eliminating one of the two software layers. In fact, a benchmark presented in Chapter 8 shows that video output directly through the BIOS is approximately two times faster than output through DOS.

Second, the BIOS functions are also at a lower level in the sense that they control many of the features that are specific to the architecture of MS-DOS machines. DOS provides a much more generic, abstract set of services, such as might be found on many other operating systems (for example, a number of the services are almost identical to those of UNIX). The BIOS, however, provides many hardware-specific features such as setting video display modes and attributes, displaying graphics, formatting disk sectors, and obtaining a list of available equipment. The BIOS is thus an essential tool for achieving optimal software performance by tapping the inherent resources of MS-DOS machines.

Note, however, that the BIOS is not at the lowest level of the layered system; at an even lower level are the specific memory addresses and ports belonging to the hardware. The BIOS is designed to provide a fair degree of hardware independence, and the interface to its services should remain constant even with modifications in the hardware. Chapter 7 discusses methods of testing for compatibility, so that the software can always use the method that is best for the specific machine.

The two primary advantages of the BIOS functions, as compared to those provided by DOS, are a higher level of performance and the availability of functions not offered by DOS. The management of textual and graphic video displays is probably the area in which the BIOS offers the greatest advantages over DOS; therefore, this set of functions is emphasized in the descriptions that follow.

Among the disadvantages of BIOS, as compared to DOS, functions are the lack of portability to non-IBM compatible MS-DOS machines (see Chapter 7), and the loss of the manageable logical resources provided by DOS, specifically the file system. The BIOS certainly provides services for performing disk I/O; these services, however, operate on the level of individual sectors. The concept of a file exists only at the MS-DOS level, and for writing a high-performance program, it is generally better to use the DOS services for disk operations (after all, this is the Disk Operating System). Not only do these services obviate the need to create an entirely new file system, but they are also quite comprehensive and efficient. For example, using the DOS COPY command can be faster than an assembler routine that directly calls the BIOS (through some performance tricks played by DOS, mentioned in Chapter 6).

General Use of BIOS Functions

This section describes some general guidelines for using the BIOS interrupt functions. Be aware that some software programs intercept the BIOS vectors, and thus modify or extend the services provided (for example, TopView, which provides additional video services through interrupt 10h). The documentation supplied with such systems may override that contained in the BIOS references.

The following are general guidelines for programming with the BIOS:

- For a given interrupt number, the function number is placed in register AH.

- In general, the BIOS services preserve all registers except AX, the flags, and those registers that are specifically stated in the documentation to return values.

- The BIOS code should always be accessed through the official interrupt numbers, and never through specific addresses, which are subject to change.

- Some of the functions described in the following section are available only in certain BIOS versions, which are identified by date. IBM and IBM-compatible BIOS versions contain a date as an 8-byte string beginning at address F000h:FFF5h. The following code fragment displays this date:

```
#include <dos.h>
...
```

```
char far *ChPtr;
int i;
FP_SEG (ChPtr) = 0xf000;
FP_OFF (ChPtr) = 0xfff5;
for (i = 1; i <= 8; ++i)
        putchar (*ChPtr++);
```

The BIOS Functions by Category

The organization of the BIOS functions is much simpler than that of the MS-DOS functions. There is far less duplication, and the services are nicely separated into categories by interrupt type. Each interrupt type controls a unique device, with a few miscellaneous utilities thrown in. See Appendix C for the calling procedures and detailed descriptions of each function. Also, the BIOS functions are documented in the *IBM Personal System/2 and Personal Computer BIOS Interface Technical Reference* and in the technical reference manuals for the IBM-PC and IBM PC-AT (these manuals are listed in the Bibliography).

Video Services: Interrupt 10h

Interrupt 10h includes a wonderful and comprehensive set of functions that are relatively efficient, directly address most of the display capabilities of the IBM-PC family, and are fun to use. They are probably the most useful of the BIOS functions for generating a high-performance program.

The video display capabilities of MS-DOS are primitive. Output consists of a simple stream of characters like those to a teletype machine, with no control over the cursor position or display attributes (unless the cumbersome and slow ANSI.SYS device driver is installed and special codes are embedded in the output). The BIOS, on the other hand, is an excellent means for exploiting the sophisticated display capabilities of IBM-PC, PC-AT, and PS/2 compatible machines.

Another excellent feature of this set of routines is their uniformity across different video display adapters: MDA (monochrome display adapter), CGA (color graphics adapter), EGA (enhanced graphics adapter), and PS/2 graphics adapters. PS/2 Models 25 and 30 come with an MCGA (multi-color graphics array) adapter, and Models 50, 60, 70, and 80 have a VGA (video graphics array) adapter. The MCGA provides a subset of the video modes supported by the VGA (see the description of interrupt 10h in Appendix C for a list of video modes). Also, functions such as setting the cursor position and writing characters to the screen work consistently in either text or graphics modes. (The general topic of video display is discussed in Chapter 8, including: a comparison of different methods of video display, the video attribute and color codes, and the interpretation of special characters sent to the screen.)

As a first example, Figure 5.1 demonstrates the use of the BIOS video services by a C program. This program contains four procedures, **getmode**, **setmode**, **getcur**, and **setcur**, and uses them to manage the basic video parameters. These C procedures all employ the service functions of interrupt 10h, and may be summarized as follows.

The procedure **getmode** uses function 0Fh to obtain:

- The current video mode.

- The number of columns displayed. Although this value is implicit in the current video mode, it is convenient to obtain it directly before using function 06h or 07h to clear the screen.

- The current video page.

The procedure **setmode** uses:

- Function 00h to set the video mode.

- Function 05h to set the video page.

The procedure **getcur** uses function 3 to obtain:

- The current cursor position. Note that row and column numbers start from 0 and that there is a separate cursor position for each video page.

- The cursor "style"; that is, the starting and stopping lines used to generate the cursor. The cursor lines are numbered beginning from the top. For a monochrome system, the range is from 0 to 12 (the default is starting line = 11, stopping line = 12). For a color system (CGA, EGA, and PS/2), the range is from 0 to 7 (the default is starting line = 6, stopping line = 7). A split cursor can be obtained by specifying a starting position greater than the stopping position.

The procedure **setcur** uses:

- Function 02h to set the cursor position. The cursor position is set for a specific video page.

- Function 01h to set the cursor style. Unlike the cursor position, the style is set for all video pages simultaneously.

```
/*
      File:      VIDEO.C

      This file contains a set of routines which use the BIOS video services
      interrupt (10h) to get and set the video mode and cursor parameters.
*/

struct cursor                                    /* Cursor parameters. */
    {
    unsigned char row;
    unsigned char col;
    unsigned char startline;
    unsigned char stopline;
    };

struct crtmode                                   /* Video mode parameters. */
    {
    unsigned char videomode;
    unsigned char columns;
    unsigned char videopage;
    };
                                /* Forward declarations for type checking. */
void getcur (struct cursor *, int);
void setcur (struct cursor *, int);
void getmode (struct crtmode *);
void setmode (struct crtmode *);


void main ()
    {
    struct cursor oldcur;                /* Structures for getting & setting */
    struct cursor newcur;                /* cursor parameters & for getting  */
    struct crtmode oldmode;              /* & setting video mode parameters. */
    struct crtmode newmode;

                           /* Save current video state and initilize new state. */

    getmode (&oldmode);                  /* Save current video mode parameters. */

    getcur (&oldcur, oldmode.videopage); /* Save current cursor parameters.*/

    if (oldmode.videomode != 7)
        {                                /* If not mono, set mode for 80 column */
        newmode.videomode = 3;           /* color text and page 0.              */
        newmode.videopage = 0;
        setmode (&newmode);
        }
                                    /* Use setcur to hide the cursor.       */
    newcur.row = 30;                /* Place cursor beyond possible position. */
    newcur.col = 80;
    newcur.startline = 32;          /* Turning on bit 5 zaps the cursor.    */
    newcur.stopline = 0;
    setcur (&newcur, 0);            /* Set cursor parmeters for video page 0. */
```

Figure 5.1: *A set of video routines using the BIOS*

```
                                        /* Place main application here ... */

                              /* Before exit, restore previous video state. */
        setmode (&oldmode);
        setcur (&oldcur, oldmode.videopage);

        } /* end main */


#include <dos.h>               /* These two lines are necessary for all of */
union REGS reg;                /* following functions.                     */


void getcur (curptr, page)     /* This function obtains the current cursor */
struct cursor *curptr;         /* position and 'type' (start and stop row) */
int page;                      /* for the specified video 'page'. Rows and */
        {                      /* columns are numbered starting from 0.    */
        reg.h.ah = 3;
        reg.h.bh = (unsigned char)page;
        int86 (0x10, &reg, &reg);
        curptr->row = reg.h.dh;
        curptr->col = reg.h.dl;
        curptr->startline = reg.h.ch;
        curptr->stopline = reg.h.cl;

        } /* end getcur */


void setcur (curptr, page) /* Sets all of the cursor parameters;  rows and */
struct cursor *curptr;     /* columns are numbered starting from 0.        */
int page;
        {
        reg.h.ah = 2;
        reg.h.dh = curptr->row;
        reg.h.dl = curptr->col;
        reg.h.bh = (unsigned char)page;
        int86 (0x10, &reg, &reg);

        reg.h.ah = 1;                   /* Note: sets cursor style for all pages. */
        reg.h.ch = curptr->startline;
        reg.h.cl = curptr->stopline;
        int86 (0x10, &reg, &reg);

        } /* end setcur */


void getmode (modeptr)         /* This function gets the current video mode, */
struct crtmode *modeptr;       /* number of display columns, and video page. */
        {
        reg.h.ah = 15;
        int86 (0x10, &reg, &reg);
        modeptr->videomode = reg.h.al;
        modeptr->columns = reg.h.ah;
```

Figure 5.1: *A set of video routines using the BIOS (continued)*

```
        modeptr->videopage = reg.h.bh;

    } /* end getmode */


void setmode (modeptr)              /* This function sets the video mode and    */
struct crtmode *modeptr;            /* display page;  note that the field       */
                                    /* 'columns' is not used, since this value  */
    {                               /* is implicit in the mode.                 */
    reg.h.ah = 0;
    reg.h.al = modeptr->videomode;
    int86 (0x10, &reg, &reg);

    reg.h.ah = 5;
    reg.h.al = modeptr->videopage;
    int86 (0x10, &reg, &reg);

    } /* end setmode */
```

Figure 5.1: *A set of video routines using the BIOS (continued)*

Note that the BIOS requires a single function to get either the current mode or cursor parameters, but two functions to set the same parameters. The C procedures provide a more uniform video interface; for example, to manage the video mode, a single procedure obtains all parameters, a single procedure sets all parameters, and the same data structure (**struct crtmode**) is used to exchange all parameter values for both procedures.

Any program that modifies the video mode or cursor style should save and restore the old values. This is especially critical for a memory-resident utility that displays a window on top of an application, and must then restore the exact video state, including cursor position. The **main** procedure of Figure 5.1 demonstrates a possible sequence of steps using these C video functions:

- The procedure **getmode** saves the current video mode parameters.

- Once the current video display page is known through the call to **getmode**, the cursor parameters for that page can be saved using **getcur**.

- If the display is not monochrome (mode 7), the mode is switched into 80-column color text (mode 3) and display page 0 using **setmode.**

- The cursor parameters are now set through **setcur** in such a way that the cursor will disappear. Cursor hiding is accomplished through setting on bit 5 of the **startline** field. To make sure the deed is done, the cursor position is also set to a point about an inch below the screen.

- The main body of the application comes next.

- Before exiting, the video mode and cursor are restored through **setmode** and **setcur**, passing these functions the values that were saved at the beginning of the program.

Note that the program in Figure 5.1 makes no provision for saving the current screen data before it switches modes and writes to the screen. Procedures for saving and restoring screen data are presented in Chapter 8, and the special problems encountered when a memory-resident program displays a window on top of a foreground application are discussed in Chapter 11.

Another example of the use of BIOS services is the procedure **printa** ("print with attributes") in Figure 5.2. Unlike the macro **prints** and the procedure **printz** in Chapter 4, **printa** offers a fine level of video display control, including the specification of the video display attribute or color, and the position on the screen where the string is displayed (rather than simply at the current cursor position). Also, as Chapter 8 will demonstrate, this function is considerably faster than display routines using DOS.

The procedure **printa** uses function 02h to position the cursor, and function 09h to write the characters with specific colors or monochrome attributes. Notice that function 09h does *not* update the cursor position, and after each character is displayed, the cursor must be repositioned with function 02h. This routine is useful mainly for displaying short messages or small amounts of data at specific points within a window design, and will correctly scroll to the next line when the last column is reached (except on the last line!). However, it is not good for displaying large amounts of information of indeterminate length because special characters such as backspace and carriage return are not handled automatically (these characters display as graphic symbols; for example, CR is a musical note). Also, the screen does not scroll after the last line is filled (the next characters simply disappear).

The following table summarizes the BIOS interrupt 10h video functions. *Function* is the number of the specific service that is placed in register AH when invoking the interrupt.

Function	Service performed
00h	Set video mode. Note that the black and white modes 0, 2, and 5 suppress the color signal only on a composite monitor and not on a standard RGB monitor or the monitors for EGA or PS/2 systems.

```
/*
     File:     PRINTA.C

     A C Function which uses a BIOS Interrupt to Display a String.
*/

void printa (char *, unsigned char, unsigned char, unsigned char);

void main ()
{
     printa ("red",0x4,1,1);
     printa ("white",0xf,2,1);
     printa ("blue",0x1,3,1);
}


#include <dos.h>

void printa (s, a, r, c)          /* Position cursor and write a string with */
char *s;                          /* specified color or video attribute.     */
unsigned char a, r, c;
/*
     s    : String to be displayed on screen.
     a    : Display attribute.
     r,c  : Starting row and column (0 .. 24, 0 .. 79) (ul corner = 0,0).
*/
     {
     union REGS cur_regs, write_regs;

     while (*s)                         /* Continue until null at end of string. */
          {
          cur_regs.h.ah = 2;            /* Update position of cursor using    */
          cur_regs.h.dh = r;            /* BIOS set cursor position function. */
          cur_regs.h.bh = 0;
          cur_regs.h.dl = c++;
          int86 (0x10, &cur_regs, &cur_regs);

          write_regs.h.ah = 9;          /* Write char & attribute at current */
          write_regs.h.bh = 0;          /* cursor position using BIOS.       */
          write_regs.x.cx = 1;
          write_regs.h.bl = a;
          write_regs.h.al = *s++;
          int86 (0x10, &write_regs, &write_regs);
          }

     } /* end printa */
```

Figure 5.2: *A C function using the BIOS to write a string*

01h	Set cursor type.
02h	Set cursor position.
03h	Read cursor position and type.
04h	Read light pen position.

05h   Set active display page. The number of pages is a function of the specific video mode, and ranges from 1 to 8. Note that data can be written to any page, and the cursor moved, whether or not that page is currently displayed. Thus, data can be slowly built up in a nondisplayed page and then instantly displayed using this function.

06h   Scroll page up.

07h   Scroll page down. Services 06h and 07h generate scrolling within a specified area of the screen, and can therefore be used to manage windows. Also, by setting AL to 0, an entire window or the whole screen can be cleared (and filled in with a specified attribute). Only the currently active display page is affected.

08h   Read character and attribute at cursor position. This function allows characters to be read directly off the screen in both text and graphics modes (plus the attribute, in text modes).

09h   Write character and attribute at cursor. See Figure 5.2 for an example. Note that although this function does not advance the cursor, when multiple copies of the same character are displayed (CX > 1), characters are placed in sequential positions on the screen and wrap around at the end of a line.

0Ah   Write character only at cursor. Service 0Ah, unlike number 09h, does not modify the existing attribute at the point on the screen where the character is written.

0Bh   Set color palette. Applies to color graphics modes.

0Ch   Write pixel.

0Dh   Read pixel.

0Eh   Write character in teletype style. Unlike service 09h, this function (a) advances the cursor automatically after each character; (b) responds correctly to ASCII 07h (bell), 08h (backspace), 0Ah (linefeed), and 0Dh (carriage return); and (c) automatically performs line wrapping when the last column is reached, and scrolling when the last line is reached. However, character attributes or colors may not be specified with this function. (But if function 09h is first used to write a blank having the correct attribute, subsequent characters written with this function will replicate the attribute.)

0Fh   Get current video mode, number of display columns, and active display page.

10h   PCjr, EGA, and PS/2 systems only: Set palette registers. (See the BIOS interface manual cited in the Bibliography for more details on this and the following functions.)

11h   EGA and PS/2 only: Character generator routine.

12h   EGA and PS/2 only: Alternate select function. This function provides a set of subfunctions for obtaining video information and setting video parameters.

13h   PC XT (dated 1/10/86 and after), AT, EGA, PC Convertible, and PS/2 only: Write character string. This function combines the best features of display services 9, 10, and 14: an entire string can be written with a single call; display attributes can be specified; and CR, LF, backspace (08), and bell (07) are treated as commands and not as printable characters.

14h   PC Convertible only: Load LCD character font or set LCD high-intensity substitute.

15h   PC Convertible only: Return physical display parameters for active display.

1Ah   PS/2 only: Read/write display combination code.

1Bh   PS/2 only: Return functionality and state information.

1Ch   PS/2 only: Save and restore video state.

Diskette Services: Interrupt 13h

Interrupt 13h provides a series of disk control functions that operate at the sector level. As mentioned earlier, these services bypass the nice logical file resources provided by MS-DOS, and are seldom needed except for writing copy protection schemes, implementing disk maintenance utilities, or other nefarious activities.

If an error is reported on one of these services, first reset the disk system using function 00h. Three tries are recommended in case the error is due to the time the disk motor requires to come to full speed when it is starting up.

The following services are provided for floppy disks:

Function	Service performed
00h	Reset diskette system. This function should be called after an error—the next disk operation will begin with a recalibration of the read/write head.
01h	Read diskette status from last operation. Even if using DOS for disk I/O, this routine can still be called to provide highly detailed information in the event of an error, and might therefore be used by a critical-error handler (see Chapter 6).
02h	Read sectors.
03h	Write sectors.
04h	Verify sectors. Tests the integrity of data in a given sector by calculating the CRC (cyclical redundancy check).
05h	Format track.
08h	Read floppy-disk drive parameters. Returns information on a specified disk drive, such as number of bytes per sector, the motor startup time, the maximum number of tracks, as well as the total number of disk drives installed.
15h	Read DASD type. Reports whether a given floppy-disk drive is present and whether a change line is installed (a *change line* is a hardware device that indicates when the disk has been changed).
16h	Obtain disk-change status. Indicates whether the disk-change signal is active.
17h	Set DASD type for format. Called in preparation for formatting a floppy disk.
18h	Set media type for format. Called in preparation for formatting a floppy disk.

The following services are provided for fixed disks:

Function	Service performed
00h	Reset disk system.
01h	Read disk status from last operation.
02h	Read sectors.
03h	Write sectors.
04h	Verify sectors.
05h	Format cylinder.
06h	Format cylinder and set bad sector flags.
07h	Format drive starting at a specified cylinder.
08h	Read fixed disk drive parameters.
09h	Initialize drive pair characteristics.
0Ch	Seek.
0Dh	Alternate disk reset.
10h	Test drive ready.
11h	Recalibrate.
15h	Read DASD type.
19h	Park heads.
1Ah	Format unit.

Serial Port Services: Interrupt 14h

These routines provide byte stream I/O to the communications port. This set of services, however, is severely limited for a high-performance communication application. Usually, such a communications program must concurrently read characters arriving at the serial port and display them on the screen *and* read characters from the keyboard, display them on the screen, and send them out the serial port.

If the BIOS services are used, however, the program must periodically poll the serial port to see if a character has been received (service 03h) while performing other tasks. Because the arrival of characters is asynchronous, there is a high probability of losing characters. The solution is to bypass the BIOS and write an interrupt-driven routine, which functions as follows:

- When a character arrives, the serial port generates a hardware interrupt.

- The interrupt handler reads the character directly from the input port and stores it in a buffer (much like the BIOS keyboard interrupt handler).

- When the main program loop requires a character, it pulls one out of the buffer.

See Chapter 6 for information on writing hardware interrupt handlers.

The following table summarizes the BIOS interrupt 14h serial port functions.

Function	Service performed
00h	Initialize communications port.
01h	Write character to communications port.
02h	Read character; wait until ready.
03h	Return communications port status.
04h	PS/2 only: Extended initialize.
05h	PS/2 only: Extended communications port control.

Cassette Services: Interrupt 15h

The following table summarizes the BIOS interrupt 14h cassette functions.

Function	Service performed
00h	Turn motor on.
01h	Turn motor off.
02h	Read cassette block.
03h	Write cassette block.

Extended Services: Interrupt 15h

Also available under the same interrupt number as the cassette functions are a series of extended services for the AT, PS/2, PC Convertible, and certain models of the PC XT, dealing with special features of the hardware. These services are listed in Appendix C; for a complete description, see the BIOS interface technical reference cited in the Bibliography.

Keyboard Services: Interrupt 16h

The keyboard services are probably the second most useful of the BIOS functions. They are simple and quite functional; if the BIOS video services are used, there is no reason not to throw these in too.

As an example, the procedure **getkey** in Figure 5.3 uses BIOS function 00h to read a key from the keyboard. Function 00h is an excellent general method for accepting keyboard data; it has several useful properties:

- If a key has not already been entered, the function waits for input. (However, function 01h can first be called to see if a character is ready.)

- The function returns immediately when a key is entered; therefore, the user need not press the Return key to continue the program. The key is not echoed.

- The function returns the ASCII value of the key, or 0 if there is no ASCII value (for example, function keys).

- The function also returns an extended code for the key. Every key (or recognized key combination such as Alt-F1) is assigned an extended code, so that it is possible to identify keys that do not have an ASCII value (i.e., an ASCII value of 0 is returned). Note that unlike the DOS services, a single function returns both the ASCII value and the extended code.

The term *extended code* is not synonymous with *scan code*. Each of the 83 physical keys on the standard IBM-PC keyboard has a unique scan code from 1 to 83 (which is the value transmitted by the hardware when the key is pressed; note that there are also unique scan codes for each of the keys of the 84-key AT keyboard and of the 101- or 102-key keyboard for the AT and PS/2). If a key is pressed by itself (the *base case*), or if the key has an ASCII value, the extended code returned will in fact be equal to the scan code of the key. However, for certain key combinations (e.g., Shift-F1), the extended code will not be the scan code, but rather some number greater than 83, so that the various key combinations can be distinguished with a single number. For example, F1 does not have an ASCII value and its scan code is 59. The extended codes returned for

```
/*
      File:    GETKEY.C

      A C Function which uses a BIOS Interrupt to Read the Keyboard.
*/
#include <stdio.h>

int getkey (void);

void main ()
      {
      int ch;

      /* demo 1 */
      printf ("press any key to continue ...");       /* Use unbuffered input */
      getkey ();                                      /* to generate pause.    */


      /* demo 2 */
      printf ("\n\nenter another key ...");
      ch = getkey ();
      if ((ch & 0x00ff) == 0)                 /* Mask off upper byte to look at  */
                                              /* ASCII code. If ASCII code = 0,  */
                                              /* must look at extended code.     */
            switch (ch >> 8)                  /* Branch on extended code.        */
                  {
                  case 59 : {
                            printf ("\nF1 pressed");
                            break;
                            }
                  case 60 : {
                            printf ("\nF2 pressed");
                            break;
                            }
                  /* etc., etc.  */
                  }


      /* demo 3 */
      printf ("\n\nenter a series of keys to see codes, <esc> ends");
      printf ("\n\nASCII code        extended code");
      do
            {
            ch = getkey ();
            printf ("\n%5d%18d", (ch & 0x00ff),(ch >> 8));
            }
      while ((ch & 0x00ff) != 0x1b);                        /* Test for <esc>. */

      } /* end main */


#include <dos.h>
```

Figure 5.3: *The function* **getkey***, which uses the BIOS keyboard service interrupt (16h) to read a key from the keyboard*

```
int getkey ()
/*

    This function waits for a key to be entered.  Input is unbuffered, so
    that the function returns immediately after the key is pressed (the
    user does not have to press CR).  Returns an integer containing:
        low order byte:   the ASCII key code (if available)
        high order byte:  the "extended" key code
*/

    {
    union REGS reg;

    reg.h.ah = 0;
    int86 (0x16, &reg, &reg);
    return (reg.x.ax);

    }  /* end getkey */
```

Figure 5.3: *The function* **getkey**, *which uses the BIOS keyboard service interrupt (16h) to read a key from the keyboard (continued)*

various combinations are:

Key	Extended code
F1	59
Ctrl-F1	94
Shift-F1	84
Alt-F1	104

Note that keys that have an ASCII value always return an extended code equal to the scan code. For example, typing either a, A, or Ctrl-A generates the extended code 30, the scan code for that key. Therefore, the proper procedure to distinguish any possible key is to first test the returned ASCII code. If it is not zero, process the key based on the ASCII value. If it is zero, then test the extended code to determine which key or key combination has been entered. The ASCII and extended code values for all keys and valid key combinations are listed in the PC or PC-AT technical reference, in the BIOS interface reference, and in the Appendix of the IBM BASIC reference.

Figure 5.3 demonstrates some of the basic uses for function 00h. The BIOS returns the ASCII value in register AL and the extended code in register AH. The function **getkey** returns both of these registers in a single integer; therefore, the C program must perform shifting and masking operations to examine the individual values. The function **main** first demonstrates two basic uses for **getkey**: creating a pause and reading function keys. The third demo simply prints out the returned values for the keys that are pressed. If there is any doubt regarding the codes for a given key, this test program provides the definitive answer.

Function 01h tests to see if a key is ready to be read (i.e., is in the BIOS keyboard buffer) and returns immediately to the calling program. Such functions can improve program efficiency by eliminating idle time spent waiting for keyboard input (function 00h, for example, does not return until a key has been entered). Instead, useful work can be accomplished while waiting. In pseudocode, the process would be:

repeat
      call function 01h to see if character is ready
      if character is ready then
            call function 00h to read character
            process character
      else
            perform another task (e.g., send characters to printer)
   until (ending condition)

The following table summarizes the BIOS interrupt 16h keyboard functions.

Function	Service performed
00h	Read character.
01h	Test if character is ready, without pausing.
02h	Return shift status. See Appendix C for the shift status codes, and Chapter 11 for an example of using the shift status to detect a **hotkey**.
03h	PCjr, AT (11/15/85 and later), PC-XT Model 286, and PS/2 only: Set typematic rate. Sets the initial delay and rate at which keys are automatically repeated by the keyboard.
04h	PCjr and PC Convertible only: Keyboard click adjustment.
05h	AT (11/15/85 and later), PC-XT (1/10/86 and later), PC-XT Model 286, and PS/2 only: Keyboard write. Places an extended code/character code combination in the keyboard buffer as if it came from the keyboard.
10h	AT (11/15/85 and later), PC-XT (1/10/86 and later), PC-XT Model 286, and PS/2 only: Extended keyboard read; similar to function 00h but returns codes unique to the 101/102 key keyboard.

11h	AT (11/15/85 and later), PC-XT (1/10/86 and later), PC-XT Model 286, and PS/2 only: Extended keystroke status; similar to function 01h but returns codes unique to the 101/102 key keyboard.
12h	AT (11/15/85 and later), PC-XT (1/10/86 and later), PC-XT Model 286, and PS/2 only: Extended shift status; similar to function 02h but returns shift states unique to the 101/102 key keyboard.

Printer Services: Interrupt 17h

Interrupt 17h provides a basic set of functions for the printer. A very useful one is number 02h, which returns the current status of the printer. The C function **prnready** in Figure 5.4 uses this function to determine whether the printer is currently ready to receive output. This routine can prevent the ungraceful program termination ("Abort, Retry, Ignore?") that occurs when attempting to write to a printer that is off-line.

The following table summarizes the BIOS interrupt 17h printer functions.

Function	Service performed
00h	Print character.
01h	Initialize printer. This function can be used to erase the current set of control codes and bring the printer back to its startup state.
02h	Obtain printer status.

Time-of-Day Services: Interrupt 1Ah

These services allow reading or modifying the time-keeping data maintained by the BIOS. The following table summarizes the BIOS interrupt 1Ah time functions.

Function	Service performed
00h	Read clock.
01h	Set clock. Services 00h and 01h report the time in clock "ticks" (which occur at the rate of 18.2 times per second) since midnight, and require calculation to find the actual hours, minutes, and seconds.

```
/*
      File:       PRNREADY.C

      A C Function using BIOS Printer Services Interrupt 17h to Read the
      Status of the Printer.
*/
#include <stdio.h>

int prnready (void);
int getkey (void);

void main ()
      {
      while (!prnready() )
            {
            printf ("\nready printer and press any key to continue ...");
            getkey ();                                              /* Pause. */
            }
      printf ("\nprinter is now online");

      } /* end main */


#include <dos.h>
union REGS reg;

int prnready ()
/*
      This function returns the 'selected' bit of the printer status byte.  It
      obtains the value via BIOS interrupt 17h.  This bit generally indicates
      that the printer is ready to receive characters without error, and using
      this function prior to writing to the printer can avoid the usual
      "Abort, Retry, Ignore?" message when attempting to write to a printer
      that is offline.  Test this function with your system, since the exact
      coding of the status bits seems to vary with different BIOS and printer
      combinations.
*/
      {
      reg.h.ah = 2;                                /* Printer status function. */
      reg.x.dx = 0;                                /* Printer 0 is LPT1.        */
      int86 (0x17, &reg, &reg);
      return (reg.h.ah & 0x10);      /* Mask all bits except 'selected' bit.  */

      } /* end prnready */


int getkey ()
      {
      reg.h.ah = 0;
      int86 (0x16, &reg, &reg);
      return (reg.x.ax);

      } /* end getkey */
```

Figure 5.4: *A C function using the BIOS to read the printer status*

02h	AT, PC-XT Model 286, PC Convertible, and PS/2 only: Read real-time clock.
03h	AT, PC-XT Model 286, PC Convertible, and PS/2 only: Set real-time clock. Unlike services 00h and 01h, the routines 02h and 03h get and set time directly in terms of hours, minutes, and seconds.
04h	AT, PC-XT Model 286, PC Convertible, and PS/2 only: Read real-time clock date.
05h	AT, PC-XT Model 286, PC Convertible, and PS/2 only: Set real-time clock date.
06h	AT, PC-XT Model 286, PC Convertible, and PS/2 only: Set real-time clock alarm.
07h	AT, PC-XT Model 286, PC Convertible, and PS/2 only: Reset real-time clock alarm.
08h	PC Convertible only: Set real-time clock–activated power-on mode.
09h	PC Convertible only: Get real-time clock alarm and status.
0Ah	PC-XT (1/10/86 and later) and PS/2 only: Get count of days since 1/1/80.
0Bh	PC-XT (1/10/86 and later) and PS/2 only: Set count of days since 1/1/80.

Miscellaneous Services

The following are a number of miscellaneous BIOS interrupt services that do not fit into any of the previous categories.

Interrupt	Service performed
Interrupt 05h	Print screen. Performs the same function as pressing Shift-PrtSc.
Interrupt 11h	Return equipment list. Returns list of peripheral equipment attached to the computer as determined by the power-on diagnostics. See Chapter 7 for an example of the use of this function.

Interrupt 12h   Return memory size. Returns the total number of kilobytes of user memory (in the IBM-PC, from the settings on the DIP switch block). See Chapter 7 for an example of the use of this function.

Interrupt 18h   Run ROM-BASIC.

Interrupt 19h   Reboot computer.

CHAPTER 6

Other Resources in MS-DOS Machines

In addition to the extensive set of routines available through the interrupt mechanism described in the last two chapters, there are many other resources in an MS-DOS machine that can enhance software performance. This chapter discusses these resources, which are provided by the hardware, the firmware (BIOS), and the software (MS-DOS), and allow you to

- Obtain information on system configuration
- Communicate with other applications
- Modify the behavior of DOS and the BIOS
- Bypass DOS and the BIOS to enhance performance
- Synchronize routines with hardware events
- Develop custom interfaces to peripheral equipment

Some of the resources discussed in this chapter are universally available on MS-DOS machines, while others are machine-specific and may function only on the IBM-PC, AT, PS/2, or close compatibles. See Chapter 7 for a discussion of compatibility testing.

In order to round out the treatment of resources with practical value for high-performance programming, this chapter comprises quite a divergent collection of topics. Among the resources discussed are the program segment prefix, system data stored in low memory, Ctrl-Break and critical-error interrupt handlers, and hardware-generated interrupts.

▪▫ The Program Segment Prefix
▫▪

When the MS-DOS loader prepares a program for execution, it sets up a 100h-byte block of data immediately preceding the program in memory. This block is known as the program segment prefix (PSP), and includes:

- Parameters stored by DOS for its own use in managing the process
- Information provided by DOS for the use of the program
- Areas for managing file I/O and exchanging file data

Appendix C delineates the overall contents of the PSP; this chapter describes only those fields that are of practical, immediate use to the programmer.

Accessing the PSP from Assembler

The techniques for accessing the PSP from assembly language depend on whether the program is written as a .COM file or an .EXE file.

.COM Files

Accessing the PSP from a .COM file is no great trick. When the operating system loads a .COM file, *all* segment registers point to the beginning of the PSP. The program does not normally alter the values of these registers, and may therefore access a field in the PSP with a simple data reference instruction. For example, the following instruction moves the one-byte field at offset 80h in the PSP into register CL:

mov cl, ds:[80h]

The DS segment override is theoretically unnecessary since DS is the default segment register for data reference instructions. However, unless the override is present, the assembler incorrectly interprets 80h as an immediate value rather than a pointer.

Figure 1.2, a format for generating a .COM file, demonstrates a better method for accessing the PSP. At the beginning of the code segment, each field of the PSP that needs to be accessed is represented by an **org** statement indicating the offset, and a **db** statement specifying the name, data type, and size of the field. For example, offset 80h contains the length of the command line, and is represented as

org 80h
parmlen db ? ;Single byte command line length.

To load this value into register CL, simply use

mov cl, parmlen

These **db** instructions appear to be normal variable definitions; however, it would be futile to try to assign initial values since *everything* preceding the entry point at offset 100h is stripped off by EXE2BIN when the file is converted to a .COM format. These definitions serve only as a temporary template so that the assembler will generate the correct offset values. (They therefore do not add any size to the .COM file on disk or in memory.)

.EXE Files

The method for accessing the PSP from .EXE files is different from the method used for .COM files in two salient ways. First, when the program is loaded, only registers DS and ES point to the PSP; furthermore, these segment registers are normally reinitialized at the beginning of the program to point to the data segment. Therefore, the segment address of the PSP should be saved in a memory variable for later use. The instructions at the beginning of the .EXE format in Figure 1.3 should be modified to include an additional instruction:

```
mov ax, dataseg
mov ds, ax
mov psp, es ;** Add this instruction. **
mov es, ax
```

PSP is defined in the data segment as

```
psp dw ?
```

If at some later point in the program the byte at PSP offset 80h is to be loaded into register CL, use the following two instructions:

```
mov es, psp
mov cl, es:[80h]
```

Second, unlike a .COM file, placing define instructions for PSP offsets at the beginning of the code segment of an .EXE file would cut into available code space and unnecessarily bloat the size of the file. Therefore, it is better to use immediate numeric offsets (such as the 80h in the example above). When using immediate values, it may be necessary to add a **ptr** instruction when the assembler has no other clues regarding the size of an operand; for example,

```
mov es, psp
cmp byte ptr es:[80h], 127 ;Compare a BYTE quantity.
```

Accessing the PSP from C

Microsoft C conveniently provides the global variable **_psp**, which contains the segment address of the program segment prefix. (It is declared as an **unsigned int** in the file STDLIB.H.) The following code demonstrates how this variable may be used to access the one-byte field at offset 80h that contains the length of the command line parameters.

```
#include <stdlib.h>                    /* For _psp. */
#include <dos.h>               /* For FP_OFF & FP_SEG. */
```

```
    .
    .
    .
unsigned char far *plptr;        /* Pointer to a single byte. */

FP_OFF (plptr) = 0x80;           /* Offset within PSP.      */
FP_SEG (plptr) = _psp;           /* Segment value of PSP.   */
printf ("length of parm line  =  %d\n", *plptr);
```

This example illustrates the following important points:

- The value is accessed through a far pointer, since it is outside of the default data segment.

- In this case, the far pointer points to an **unsigned char** because we want to read a single byte quantity.

- The predefined macros **FP_OFF** and **FP_SEG** are used to assign the offset and segment values to the far pointer (which is four bytes long).

- The actual value from the PSP field is derived by a single indirection: ***plptr**.

A last note regarding access to the program segment prefix: For versions of DOS 3.0 and later, function 62h returns the segment address of the PSP for the currently executing process.

Important PSP Fields

This section discusses the structure and use of a subset of the fields within the program segment prefix that has practical significance for the programmer: the top-of-memory address, the segment size, the DOS file table, the environment address, the file control blocks, the command line, and the default disk transfer address.

Offset 02h: Top of Memory

This field contains the segment address of the top of the block of memory that is currently allocated to the program. The byte at offset 0 with respect to this segment is actually the first byte of *un*allocated memory. Note that this field does *not* necessarily contain the address of the top of *user memory* (the total amount of conventional memory installed in the system). The significance of this field depends on whether the program is a .COM file or an .EXE file.

If the program is a .COM file, it is allocated all possible memory when it is loaded, and therefore the top-of-memory field will in fact contain the address of the top of user memory (unless the program explicitly frees memory). There would therefore be no obtainable memory at or above this address.

An .EXE file may not have been allocated all possible memory, and might therefore be able to obtain additional memory beyond the top-of-memory address by using DOS function 48h (allocate memory). The amount of memory initially allocated to an .EXE file depends on the value in the *maximum paragraphs* field of the file header; this value can be modified either at link time using the **/CP** flag, or on an existing .EXE file using the Microsoft EXEMOD utility with the **/MAX** option.

The BIOS interrupt 12h returns the total number of kilobytes of user memory (in the IBM-PC, from the dip switch settings). However, note that some RAM disks and other utilities load themselves into high memory; these programs adjust downwards the end of user memory address maintained by DOS, but do not affect the value returned by the BIOS, which would therefore be too large. The following is a general strategy for reliably determining the total amount of available memory, allocated and unallocated, for either a .COM or an .EXE program:

1. Examine the field at offset 02 in the PSP to determine the amount of memory already allocated to the program. A .COM program may stop at this step, because no further memory will be available.

2. An .EXE file can determine the additional amount of memory available for allocation by invoking DOS interrupt 21h, function 48h (allocate memory), and requesting an impossible amount of memory by loading FFFFh into register BX. When the function returns, the carry flag will be set (indicating that the request could not be filled), and register BX will contain the largest block of memory available (in paragraphs).

Offset 06h: Segment Size

For .COM files, this field contains the number of bytes available in the program segment. Normally, this value is close to 64K (the maximum segment size); however, if there is insufficient free memory, the value might be less. Therefore, it is a good idea to check this field before making assumptions about available memory within the program segment.

Offset 18h–Offset 2Bh: DOS File Table

Note that this 20-byte area of the PSP is officially designated as "reserved." The following information is undocumented and is therefore subject to change in future versions of the operating system. The methods should be used cautiously.

MS-DOS versions 3.3 and later provide a function (number 67h, accessed through interrupt 21h) that allows you to specify the maximum number of file handles that may be open at the same time by a given process. Under versions of MS-DOS prior to 3.3, the number of open file handles for a single process is limited to 20 (assuming that the number specified in the **FILES =** line of the configuration file is 20 or greater). However, by directly manipulating the DOS file table in the PSP, it is possible to have as many as 255 file handles open simultaneously under DOS 2.0 or any later version.

The structure and use of the DOS file table   A file handle returned by DOS on an open command is a number between 0 and 19, and serves as an index into the 20-byte file table at PSP offset 18h. Each one-byte entry in this table contains either FFh, indicating that the table entry is unused, or a value between 0 and FEh, which is an internal number used by DOS to refer to the actual file or device. This number will be called the *internal DOS number* to distinguish it from the file handle. When DOS is passed a file handle, it does not use the file handle to identify the actual file, but rather uses the internal DOS number obtained from the file table. Internal DOS numbers have the following values:

Internal DOS number	File/Device
00	AUX
01	CON
02	PRN
03 and greater	Files/devices opened by program

When a program is loaded, the file table has the following initial values:

Offset	Handle name	Value
0	Standard input	01
1	Standard output	01
2	Standard error	01
3	Standard auxiliary device	00
4	Standard printer device	02
5 and greater	Free handles	FF

The first five entries correspond to the standard preopened file handles (see the section on File-Level Management in Chapter 4). Note that standard input, standard output, and standard error all refer to the console device.

A benefit of this scheme is that DOS may redirect a file handle simply by changing the corresponding entry in the file table. For example, the table entry at offset 1 (corresponding to the standard output file handle) normally contains the internal DOS number for the console (01); if the operating system replaces this entry by an internal DOS number referring to a disk file, then all subsequent writes to standard output will go to the disk file.

By default, DOS reserves space for eight internal file numbers. If, however, the configuration file contains a **FILES = nn** line (see the DOS manual), DOS reserves space for the specified number of files, which can be as large as 255. Thus, if CONFIG.SYS contains the line

FILES = 255

DOS will reserve internal space to allow 255 open files, numbered from 0 to FEh. The 20-file limit stems only from the fact that the handle table in the PSP is 20 bytes long, and when there are no more free entries (i.e., those marked FFh), DOS will open no further files, and will return error code 4.

Beating the system   To demonstrate a method for circumventing the DOS 20-handle limit, Figure 6.1 lists a C program in which 31 files are opened at the same time. The same method could be used to open as many as 255 files. The basic technique is to reference a file by internal DOS number rather than by file handle. The steps are as follows:

1. Place the line **FILES = 31** in CONFIG.SYS and reboot the system. (Use a larger number to open more files; the limit is 255.)

2. The variable **ftptr** is declared as a far pointer and is initialized to point to the file table entry for handle 5. Thus, the five preopened device handles are left intact, and all subsequent files will be opened and closed using the single file handle number 5.

3. The array **dosnum** will hold the 26 internal DOS numbers for the 26 new files to be opened.

4. Each of the files is opened as follows:

   a. The file table entry for handle 5 is assigned FFh to mark it as available.

   b. The file is opened using **creat**. Note that the file handle is not saved since we already know that the number will be 5 (DOS uses the *first* available handle).

c. The internal DOS number is saved in the **dosnum** array, and will be used subsequently to access the file.

5. Each of the files is closed using the following method, which demonstrates how files must be referenced:

a. The file table entry for handle 5 is assigned the internal DOS number for the file to be closed.

b. File handle 5 is closed using the **close** function.

Offset 2Ch: Segment Address of the Environment

The environment is an area in memory used primarily to store the parameters set by the DOS PATH, PROMPT, and SET commands. It consists of a sequence of 0 terminated strings (ASCIIZ strings—the last byte is a binary zero, *not* the ASCII code for the 0 character), which have the format:

name = parameter

The entire set of strings is terminated by an additional 0 byte. Note that for DOS 3.*x*, the following fields come after the terminating 0:

- A **word** count of the number of following strings.
- An ASCIIZ string containing the full path name of the program, so the program can find out its own name and the directory where it was loaded. In C, for DOS version 3.*x*, **argv[0]** contains the program name, but for earlier versions of DOS, **argv[0]** contains only the character C.
- Possible additional strings that have been made available to the program.

Each process has its own copy of the environment in the memory block immediately preceding its PSP. The manner in which the environment is copied from process to process is as follows: The command processor maintains its own copy of the environment, which contains an entry indicating the location of COMMAND.COM; for example,

COMSPEC = C:

plus any additional entries resulting from the PATH, PROMPT, and SET commands. When a program is loaded, it receives a copy of the command processor's environment. The program may modify its copy of the environment, but this will *not* affect the environment maintained by the command processor and passed on to other programs. If the program invokes a child process, it may pass the process an exact copy of its own

```
/*
      File:     FILES31.C

      A C demonstration which uses handle functions and has 31 files open at
      the same time:  the 5 standard handles plus 26 new files named
      'FILEA' ... 'FILEZ'.
*/

#include <stdlib.h>
#include <dos.h>
#include <sys\types.h>
#include <sys\stat.h>
#include <io.h>

void main ()
      {
      unsigned char far *ftptr;          /* Far pointer to file table entry.  */
      unsigned char dosnum[26];          /* Storage for internal DOS numbers. */
      static char filename[6] = "testx";
      int i;

      FP_SEG (ftptr) = _psp;             /* Beginning of the PSP.             */
      FP_OFF (ftptr) = 0x1d;             /* Entry in file table for handle 5; */
                                         /* leave 5 standard handles alone.   */

      for (i=0;i<26;++i)                      /* Open 26 new files.           */
            {
            *ftptr = 0xff;               /* Mark handle 5 free.              */
            filename[4] = (char) ('a'+i);  /* Create unique file name.       */
            creat (filename, S_IWRITE);    /* Open file, don't save handle   */
                                           /* since we know the handle is 5. */
            dosnum[i] = *ftptr;          /* Save the internal DOS number.    */
            }

                                             /* 31 files are now open!       */

      for (i=0;i<26;++i)                      /* Close the 26 new files.      */
            {
            *ftptr = dosnum[i];          /* Replace internal DOS number.     */
            close (5);                   /* All files use handle 5.          */
            }

      } /* end main */
```

Figure 6.1: *A C program that uses file handle functions but has 31 files open simultaneously*

environment (like the example program in Figure 4.10) or it may pass an entirely different environment. Thus, the environment is a one-way channel of communication from a parent to a child process. A process that remains resident in memory will retain its copy of the environment, but this area will *not* be updated by subsequent commands that alter DOS's copy of the environment.

The field at offset 2Ch of the program segment prefix contains the two-byte segment address of the copy of the environment belonging to the program; the first byte is at offset 0 within this segment. Accessing the environment through this address from an assembler program is similar to the previous examples for accessing the PSP; however, another level of indirection is required. For example, the following code would move the first byte of the environment into register AL:

```
mov  es, psp        ;Saved PSP segment address.
mov  ax, es:[2Ch]   ;Move segment address of environment into
                    ;AX.
mov  es, ax         ;Now ES has environment segment address.
mov  al, es:[0]     ;Access first byte of environment.
```

A C program could access the environment through the predefined **_psp** variable, using far pointers and several levels of indirection. However, Microsoft C provides three alternative methods:

1. The library function **getenv** retrieves strings from the environment, and the function **putenv** adds strings to the environment. Note that **putenv** may result in the environment being moved to another address.

2. C maintains the predefined variable **environ**, which always points to the environment (even if it has moved) and may be used to access environment strings. This variable is an array of pointers to the strings that constitute the program's environment and is declared as **char *environ[]**.

3. In addition to **argc** and **argv**, a third parameter, **envp**, is passed to the **main** function. This parameter is also a pointer to the environment table (**char *envp[]**), but unlike **environ**, it is not automatically updated if the environment is moved. Therefore, it is safer to use **environ**.

Offsets 5Ch and 6Ch: File Control Blocks

If the first two parameters that are entered on the command line when the program is run are valid file names, *not* containing directory paths, they will appear at offsets 5Ch and 6Ch, parsed into standard format:

Position	Contents
Byte 0	Drive code (0 = default, 1 = A:, 2 = B:, etc.)
Bytes 1–8	File name
Bytes 9–11	File extension

How can the programmer determine whether these fields contain valid file names? If the first parameter is a valid file name, register AL will be set to 00h when the program begins (FFh indicates an invalid name). Likewise, if the second parameter is a valid file name, then register AH is set to 00h (FFh otherwise). DOS performs this service to assist programs in opening file control blocks, and the main limitation is the lack of support for directory paths. However, even a program that does not use FCBs may find a use for these areas.

One additional note about offset 5Ch is that this position marks the beginning of the dispensable portion of the PSP. DOS does not require the PSP from offset 5Ch to the end for its normal functioning, and therefore this area may safely be used for other purposes.

Offset 80h: Command Line Length/Default Disk Transfer Area

The one-byte field at offset 80h initially contains the length of the command line, which is stored at offset 81h.

This area serves a double purpose. It is also the beginning of the default disk transfer area (DTA), and therefore you should save the command line length and command line before invoking any routines that use the DTA. The disk transfer area (DTA) is the buffer used by file control block commands to exchange data with files. The default DTA is a 128-byte buffer in the PSP, starting at offset 80h. This area is not too exciting for users of handle functions, since handle I/O takes place in a programmer specified buffer, typically in the data segment. There is one exception, however: handle functions 4Eh and 4Fh use the DTA to store and return information when searching for matching files. See Figure 4.7 for an example of using the default DTA for file searches with functions 4Eh and 4Fh.

Offset 81h: The Command Line

The field at offset 81h contains an unformatted copy of the command line beginning with the first blank entered after the program name. This area can contain a maximum of 127 bytes (it extends to the end of the PSP) and is a literal copy of the command line, with one exception: redirecting (<, >) and piping (¦) symbols, and the file names that are associated with them, are removed by the command processor. (Redirection and piping are handled by the operating system, not the application program; therefore, this information should not be visible to the program.)

Low-Memory Data Areas

The block of memory from 0000:0400h to 0000:05FFh is reserved as a communication area: the BIOS, DOS, and user applications use specific fields in this region for storing parameters, flags, and other data. Programmers can directly access these areas to obtain inside information on the system status, modify the behavior of the system, and exchange information with other applications.

The following addresses are given as hexadecimal offsets from segment 0000h. As an example of the code needed to access one of these specific memory locations, the following instructions load the value at offset 500h into register AL:

```
xor   ax, ax          ;Quickly zero out AX.
mov   es, ax          ;Segment = 0000h.
mov   ax, es:[500h]   ;AX gets value at 0000h:0500h.
```

400h–4ABh: BIOS Communication Area

The BIOS uses the area of memory from offsets 400h to 4ABh to store an extensive set of parameters and status flags. These fields are defined at the beginning of the assembler listing in the PC/AT technical reference. Many of the values can be manipulated through the preferred method of BIOS function calls; others, however, are profitably read or written using direct memory access. The following is the basic layout of this area, with emphasis on those fields that are of practical significance to the programmer (all the following offsets are in hexadecimal):

Offset	Contents
400–407	Addresses of RS232 adapters.
408–40F	Addresses of printers.
410–411	Equipment flag. This is the same value returned by interrupt 11h and is documented in Appendix C. These values are normally set only at startup; however, programs that switch video adapters (or switch modes on multiadapter video cards) must correctly set bits 5:4 of this word as follows:

> 00: Not used
> 01: CGA card 40 columns
> 10: CGA card 80 columns
> 11: mono card

412	Initialization flag.
413–414	Memory size. Returned by interrupt 12h.
415–416	Amount of memory in I/O channel.
417–43D	Keyboard data area 1. This area contains the keyboard status flags and the 15-byte keyboard buffer. Normally, keyboard I/O is performed, and keyboard status is determined through interrupt 16h. (See Appendix C.) Some special utilities, however, such as those that speed up the PC typematic rate of keyboard input (the rate at which keys are repeated when held down), bypass the BIOS and read or write directly to this buffer.
43E–448	Diskette data.
449–466	Video control data area 1. These values are conveniently read or set through interrupt 10h.
467–46B	In the PC: Cassette data. In the PS/2, except Models 25 and 30, 467h is the **far** (double word) address of the code that resets the computer, preserving memory.
46C–470	Time data. The BIOS timer information is managed through interrupt 1Ah.
471	Break flag. This flag is set to 1 if the break key has been pressed.
472–473	Reset flag. If this word flag is set to 1234, the BIOS initialization routine, starting at segment FFFFh, will bypass the lengthy memory check normally performed during a cold boot. Therefore, an easy way to generate a quick warm boot is demonstrated by the following code fragment:

```
bios        segment at 0ffffh
reboot      label far
bios        ends
            .
            .
            .
xor ax, ax
mov es, ax
mov word ptr es:[472h], 1234h
jmp reboot
```

Note that in the PS/2, except Models 25 and 30, if the reset flag is set to 4321h, the system will perform a reset operation without erasing the contents of memory.

474–477	Fixed disk data area.
478–47F	Printer and serial port timeout counters. Used in the IBM PCjr.
480–483	Keyboard data area 2. Word values for the start and stop offsets of the keyboard buffer.
484–48A	Video control data area 2 (EGA and PS/2).
48B–495	Diskette drive/fixed disk drive control data area (AT and PS/2).
496–497	Keyboard data area 3 (AT and PS/2).
498–4A0	Real-time clock data area (AT and PS/2).
4A1–4A7	Reserved for network adapters.
4A8–4AB	Double word pointer to video parameters and overrides (EGA and PS/2).

4ACh–4EFh: Reserved

Although the offsets from 4ACh to 4EFh are not currently used for storing data, this area is reserved for the BIOS.

4F0h–4FFh: User Communication Area

Known as the "intra-application communication area," the region from 4F0h to 4EFh may be used freely by any program. For example, several independent but related application programs could exchange data through this area, or a single program could store data to be used each time it is run. The problem is that anarchy prevails—since any application can write to this section of memory, information is always subject to corruption. A safer method of establishing globally available configuration information is through the DOS environment; however, environment data must be set by the user at the command level, and cannot be assigned by a program (a program has access only to a temporary, private copy of the environment, while COMMAND.COM manages the global environment).

⊞ 500h–5FFh: DOS Communication Area

Some of the addresses between 500h and 5FFh are reserved for DOS and some are reserved for BASIC. One interesting field is the following:

> 500h   Print screen status flag.

This one-byte field is used to record the status of the print screen function as follows:

> 0   Print screen not active/successful termination.
>
> 1   Print screen in progress.
>
> 255   Error occurred during print screen.

By placing 1 in this field, you can disable the print screen function by making the system think that the process is already active.

⊞ Ctrl-Break and Critical-Error Interrupts

When the system detects a Ctrl-Break keyboard combination, or when it encounters a critical hardware error, rather than simply handling the situation in an arbitrary fashion, it generates a software interrupt to allow your application to control the action taken. If your program does not provide appropriate interrupt handlers, DOS will take its default action, which can easily lead to a premature and ungraceful termination of the program.

The main problem with an uncontrolled program exit under MS-DOS is that data written to any unclosed files can be lost (data are written to the disk each time a buffer is flushed, but the directory entry is not updated until the file is properly closed). Techniques already discussed to help prevent this occurrence include:

- Periodically close all modified files (close a *duplicate* file handle to avoid the overhead of reopening the file, or under DOS versions 3.3 and later use function 68h of interrupt 21h; see Chapter 4). This is an important measure (even if the other safeguards listed below are implemented) because of the ever-present possibility of a power loss.

- Use BIOS interrupt 16h to make sure the printer is online before attempting a write (see Chapter 5).

- To prevent program termination through Ctrl-Break, disable Ctrl-Break checks through DOS function 33h (this function does *not* disable Ctrl-Break checks during I/O functions), and perform keyboard input using either (a) traditional functions 06h and 07h; or

(b) handle function 3Fh, after setting the console device to the raw mode (see Chapter 4).

The most important technique, however, is to write interrupt handlers to directly intercept a Ctrl-Break or critical error, and either prevent program termination or close all open file handles before program termination. The invocation of these interrupts by DOS and the BIOS is thus a very important resource for a robust application, and it is surprising how few programs and high-level languages take advantage of it.

Ctrl-Break

Both the BIOS and DOS check for the Ctrl-Break key combination. The BIOS checks only for Ctrl-Break; DOS, however, responds equally to Ctrl-Break or Ctrl-C.

When the BIOS keyboard routine detects that a Ctrl-Break has been entered, it generates interrupt 1Bh. At initialization, this vector is set to point to a routine that simply returns; the programmer, however, can set this interrupt to the address of a procedure that is to be invoked every time Ctrl-Break is detected by the BIOS.

MS-DOS also checks for Ctrl-Break (and Ctrl-C) at various times. If the DOS BREAK flag is set ON, then the break key is checked whenever any DOS function is called. If this flag is set OFF, then checking occurs only during input/output operations to the standard character devices. When DOS detects a Ctrl-Break, it invokes interrupt 23h.

There are two important differences between Ctrl-Break handling at the BIOS and DOS levels:

- DOS is able to check for Ctrl-Break only when a DOS function is called. The BIOS keyboard routine, however, is interrupt-driven and will almost always respond to a break key (unless interrupts are disabled, or the BIOS routine has been replaced by another program). Therefore, the BIOS vector is a better choice for a Ctrl-Break routine that is to be globally available.

- If you do not install an interrupt 1Bh handler, the BIOS will simply do nothing when Ctrl-Break is entered. However, if you do not install an interrupt 23h handler, DOS will perform its default action, which is to summarily abort the current program, with the possible dire consequences discussed above. Therefore it is most important for a robust application to provide an interrupt 23h handler.

An Assembler Ctrl-Break Handler

Figure 6.2 provides an example of setting up an interrupt 23h Ctrl-Break handler for an assembler program. The **main** procedure uses DOS function 25h to set vector 23h to point to the interrupt handler **cbhandler**. It then invokes a DOS keyboard function that tests for Ctrl-Break (01) and invites the user to go ahead and try it. Next, it calls the procedure **wrapup**, which in a real application would close files, restore interrupts, and perform other final cleaning up. It finally terminates without restoring the interrupt 23h vector. Normally, an application should restore all modified vectors; however, DOS automatically restores interrupt vectors 23h and 24h from the former values that are stored in the program segment prefix.

The interrupt handler **cbhandler** queries the user to determine if the program should be aborted. If the program is not to be aborted, it simply uses an **iret** instruction, which forces DOS to continue the program. If the program is to be aborted, **cbhandler** first calls the **wrapup** procedure to provide a graceful exit, and then signals DOS to abort the program by setting the carry flag and returning with a far return (note that the procedure must be declared as **far**). Using a **ret** rather than a **iret** preserves the current value of the flags so that DOS can detect the set carry flag.

A C Ctrl-Break Handler

Figure 6.3 demonstrates the use of a Ctrl-Break handler in a C program. The program functions much as the example above; however, the process is greatly simplified through use of the **signal** C library function.

The function **ctrlbrk** is the Ctrl-Break handler. This routine performs the same actions as the assembler procedure **cbhandler** above. If the program is *not* to be aborted, the function simply returns, which forces DOS to continue the process. If the program is to be aborted, the function does not return, but rather calls **lastrites**, which closes all open streams in order to preserve data, and then calls **exit** to abort the program with an error level of 1.

The **signal** library function installs the Ctrl-Break handler. The first parameter is the manifest constant SIGINT, which specifies interrupt 23h. The second parameter is the address of the handler to be installed, **ctrlbrk**. The second parameter could also be replaced by two constants with special meanings:

- SIG_IGN: Ctrl-Break would be ignored, and thus the user could not terminate the program using this key combination.

```
page 50,130

;file:    CTRLBRKA.ASM

;An .EXE format for an example Ctrl-Break handler
;
;    To generate .EXE file from CTRLBRKA.ASM:
;        MASM CTRLBRKA;
;        LINK CTRLBRKA;

public    main                        ;Declarations for CodeView.
public    cbhandler
public    c01
public    wrapup

include   DISPLAY.MAC                 ;Include file containing 'prints',
                                      ;Figure 4.4.

codeseg   segment 'CODE'
codeseg   ends

dataseg   segment 'DATA'
dataseg   ends

stackseg  segment stack 'STACK'
          db      128 dup ('stack   ')
stackseg  ends

          assume  cs:codeseg
          assume  ds:dataseg
          assume  es:dataseg
          assume  ss:stackseg

codeseg   segment 'CODE'

main      proc    far

          mov     ax, dataseg         ;Standard .EXE initialization.
          mov     ds, ax
          mov     es, ax

          push    ds                  ;Set interrupt 23h vector to
          mov     ax, cs              ;point to the interrupt routine
          mov     ds, ax              ;'cbhandler'.
          mov     ah, 25h
          mov     dx, offset cbhandler
          mov     al, 23h
          int     21h
          pop     ds
                                      ;Test the ctrl-break handler.
          prints  <10,13,"press control-break ... ">
          mov     ah, 01              ;This function checks for ctrl-break.
          int     21h

          prints  <10,13,"program did not abort">

          call    wrapup              ;Standard wrapup routine which is
                                      ;also called by 'cbhandler'.

          mov     ah, 4ch             ;Exit w/ errorlevel 0.
          mov     al, 0
          int     21h

main      endp


cbhandler proc    far                 ;Interrupt 23h handler.  DOS invokes
                                      ;this interrupt when it detects a
                                      ;control-break or control-c.

          push    ax                  ;Save all modified registers here.
```

Figure 6.2: *An assembler Ctrl-Break handler in .EXE format*

```
                                         ;See if user really wants to abort.
              prints   <10,13,"abort program? (y/n): ">
              mov      ah, 07h            ;Use a read function that does NOT
              int      21h                ;check for ctrl-brk -- we don't need
              cmp      al, 'Y'            ;recursion at this point!
              je       c01
              cmp      al, 'y'
              je       c01

                                          ;User does not want to abort.
              pop      ax                 ;Restore any saved registers here.
              iret                        ;Simple interrupt return makes DOS
                                          ;continue program.

  c01:                                    ;User wants to abort.
              call     wrapup             ;Tie up loose ends -- save all data.
              stc                         ;DOS aborts if carry flag set.
              pop      ax                 ;Restore any saved registers here.
              ret                         ;Simple return preserves current flags.

  cbhandler   endp


  wrapup      proc     near               ;Close all open files, restore
                                          ;interrupt vectors, and perform any
                                          ;other final tasks.  This routine is
                                          ;called at end of 'main' & by 'cbhandler'.

              prints   <10,13,"wrapup called">
              ret

  wrapup      endp

  codeseg     ends

              end      main
```

Figure 6.2: *An assembler Ctrl-Break handler in .EXE format (continued)*

- SIG_DFL: Ctrl-Break will immediately terminate the process. This parameter serves no purpose, since this is the default action if no handler is installed.

The program opens TESTFILE and sends it a line of data in order to determine whether the file is successfully closed when Ctrl-Break is entered. Note that if the Ctrl-Break handler is not installed, data are written to the file, but if the program is prematurely aborted through Ctrl-Break, the resulting file will have a length of 0. When the handler is installed and Ctrl-Break is pressed, the file is properly closed and its directory entry correctly updated.

Critical Error

When MS-DOS encounters a *critical error,* such as an open disk door when trying to access a file, or an offline printer when trying to print a character, one of the actions it performs is to call interrupt 24h. At initialization, this vector points to a routine that prints the familiar "Abort,

```
/*
      File:    CTRLBRK.C

      A C Program Demonstrating a Control-Break Handler.
*/

#include <stdio.h>
#include <signal.h>
#include <conio.h>
#include <process.h>

void main ()
    {
    FILE *testf;
    void ctrlbrk (void); /* Must declare function for passing as parameter.*/

    signal (SIGINT, ctrlbrk);          /* Install the control-break handler. */

                              /* Test file to see if stream closed properly. */
    testf = fopen ("testfile","w");
    fprintf (testf,"this data will not get recorded in the file's ");
    fprintf (testf,"directory entry if the program terminates abnormally\n");

    printf ("go ahead and hit control-c ... ");
    getche ();

    printf ("\nprogram continued normally ... not aborted");
    fclose (testf);

    } /* end main */


void ctrlbrk ()        /* Control break interrupt handler -- simply returning */
                       /* from this function causes DOS to continue program.  */
    {
    void lastrites (void);

    signal (SIGINT, ctrlbrk);                    /* Must reinstall 'ctrlbrk'.*/
    fprintf (stderr, "Abort program? (y/n): ");
    switch (getche ())
        {
        case 'y' :
        case 'Y' : lastrites ();       /* Prepare program for the end.     */
                   exit (1);           /* Abort program with errorlevel 1. */
        }
    fprintf (stderr,"\nContinue input: ");                    /* Don't abort. */

    } /* end ctrlbrk */


void lastrites ()        /* This function should perform the minimum set of */
                         /* tasks required to cleanup and save data before  */
                         /* termination due to control-c or critical error. */
    {
    fcloseall ();                              /* Closes all open streams. */
    }
```

Figure 6.3: *A Ctrl-Break handler for C*

Retry, Ignore?," and then returns a code to DOS informing it which of these three actions to take. The problem is that if the user chooses to abort, the program has no opportunity to prepare for its untimely demise, with the possible loss of data. By writing your own interrupt 24h handler you can control the critical-error handling process. Among the advantages of a custom interrupt handler are the following:

- The opportunity to print a more detailed and helpful error message.

- The ability to display the error message in a format that is consistent with the screen design. (DOS simply overwrites the screen at the current cursor position, giving the user the impression that the program has lost control, which, in fact, it has.)

- The opportunity to close files and perform any other final cleaning up if the user chooses to abort.

Again, the methods and options for installing a critical-error handler are best described through an example. Microsoft C does not have a convenient library function to install a critical-error handler as it did for a Ctrl-Break handler (**signal**). Therefore, the example program consists of an assembler critical-error handler and installation procedure that can be linked to a C program. Figure 6.4 lists a C program that installs the critical-error handler and tests its operation. Figure 6.5 is the assembler module containing the installation routine **ce_init** and the critical-error handler itself, **ce_hand**.

In order to install and test the critical-error handler, the C program first opens a data file and writes a line of data. It then calls the assembler routine **ce_init** to install the critical-error handler. This function takes a single argument: the address of a function that is to be called before program termination if the user chooses to abort. The C program passes the address of **lastrites**, a C function that simply closes all open streams. Once the critical-error handler is safely installed, the program tests its operation by first trying to open a file on drive A: and then trying to write to the printer. Before running this program, leave the door to drive A: open and turn the printer offline to generate critical-error conditions.

The procedure **_ce_init** in Figure 6.5 installs the critical-error handler. It first saves the address of the function that was passed as an argument, so that this function may be called by **_ce_hand** before aborting the program. It then saves the C data segment value for later use by **_ce_hand**. Because the critical-error handler is called by DOS, the DS register will not contain the proper value to access the C data group; therefore, DS must be saved, set to the correct value, and restored by **_ce_hand** to allow access to C data. Finally, DOS function 25h is used to set interrupt vector 24h to point to **_ce_hand**.

```
/*

        File:    CRITERR.C

        A C Program Demonstrating a Critical Error Handler

        This program must be linked with the assembler module CRITERRA.ASM
        (Figure 6.5).  To generate program from CRITERR.C and CRITERRA.ASM:
             cl /c CRITERR;
             masm CRITERRA;
             link CRITERR+CRITERRA;
*/

#include <stdio.h>

void main ()
     {
     FILE *testf;                     /* File to test if data is preserved.   */
     void lastrites (void);           /* Declare function for passing as parm. */
     void ce_init (void (*)());       /* Assembler routine: initializes       */
                                      /* error handler.                       */

                                  /* Test file to see if stream closed properly. */
     testf = fopen ("testfile","w");
     fprintf (testf,"this data will not get recorded in the file's ");
     fprintf (testf,"directory entry if the program terminates abnormally\n");

     ce_init (lastrites); /* Initialize crit. error handler & pass address  */
                          /* of function to prepare program for termination.*/

     fprintf (stdprn,"crash");              /* Note: take printer off line.  */
     fopen ("a:crash","w");                 /* Note: leave drive A: door open. */

     fclose (testf);
     printf ("\nprogram continued normally ... not aborted");

     } /* end main */


void lastrites ()            /* This function should perform the minimum set of */
                             /* tasks required to cleanup and save data before  */
                             /* termination due to control-c or critical error. */
     {
     fcloseall ();                                  /* Closes all open streams. */
     }
```

Figure 6.4: *A C program that installs and tests a critical-error handler*

The procedure **_ce_hand**, also in Figure 6.5, handles critical errors as follows. When DOS invokes interrupt 24h, register DI contains an error code ranging from 0h to Ch. These error codes correspond to the messages listed in **mess_table**. The procedure prints out the error message by multiplying the value of DI by the length of a single error message (note that all messages are conveniently the same length), and then adding this value to the

```
page 50,130

;File:      CRITERRA.ASM

;Assembler routines for critical error handler
;           Called f.om the C program CRITERR.C

public      _ce_init                    ;Called from C.
public      ce_hand                     ;Declare other symbols for CodeView.
public      terminate
public      c01, c02, c03, c04

_data       segment word public 'DATA'
                                        ;Error message table for 'ce_hand':

mess_table db        10,13,'critical error: write-protected diskette    $'
mess_len   equ       $ - mess_table
           db        10,13,'critical error: unknown unit                $'
           db        10,13,'critical error: drive not ready             $'
           db        10,13,'critical error: unknown command             $'
           db        10,13,'critical error: data error (CRC)            $'
           db        10,13,'critical error: bad request structure length$'
           db        10,13,'critical error: seek error                  $'
           db        10,13,'critical error: unknown media type          $'
           db        10,13,'critical error: sector not found            $'
           db        10,13,'critical error: printer out of paper         $'
           db        10,13,'critical error: write fault                 $'
           db        10,13,'critical error: read fault                  $'
           db        10,13,'critical error: general failure             $'

mess01     db        10,13,'abort, ignore, retry? $'
terminate  dw        ?                  ;Address of C terminate routine.

_data       ends

dgroup      group     _data
assume      cs:_text, ds:dgroup

_text       segment byte public 'CODE'

_ce_init    proc      near             ;** Initilizes Critical Error Handler **
                                       ;void ce_init (func);
                                       ;void (*func)();

sframe      struc                      ;Template to access stack frame.
bptr        dw        ?                ;Position of saved BP register.
ret_ad      dw        ?
parm1       dw        ?                ;Address of C function called on crit.err.
sframe      ends

frame       equ       [bp - bptr]      ;Base for accessing stack frame.

            push      bp               ;Standard module initialization.
            mov       bp, sp
            sub       sp, bptr

            push      di
            push      si

            mov       ax, frame.parm1  ;Save address of terminate routine to
            mov       terminate, ax    ;be called by 'ce_hand'.

            mov       cs:dataseg, ds   ;Save the C data segment for 'ce_hand'.

            push      ds               ;Initialize interrupt 24h to point to
            mov       ah, 25h          ;'ce_hand'.
            push      cs
            pop       ds
            mov       dx, offset ce_hand
            mov       al, 24h
            int       21h
            pop       ds
```

Figure 6.5: *Assembler critical-error routines that can be called by a C program*

```
                pop     si                  ;Restore registers.
                pop     di
                mov     sp, bp
                pop     bp
                ret                         ;Return to C program.
_ce_init        endp


ce_hand         proc    near                ;The critical error handler --
                                            ;activated by interrupt 24h.

                sti                         ;Turn interrupts back on.
                push    ax                  ;Save registers.
                pushf

                push    bx                  ;Save registers for writing messages.
                push    ds
                push    dx

                mov     ax, di              ;Write error message using code passed
                mov     bx, mess_len        ;in DI as pointer to message table.
                mul     bx
                mov     ds, cs:dataseg
                mov     dx, offset dgroup:mess_table
                add     dx, ax
                mov     ah, 09h
                int     21h

                mov     ah, 09              ;Prompt user for decision.
                mov     dx, offset dgroup:mess01
                int     21h

                pop     dx                  ;Done with messages: restore registers.
                pop     ds
                pop     bx
c01:            mov     ah, 07h             ;Read user response.

                int     21h
                cmp     al, 'a'             ;Branch on response value.
                je      c02
                cmp     al, 'A'
                je      c02
                cmp     al, 'r'
                je      c03
                cmp     al, 'R'
                je      c03
                cmp     al, 'i'
                je      c04
                cmp     al, 'I'
                je      c04
                jmp     c01                 ;Go back if invalid response.

c02:            popf                        ;Abort.
                pop     ax
                mov     ds, cs:dataseg      ;Restore C data segment value.
                call    word ptr cs:terminate    ;Call C terminate function.

                mov     ax, 4C01h           ;Exit w/ errorlevel 1.
                int     21h

c03:            popf                        ;Retry
                pop     ax
                mov     al, 1               ;1 => retry.
                iret                        ;Back to DOS.

c04:            popf                        ;Ignore.
                pop     ax
                mov     al, 0               ;0 => ignore.
                iret                        ;Back to DOS.
```

Figure 6.5: *Assembler critical-error routines that can be called by a C program (continued)*

```
    dataseg    dw      ?                    ;Store C DS value where addressible
                                            ;by 'ce_hand'.
    ce_hand    endp

    _text      ends                         ;End of code segment.
               end
```

Figure 6.5: *Assembler critical-error routines that can be called by a C program (continued)*

offset of **mess_table**; the resulting offset is passed to the DOS print string function 09h.

The procedure **_ce_hand** now elicits the user's decision and branches according to the response. If the user chooses to abort, then the programmer's termination routine is called (in this example, the actual routine called is the C function **lastrites**), and the program is ended through DOS function 4Ch (with an **errorlevel** value of 1). If the user chooses to retry, then register AL is given a value of 1, which is the code for DOS to retry the operation, and control is returned to DOS through an interrupt return. If the user chooses to ignore, then AL is given a value of 0 and an interrupt return is issued.

There are two additional values that may be returned to DOS through register AL:

AL = 2

AL = 3

AL = 2 terminates the program through interrupt 23h. The example procedure **ce_hand** does not employ this particular option because a Ctrl-Break handler might also be installed, which would again query the user and only complicate the situation.

AL = 3 fails the system call that is in progress; in other words, DOS returns to the application program and passes back an error message without completing its service. The procedure **ce_hand** also avoids this option because under DOS 3.*x* a **fail** request might not be allowed, and is automatically converted to an **abort**, bypassing the terminate routine and defeating the purpose of the handler. With some applications, however, it may be necessary to keep the program running even if an error condition cannot be corrected. In this case, setting AL = 3 might be the best response.

A critical-error handler should perform whatever actions are necessary to gracefully handle an error situation, but there are two important rules:

- Preserve the contents of all registers.
- Do not make DOS function calls except 01h to 0Ch, or 59h.

The example critical-error handler in Figure 6.5 prints a simple error message and performs the minimal tasks. A much more sophisticated error handler, however, could be written using this basic design. A great deal of error information is available to an interrupt 24h handler, including the following:

- Register DI contains a simple error code, as previously explained. Note that these error codes, ranging from 0h to Ch, correspond exactly to the standard "extended error codes" 19 (decimal) to 31 (decimal).

- Registers BP:SI contain the address of the device header control block. This header contains information on the device involved in the error. See Chapter 9 for the layout of the fields.

- Bit 7 of register AH is set to 0 to indicate a disk error. Bit 7 of AH = 1 indicates a nondisk error (or a bad memory image of the FAT associated with a disk, which would be indicated if the device header control block specifies a block device).

If bit 7 of AH is 0, indicating a disk error, then the following additional information is available:

- Register AL contains the offending drive number, starting with 0 for drive A:.

- AH bit 0 = 0 if the operation is a read, and 1 if it is a write.

- AH bits 2:1 indicate the affected disk area:

  0 0 DOS area
  0 1 FAT
  1 0 directory
  1 1 data area

- AH bit 3 = 0 if **fail** is not allowed, and 1 if **fail** is allowed.

- AH bit 4 = 0 if **retry** is not allowed, and 1 if **retry** is allowed.

- AH bit 5 = 0 if **ignore** is not allowed, and 1 if **ignore** is allowed.

Note that the above information is returned in bits 3, 4, and 5 only in DOS versions 3.0 and later.

Hardware-Generated Interrupts

Chapter 4 provided a brief description of the interrupt mechanism and explained the difference between software interrupts, internal hardware interrupts, and external hardware interrupts. This section discusses external hardware interrupts as important resources for enhancing program efficiency.

There is a significant fundamental difference between software and hardware interrupts, aside from their origin. A software interrupt must be explicitly invoked by a process at the appropriate point in the flow of logic; it is thus a synchronous event under the control of the calling program, and in this sense is very much like a subroutine call. A hardware interrupt, however, is generated by an autonomous device; it is thus an asynchronous event, initiated by a separate process and not under the control of the interrupted program. This fact has an important implication for performance programming: the hardware interrupt mechanism can be used to create a limited form of multitasking that can enhance program efficiency.

For example, a communications program must respond quickly when a character arrives at the serial port. If this program must make frequent function calls to determine if a character is ready, much time, which could be spent on other tasks, is wasted. However, if a hardware interrupt notifies the program of the arrival of a character, no time is wasted and the response time is minimal. The hardware interrupt mechanism constitutes a distinct parallel process, which increases overall efficiency. (See discussion of the BIOS serial port services in Chapter 5.)

Another example is a program that performs a lengthy internal process, such as sorting, compiling, or numerical calculations. Such a program cannot respond quickly to the keyboard unless it makes frequent function calls to poll the keyboard status. If, however, a hardware interrupt informs the program when a key is pressed, keyboard function calls need not be interspersed in the code.

A final example is a program that displays constant status information, such as the time of day or the shift state of keys such as Caps-Lock. By using hardware interrupts from the clock or the keyboard, these applications can update the display without making frequent function calls.

External Hardware Interrupts

Before describing the design of a hardware interrupt handler, this section discusses some of the basic features of this type of interrupt on MS-DOS machines. The external hardware interrupts are divided into two categories: nonmaskable and maskable.

Nonmaskable Hardware Interrupts

Only one interrupt type, 02h, is *nonmaskable,* meaning that it is not disabled by the **cli** software instruction. This interrupt is generated by a signal on the processor's NMI pin and is normally used to report memory parity errors. Additionally, some debuggers use this interrupt to regain control when the program crashes and normal interrupts are disabled. There are two components to this debugging mechanism: an external button that directly triggers a NMI, and an interrupt 02h handler that receives control when the button is pressed, and resumes the debugger. (See Chapter 3 for more information on these debuggers.)

Maskable Hardware Interrupts

A *maskable* hardware interrupt is generated by a signal on the processor's INTR pin. Since there are several sources for this category of interrupt and only one pin, the device interrupt requests are routed through the *programmable interrupt controller* (8259A PIC). This chip handles eight interrupt request lines, which are labeled IRQ0 through IRQ7. Conflicting requests are resolved according to priority, with IRQ0 having the highest priority and IRQ7 the lowest. The IRQ0 and IRQ1 lines originate from the motherboard, and IRQ2 through IRQ7 come from adapter cards on the I/O channel. Table 6.1 summarizes these interrupts as they are configured on a typical MS-DOS machine.

The PIC services the highest priority interrupt line by sending an INTR signal to the processor. When the processor acknowledges the request, the PIC places the interrupt number on the data bus. The processor then generates the interrupt. As shown in Table 6.1, the actual interrupt number is derived by adding 8 to the number of the IRQ line. IRQ lines are individually enabled by clearing the corresponding bits at the PIC port 21h. For example, to enable IRQ3, read in the value at port 21h, turn off bit 3, and write the value back to port 21h. At system startup, IRQ3 and IRQ4 are both disabled.

Note that the AT uses two 8259A controllers and thus has 15 available lines. The two controllers are connected in series—one input line, IRQ2 is used to receive the output from the second 8259A. See Appendix A for a table of the interrupt vectors.

Hardware Interrupt Service Routines

As an example of the process of installing and using a hardware interrupt service routine, Figure 6.6 lists a C program that makes use of a keyboard interrupt (09h) handler. The installation routine (**init_kbrk**) and

PIC line	Origin	Interrupt number	Use of interrupt
IRQ0	8253-5 timer	08h	BIOS time-keeping functions; generates an interrupt 18.2 times/sec
IRQ1	Keyboard	09h	Signals keyboard input
IRQ2	Reserved		(On AT, gate from controller 1)
IRQ3	COM2	0Bh	Communications, secondary
IRQ4	COM1	0Ch	Communications, primary
IRQ5	Hard disk	0Dh	Signal from hard disk controller
IRQ6	Diskette	0Eh	Signal from floppy controller
IRQ7	Printer	0Fh	Signal from printer controller

Table 6.1: *Maskable hardware interrupts*

interrupt handler itself (**kb_brk**) are contained in the assembler file listed in Figure 6.7.

The purpose of this interrupt handler is to enhance a program's efficiency and simplify its coding. The basic structure of the C program is common to many applications: a main menu that permits either the selection of one of several functions or exiting to DOS. In a real application, a selected function may be quite lengthy, and the user should be able to return to the main menu at any time and either select another procedure or quit the program. The function, however, may not involve user input; for example, a program demonstration displaying a series of screens, a lengthy graphics display, or a long internal process such as a sort routine or numerical computation. Another example would be a compiler.

In order for the user to be able to interrupt such a process, function calls that poll the keyboard must normally be interspersed with the code. This

```
/*
        File:     KBRK.C

        A C program demonstrating the use of a keyboard interrupt handler

        This program must be linked with the assembler module KBRKA.ASM
        (Figure 6.7).  To generate an .EXE file from KBRK.C and KBRKA.ASM:
                MSC KBRK;
                MASM KBRKA;
                LINK KBRK+KBRKA
*/

#include <setjmp.h>
#include <dos.h>

jmp_buf mark;
int  menu (void);                                /* C function declarations. */
void demo1 (void);
void demo2 (void);
void printa (char *,int,int,int);
void cls (int,int,int,int);

void init_kbrk (void);                              /* Assembler function. */

main ()
     {
     int choice;

     while (setjmp (mark))           /* Sets return point for 'longjmp ()'. */
          ;
     choice = menu ();               /* Display main menu, get choice.      */
     switch (choice)
          {
          case 1:
               init_kbrk ();     /* Activate the keyboard interrupt routine. */
               demo1 ();
               break;
          case 2:
               init_kbrk ();     /* Activate the keyboard interrupt routine. */
               demo2 ();
               break;
          case 3:
               cls (0,0,24,79);
               exit (0);
          } /* end switch */

     } /* end main */


int menu ()
     {
     int ch;
```

Figure 6.6: *A C program demonstrating the use of a keyboard interrupt handler*

```
   cls (0,0,24,79);
   printa ("----------------------------------------------------------",64,7,15);
   printa ("|                      MAIN MENU                         |",64,8,15);
   printa ("|     (1)   DEMO ONE                                     |",64,9,15);
   printa ("|                                                       |",64,10,15);
   printa ("|     (2)   DEMO TWO                   ENTER CHOICE:     |",64,11,15);
   printa ("|                                                       |",64,12,15);
   printa ("|     (3)   EXIT TO DOS                                  |",64,13,15);
   printa ("----------------------------------------------------------",64,14,15);
   printa (" ",64,11,60);
   while ((ch = getch()) < '1' || ch > '3')
        ;
   return (ch - 48);

   } /* end menu */



void demo1 ()
    {
    cls (0,0,24,79);                          /* Clear the whole screen. */

    printa ("----------------------------------------------------",64,7,15);
    printa ("|                                                   |",64,8,15);
    printa ("|                 THIS IS DEMO ONE                  |",64,9,15);
    printa ("|                                                   |",64,10,15);
    printa ("|           PRESS ANY KEY TO INTERRUPT              |",64,11,15);
    printa ("|                                                   |",64,12,15);
    printa ("----------------------------------------------------",64,13,15);

    for (;;)                                   /* This is forever. */
        ;

    } /* end demo1 */



void demo2 ()
    {
    cls (0,0,24,79);                          /* Clear the whole screen. */

    printa ("----------------------------------------------------",64,7,15);
    printa ("|                                                   |",64,8,15);
    printa ("|                 THIS IS DEMO TWO                  |",64,9,15);
    printa ("|                                                   |",64,10,15);
    printa ("|           PRESS ANY KEY TO INTERRUPT              |",64,11,15);
    printa ("|                                                   |",64,12,15);
    printa ("----------------------------------------------------",64,13,15);

    for (;;)                                   /* This is forever. */
        ;

    } /* end demo2 */
```

Figure 6.6: *A C program demonstrating the use of a keyboard interrupt handler (continued)*

```
void brkdisp ()    /* Display function called by keyboard interrupt handler. */
    {
    printa ("------------------------------------------------------",30,22,15);
    printa ("| CONTINUE (C) OR RETURN TO MAIN MENU (R) ?         |",30,23,15);
    printa ("------------------------------------------------------",30,24,15);
    printa (" ",30,23,61);                        /* Place cursor for reply. */

    } /* end brkdisp */


void printa (s, a, r, c)         /* Position cursor and write a string with */
char *s;                         /* specified color or video attribute.     */
int a, r, c;
/*
    s    : String to be displayed on screen.
    a    : Display attribute.
    r,c  : Starting row and column (0 .. 24, 0 .. 79) (ul corner = 0,0).
*/
    {
    union REGS cur_regs, write_regs;

    while (*s)                   /* Continue until null at end of string. */
        {
        cur_regs.h.ah = 2;          /* Update position of cursor using     */
        cur_regs.h.dh = r;          /* BIOS set cursor position function. */
        cur_regs.h.bh = 0;
        cur_regs.h.dl = c++;
        int86 (0x10, &cur_regs, &cur_regs);

        write_regs.h.ah = 9;        /* Write char & attribute at current  */
        write_regs.h.bh = 0;        /* cursor position using BIOS.        */
        write_regs.x.cx = 1;
        write_regs.h.bl = a;
        write_regs.h.al = *s++;
        int86 (0x10, &write_regs, &write_regs);
        }

    } /* end prints */

void cls (row1,col1,row2,col2)    /* This function uses BIOS interrupt 10h  */
int row1,col1,row2,col2;          /* to clear the specified area of screen. */
/*
    row1, col1 : Upper left corner of window to be cleared.
    row2, col2 : Lower right corner of window to be cleared.
*/
    {
    union REGS reg;

    reg.h.ah = 6;
    reg.h.al = 0;                              /* Blank the whole window. */
    reg.h.ch = row1;
    reg.h.cl = col1;
    reg.h.dh = row2;
    reg.h.dl = col2;
    reg.h.bh = 7;


    int86 (0x10, &reg, &reg);

    } /* end cls */
```

Figure 6.6: *A C program demonstrating the use of a keyboard interrupt handler (continued)*

method, however, complicates programming, decreases efficiency, and provides a sluggish response. The keyboard interrupt handler of Figures 6.6 and 6.7 is an alternative that provides instant response to user input and obviates the need to place keyboard function calls within the routine.

Basic Features of the Interrupt Handler

This section describes the workings of the functions found in the program of Figures 6.6 and 6.7.

The C library functions **setjmp** and **longjmp** are used to allow the program to jump back to the beginning of **main** from an arbitrary point in the code (which may be deeply nested in function calls). The function **setjmp** saves the current state of the registers and stack in the external array **mark**. When **longjmp** is called at some later point, the complete machine state is restored, and the program continues at the instruction immediately following **setjmp**.

The main menu allows selection of one of two major program divisions: **demo1** and **demo2**. Immediately before branching to either of these two functions, the assembler procedure **init_kbrk** is called to initialize the keyboard interrupt handler. Then **init_kbrk** saves the old value of the interrupt 09h vector, and resets this vector to point to **kb_brk**. The next hardware interrupt generated by keyboard action will now branch to **kb_brk**.

Meanwhile, back in the C program, a demo routine is called. After displaying a message, this routine simply goes into an endless loop to simulate a long, noninteractive process. When the user presses a key, **kb_brk** immediately receives control. This function now performs the following steps:

- It tests the flag **kb_act** to see if **kb_brk** has already been entered; if true, it *jumps* immediately to the original interrupt routine to avoid a recursive call.

- It sets the **kb_act** flag to prevent recursive calls.

□□■□

```
page 50,130

;File:       KBRKA.ASM

;Keyboard interrupt routines callable from a C program
;            Called from the C program KBRK.C

public       _init_kbrk
public       c_ds
public       int09_off
public       int09_seg
public       kb_act
public       kb_brk
public       k00, k01, k02, k03, k04, k05
public       acls

_data        segment word public 'DATA'
extrn        _mark:word
_data        ends

dgroup       group   _data
assume       cs:_text, ds:dgroup

_text        segment byte public 'CODE'

extrn        _brkdisp:near               ;List of all C functions called.
extrn        _longjmp:near

_init_kbrk proc     near                 ;** Initializes keyboard interrupt handler.
                                         ;void init_kbrk ();
             assume  cs:_text

             mov     cs:c_ds, ds         ;Save C data segment for use by kb_brk.

             mov     ah, 35h             ;Save old int 09h vector, called by
             mov     al, 09h             ;kb_brk.
             int     21h
             mov     cs:int09_off, bx
             mov     cs:int09_seg, es

             mov     ah, 25h             ;Set int 09h to point to kb_brk.
             push    cs
             pop     ds
             mov     dx, offset kb_brk
             mov     al, 09h
             int     21h

             mov     ds, cs:c_ds         ;Restore data segment.
             ret                         ;Return to C program.
_init_kbrk endp

                                         ;** Code segment data. **
c_ds         dw      ?                   ;Stores C data segment.
int09_off    dw      ?                   ;Stores old int 09 vector.
int09_seg    dw      ?
kb_act       db      0                   ;Flag: 1 => kb_brk already active.

kb_brk       proc    far                 ;** Keyboard interrupt handler. **
             assume  cs:_text

k00:         cmp     cs:kb_act, 0        ;Test if routine already active.
             je      k01                         ;If active:
             jmp     dword ptr cs:int09_off   ;branch to original vector.
k01:         mov     cs:kb_act, 1        ;Set active flag.
             pushf                       ;Simulate interrupt to original vector.
             call    dword ptr cs:int09_off
             push    ax
             mov     ah, 01h             ;Test if key available.
             int     16h
             jnz     k02
             pop     ax                  ;No key available -- restore & go back.
             mov     cs:kb_act, 0
             iret
```

Figure 6.7: *Keyboard interrupt routines that can be called from a C program*

```
k02:                                    ;Key is available.
           mov     ah, 0                ;Read it.
           int     16h
           sti                          ;Enable interrupts.
           push    bx                   ;Save more registers.
           push    cx
           push    dx
           call    _brkdisp             ;Display message.
k03:       mov     ah, 0                ;Read user's response.
           int     16h
           cmp     al, 'C'              ;Test response.
           jz      k04
           cmp     al, 'c'
           jz      k04
           cmp     al, 'R'
           jz      k05
           cmp     al, 'r'
           jz      k05
           jmp     k03                  ;Invalid key entered, go back.
k04:                                    ;** Continue. **
           call    acls                 ;Assembler version of clear screen.
           pop     dx                   ;Restore registers.
           pop     cx
           pop     bx
           pop     ax
           cli                          ;Prevent recursive call.
           mov     cs:kb_act, 0         ;Indicate routine not active.
           iret                         ;Go back.
k05:                                    ;** Return to main menu. **
           mov     ah, 25h              ;Restore interrupt 09 vector.
           lds     dx, dword ptr cs:int09_off
           mov     al, 09h
           int     21h
                                        ;Call 'longjmp'.
           mov     ax, 1                ;Second parm is 1.
           push    ax
                                        ;First parm is address of 'mark' array.
           mov     ax, offset dgroup:_mark
           push    ax
           mov     ds, c_ds             ;Restore C data segment.
           mov     cs:kb_act, 0         ;Indicate routine not active.
           call    _longjmp             ;Back to instruction after 'setjmp'.

kb_brk     endp

acls       proc    near                 ;Routine which uses BIOS interrupt 10h,
           assume  cs:_text             ;function 6, to clear last three rows
                                        ;of the screen.
           mov     ah, 6                ;Scroll active page up function.
           mov     al, 0                ;0 => blank entire window.
           mov     ch, 22               ;UL row.
           mov     cl, 0                ;UL column.
           mov     dh, 24               ;LR row.
           mov     dl, 79               ;LR column.
           mov     bh, 7                ;Normal/b & w attribute.
           int     10h                  ;BIOS video services.
           ret

acls       endp

_text      ends                         ;End of code segment.
           end
```

Figure 6.7: *Keyboard interrupt routines that can be called from a C program (continued)*

- It *calls* the original interrupt routine to allow it to process the scan code received from the keyboard.

- Upon return, it calls the BIOS (function 16h) to see if a key is ready to be read (a keyboard interrupt does not necessarily mean that a complete key has been entered).

- If no key is entered, it restores AX, resets **kb_act**, and returns control to the demo function.

- If a key is ready, it is read, interrupts are enabled, and the user is prompted to enter a C to continue the demo, or an R to return to the main menu.

- If the user opts to continue, the state is restored and an **iret** issued.

- If the user decides to return to the main menu, the interrupt 09h vector is restored so that the main program can perform normal keyboard input. Finally, **longjmp** is called and control returns immediately to the beginning of **main**. Note that the registers need not be popped off the stack since **longjmp** restores the original stack.

General Guidelines for Hardware Interrupt Handlers

The model program in Figure 6.6 and 6.7 demonstrates several important guidelines for writing hardware interrupt handlers. First, an interrupt handler should chain back to the original routine to avoid blocking other elements of the system. Thus, the old interrupt 09h vector is saved and the routine at this address is called with every interrupt.

Another important reason for chaining back to the original interrupt 09h routine at the beginning of the procedure is that, as mentioned earlier, hardware interrupts are routed through the 8259A PIC. Until an end of interrupt signal is sent to this chip, all further interrupts of the same or lower priority than the current one are disabled (regardless of the state of the interrupt flag). This function is conveniently performed by the original BIOS routine. If, however, it is not possible to chain to a routine that signals the PIC, the following port output can be used to signal an end of interrupt:

```
mov al, 20h          ;PIC port is 20h.
out 20h, al          ;20h signals end-of-interrupt.
```

(Note that PS/2 machines may require you to clear the current interrupt-in-progress explicitly before sending an end-of-interrupt signal. See the IBM hardware system manual for the appropriate PS/2 machine for further details on writing hardware interrupt handlers, as well as for other programming considerations specific to the Micro Channel architecture used by these machines.)

When an interrupt routine receives control, the interrupts are disabled and should be enabled with the **sti** instruction as soon as possible to prevent blocking other processes (such as the clock interrupt 08h, which calls the BIOS time-keeping functions).

When designing an interrupt handler, you should carefully consider the points at which interrupts are enabled and disabled. The issues are very similar to those encountered when managing the asynchronous processes of a multitasking system. In general, interrupts are temporarily disabled at a critical point in the code to prevent another process from gaining control and interfering with the current task, or corrupting data that is currently being modified. For example, in the interrupt handler of Figure 6.7, immediately above the label **k05:**, interrupts are disabled to prevent reentry into the code once the **kb_act** semaphore is reset to 0.

■. Other Resources

There are a few final resources in an MS-DOS machine that deserve mention. These include the data interrupt vectors, hardware ports, video memory, and installable device drivers.

▫. Data Interrupt Vectors

Not all of the interrupt vectors contain the addresses of executable routines; several of them contain the memory locations of tables storing input/output parameters used by the BIOS. The reason that the BIOS places the addresses of some of its data in the interrupt vector table is that this mechanism allows these addresses to be replaced with the memory locations of alternative data tables supplied by the programmer. Therefore, just as a system interrupt routine may be replaced or trapped by changing an address in the interrupt table, some internal data may also be replaced to modify the behavior of the system. The recommended procedure is to first copy the existing data to an area within your program, make the required modifications, and then reset the appropriate interrupt vector to point to the modified table. The following sections describe the data interrupt vectors used by the BIOS.

1Dh: Video Parameters

Vector 1Dh normally points to a table of parameters used to initialize the 6845 chip on the video controller. At system startup, the vector points to data contained in the ROM BIOS (in the PC at F000h:F0A4h; see the BIOS listing for the layout). However, this vector may be changed to point to an alternate table. For example, the BIOS of an EGA controller may adjust the vector to point to a modified table contained in the C000h segment.

1Eh: Disk Base

At system startup, vector 1Eh points to a table of data in the standard ROM BIOS (in the PC at F000h:EFC7h; see the BIOS listing for the layout). However, it may be replaced by the address of a modified block of diskette parameters. When MS-DOS loads, it resets this vector to point to its own table (for version 2.1, at address 0000f:0522h). MS-DOS dynamically modifies these parameters to enhance disk performance; this technique may also be employed by the performance-minded programmer writing nonDOS disk routines. Specifically, modifying the following two fields may improve disk performance:

Offset 9h: Head settle time   The default value in the PC/XT is 25 (milliseconds). Temporarily setting this value to 0 on all read operations can improve disk access speed (leave it at 25 for write operations).

Offset Ah: Motor startup time   The default value is 4 (× 1/8 seconds). You can experiment with reducing this value to improve performance, although errors may occur if it is too small.

1Fh: Extended Graphics Character Table

Vector 1Fh points to a table of bit map data to be used for generating the characters with ASCII codes from 128 to 255, when in a graphics mode. The ROM BIOS contains the data for generating the first 128 characters (in the PC at F000h:FA6Eh), but does not contain data for the higher 128 characters. At system startup this vector is set to F000h:0000h, indicating that no data are available. The programmer must create a new table and reset the vector to point to it. Consult the ROM BIOS listings for the layout required to generate characters (in the PC, at offset FA6Eh).

41h: Fixed Disk Parameters (First Fixed Disk)

Vector 41h points to a table of data used to control the first fixed disk.

43h: EGA Graphics Video Parameters

When an EGA controller is installed, vector 43h points to a table containing video initialization parameters. At system startup, the vector is set to point to a table of default parameters contained in the EGA ROM in segment C000h (see the ROM listing in the EGA manual mentioned in Appendix H for the format).

44h: EGA Graphics Character Table

When an EGA controller is installed, vector 44h points to a table containing the dot patterns used to generate graphics characters. In video modes 4, 5, and 6, the table is used for the first 128 characters (the table for the higher 128 characters is pointed to by vector 1Fh). However, in all other EGA graphics modes, the table is used for the full 256 characters.

46h: Fixed Disk Parameters (Second Fixed Disk)

Vector 46h points to a table of data used to control the second fixed disk in a system with more than one fixed disk.

Ports

The 8086 family of processors are capable of addressing 64K I/O ports. Programs that write to specific ports are the ultimate in nonportability. Generally, I/O can be handled through DOS or the BIOS; however, some special purpose functions may not be able to achieve sufficient performance without port access, and some portions of the port interface are quite likely to remain constant among compatible machines and with future hardware versions. See Chapter 7 for a general discussion of the topic of performance and compatibility.

Video Memory

The presence of the video refresh buffer in directly addressable RAM has important implications for performance programming. Chapter 8 discusses this topic.

Installable Device Drivers

A final important resource offered by MS-DOS versions 2.0 and higher is the provision for installing custom device drivers. This topic is discussed in Chapter 9.

CHAPTER 7

COMPATIBILITY VS. PERFORMANCE

Compatibility is a constant concern for the performance-conscious programmer. A program written for a specific target machine may of course use any reliable feature of that machine. If, however, the program is designed for a broad market and is expected to have a long lifetime, it must be compatible with a wide variety of present and future hardware and software environments. Unfortunately, many of the highest performance techniques may not be compatible with

- Certain versions of the operating system, present and future
- Non-IBM compatible MS-DOS machines
- Newly developed peripheral equipment
- Network systems
- Multitasking environments such as Windows and TopView

Does this imply that a programmer writing a portable application must give up performance-rich features and reduce the program to the lowest common denominator of universally available resources? Absolutely not. Rather, the contention of this chapter is that performance and compatibility are *not* mutually exclusive. By analyzing the resources present in the computing environment at runtime, it is possible to the select the highest performance techniques compatible with that environment.

The first section presents some general guidelines for developing applications compatible with present and future machines and operating systems, all of which can normally be followed without loss of software performance. The next section delineates methods for a program to determine the specific hardware and software environment in which it is running. The last section discusses making optimal use of the existing resources once the nature of the environment has been established.

The methods presented in this chapter offer a general approach to maintaining compatibility in a high-performance program. However, this information is only a starting point; with the rapid influx of new processing hardware, peripherals, and operating systems, continuing research is needed to assure that an application retains its compatibility while using the most advanced features available.

▪▪ General Compatibility Guidelines

The literature on MS-DOS programming abounds with rules for writing compatible applications. This section presents only those general rules that do not normally impact software performance, and therefore may be used for most applications. Rules that tend to limit software performance (such as not addressing absolute memory locations) are discussed in the following section, where they are presented not as general dictums, but rather as possible requirements for certain specific computer systems.

A common theme of many of the following guidelines is to use MS-DOS whenever possible. With the advent of multitasking environments and memory-resident utilities, a program can no longer assume that it is the only process in memory, and therefore it is especially important to use official channels and keep DOS informed of the program's actions.

Use the MS-DOS file system whenever possible. As mentioned before, the file system is one of MS-DOS's strong points, and disk I/O through the file system is preferred to direct manipulation of specific sectors using DOS interrupts 25h and 26h, BIOS interrupt 13h, or programmer-written routines.

Use DOS handle function calls rather than FCB functions or the traditional character device I/O functions 01h through 0Ch. (For some exceptions, see Chapter 4.)

Let DOS manage processes. Use the EXEC function to load program overlays and execute child processes, allowing DOS to handle relocation and other details of program loading. Employing DOS functions also keeps the system informed of the identity of the current process (the operating system keeps an internal record of the current process, which is identified through the address of its program segment prefix).

Let DOS manage memory allocation. Allocate and deallocate memory through functions 48h, 49h, and 4Ah, and do not use memory not allocated to the process.

Release unused memory. It is especially important in a multitasking environment that a program release any unused memory that is allocated to it by the loader. Note that .COM files are always allocated all free user memory, and must explicitly deallocate memory through DOS function 4Ah. .EXE files, however, are allocated additional memory above the program according to the instructions in the .EXE file header. By default, the linker generates an .EXE file header that demands all available memory; the amount can be reduced using the **/CP:n** LINK command line option, where **n** stands for the number of 16-byte paragraphs of additional memory desired. Setting this value to 1 will reduce memory allocation to the minimum. (By default, the value is set to 65535, an impossibly large amount that results in the maximum allocation.)

Use the newer DOS exit functions 4Ch **(terminate)** *and 31h* **(terminate and stay resident)** *rather than the older functions 00h* **(terminate)**, *interrupt 20h (identical to function 00h), and interrupt 27h* **(terminate and stay resident)**. The advantages of these functions are discussed in Chapter 4.

When using interrupts, get and set interrupt vectors through the DOS functions 25h and 35h, rather than writing directly to memory. Using these functions will notify DOS of your intentions and properly disable interrupts when the vector is in a state of transition. Also save the prior contents of any modified interrupt vector and restore its value before program termination. Exceptions to this rule are interrupts 23h and 24h, which are restored automatically by DOS from values stored in the program segment prefix.

Use the MS-DOS environment to communicate information from the user to an application (for example, the location of configuration files and overlays). See Chapter 6 for the use of the environment.

Use the system time functions (DOS function 2Ch or BIOS interrupt 1Ah) or the 8253 programmable timer, rather than software timing loops, the duration of which depends on the processor speed.

Access BIOS functions through the documented interrupt vectors and not through absolute memory addresses, which are subject to change.

Establishing the Computer Environment

The first step toward achieving the highest possible degree of performance is to develop a systematic and reliable method for determining and recording the hardware and software environment present at runtime. Once this information is obtained, it may be used throughout the remainder of the program to make the optimal choice of alternative methods. The specific approach recommended in this chapter is to set up a table of resources, filling in the values either through dynamic runtime testing or through a user installation procedure.

The Resource Table

A resource table is a data structure used to store information about the current computing environment, and should be in a form that simplifies the subsequent testing of its fields. The structure **resources**, beginning on line 51 of the C program in Figure 7.1, is an example of a simple resource table. Most fields are defined as **unsigned char** rather than as **int** in order to use only a single byte where no possible value is over 255. There are two basic types of fields according to the values they store.

First, some fields indicate the presence of a resource that is one of a set of mutually exclusive possibilities; for example, the processor type (**cpu**) or the machine name (**machine**). In order to simplify setting and testing these fields, manifest constants are defined for each possible value (see lines 20–39). These constants are numbered sequentially.

Second, other fields indicate the presence of one or more resources that can exist simultaneously; for example, the video features field (**video**). The manifest constants for this field are not numbered sequentially, but rather as 1, 2, 4, and so on, so that each resource has its own bit. This allows more than one feature to be indicated in a single byte, because it is possible for several of these features to coexist in a system. For example, a system can have both normal color graphics capability (**VCGA**) *and* enhanced graphics capability (**VEGAC**). See lines 43–48.

You should design your own version of the resource table to contain information pertinent to the particular application. Once the fields in this table are set, it is a simple matter to use the values to select the optimal routine. For example,

```
if (resources.machine == MUNK) /* Unknown machine,        */
                               /* can't use BIOS.         */
    printf ("plain message");  /* Must use slow, dumpy    */
                               /* printf.                 */
else                           /* IBM-compatible machine; */
                               /* therefore can use fast, */
                               /* slick BIOS function.    */
    printa ("attractive message",112,24,0,7);
```

There are two basic approaches to setting the values of the resource table: dynamic testing by the program at runtime and user installation.

Dynamic Testing

By performing appropriate tests, the program itself can determine a great deal about the computing environment in which it is running. This method of setting the resource table provides the greatest convenience for the user, and is exemplified by the C program in Figure 7.1.

```
 1:  /*
 2:
 3:          File:     RESRC.C
 4:
 5:          A C program which obtains and Stores the Resources of the Current
 6:          Computing Environment.
 7:
 8:          This program must be linked with the assembler module RESRCA.ASM (Figure
 9:          7.2). You can use the following commands to generate the executable
10:          program from RESRC.C and RESRCA.ASM:
11:
12:                  cl /c RESRC.C
13:                  masm RESRCA;
14:                  link RESRC+RESRCA;
15:  */
16:  #include <stdio.h>
17:
18:                                      /* Manifest constants for 'resources' structure. */
19:                                              /* resources.cpu                  */
20:  #define     P86        0             /* Intel 8086 or 8088             */
21:  #define     P186       1             /* Intel 80186 or 80188           */
22:  #define     P286       2             /* Intel 80286                    */
23:  #define     P386       3             /* Intel 80386                    */
24:
25:                                              /* resources.machine              */
26:  #define     MUNK       0             /* Unknown machine                */
27:  #define     MIBMPC     1             /* IBM-PC                         */
28:  #define     MIBMXT     2             /* IBM-XT or Portable PC          */
29:  #define     MIBMJR     3             /* IBM-PCjunior                   */
30:  #define     MIBMAT     4             /* IBM-AT                         */
31:  #define     MIBMXT2    5             /* IBM-XT 286                     */
32:  #define     MIBMCONV   6             /* IBM-CONVERTIBLE                */
33:  #define     IBMMOD30   7             /* IBM PS/2 Model 30              */
34:  #define     IBMMOD50   8             /* IBM PS/2 Model 50              */
35:  #define     IBMMOD60   9             /* IBM PS/2 Model 60              */
36:  #define     IBMMOD80   10            /* IBM PS/2 Model 80              */
37:  #define     MIBMUN     11            /* IBM-unknown model              */
38:  #define     MCOMPAQ    12            /* COMPAQ                         */
39:  #define     MATT       13            /* AT&T                           */
40:
41:                                              /* resources.video                */
42:                                              /* MODES SUPPORTED:               */
43:  #define     VMDA       1             /* 7.                             */
44:  #define     VHGC       2             /* Hercules 720 x 348 mono.graphics.*/
45:  #define     VCGA       4             /* 0, 1, 2, 3, 4, 5, 6.           */
46:  #define     VEGAM      8             /* 7, F.                          */
47:  #define     VEGAC      16            /* 0, 1, 2, 3, 4, 5, 6, D, E, 10. */
48:  #define     VPS2       32            /* Call int 10h, function 1bh to  */
49:                                              /* list of supported modes.       */
50:
51:  struct      /* Table of resources present in current computing environment. */
52:       {
53:          unsigned char cpu;          /* Processor type.                */
54:          unsigned char machine;      /* Brand of machine.              */
55:          struct dos                  /* Version of MS-DOS.             */
```

Figure 7.1: *A C program that tests the current computer environment*

```
 56:               {
 57:               unsigned char major;        /* Major version number = 1, 2, 3, etc.  */
 58:               unsigned char minor;        /* Minor version number                   */
 59:               }
 60:          dos;
 61:     unsigned char video;                  /* Active display adapter features.       */
 62:     unsigned char ncp;                    /* Boolean: numeric coprocessor present?  */
 63:     unsigned char gameport;               /* Boolean: game port attached?           */
 64:     unsigned int memsiz;                  /* Total system memory in kilobytes.      */
 65:     unsigned char numprn;                 /* Number of printers attached.           */
 66:     unsigned char numserial;              /* Number of serial ports attached.       */
 67:     unsigned char numdisk;                /* Number of diskette drives present.     */
 68:          }
 69:     resources;
 70:
 71:                                           /* Assembler functions.                   */
 72:     unsigned char cur_cpu (void);         /* Returns resources.cpu                  */
 73:     unsigned char cur_mach (void);        /* Returns resources.machine              */
 74:     void dos_ver (struct dos *);          /* Sets resources.dos                     */
 75:     unsigned char cur_video (void);       /* Returns resources.video                */
 76:     unsigned char cur_ncp (void);         /* Returns resources.ncp                  */
 77:     unsigned char cur_gameport (void);    /* Returns resources.gameport             */
 78:     unsigned int cur_memsiz (void);       /* Returns resources.memsiz               */
 79:     unsigned char cur_numprn (void);      /* Returns resources.numprn               */
 80:     unsigned char cur_numser (void);      /* Returns resources.numserial            */
 81:     unsigned char cur_numdisk (void);     /* Returns resources.numdisk              */
 82:
 83:
 84:     void main (argc, argv)
 85:     int argc;
 86:     char *argv[];
 87:          {
 88:          static char *cpuid [] =
 89:               {
 90:               "Intel 8086/88",
 91:               "Intel 80186/8",
 92:               "Intel 80286",
 93:               "Intel 80386"
 94:               };
 95:          static char *machid [] =
 96:               {
 97:               "unknown",
 98:               "IBM-PC",
 99:               "IBM-XT",
100:               "IBM JUNIOR",
101:               "IBM-AT",
102:               "IBM XT 286",
103:               "IBM CONVERTIBLE",
104:               "IBM PS/2 Model 30",
105:               "IBM PS/2 Model 50",
106:               "IBM PS/2 Model 60",
107:               "IBM PS/2 Model 80",
108:               "IBM-unknown model",
109:               "COMPAQ",
110:               "AT&T"
```

Figure 7.1: *A C program that tests the current computer environment (continued)*

```
111:              );
112:         unsigned char ibmcom;            /* Boolean variable => IBM-compatibility. */
113:
114:         resources.cpu = cur_cpu ();                    /* Set resource table. */
115:         resources.machine = cur_mach ();
116:         dos_ver (&resources.dos);
117:                                          /* Set IBM-compatibility variable.*/
118:         ibmcom = (unsigned char)(resources.machine != MUNK
119:              || *argv[1] == 'i'                        /* Allow user override. */
120:              || *argv[1] == 'I');
121:
122:                                     /* The following tests use BIOS,         */
123:                                     /* therefore must have IBM-compatibility. */
124:         if (ibmcom)
125:              {
126:              resources.video = cur_video ();
127:              resources.ncp = cur_ncp ();
128:              resources.gameport = cur_gameport ();
129:              resources.memsiz = cur_memsiz ();
130:              resources.numprn = cur_numprn ();
131:              resources.numserial = cur_numser ();
132:              resources.numdisk = cur_numdisk ();
133:              }
134:         else        /* Can't perform tests, therefore must assume the worst. */
135:              {
136:              resources.video = 0;
137:              resources.ncp = 0;
138:              resources.gameport = 0;
139:              resources.memsiz = 0;
140:              resources.numprn = 0;
141:              resources.numserial = 0;
142:              resources.numdisk = 0;
143:              }
144:                                                   /* Print out resource table. */
145:         printf ("\ncurrent computing environment\n");
146:         printf ("------- --------- ----------\n");
147:         printf ("current processor:      %s\n",cpuid [resources.cpu]);
148:         printf ("machine make:           %s\n",machid [resources.machine]);
149:         printf ("MS-DOS version:         %1d.%2d\n",
150:              resources.dos.major,
151:              resources.dos.minor);
152:                                          /* The following have meaningful  */
153:         if (ibmcom)                      /* values only if IBM-compatible. */
154:              {
155:              printf ("active display adapter:%s%s%s%s%s%s\n",
156:                   resources.video & VMDA  ? " MDA"           : "",
157:                   resources.video & VHGC  ? " HERCULES"      : "",
158:                   resources.video & VCGA  ? " CGA"           : "",
159:                   resources.video & VEGAM ? " EGA/MONOCHROME" : "",
160:                   resources.video & VEGAC ? " EGA/COLOR"     : "",
161:                   resources.video & VPS2  ? " PS/2"          : "");
162:              printf ("numeric coprocessor?:   %s\n", resources.ncp?"yes":"no");
163:              printf ("gameport attached?:     %s\n",
164:                   resources.gameport?"yes":"no");
165:              printf ("memory size:            %d kilobytes\n",resources.memsiz);
```

Figure 7.1: *A C program that tests the current computer environment (continued)*

```
166:                printf ("number of printers:      %d\n",resources.numprn);
167:                printf ("number serial devices:   %d\n",resources.numserial);
168:                printf ("number diskette drives:  %d\n",resources.numdisk);
169:                }
170:
171:        ) /* end main */.
```

Figure 7.1: *A C program that tests the current computer environment (continued)*

The program begins by first calling those assembler functions that do not use BIOS services and that should work on any MS-DOS machine: **cur_cpu**, **cur_mach**, and **dos_ver** (lines 85–87).

Once the **resources.machine** field is set (by calling **cur_mach**), the program can use its value to set the flag for IBM compatibility, **ibmcom**. The only value of **resources.machine** that would indicate non-IBM compatibility in this particular example is **MUNK** (unknown machine type; see line 118). Notice that the expression that sets the IBM-compatibility flag will also evaluate to true if the first command line parameter begins with an **i** or **I**. This feature allows the user to override the type of compatibility determined by the program. Providing user override capability is very important, since compatibility is typically determined by testing a limited number of machines (especially in this example! See lines 119 and 120).

Once IBM-compatibility has been determined, it is possible to call the testing functions that use BIOS services. If these functions cannot be called (and no other means are available for finding the information), then the program must assume the worst case, and set all the applicable resource fields to 0 (lines 124–143). Finally, the program prints the results: the list of resources found in the machine.

Figure 7.2 contains the listings of the assembler functions that are called from the C program. This file begins with a definition of the same manifest constants defined in the C file. The next several sections describe the functions that are included.

_cur_cpu

The function **_cur_cpu** returns the identity of the current processor, and is used to set the value of **resources.cpu**. It uses the following sequence of tests to discriminate among a small set of possible processors: the 8086/88, the 80186, the 80286, and the 80386. As new processors, such as the 80486, become available, other tests should be added to this routine to detect their presence.

```
page 50,130

;Figure:     7.2
;File:       RESRCA.ASM

;Assembler Routines which Test the Current Computer Environment.
;            Called from the C program RESRC.C.

                                          ;Manifest constants for resource table.
                                          ;resources.cpu
P86         equ     00                    ;Intel 8086 or 8088.
P186        equ     01                    ;Intel 80186 or 80188.
P286        equ     02                    ;Intel 80286.
P386        equ     03                    ;Intel 80386.


                                          ;resources.machine
MUNK        equ     00                    ;Unknown machine.
MIBMPC      equ     01                    ;IBM-PC.
MIBMXT      equ     02                    ;IBM-XT or Portable PC.
MIBMJR      equ     03                    ;IBM-PCjunior.
MIBMAT      equ     04                    ;IBM-AT.
MIBMXT2     equ     05                    ;IBM-XT 286.
MIBMCONV    equ     06                    ;IBM-CONVERTIBLE.
MIBMMOD30   equ     07                    ;IBM PS/2 Model 30.
MIBMMOD50   equ     08                    ;IBM PS/2 Model 50.
MIBMMOD60   equ     09                    ;IBM PS/2 Model 60.
MIBMMOD80   equ     10                    ;IBM PS/2 Model 80.
MIBMUN      equ     11                    ;IBM-unknown model.
MCOMPAQ     equ     12                    ;COMPAQ.
MATT        equ     13                    ;AT&T.


                                          ;resources.video
                                          ;MODES SUPPORTED:
VMDA        equ     01                    ;7.
VHGC        equ     02                    ;Hercules 720 x 348 mono. graphics.
VCGA        equ     04                    ;0, 1, 2, 3, 4, 5, 6.
VEGAM       equ     08                    ;7, F.
VEGAC       equ     16                    ;0, 1, 2, 3, 4, 5, 6, D, E, 10.
VPS2        equ     32                    ;Call int 10h, function 1bh to get
                                          ;list of supported modes.
            public      _cur_cpu
            public      a01,a02,a03
            public      _cur_mach
            public      b00,b01,b02,b03,b04,b05,b06,b07,b08,b09
            public      _dos_ver
            public      c01,c02
            public      _cur_video
            public      d01,d02,d03,d04,d05
            public      _cur_ncp
            public      _cur_gameport
            public      _cur_memsiz
            public      _cur_numprn
            public      _cur_numser
            public      _cur_numdisk
            public      ibm, lenibm, compaq, lencompaq, att, lenatt
```

Figure 7.2: *Assembler routines for testing the current computer environment*

```
                                             ;Masks for BIOS interrupt 11h.
  equipment    record  prn:2,r1:1,game:1,ser:3,r2:1,drv:2,mode:2,ram:2,ncp:1,ipl:1

  _data        segment word public 'DATA'

  ibm          db      "IBM"
  lenibm       equ     $-ibm
  compaq       db      "COMPAQ"
  lencompaq    equ     $-compaq
  att          db      "OLIVETTI"
  lenatt       equ     $-att
  video        dw      ?                      ;Build up video attributes.

  _data        ends

  dgroup       group   _data
               assume  cs:_text, ds:dgroup

  _text        segment byte public 'CODE'


  _cur_cpu     proc    near                   ;** returns resources.cpu **
                                              ;unsigned char cur_cpu ();

               assume  cs:_text

               pushf                          ;Save flags.

                                              ;** Test for the 8086/88. **
               xor     ax, ax                 ;Place 0 in AX.
               push    ax                     ;Try to load FLAGS with 0.
               popf
               pushf                          ;Now test contents of FLAGS.
               pop     ax                     ;Place FLAGS in AX.
               and     ax, 0f000h             ;Isolate 4 high-order bits.
               cmp     ax, 0f000h             ;Test whether high-order bits are set.
               jne     a01
               mov     ax, P86                ;Bits set indicates 86/88 processor.
               jmp     a04
  a01:
                                              ;** Test for the 80186. **
               push    sp                     ;Test whether SP is decremented before
               pop     ax                     ;or after it is written to stack;
               cmp     ax, sp                 ;186 decrements BEFORE, 286/386
               je      a02                    ;decrement AFTER SP is written.
               mov     ax, P186               ;Must be the 80186.
               jmp     a04
  a02:
                                              ;** Test for the 80286. **
               mov     ax, 0f000h             ;Attempt to set 4 high-order bits of
               push    ax                     ;FLAGS.
               popf
               pushf                          ;Test the 4 high-order bits.
               pop     ax
               and     ax, 0f000h
               jnz     a03
               mov     ax, P286               ;No bits set, must be the 80286.
```

Figure 7.2: *Assembler routines for testing the current computer environment (continued)*

```
            jmp      a04
a03:                                      ;** Must be the 80386. **
            mov      ax, P386
a04:                                      ;Exit point.
            popf                          ;Restore flags.
            ret


_cur_cpu    endp


_cur_mach   proc     near                 ;** Returns resources.machine. **
                                          ;unsigned char cur_mach ();

            assume   cs:_text

            push     si                   ;Save registers.
            push     di
            push     es

            mov      si, offset dgroup:ibm     ;** Test for IBM logo. **
            mov      ax, 0f000h
            mov      es, ax
            mov      di, 0e00eh
            mov      cx, lenibm
            repe     cmpsb
            je       b00                  ;Now test for specific IBM model.
            jmp      b16                  ;Not IBM, test for other logos.

b00:                                      ;** Test for PC. **
            cmp      byte ptr es:[0fffeh], 0ffh
            jne      b01
            mov      ax, MIBMPC
            jmp      b19                  ;Exit.
b01:                                      ;** Test for XT. **
            cmp      byte ptr es:[0fffeh], 0feh
            je       b02
            cmp      byte ptr es:[0fffeh], 0fbh
            je       b02
            jmp      b03
b02:
            mov      ax, MIBMXT
            jmp      b19                  ;Exit.
b03:                                      ;** Test for Junior. **
            cmp      byte ptr es:[0fffeh], 0fdh
            jne      b04
            mov      ax, MIBMJR
            jmp      b19                  ;Exit.
b04:                                      ;** Test for 286 machines. **
            cmp      byte ptr es:[0fffeh], 0fch
            jne      b12                  ;Not a 286 machine.
            mov      ah, 0c0h             ;BIOS:  return system configuration
            int      15h                  ;(ES:BX points to system descriptor).
            cmp      ah, 86h              ;FCh model and 86h code means an AT
            jne      b05                  ;dated 1/10/84.
            mov      ax, MIBMAT
            jmp      b19                  ;Exit.
```

Figure 7.2: *Assembler routines for testing the current computer environment (continued)*

```
b05:
            cmp     ah, 0
            je      b06                 ;0 code indicates a 286 machine.
            mov     ah, MIBMUN          ;Code neither 86h nor 00h is unexpected
            jmp     b19                 ;at this point;  jump to exit.
b06:
                                        ;Test for specific 286 model.
            add     bx, 3               ;Get to offset of submodel byte.
            cmp     byte ptr es:[bx], 0 ;0 or 1 means AT dated 6/10/85 or
            je      b07                 ;11/15/85.
            cmp     byte ptr es:[bx], 1
            je      b07
            jmp     b08
b07:
                                        ;AT
            mov     ax, MIBMAT
            jmp     b19                 ;Exit.
b08:
            cmp     byte ptr es:[bx], 2 ;2 means XT 286.
            jne     b09
            mov     ax, MIBMXT2
            jmp     b19                 ;Exit.
b09:
            cmp     byte ptr es:[bx], 4 ;4 means Model 50.
            jne     b10
            mov     ax, MIBMMOD50
            jmp     b19                 ;Exit.
b10:
            cmp     byte ptr es:[bx], 5 ;5 means Model 60.
            jne     b11
            mov     ax, MIBMMOD60
            jmp     b19                 ;Exit.
b11:
            mov     ax, MIBMUN          ;Unknown IBM model.
            jmp     b19                 ;Exit.

b12:
                                        ;** Test for Model 30. **
            cmp     byte ptr es:[0fffeh], 0fah
            jne     b13
            mov     ax, MIBMMOD30
            jmp     b19                 ;Exit.
b13:                                    ;** Test for Convertible. **
            cmp     byte ptr es:[0fffeh], 0f9h
            jne     b14
            mov     ax, MIBMCONV
            jmp     b19                 ;Exit.
b14:                                    ;** Test for Model 80. **
            cmp     byte ptr es:[0fffeh], 0f8h
            jne     b15
            mov     ax, MIBMMOD80
            jmp     b19                 ;Exit.
b15:                                    ;** Unknown IBM model. **
            mov     ax, MIBMUN
            jmp     b19                 ;Exit.
b16:                                    ;** Test for COMPAQ. **
            mov     si, offset dgroup:compaq
            mov     di, 0feah
```

Figure 7.2: *Assembler routines for testing the current computer environment (continued)*

```
                mov     cx, lencompaq
                repe    cmpsb
                jne     b17
                mov     ax, MCOMPAQ
                jmp     b19                     ;Exit.
                                                ;** Test for AT&T. **
    b17:
                mov     si, offset dgroup:att
                mov     di, 0c050h
                mov     cx, lenatt
                repe    cmpsb
                jne     b18
                mov     ax, MATT
                jmp     b19                     ;Exit.
                                                ;** Unidentified machine. **
    b18:
                mov     ax, MUNK
                jmp     b19                     ;Exit.
    b19:                                        ;Exit point.
                pop     es
                pop     di
                pop     si
                ret


    _cur_mach   endp


    _dos_ver    proc    near                    ;** Assigns values to 'resources.dos'. **
                                                ;void dos_ver (version);
                                                ;struct dos *version;

                assume  cs:_text

    sframe      struc                           ;Template to access stack frame.
    bptr        dw      ?
    ret_ad      dw      ?
    parm1       dw      ?
    sframe      ends
    frame       equ     [bp - bptr]             ;Base for accessing stack frame.

                push    bp                      ;Set up base pointer to access frame.
                mov     bp, sp

                mov     ah, 30h                 ;Call dos to get version number.
                int     21h
                mov     bx, frame.parm1         ;Move 'dos' structure address into BX.
                cmp     al, 0
                jne     c01
                mov     byte ptr [bx], 1        ;Use BX as a pointer to access the
                mov     byte ptr [bx+1], 0      ;actual 'dos' structure fields.
                jmp     c02
    c01:        mov     byte ptr [bx], al
                mov     byte ptr [bx+1], ah
    c02:
                pop     bp
                ret

    _dos_ver    endp
```

Figure 7.2: *Assembler routines for testing the current computer environment (continued)*

```
_cur_video proc    near              ;** Returns resources.video **
                                     ;unsigned char cur_video ();
                                     ;Note: this function uses the BIOS and
                                     ;therefore should be called only if
                                     ;IBM compatibility is established.

           assume  cs:_text

           push    si
           push    di
           mov     video, 0          ;Initialize video flag w/ no attributes.

                                     ;*** Test for MDA. ***
                                     ;Test for 6845 monochrome registers.
           mov     dx, 03b4h         ;Index register.
           mov     al, 0fh           ;Select register 0fh.
           out     dx, al
           mov     dx, 03b5h         ;Data register.
           in      al, dx            ;Read register 0fh.
           mov     ah, al            ;Store value read in AH.
           mov     al, 99h           ;Write a number to the register.
           out     dx, al
           mov     cx, 512           ;Pause.
d01:
           loop    d01
           in      al, dx            ;Now read the register back.
           xchg    ah, al            ;Restore saved register value.
           out     dx, al
           cmp     ah, 99h           ;Compare value read to value written.
           jne     d02               ;No MDA;  go on to test for CGA.
           or      video, VMDA       ;Set MDA bit.
d02:                                 ;CGA test.
                                     ;Test for 6845 CGA registers.
           mov     dx, 03d4h         ;Index register.
           mov     al, 0fh           ;Select register 0fh.
           out     dx, al
           mov     dx, 03d5h         ;Data register.
           in      al, dx            ;Read register 0fh.
           mov     ah, al            ;Store in AH.
           mov     al, 99h           ;Write a number to the register.
           out     dx, al
           mov     cx, 512           ;Pause.
d03:
           loop    d03
           in      al, dx            ;Now read the register back.
           xchg    ah, al            ;Restore saved register value.
           out     dx, al
           cmp     ah, 99h           ;Compare value read to value written.
           jne     d04               ;No CGA;  go on to test for Hercules.
           or      video, VCGA       ;Set CGA bit.
d04:                                 ;** Test for HERCULES. **
                                     ;This routine supplied courtesy of
                                     ;Hercules Computer Technology.
           mov     dx, 03bah         ;Display status port.
           xor     bl, bl            ;Clear counter.
```

Figure 7.2: *Assembler routines for testing the current computer environment (continued)*

```
              in      al, dx              ;Read port.
              and     al, 80h             ;Mask off all bits except 7.
              mov     ah, al              ;Save bit 7 in AH.
              mov     cx, 8000h           ;Set loop counter.
d05:
              in      al, dx              ;Read port again.
              and     al, 80h             ;Mask out bit 7.
              cmp     al, ah              ;Test if bit has changed.
              je      d06                 ;Bit not yet changed.
              inc     bl                  ;Bit changed, increment counter.
              cmp     bl, 10              ;Want to see it change 10 times.
              jb      d06                 ;Need to see more changes.
              or      video, VHGC         ;Yes, it is a HCG.
              jmp     d07                 ;Go on to EGA test.
d06:
              loop    d05                 ;Continue testing for changes.

d07:                                      ;** Test for EGA. **
              mov     bh, 0ffh            ;Impossible return value.
              mov     ah, 12h             ;BIOS alternate select function.
              mov     bl, 10h             ;Request EGA information.
              int     10h                 ;BIOS video services interrupt.
              cmp     bh, 0               ;Test for EGA/color.
              jne     d08
              or      video, VEGAC
              jmp     d09
d08:                                      ;Test for EGA/monochrome.
              cmp     bh, 1
              jne     d09
              or      video, VEGAM
d09:                                      ;** Test for PS/2 display **
              mov     ah, 1ah             ;BIOS video display combination service.
              mov     al, 0               ;Return display combination subfunction.
              int     10h
              cmp     al, 1ah             ;Test whether function is supported.
              jne     d10                 ;Function not supported.
              or      video, VPS2         ;PS/2 functions supported.
d10:                                      ;Exit point.
              pop     di
              pop     si
              mov     ax, video
              ret

_cur_video endp


_cur_ncp      proc    near                ;** Returns resources.ncp **
                                          ;unsigned char cur_ncp ();
                                          ;Note: this function uses the BIOS and
                                          ;therefore should be called only if
                                          ;IBM compatibility is established.

              assume  cs:_text

              int     11h                 ;BIOS equipment service --
```

Figure 7.2: *Assembler routines for testing the current computer environment (continued)*

```
            and     ax, mask ncp        ;       bit 1 = 0 : no num. coprocessor
            mov     cl, ncp             ;       bit 1 = 1 : num. coprocessor found
            shr     ax, cl              ;Move significant bit to rightmost position.
            ret

_cur_ncp    endp


_cur_gameport proc near                 ;** Returns 'resources.gameport'. **
                                        ;unsigned char cur_gameport ();
                                        ;Note: this function uses the BIOS and
                                        ;therefore should be called only if
                                        ;IBM compatibility is established.

            assume  cs:_text

            int     11h                 ;BIOS equipment service --
            and     ax, mask game       ;       bit 12 = 0 : no game port
            mov     cl, game            ;       bit 12 = 1 : game port
            shr     ax, cl              ;Move significant bit to rightmost position.
            ret

_cur_gameport endp


_cur_memsiz proc near                   ;** Returns 'resources.memsiz' **
                                        ;unsigned int cur_memsiz ();
                                        ;Note: this function uses the BIOS and
                                        ;therefore should be called only if
                                        ;IBM compatibility is established.

            assume  cs:_text

            int     12h                 ;BIOS memory size service.
            ret                         ;Returns kilobytes of memory in AX.

_cur_memsiz endp


_cur_numprn proc near                   ;** Returns 'resources.numprn' **
                                        ;unsigned char cur_numprn ();
                                        ;Note: this function uses the BIOS and
                                        ;therefore should be called only if
                                        ;IBM compatibility is established.

            assume  cs:_text

            int     11h                 ;BIOS equipment service.
            and     ax, mask prn        ;Bits 15:14 = number of printers.
            mov     cl, prn
            shr     ax, cl
            ret

_cur_numprn endp


_cur_numser proc near                   ;** Returns 'resources.numserial' **
                                        ;unsigned char cur_numser ();
```

Figure 7.2: *Assembler routines for testing the current computer environment (continued)*

```
                                           ;Note: this function uses the BIOS and
                                           ;therefore should be called only if
                                           ;IBM compatibility is established.

            assume  cs:_text

            int     11h                    ;BIOS equipment service --
            and     ax, mask ser           ;    bits 11:10:9 = num serial devices.
            mov     cl, ser
            shr     ax, cl
            ret

_cur_numser endp


_cur_numdisk proc near                     ;** Returns 'resources.numdisk' **
                                           ;unsigned char cur_numdisk ();
                                           ;Note: this function uses the BIOS and
                                           ;therefore should be called only if
                                           ;IBM compatibility is established.

            assume  cs:_text

            int     11h                    ;BIOS equipment service --
            test    ax, mask ipl           ;    bit 0 => diskette dirve(s) present
            jnz     j01                    ;    bits 7:6 = num diskette drives
            xor     ax, ax                 ;        00 = 1
            ret                            ;        01 = 2
j01:        and     ax, mask drv           ;        10 = 3
            mov     cl, drv                ;        11 = 4
            shr     ax, cl
            inc     ax

            ret

_cur_numdisk endp


_text       ends                           ;End of code segment.
            end
```

Figure 7.2: *Assembler routines for testing the current computer environment (continued)*

First, it tests for the 8086/88 processor by attempting to clear the four high-order bits of the **flags** register. If all four of these bits remain set, the processor must be an 8086/88 (only in the 8086 or 8088—from among the processors that are being tested—do these bits always remain set).

Next, the routine tests for an 80186 processor by determining whether the PUSH machine instruction decrements the stack pointer (SP) before or after the value is written to the stack. If the stack pointer is decremented before its value is written to the stack, then the processor must be an 80186, since the 80286 and 80386 both decrement SP after it is written to the stack.

Finally, the 80286 and 80386 processors are distinguished by attempting to set the four high-order bits of the **flags** register. If none of these bits can be set, then the processor must be an 80286; in the 80286 these bits are always clear, while in the 80386 the bits may be set.

This example serves only to illustrate one basic method for identifying the processor. In addition to adding new processors such as the 80486, it would also be possible, for example, to distinguish between the 8086 and 8088. Further distinctions can be researched and added if they become critical to the operation of the program.

_cur_mach

The function **_cur_mach** returns the identity of the computer, and is used to set **resources.machine**. This function tests for machines manufactured by IBM, Compaq, and AT&T. If none of these machines is found, the value **MUNK** is returned, indicating an unknown machine type. If the machine is determined to be an IBM, the function attempts to identify the specific model (if the model cannot be identified, it returns **MIBMUN**, indicating an unknown IBM model).

The routine first determines whether the machine is an IBM model by looking for the string "IBM" that is placed in the BIOS of all IBM machines at the address F000h:E00Eh. If this string is not found it goes on to test for a Compaq or an AT&T machine using a similar method. If the machine is an IBM, the function then tests the *model byte* at address F000h:FFFEh, which in all IBM machines contains a code for the specific model. Each of the possible code values indicates a distinct IBM model with one exception: the value FCh is used for all models employing the 80286 processor. Therefore, if the model byte equals FCh, the following tests are performed to distinguish among the various 80286 machines:

1. The BIOS "return system configuration" service is invoked (interrupt 15h, function C0h).

2. If this service returns 86h in register **ah**, then the machine must be either an XT (dated 11/08/82) or an AT (dated 1/10/84). If the machine were an XT, however, the function would already have returned, since the test for the XT precedes the test for the AT. Therefore, the machine must be an AT and the value **AT** is returned.

3. If interrupt 15h returns a 0, then the machine must be an AT (dated after 1/10/84), an XT-286, a Model 50, or a Model 60. In this case, the address of a system descriptor is contained in registers **es:bx**. A submodel byte is located at an offset of 3 within this descriptor, and is used to identify the specific model.

4. If the submodel byte does not contain a meaningful code, or if interrupt 15h fails to return a sensible value, then the code **UKIBM** is returned to the calling program to indicate an unknown IBM model.

Note that many IBM "clones" will be detected as IBM machines since the manufacturers of IBM-compatible BIOS chips often place the IBM logo and model numbers at the appropriate addresses in the BIOS. The function **_cur_mach** tests for only a few common machines; you could test for additional brands once you have determined the content and location of their identifying logos. Note, however, that although the machine may not be identified, it may still be IBM-compatible; you should therefore allow the user to manually specify that the machine is IBM-compatible, as shown in Figure 7.1.

_dos_ver

The procedure **_dos_ver** uses DOS function 30h, which returns the current version of the operating system. Since this function was not extant with DOS 1.*x*, it does not return a proper value for this version; however, it will consistently return a 0. Note that **_dos_ver** does not return a value, but rather directly alters the structure whose address is passed as a parameter. Since both fields of the structure are one-byte values, you can assume that they are contiguous in memory; however, do not make this assumption in general because C often leaves gaps between structure elements, making them difficult to manage in an assembler routine (see the section Accessing External C Data in Chapter 2).

_cur_video

The function **_cur_video** returns a code indicating the video adapter type or types currently installed in the machine; this code allows you to determine the video modes that are supported by the hardware. Table 7.1 lists the codes that may be returned by this function, their meanings, and the supported video modes. (See the description of video modes in Appendix C, under interrupt 10h, function 00h.) The constants for the return codes are defined in Figures 7.1 and 7.2; since each code corresponds to a single bit in the returned value, more than one code may be returned. For example, it is possible to have both a monochrome display adapter (**VMDA**) and a color graphics adapter (**VCGA**) installed in the same machine. To test for a particular code, you can use the AND operator on the returned value, as in the following example:

```
if (cur_video () & VEGAM)
    /* then modes 07h and 0Fh are available */
```

Code Returned	Meaning	Modes Supported
VMDA	Monochrome display adapter	7
VHGC	Hercules graphics card	720 × 348 monochrome graphics
VCGA	Color graphics adapter	00h,01h,02h,03h,04h,05h,06h
VEGAM	EGA adapter/mono-chrome monitor	07h,0Fh
VEGAC	EGA adapter/color monitor	00h,01h,02h,03h,04h,05h,06h,0Dh,0Eh,10h
VPS2	PS/2 video BIOS supported	Call interrupt 10h, function 1Bh, to get a complete list of supported modes

Table 7.1: *Video Codes Returned by* **_cur_video**

Note that if the value **VPS2** is included in the returned byte, then the PS/2 video BIOS functions are supported. In this case you should call interrupt 10h, function 1Bh, for a complete list of the supported video modes (see Appendix C).

The function **_cur_video** performs the following sequence of tests:

1. The function determines whether a monochrome display adapter is installed by performing a presence test for the 6845 video controller registers that are used by this adapter. The routine attempts to write to the data register at address 3B5h; if the value can be successfully read back, then the register is present and the monochrome adapter must be installed.

2. The function performs a similar test for the color graphics adapter (the data register for this adapter is located at address 3D5h).

3. The function tests for the presence of a Hercules graphics adapter. This test (supplied courtesy of Hercules Computer Technology) determines whether bit 7 of the "display mode status" port (3BAh) changes at least 10 times during the execution of a loop (8000h repetitions). On a Hercules card this bit goes low with

each vertical retrace (see Chapter 8), while IBM cards do not use the bit.

4. The function tests for an EGA adapter by calling BIOS interrupt 10h, function 12 (the "alternate select" function). This service returns 0 in register BH if an EGA adapter attached to a color monitor (an enhanced display) is present. It returns 1 in register BH if an EGA adapter attached to a monochrome monitor is present. If neither 0 nor 1 is returned in BH, then an EGA system is not installed.

5. The function determines whether the PS/2 video BIOS services are supported by calling interrupt 10h, function 1Ah ("read/write display combination code"), passing a subfunction code of 00h in AL (to read the display combination). If this function is supported, it returns 1Ah in register AL. In this case, **_cur_video** sets the **VPS2** bit of the return value; when your program receives this value, it can call interrupt 10h, function 1Ah, to determine the active and secondary display adapters, and it can call interrupt 10h, function 1Bh, to obtain a complete list of all supported video modes (as well as other detailed video information). See the description of these functions in Appendix C and in the IBM BIOS interface reference cited in the Bibliography.

_cur_ncp

The function **_cur_ncp** returns a 1 if either the 8087 or 80287 coprocessor is present, and a 0 if no numeric coprocessor is present. It is used to set **resources.ncp**. The function simply calls the BIOS equipment list service (interrupt 11h). Bit 1 of the value returned in register AX indicates the presence of a numeric coprocessor. This bit is shifted to the right-most position and its value returned. In the IBM-PC/XT, this test is not infallible because the BIOS obtains the value directly from the switch block, which may be improperly set. There are more sophisticated methods using x87 instructions.

_cur_gameport

The function **_cur_gameport** returns a 1 if a game adapter is installed, and 0 otherwise. It works exactly like **_cur_ncp**.

_cur_memsiz

The function **_cur_memsiz** uses the BIOS interrupt 12h memory size service. The value returned is in kilobytes, and is obtained directly from the switch block (in the PC/XT). See comments regarding possibly more accurate methods for determining usable memory in Chapter 6, under the discussion of the program segment prefix.

_cur_numprn

The function **_cur_numprn** also uses BIOS interrupt 11h to return the number of printers currently installed. It will report only printers attached to separate parallel ports, not those that share a single port and use a switching device.

_cur_numser

The function **_cur_numser** returns the number of serial devices that are installed, such as modems and serial printers. It uses the same method as **_cur_numprn**.

_cur_numdisk

The function **_cur_numdisk** returns the number of floppy disk drives that are installed (it does *not* include hard disks or RAM disks). It uses the same basic method as the previous two functions, except that the information requires slightly more decoding. See the explanation of **_cur_numdisk** in Figure 7.2.

User Installation

Another method for setting the values of the resource table is to call upon the user to supply the necessary information. Many applications use this approach, and it has several advantages. First, this method can simplify software development, obviating the need to research and design testing routines. Also, user installation can be more reliable in some situations, such as with a new or unrecognized IBM-compatible machine, or if there are factors that are difficult to detect (for example, a program that is going to be run in Windows or another multitasking environment). Finally, user-installed programs can be smaller and faster due to the elimination of testing code, and possibly the elimination of alternative routines.

There are also several disadvantages to user installation. First, the method places a greater burden on the user, who is often technically unknowledgeable and anxious to run the program. Also, the program must generally be reinstalled whenever the machine or peripheral equipment change. For example, when a display adapter is changed, the user must remember which programs need manual reinstallation; programs that are not reinstalled typically fail miserably and hang the system.

The best compromise for many situations is to include a dynamic runtime test, but also allow the user to override any of the features. This approach should function automatically in the great majority of cases, but still allow the user final control over program behavior.

Among the methods that can be used to obtain information from the user, either to install features or override those set by the program, are the following: command line switches entered when the program is run; environment variables; and an installation procedure, either as part of the main application or as a freestanding program. See the section on the program segment prefix in Chapter 6 for information on accessing the command line and the environment.

Once the information has been gathered from the user, it may be stored and processed in one of several different ways. First, you could use program patches: Write the values directly into the executable file, for example, directly into the resource table in the data segment. Second, you could use the information to select one of several different versions of the program, which might then be copied onto the runtime disk. A third method is to write the information to a configuration file that is read by the program each time it is run. A fourth and final approach is to separate out sections of code that are highly machine specific into small freestanding device drivers, with a separate driver for each type of device. When the user selects a particular device (such as a Hercules display adapter), rename or copy the appropriate driver so that it will subsequently be used by the program.

Using the Available Resources

When a program obtains information concerning its runtime environment, many of the rules for software compatibility become relative rather than absolute—they depend on the specific set of resources available. How is the resource information used once it has been collected, and what are the implications of the various fields? This question will be addressed for specific runtime resources, the type of machine that is present, the operating system version, and the presence of operating environments such as Microsoft Windows.

Using Specific Resources

The implication of a resource table field that refers to a specific resource is obvious: if the resource is present, you can use it; if it isn't, you can't.

For example, if the field **resources.cpu** in the resource table indicates an 8086/88 processor, you cannot use instructions specific to the 80286 (such as **pusha**). Likewise, if the field **resources.video** indicates a monochrome system, you should assign display attributes rather than colors for all video output. Other fields of the **resource** structure in this category are:

ncp

gameport

memsiz

numprn

numserial

numdisk

Using the Machine-Type Information

The implications of the machine-type field (**machine**) of the resource table are not as obvious. Specific machine brands have specific resources, but for the sake of simplicity, you can divide machines into two categories: non-IBM compatible and IBM-compatible.

Non-IBM Compatible

If the program cannot identify the machine or the machine is known to be non-IBM compatible and you have no other information regarding resources that are present (for example, through a user override), then you must assume the worst. Specifically, in order to allow the program to run on virtually any MS-DOS machine, you should *not* use any of the following features:

- The IBM extended character set (ASCII codes 127–255)
- Cursor keys or function keys (like WordStar, the program could offer alternate keys, such as the left-arrow key or ^S)
- BIOS interrupt services
- System data stored in low memory (discussed in Chapter 6)
- Direct hardware access through I/O ports
- Direct output to video memory (see Chapter 8)
- Bitmapped graphics

All input/output should be performed through DOS functions because this is the only resource known to be present.

Note that these restrictions are rather extreme, and the antithesis of high-performance programming. However, with the increasing number of closely compatible IBM clones that are now available, such restrictive guidelines are seldom necessary; also, the user should always be given the opportunity to override the decision of the program.

IBM-Compatible

Once the presence of an IBM-compatible machine is established, a plethora of high-performance resources becomes available. The exact list depends on the particular machine model. IBM has suggested (but not guaranteed) that the following features will be maintained over the family of IBM computers, and that an application that uses them will remain IBM-compatible. Therefore, the following should be available for IBM-compatible machines. (See the *IBM Personal Computer Seminar Proceedings*, pp. 23–26. The complete reference is in the Bibliography.)

- The BIOS interrupt services, provided they are accessed through the interrupt vector table and *not* by absolute address (see Chapter 5).

- The interrupt vector table. A vector may be replaced by one pointing to an alternative routine; however, the handler should save the original address and call the original routine each time it receives control (see Chapters 6 and 11).

- The BIOS data variables stored at low-memory addresses from 400h to 48Fh. Most of these fields should retain their current meanings. However, it is best to access the values whenever possible through the BIOS service routines (see Chapter 6).

- Video memory at B0000h for text mode 7, and B8000h for color graphics adapter modes (text or graphics). In general, the buffer location for a given video mode will remain the same; if a new location is used, it will be associated with a new mode number (for example, the new modes available with the EGA). See Chapters 6 and 8.

- The following I/O ports:

021h	8259A interrupt controller mask register (see the section External Hardware Interrupts in Chapter 6).
040h, 042h, and 043h	8253 timer, channels 0 and 2. A program should never modify port 41h. A constant input frequency of 1.19 MHz will be maintained so that the timer may be used in lieu of program loops.

061h	Sound control 8255A-5.
201h	Game control.
3BAh and 3DAh	Monochrome and color video status registers (see Chapter 8).
2F8h–2FFh and 3F8h–3FFh	The asynchronous communications adapter ports beginning at 2F8h and 3F8h may be programmed to enable interrupt driven communication; however, the BIOS services should be used to set communication parameters.

Programming for the Appropriate Operating System Version

Each new version of MS-DOS has introduced functionally equivalent but enhanced versions of basic service routines. Once the operating system version has been established at runtime using the procedure **_dos_ver**, it is possible to select the optimal DOS function.

DOS Version 2.0 or Later

If the version of DOS is 2.0 or later, you should use the enhanced terminate and stay-resident function 31h rather than the older interrupt 27h method, and also the terminate with error code function 4Ch rather than the older function 00h. You should also use the file handle services rather than the more limited FCB commands and the EXEC function 4Bh rather than the old "create program segment prefix" function 26h.

DOS Version 3.0 or Later

If the version is 3.0 or later, be sure to take advantage of the "get extended error" function 59h. Ideally, function 59h should be called in these cases:

- After a traditional function signals an error by returning FFh (or other error code) in register AL

- After a function that signals an error with the carry flag returns with the carry flag set

- By an interrupt 24h critical-error handler (see Chapter 6)

See Appendix B for a list of DOS functions present with each version. Chapter 4 provides a more detailed discussion of the MS-DOS functions.

Programming for Operating Environments

Another increasingly important compatibility consideration is the presence of multitasking operating environments such as Microsoft Windows, IBM TopView, Quarterdesk DESQview, and DRI GEM. Even when a program tests for the presence of a machine resource and uses it properly, the resulting behavior may prove incompatible with one or more of these environments. (See also Chapter 12 for a discussion of the rules for writing MS-DOS programs that run within the DOS compatibility environment provided by OS/2.)

For example, consider a program that is to run under Microsoft Windows. If video output is accomplished either through DOS functions or direct BIOS calls, the program can be run within a window, and the screen display will be properly managed. If, however, the program uses direct writes to video memory (see Chapter 8), it cannot run within a window, but must be given control of the entire screen, which causes the suspension of all other applications.

Each of these environments has its own particular definition of a "well-behaved" program. The general guidelines listed at the beginning of this chapter go a long way toward achieving compatibility with these systems. However, before giving up such a performance-rich feature as direct video memory access, it might be best to first determine (through one of the methods discussed earlier) whether the user intends to use the program within a multitasking environment.

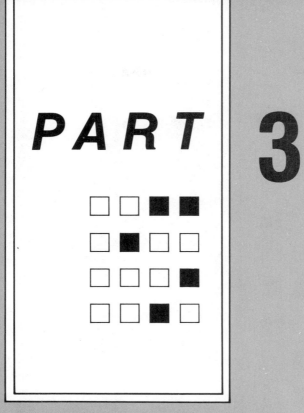

PART 3

DEVICES

Fast Video Display

A fast and attractive video display is one of the most important elements of a high-performance program. There are a number of reasons for the unique importance of this topic. First, the video display is the most immediate and visible aspect of a program. Also, standard methods for producing video output often create performance bottlenecks, slowing otherwise efficient programs, whereas alternative methods for writing to the screen can dramatically improve both the speed and level of control. Finally, writing efficient and reliable video drivers is a relatively simple task. Thus, unlike attempting to replace DOS file management functions, writing custom video routines that bypass both MS-DOS and the BIOS can be a rewarding activity.

Three Basic Methods of Video Display

The simplest type of video output consists of a stream of characters written at the current cursor position, using the default display attribute or color. When the end of a line is reached, the next character is written in the first column of the next line, and when the last line is reached, the entire screen scrolls up. Many programs, including the MS-DOS utilities, use this type of video display. Known as *teletype output,* it is generated by the following frequently used methods for writing to the screen:

- C functions that write to standard output or to the CON device (the console, consisting of the screen and keyboard), such as **printf** or **fprintf**.

- MS-DOS function calls that write to the standard output or to the CON device, such as service numbers 09h and 40h.

- BIOS interrupt 10h, service 14.

IBM-PC compatible machines, however, provide a much greater level of control over video output. In addition to being able to display standard ASCII characters in teletype fashion, these machines can:

- Display 254 different characters, exploiting almost the full range of values that can be encoded in an eight-bit byte. Codes outside the

□□■□

range of standard ASCII characters are used for a variety of foreign, mathematical, graphic, and purely whimsical symbols.

- Directly place a given character at any position in the 25-line by 80-column screen matrix.

- Display a character in any of a variety of attributes on a monochrome system, or with a specified background and foreground color on a color system.

- Save, overwrite with new data, restore, clear, or scroll selected portions of the screen in order to create and manage windows.

These enhanced display capabilities are very important for generating attractive and responsive applications. This chapter compares three basic methods (ANSI.SYS, BIOS, and direct video writes) that are capable of achieving most or all of these modes of video control. Techniques that produce only teletype output do not enter into the comparisons.

In addition, depending on the type of monitor and controller, some MS-DOS systems can display bit-mapped graphic images in a variety of resolutions, using varying numbers of colors (or shades of grey on monochrome monitors). The methods treated in this chapter, however, are for displaying text only. Note that a number of the IBM *extended* characters (those in addition to the standard ASCII set) can be juxtapositioned to produce lines, boxes, or textures, and can be used to generate striking screen displays without a graphics mode. The advantages of text modes over graphics modes are greater processing speed and lower data storage requirements. The programs presented in this chapter are compatible with the text modes provided by all adapter types for IBM-compatible computers that were discussed in the last chapter: MDA, Hercules, CGA, EGA, and the MCGA and VGA adapters present in PS/2 models.

░ Video Display through DOS/ANSI.SYS

The highest level method for producing controlled video output is using MS-DOS function calls in conjunction with the installable device driver ANSI.SYS, which is supplied with the operating system. The MS-DOS functions normally produce simple teletype video output; however, when ANSI.SYS is installed, a fine level of control is available for video output (and keyboard input as well).

You must take three steps to use the video display features of ANSI-.SYS. First, include the following line in the CONFIG.SYS file, which must be present in the root directory of the boot disk:

DEVICE = ANSI.SYS

A full path name may precede the file name ANSI.SYS, provided the file is present in the specified location at boot time. The second step is to use one of the following MS-DOS function calls for video output:

- Traditional functions 02h, 06h, and 09h, which write automatically to the standard output device

- Traditional FCB functions 15h, 22h, and 28h, writing to a file opened under the name *CON*

- Handle function 40h, writing to standard output (handle 01), standard error (handle 02), or a file opened under the name *CON*

Note that console output generated by C library functions is routed through MS-DOS functions within the above group, and thus will work with ANSI.SYS. The third step is to embed the appropriate control sequences in the output stream. The ANSI.SYS control codes are known as escape sequences and all begin with the two characters

ESC [

or, in hexadecimal, the two bytes

1Bh 5Bh

The codes are thoroughly documented in the DOS technical reference, Chapter 3, and will not be duplicated here. ANSI.SYS can perform the following types of video control:

Cursor position and movement   The cursor may be placed at any absolute position on the screen, or may be moved a specified distance in any direction from its present position. Also, the current cursor position can be saved and restored.

Erasing   Either the entire screen or specific lines may be erased.

Display attributes   Colors or monochrome display attributes, which will be used for all characters written to the screen until the next command is received, may be specified. On monochrome systems, the following attributes can be selected:

- High intensity
- Underlining
- Blinking
- Reverse video
- Invisible characters
- Normal display (all special attributes off)

On color systems, the following characteristics can be chosen:

- Sixteen foreground colors and eight background colors
- Blinking
- Normal display (white on black, no blinking)

The numeric codes used for the above attributes are distinct from those used by the BIOS and the video controller hardware discussed in the following sections.

Video mode   Finally, the video mode may be set.

The following section of code illustrates the use of the ANSI.SYS driver from a C program. Since **printf** uses MS-DOS function calls to generate output, simply embed the appropriate escape sequences directly within the string that is to be displayed; for example,

```
printf ("\x1b[41;30m");  /* Red background, black foreground.  */
printf ("\x1b[10;5H");   /* Position cursor at row 10, column 5. */
printf ("Row 10, column 5, black on red.");
printf ("\x1b[0m");      /* Restore normal display: white      */
                         /* on black.                          */
```

There are several advantages to using ANSI.SYS. The main advantage is its high degree of portability. Since ANSI.SYS is available with all MS-DOS machines, it provides a convenient device-independent video interface. Also, since the ANSI.SYS method uses the MS-DOS functions, video output can be redirected, provided it is sent to standard output. Finally, using ANSI.SYS is compatible with multitasking environments. For example, an application that controls video output through ANSI-.SYS escape codes may run within a window under Microsoft Windows and will behave properly, although Windows may interpret instructions for specific colors differently than ANSI.SYS.

The ANSI.SYS method also has two primary disadvantages. First, its use entails modification of the user's configuration file and rebooting the system before an application will run properly. Second, ANSI.SYS is rather slow, especially in the default *cooked* mode, as the benchmark in Figure 8.8 will demonstrate.

Therefore, ANSI.SYS is not the best choice for a high-performance program. However, if it is used, the output speed may be significantly increased by converting to the raw mode, as described in Chapter 4 (see the **rawmode** procedure in Figure 4.8). Remember to restore the device mode before the program terminates (using **cookmode**, also in Figure 4.8).

Video Display through the BIOS and the Attribute Codes

As described in Chapter 5, the BIOS interrupt 10h provides a wealth of video services that fully exploit the display capabilities of IBM-PC compatible machines and that are generally more efficient than the MS-DOS functions used with ANSI.SYS. The procedure **printa** in Figure 5.2 demonstrates the use of BIOS video display services within a C program, and shows the degree of control that can be achieved.

Although quite convenient for displaying small amounts of information and for managing windows, these functions are considerably less efficient than the direct video write method discussed in the next section for displaying entire screens of data.

The BIOS video services and the direct video write method use the same one-byte code to specify the video display attribute. (This is the value passed as the second parameter to the function **printa**.) Before moving on to the next method of screen display, it is important to understand the meaning and use of this code. The 256 possible code values, along with their meanings for both color and monochrome systems, are listed exhaustively in the PC and AT technical references. These codes, however, are not arbitrary—each bit has a specific meaning. Therefore, it is possible to use a few constant definitions to produce the desired effect without looking up each value in the technical reference. The interpretation of a specific code depends on whether the system has a monochrome or a color display adapter.

Color Systems

The bits of the attribute code for color systems have the meanings shown in Figure 8.1.

The three background bits allow eight possible background colors, and the four foreground bits allow 16 possible foreground colors. The blinking bit will cause any color combination to begin blinking. If you know something of the way the three primary colors red, green, and blue combine, the following constant definitions can simplify the process of specifying color codes (remember that **ORing** in the intensity bit has the effect of lightening the selected color):

```
#define BLINK      0x80    /* Blinking.             */
#define BG_R       0x40    /* Background red, green, */
                           /* and blue.             */

#define BG_G       0x20
#define BG_B       0x10
```

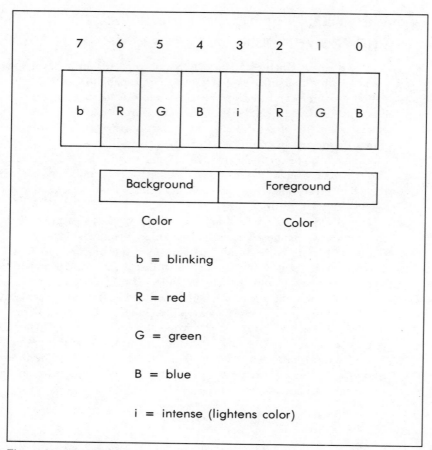

Figure 8.1: *Attribute code for color systems*

```
#define FG_I        0x08    /* Foreground intensity bit.  */
#define FG_R        0x04    /* Foreground red, green      */
                           /* and blue.                  */
#define FG_G        0x02
#define FG_B        0x01
```

The desired foreground and background colors can be produced by **ORing** together the appropriate constants; for example,

```
printa ("Red on black.", FG_R,10,0);
printa ("Cyan on black.", FG_G | FG_B,11,0);
printa ("Yellow on magenta.", FG_I | FG_R | FG_G |
        BG_R | BG_B,12,0);
```

Monochrome Systems

The meanings of the bits of the attribute code for monochrome systems are shown in Figure 8.2. All possible attribute combinations can be specified by defining five constants:

```
#define BLINK        0x80    /* Blinking.                */
#define BG           0x70    /* Turn on background.      */
#define INTENSE      0x08    /* High intensity           */
                             /* characters.              */
#define
FG_NORMAL        0x07    /* Turn on normal           */
                             /* foreground.              */
#define FG_UL        0x01    /* Turn on underlined       */
                             /* foreground.              */
```

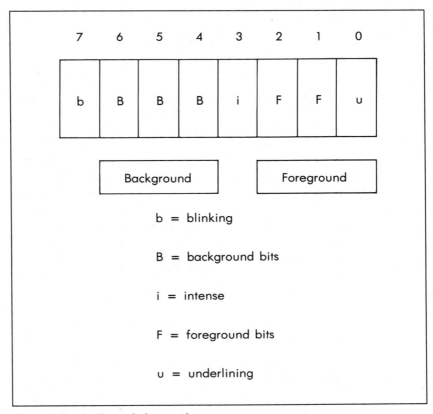

Figure 8.2: *Attribute code for monochrome systems*

and following several guidelines:

- Attributes are combined by **ORing** together the above constants. For example, to produce a normal foreground with blinking, use:

  FG_NORMAL | BLINK

- There is one type of background, **BG**, but two types of foreground, **FG_NORMAL** and **FG_UL**. Only one type of foreground may be selected, depending on whether underlining is desired (they are *not* combined).

- If neither the background (**BG**), nor a foreground (**FG_NORMAL** and **FG_UL**) is selected, then the characters will be black on black (i.e., invisible).

- If only a foreground is selected, then the characters will be white on black (either normal or underlined.)

- If only the background is selected, then the characters will be black on white (i.e., reverse video). The intensity bit selected in combination with reverse video may make a visible difference only with certain adapters.

- If *both* the background *and* a foreground are selected, then the foreground takes precedence and the characters will be white on black. (Thus it is impossible to have reverse video and underlined characters, since this would necessitate selecting both the background and a foreground).

If the above guidelines are followed, the results should be predicable with almost any monochrome system. Certain systems may allow other combinations of attributes (such as a white background with high-intensity white foreground, i.e., 0x7f; or high-intensity reverse video, i.e., 0x78). However, these special combinations will not produce predictable results among different systems, and their results may even vary on a single system if register settings are changed.

The monochrome constants are used in the same way as the color constants. For example,

```
printa ("row 10, column 5, reverse video, blinking",
        BLINK | BG,10,5);
```

Video Display through Direct Writes to Video Memory

You can achieve the ultimate degree of performance in screen output by writing directly to video memory. Video memory is a reserved area of

RAM used as a mapping of the characters and attributes displayed on the screen (or pixels in a bit-mapped graphics mode). A program may read or write to this area just as to any other area of RAM. The video controller hardware also has direct access to this memory, and constantly scans it, so that whatever is written here instantly appears on the screen.

In an 80-column text mode, video memory (see Figure 8.3) consists of 4000 bytes. The first byte contains the ASCII value of the character that appears at the upper-left corner of the screen (row 0, column 0). The second byte contains the display attribute for this character. The third byte contains the ASCII value for the character in row 0, column 1, and the fourth byte contains its display attribute. This pattern continues for the entire 2000 characters of a 25-row by 80-column screen. The ordering is thus row major: all characters of a given row precede the characters of the next row. In Figure 8.3, CHARmn means the character in row m, column n. The display attribute values, monochrome or color, are the same as those described above for the BIOS services.

There are some differences between video memory in a monochrome system and in a color system. With a monochrome adapter (standard MDA, Hercules in text mode, or EGA attached to a monochrome monitor and in mode 7), there is only one 4000 byte page of video memory

CHAR00	ATTR00	CHAR01	ATTR01	CHAR03	ATTR03	...
CHAR10	ATTR10	CHAR11	ATTR11	CHAR13	ATTR13	...
CHAR20	ATTR20	CHAR21	ATTR21	CHAR23	ATTR23	...

Figure 8.3: *Layout of video memory*

located at segment B000h. (Thus, the first ASCII value is located at address B000h:0000h.) However, with a color adapter (standard CGA, EGA, or a PS/2 adapter in text mode), in an 80-column text mode (modes 2 and 3), there are four 4000 byte pages of video RAM, beginning at the following segment addresses:

Page 0   B800h

Page 1   B900h

Page 2   BA00h

Page 3   BB00h

Data may be written directly to any page (also, the BIOS video services can be used to read or write data to any page, or to get or set the cursor position associated with any page). However, only one page is displayed at a given time (the *active display page*); by default, this is page 0, but the active display page may be changed through BIOS video function 5. This mechanism allows a program to gradually build up data in a nonactive page, and then instantly display the entire page by making it active.

Note that video memory is physically located on the monitor adapter card and is not part of the 640K maximum user memory (addresses 0 through 9FFFFh). (The IBM PCjr is an exception; video memory is actually contained in user memory. However, it may be accessed through the standard CGA addresses due to hardware rerouting of read/write requests.)

There are many advantages to using direct access to video memory. First, the method is incredibly fast, as the benchmark in Figure 8.8 will show. The method also yields a fine level of control over the video display, since each character has its own associated attribute value. And finally, the method is easily implemented in both high- and low- level languages. Writing a character and its attribute to video memory is no more difficult than writing to a variable. Data structures can be superimposed as templates over video memory, and thus standard assignment and data movement instructions can effect complex screen manipulations, such as screen saving and restoring, and the stacking and moving of windows.

There are, however, a few possible penalties for using direct access to video memory. First, non-IBM compatible architectures may use different video display schemes that would not work with this method. However, the number of closely compatible machines is increasing, and as described in Chapter 7, the machine type may be determined at runtime or specified by the user. A second and more serious problem is that direct writes to video memory restrict the use of a program within multitasking environments such as Microsoft Windows and IBM TopView. Such a program cannot be displayed within a Microsoft window, but must receive total control of the screen, suspending multitasking. Top-View provides a function call that returns the address of an alternate buffer (a *shadow buffer*) so that a program may write to this buffer rather than directly to video memory, and yet retain a performance advantage and avoid major rewriting of code. The alternate buffer is then used to update the actual display window in a well-behaved manner, under the control of TopView. A third problem is that direct video memory access can cause "snow" with the color graphics adapter (CGA). The snow effect occurs when both the program and the controller access video memory simultaneously. Only the standard CGA controller seems to have this problem; it does not occur with the EGA, or in the PS/2, IBM-PCjr, Compaq, or AT&T systems. The example routines below show how to avoid snow by synchronizing video memory writes with the horizontal and vertical retrace periods, during which the display is temporarily suppressed (this method, however, exacts a high cost on performance).

The next sections describe two types of direct video display functions: those for writing individual strings, and those for writing windows; i.e., entire screens or sections of screens.

String Functions

Figure 8.4 lists two separate functions for writing strings directly to video memory: one function for CGA displays and a separate function for all other display types. These functions are analogous to **printa** (which uses BIOS interrupt services), and are passed the same parameters, namely:

- The address of the null-terminated string to be displayed
- The display attribute
- The starting row
- The starting column

The main advantage of **printv** over the functionally similar **printa** is a phenomenal improvement in speed (**printv** is approximately 92 times faster than **printa**!).

printv   The function **printv** should be used only for controllers that do not cause snow. It performs the following main steps. First, it sets SI to point to the start of the source string. (DS already contains the appropriate segment address.) Next, it examines the BIOS video mode flag at address 0000h:0440h in order to assign the correct segment address for video memory to ES. It then sets DI to point to the offset within

```
page 50,130

;File:      PRINTV.ASM

;Assembler routines for displaying a string by direct writes to video memory
;These routines may be called from a C program.

public     _printv
public     a01,a02,a03,a04
public     _printvcga
public     c01,c02

_data      segment word public 'DATA'
_data      ends

dgroup     group    _data
assume     cs:_text, ds:dgroup

_text      segment byte public 'CODE'

_printv    proc     near             ;** Displays a string on screen. **

comment    /*
           This procedure writes a null terminated string directly to video
           memory, and should be used only with IBM-compatible systems with
           controllers that do not produce "snow."

           void printv (str,att,row,col);
           char *str;
           int att;
           int row;
           int col;

           */

sframe     struc                     ;Stack frame template.
bptr       dw       ?
ret_ad     dw       ?
str_ad     dw       ?                ;String address.
att        dw       ?                ;Display attribute.
row        dw       ?                ;Starting row.
col        dw       ?                ;Starting column.
sframe     ends

frame      equ      [bp]

           push     bp
           mov      bp, sp
           push     di
           push     si

           mov      si, frame.str_ad ;DS:SI point to start of source string.

           xor      ax, ax           ;Set ES to correct video buffer segment.
           mov      es, ax
           cmp      byte ptr es:[449h], 7   ;Test video mode.
           je       a01
           mov      ax, 0b800h       ;Color buffer.
           jmp      a02
a01:       mov      ax, 0b000h       ;Monochrome buffer.
a02:       mov      es, ax

                                     ;Starting offset in video memory =
                                     ;   (row * 160) + (col * 2)
           mov      di, frame.row    ;Place row in DI and multiply by 160.
           mov      ax, di
           mov      cl, 7
           shl      di, cl
           mov      cl, 5
           shl      ax, cl
           add      di, ax
```

Figure 8.4: *Assembler routines for writing a string directly to video memory*

```
                mov     ax, frame.col        ;Multiply col by 2.
                shl     ax, 1
                add     di, ax          ,    ;Add (col * 2) to DI.

                                             ;Attribute in AH.
                mov     ah, byte ptr frame.att
                cld
a03:            cmp     byte ptr [si], 0     ;Test for null termination.
                je      a04
                lodsb                        ;Load a single character from source.
                stosw                        ;Write a char AND attribute to dest.
                jmp     a03

a04:            pop     si                   ;Restore registers.
                pop     di
                mov     sp, bp
                pop     bp
                ret                          ;Return to C program.

_printv         endp


h_retrace       macro                        ;Pauses until the beginning of a
                local   b01, b02             ;horizontal retrace.
b01:            in      al, dx               ;Loop to complete any retrace period
                test    al, 1                ;in progress.
                jnz     b01
b02:            in      al, dx               ;Loop until start of a new horizontal
                test    al, 1                ;retrace.
                jz      b02
                endm


_printvcga      proc    near                 ;** Displays a string on screen. **

comment         /*
                This procedure is a special version of '_printv' designed especially
                for color graphics adapters that produce "snow" when writing to
                video memory.  Same parameters as '_printv'.

                */
                push    bp
                mov     bp, sp
                push    di
                push    si

                mov     si, frame.str_ad     ;DS:SI point to start of source string.

                mov     ax, 0b800h           ;Set ES to CGA buffer.
                mov     es, ax
                                             ;Starting offset =
                                             ;    (row * 160) + (col * 2)
                mov     di, frame.row        ;Place row in DI and multiply by 160.
                mov     ax, di
                mov     cl, 7
                shl     di, cl
                mov     cl, 5
                shl     ax, cl
                add     di, ax

                mov     ax, frame.col        ;Multiply col by 2.
                shl     ax, 1
                add     di, ax               ;Add (col * 2) to DI.

                                             ;Attribute in BH.
                mov     bh, byte ptr frame.att
                mov     dx, 03dah            ;CRT status register.
```

Figure 8.4: *Assembler routines for writing a string directly to video memory (continued)*

```
c01:        cmp     byte ptr [si], 0    ;Test for null termination.
            je      c02
            mov     bl, [si]            ;Move next character to BL.
            inc     si
            cli                         ;Disable interrupts.
            h_retrace                   ;Wait for horizontal retrace.
            mov     es:[di], bl         ;Move ASCII.
            inc     di
            h_retrace                   ;Wait again.
            mov     es:[di], bh         ;Move ATTRIBUTE.
            sti                         ;Restore interrupts.
            inc     di
            jmp     c01                 ;Go back for another character.

c02:        pop     si                  ;Restore registers.
            pop     di
            mov     sp, bp
            pop     bp
            ret                         ;Return to C program.

_printvcga  endp

_text       ends                        ;End of code segment.
            end
```

Figure 8.4: *Assembler routines for writing a string directly to video memory (continued)*

the video segment where the string is to be displayed. This value is calculated from the starting row and column passed as parameters. (Note that the arithmetic routine manages to avoid the use of the costly **mul** operation.) Finally, the source string together with the specified attribute are written to video memory using the string primitives **lodsb** and **stosw**.

printvcga   The function **printvcga** is a special version of **printv** to be used only if the current video controller produces snow (i.e., a CGA). This function is considerably less efficient than **printv** and should therefore not be used unless necessary—test the display type using the techniques in Chapter 7, and always allow the user to override the use of this routine. It differs from **printv** in two ways. First, since this routine is used only for CGA cards, the segment address of video RAM is assumed to be at B800h and the video mode is not tested. Second, before writing each byte, the function waits for the beginning of a horizontal retrace period.

Horizontal retrace is the time during which the electron beam is turned off, as it returns to the opposite side of the screen to begin another horizontal scan. During this period, bit 0 of the video status port at 3DAh is turned on. The macro **h_retrace** causes a delay until the *beginning* of a horizontal retrace. Note that two test loops are necessary:

1. The first loop waits until the end of a horizontal retrace in case one is currently active. If this loop were not present, the program could proceed in the middle of a retrace, which might not allow sufficient time to transfer a byte to video memory.

2. The second loop waits until a new horizontal retrace begins.

During horizontal retrace, there is sufficient time to transfer only a single byte. This is the reason that the ASCII value and the attribute are transferred separately, and the delay macro **h_retrace** is invoked twice.

Window Functions

The string display functions are suitable for writing small amounts of data to specific locations on the screen, where each string is to be displayed with only a single attribute. For displaying entire screens or large blocks of data, the functions **printw** (print window) and **printwcga** (special version for the CGA) provide a more efficient and convenient method. These two functions are listed in Figure 8.5.

The window functions work as follows. The program stores data for generating an entire screen in a 4000-byte array. This array is an exact image of video memory (organized as alternating ASCII codes and attributes, as described above). The window function **printw** or **printwcga** then transfers a contiguous block of data from the program array directly to video memory, causing the almost instantaneous appearance of all included characters and display attributes. For example, the following initialized C array could be used to store video data (note that an initialized array must be declared externally, or as **static** within a function):

```
char screen [4000] =
    {'h',15,'e',15,'h',15,'h',15,'o' . . . etc };
```

This buffer begins with the string **hello** in white on black. In an actual program, all 4000 bytes for an entire screen should be initialized. Then **printw** or **printwcga** can be used to display any portion of this array at any position on the screen. For example, to display the entire array, use the following function call:

```
printw (screen,0,0,24,79,0,0);
```

The astute reader may have already perceived a serious impracticality to this method: the initialization of the entire 4000-byte array in the source code file. Notice the number of characters required simply to encode the word **hello**. The prospect of coding an entire screen by hand is grim.

The solution is to design an entire screen using an interactive screen designer, which then automatically generates the C source code necessary to initialize a 4000-byte array. A simple version of such a utility is presented in Figure 8.9. Using a screen designer to generate video data, and then **printw** or **printwcga** to display it, has three paramount advantages. First, the screen display is extremely fast. All screen data are stored

```
                page 50,130

                ;File:      PRINTW.ASM

                ;Assembler routines for displaying windows
                ;These routines may be called from a C program.

                public      _printw
                public      a01,a02,a03
                public      _printwcga
                public      b01,b02,b03,b04,b05,b06

                _data       segment word public 'DATA'
                _data       ends

                dgroup      group    _data
                assume      cs:_text, ds:dgroup

                _text       segment byte public 'CODE'

                _printw     proc      near             ;** Displays a window. **
                comment     /*
                            This procedure transfers data from a program buffer directly to
                            video memory, and should be used only with IBM-compatible systems
                            with controllers that do not produce "snow."

                            void printw (buf,ulr_s,ulc_s,lrr_s,ulr_d,ulc_d);
                            char *buf;
                            int ulr_s;
                            int ulc_s;
                            int lrr_s;
                            int lrc_s;
                            int ulr_d;
                            int ulc_d;
                            */
                sframe      struc                      ;Stack frame template.
                bptr        dw       ?
                ret_ad      dw       ?
                buf_ad      dw       ?                 ;Address of source buffer.
                ulr_s       dw       ?                 ;Upper-left row source.
                ulc_s       dw       ?                 ;Upper-left column source.
                lrr_s       dw       ?                 ;Lower-right row source.
                lrc_s       dw       ?                 ;Lower-right column source.
                ulr_d       dw       ?                 ;Upper-left row destination.
                ulc_d       dw       ?                 ;Upper-left column destination.
                sframe      ends

                frame       equ      [bp]              ;Base for accessing stack frame.

                            push     bp                ;Set up base pointer to access frame.
                            mov      bp, sp
                            push     di
                            push     si

                            mov      si, frame.buf_ad  ;Assign SI start of source buffer.

                                                       ;Calculate source buffer offset in BX
                                                       ;    = (row * 160) + (col * 2)
                            mov      ax, frame.ulr_s   ;Multiply starting row by 160.
                            mov      bx, ax
                            mov      cl, 7
                            shl      ax, cl
                            mov      cl, 5
                            shl      bx, cl
                            add      bx, ax

                            mov      ax, frame.ulc_s   ;Multiply starting column by 2.
                            shl      ax, 1
                            add      bx, ax            ;Total offset in BX.

                            add      si, bx            ;Add offset to SI.
                                                       ;SI now contains offset in source buffer.
```

Figure 8.5: *Assembler routines for displaying windows from a C program*

```
            xor     ax, ax                  ;Set ES to correct video buffer segment.
            mov     es, ax
            cmp     byte ptr es:[449h], 7   ;Test video mode.
            je      a01
            mov     ax, 0b800h              ;Color buffer.
            jmp     a02
a01:        mov     ax, 0b000h              ;Monochrome buffer.
a02:        mov     es, ax

                                            ;Calculate video memory offset
                                            ;    = (row * 160) + (col * 2)
            mov     di, frame.ulr_d         ;Place row in DI and multiply by 160.
            mov     ax, di
            mov     cl, 7
            shl     di, cl
            mov     cl, 5
            shl     ax, cl
            add     di, ax

            mov     ax, frame.ulc_d         ;Multiply col by 2.
            shl     ax, 1
            add     di, ax                  ;Add (col * 2) to DI.
                                            ;DI now contains video memory offset.

                                            ;Calculate number of rows in BL.
            mov     bl, byte ptr frame.lrr_s
            sub     bl, byte ptr frame.ulr_s
            inc     bl

            mov     dx, frame.lrc_s         ;Calculate number of bytes/row in DX.
            sub     dx, frame.ulc_s
            inc     dx
            shl     dx, 1
            mov     ax, 160                 ;Calculate SI, DI increment in AX.
            sub     ax, dx

            cld
a03:        mov     cx, dx                  ;Load(reload) bytes/row into CX.
            rep     movsb                   ;Move one row.
            add     si, ax                  ;Adjust SI, DI to start of next row.
            add     di, ax
            dec     bl                      ;Decrement row counter.
            jnz     a03                     ;If more rows, move another one.

            pop     si                      ;Restore registers.
            pop     di
            mov     sp, bp
            pop     bp
            ret                             ;Return to C program.

_printw     endp

_printwcga  proc    near                    ;** Displays a window. **
comment     /*
            This procedure is a special version of '_printw' designed especially
            for color graphics adapters that produce "snow" when writing
            to video memory.  Same parameters as '_printw'.
            */

            push    bp                      ;Set up base pointer to access frame.
            mov     bp, sp
            push    di
            push    si

            mov     si, frame.buf_ad        ;Assign SI start of source buffer.

                                            ;Calculate source buffer offset in BX
                                            ;    = (row * 160) + (col * 2)
            mov     ax, frame.ulr_s         ;Multiply starting row by 160.
            mov     bx, ax
            mov     cl, 7
            shl     ax, cl
            mov     cl, 5
            shl     bx, cl
            add     bx, ax
```

Figure 8.5: *Assembler routines for displaying windows from a C program (continued)*

```
           mov      ax, frame.ulc_s        ;Multiply starting column by 2.
           shl      ax, 1
           add      bx, ax                 ;Total offset in BX.

           add      si, bx                 ;Add offset to SI.
                                           ;SI now contains offset in source buffer.

           mov      ax, 0b800h             ;Set ES to CGA video buffer.
           mov      es, ax

                                           ;Calculate video memory offset
                                           ;   = (row * 160) + (col * 2)
           mov      di, frame.ulr_d        ;Place row in DI and multiply by 160.
           mov      ax, di
           mov      cl, 7
           shl      di, cl
           mov      cl, 5
           shl      ax, cl
           add      di, ax

           mov      ax, frame.ulc_d        ;Multiply col by 2.
           shl      ax, 1
           add      di, ax                 ;Add (col * 2) to DI.
                                           ;DI now contains video memory offset.

                                           ;Calculate number of rows in BL.
           mov      bl, byte ptr frame.lrr_s
           sub      bl, byte ptr frame.ulr_s
           inc      bl
                                           ;Calculate number of bytes/row in BH.
           mov      bh, byte ptr frame.lrc_s
           sub      bh, byte ptr frame.ulc_s
           inc      bh
           shl      bh, 1

           mov      ah, 160                ;Calculate SI, DI increment in AH.
           sub      ah, bh

           mov      dx, 3dah               ;Keep crt status register in DX.

           cld
           mov      ch, 0                  ;Only need LSB of CX.
b01:       mov      cl, bh                 ;Load bytes/row into CX.

                                           ;Pause until the beginning of a
                                           ;vertical retrace.
b02:       in       al, dx                 ;Loop to complete any retrace period
           test     al, 8                  ;in progress.
           jnz      b02
b03:       in       al, dx                 ;Loop until start of a new vertical
           test     al, 8                  ;retrace.
           jz       b03

           rep      movsb                  ;Move entire row during vertical retrace.
           mov      cl, ah                 ;AH stores SI, DI increment value.
           add      si, cx                 ;Adjust SI, DI to start of next row.
           add      di, cx
           dec      bl                     ;Decrement row counter.
           jz       b06                    ;Quit if no more rows.

                                           ;Move another row, byte by byte, while
                                           ;waiting for next vertical retrace.
                                           ;Pause until the beginning of a
                                           ;horizontal retrace.
           mov      cl, bh                 ;Loop to complete any retrace period
b04:       in       al, dx                 ;in progress.

           test     al, 1
           jnz      b04
           cli
b05:       in       al, dx                 ;Loop until start of a new horizontal
           test     al, 1                  ;retrace.
           jz       b05
```

Figure 8.5: *Assembler routines for displaying windows from a C program (continued)*

```
             movsb                        ;Move one byte.
             sti
             loop      b04                ;Loop until entire row is moved.
             mov       cl, ah
             add       si, cx             ;Adjust SI, DI to start of next row.
             add       di, cx
             dec       bl                 ;Decrement row counter.
             jz        b06                ;Quit if no more rows.
             jmp       b01                ;Go back to move another row during the
                                          ;next vertical retrace.

  b06:       pop       si                 ;Restore registers.
             pop       di
             pop       bp
             ret                          ;Return to C program.

_printwcga   endp

_text        ends
             end
```

Figure 8.5: *Assembler routines for displaying windows from a C program (continued)*

within the executable program in its final format, and thus may be quickly transferred to video memory without further internal processing. A second advantage is that the array stores a separate attribute code for each character, thus allowing maximum flexibility in screen design. The third important advantage is that it is easy to design an attractive screen using an interactive designer, where what you see is exactly what you get. It is difficult to generate a coherent screen design by issuing a series of commands that display individual strings.

By this point the astute reader may have perceived yet another difficulty: the need to compile and store the massive amount of data required for multiple screens. Each screen consumes 4000 bytes of data space at runtime, and several times this amount in the source code file. Fortunately, the amount of disk space and RAM available in most systems is increasing, and large memory requirements are becoming common. There are also several steps that can be taken to help obviate this problem:

First, place all screen data in a separate source code file, which is then joined to the main application at link time. This data need not be processed each time the main section of code is compiled.

Second, when designing display windows that are smaller than the 25 × 80 screen, pack as many windows as possible into a single array. For example, consider an application that displays four windows all in the upper-left quadrant of the screen, as shown in Figure 8.6.

In this case, the four windows may be placed in a single array, as shown in Figure 8.7.

As an additional measure to help minimize storage requirements, screen data can be stored in separate files on disk, each file containing one or more screens. The program can reserve one or more 4000-byte

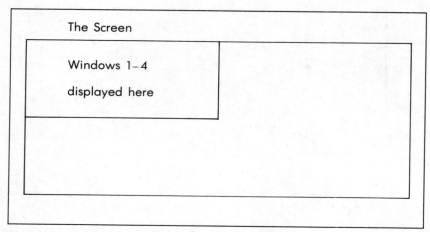

Figure 8.6: *Position of windows on the screen*

The Array

| Window 1 | Window 2 |
| Window 3 | Window 4 |

Figure 8.7: *Position of windows within the program array*

arrays. At runtime, the screen data can be read into the program array(s) and then displayed at some later point using **printw** or **printwcga**. Obviously, this process will slow program execution, and should not be used unless there is a definite lack of RAM space; however, once the data have been read, the actual display of the windows will still be instantaneous. Chapter 10 describes using expanded memory (Lotus-Intel-Microsoft standard) to store screen data beyond the 640K DOS limit.

Unfortunately, even though a screen may contain many repeated characters (especially space characters), the array itself will typically not contain repeated characters because attribute codes alternate with ASCII values. Therefore, it is generally not beneficial to use compaction schemes that eliminate repeated characters, such as Microsoft's EXEPACK utility.

printw   The function **printw** transfers a block of data from a program array directly to video memory, and should be used only if the display adapter is not a CGA. The desired block is specified by passing the upper-left row and column, and the lower-right row and column within the source array. The block can be displayed at any position on the physical screen, which is specified by passing the starting row and column. The function is passed the following seven parameters:

- The address of the source array
- The upper-left row within the source array of the block of data to be displayed (from 0 to 24)
- The upper-left column of the block (from 0 to 79)
- The lower-right row of the block
- The lower-right column of the block
- The starting row of the destination on the screen
- The starting column of the destination on the screen

For example, to display window 4 shown in Figures 8.6 and 8.7 at the upper-left corner of the screen, use the following function call:

printw (screen,12,40,24,79,0,0);

The function **printw** performs the following main steps. It first uses the initial two parameters to calculate the offset of the beginning of the block of source data within the **screen** array, and places the result in register SI. Next, it assigns the segment address of video memory to register ES, obtaining the appropriate value by testing the video mode flag maintained by the BIOS at address 0000h:0440h. Then it uses the last two parameters to calculate the starting offset within video memory, and places the result in register DI. Next, the function uses the first four parameters to calculate the number of rows to be moved (placing the value in register BL), and the number of bytes per row (in register DX). Finally, **printw** uses the **rep movs** instruction repeatedly to move each row as a block. Unfortunately, a single block move cannot be used since the data to be transferred are not necessarily contiguous (the data would be contiguous only if the block were 80 columns wide).

printwcga   The function **printwcga** is a special version of **printw** for the CGA controller. Like the function **printvcga**, it must synchronize writes to video memory with retrace periods. However, **printwcga** uses both the horizontal and vertical retrace periods, transferring data in two stages:

1. Before the first row is transferred, the program pauses until the beginning of a vertical retrace, which is indicated by a 1 value in bit 3 of the status register at port address 3DAh. The process of pausing for a vertical retrace is basically the same as that described earlier for a horizontal retrace. A vertical retrace, however, is a much longer event; while only a single byte could be transferred during a horizontal retrace, it is possible to transfer more than 400 bytes during a vertical retrace. The maximum size of a row is 160 bytes, which is safely within this limit.

2. While the routine is waiting for the next vertical retrace, it has time to transfer more than 150 bytes, one at a time, pausing for the beginning of a horizontal retrace before each transfer. The routine therefore has no problem transferring another row of data during this period.

The program now loops back and again waits for a vertical retrace, before transferring the third row. This process—alternately transferring an entire row during vertical retrace and then transferring the next row byte-by-byte during horizontal retrace periods—continues until all rows have been moved.

A Benchmark

The program in Figure 8.8 was written to obtain a quantitative comparison of the efficiency of the various methods for displaying data on the screen. Seven different methods are tested; each is used to write ten entire screens of data. Each screen consists of 2000 x characters displayed with a given attribute. Timing is accomplished by calling the function **gettime** immediately before and after the screens are displayed. The elapsed time is then calculated and stored in the floating point array **time**. The function **gettime** uses DOS function 2Ch to obtain the system time to the nearest 1/100 second.

Note that Figure 8.8 does not contain the entire program: both the screen data array **scr** and all functions except **main** and **gettime** are presumed to exist in other object modules. The screen data can be generated with a screen designer and included in another C source file as shown

```
/*
        File:       BMARK.C

        A C Program Comparing Methods for Generating Video Output

        This program must be linked with object modules containing the external
        functions called.  All of these functions are listed in other figures.

        The program prints 10 screens of data for each of 7 different methods
        of video output, measures the elapsed times, and displays the results.
*/

#include <stdio.h>

extern char scr[4000];                                    /* Contains screen data. */

                                            /* Declarations of external functions. */
void rawmode    (void);                                        /* Figure 4.8 */
void cookmode   (void);                                        /* Figure 4.8 */
void printa     (char *, int, int, int);                       /* Figure 5.2 */
void cls        (int, int, int, int);                          /* Figure 6.6 */
void printv     (char *, int, int, int);                       /* Figure 8.4 */
void printvcga  (char *, int, int, int);                       /* Figure 8.4 */
void printw     (char *, int, int, int, int, int, int);        /* Figure 8.5 */
void printwcga  (char *, int, int, int, int, int, int);        /* Figure 8.5 */

void gettime    (int *,int *,int *,int *);                /* Internal function. */

void main ()
    {
    register int s, r;                            /* Loop counters.            */
    float time[7];                                /* Stores elapsed times.     */
    int h1, h2, m1, m2, s1, s2, c1, c2;           /* Temporary variables to    */
    float timebefore, timeafter;                  /* calculate times.          */
    static char *mess [] =
        {                                         /* Method description table. */
        "dos/ansi.sys, cooked:",
        "dos/ansi.sys, raw:  ",
        "bios:               ",
        "direct video:       ",
        "direct video, CGA:  ",
        "block move:         ",
        "block move, CGA:    "
        };

    gettime (&h1,&m1,&s1,&c1);     /* DOS/ANSI.SYS method, cooked file mode. */
    for (s=1;s<=10;++s)            /* Write 10 screens of 'x' in red.        */
        for (r=1;r<=25;++r)        /* Write 25 lines.                        */
            {                      /* Set color to red and position cursor.  */
            printf ("\x1b[31m\x1b[%1d;1H",r);
            printf ("xxxxxxxxxxxxxxxxxxxxxxxxxxxxxxxxxxxxxxxxxxxxxxxxxxxx"
                    "xxxxxxxxxxxxxxxxxxxxxxxxxxxx");
            }
    gettime (&h2,&m2,&s2,&c2);
    timebefore = (float)(h1*3600.0 + m1*60.0 + s1 + c1/100.0);
```

Figure 8.8: *A C benchmark program testing methods for generating video output*

```
timeafter  = (float)(h2*3600.0 + m2*60.0 + s2 + c2/100.0);
time[0] = timeafter - timebefore;
printf ("\x1b[0m");                  /* Restore display attributes.     */
cls (0,0,24,79);                     /* Clear screen.                   */

rawmode ();                          /* DOS/ANSI.SYS method, raw file mode. */
gettime (&h1,&m1,&s1,&c1);
for (s=1;s<=10;++s)                  /* Write 10 screens of 'x' in magenta. */
    for (r=1;r<=25;++r)              /* Write 25 lines.                 */
        {                            /* Set color to magenta and position */
                                     /* cursor.                         */
            printf ("\x1b[35m\x1b[%1d;1H",r);
            printf ("xxxxxxxxxxxxxxxxxxxxxxxxxxxxxxxxxxxxxxxxxxxxxxxxxxxx"
                    "xxxxxxxxxxxxxxxxxxxxxxxxxxxxxx");
        }
gettime (&h2,&m2,&s2,&c2);
timebefore = (float)(h1*3600.0 + m1*60.0 + s1 + c1/100.0);
timeafter  = (float)(h2*3600.0 + m2*60.0 + s2 + c2/100.0);
time[1] = timeafter - timebefore;
printf ("\x1b[0m");                  /* Restore display attributes.     */
cookmode ();                         /* Restore file mode.              */
cls (0,0,24,79);                     /* Clear screen.                   */

gettime (&h1,&m1,&s1,&c1);           /* BIOS method.                    */
for (s=1;s<=10;++s)                  /* Write 10 screens of 'x' in green. */
    for (r=0;r<=24;++r)              /* Write 25 lines.                 */
        printa ("xxxxxxxxxxxxxxxxxxxxxxxxxxxxxxxxxxxxxxxxxxxxxxxxxxxx"
                "xxxxxxxxxxxxxxxxxxxxxxxxxxxxxx",02,r,0);
gettime (&h2,&m2,&s2,&c2);
timebefore = (float)(h1*3600.0 + m1*60.0 + s1 + c1/100.0);
timeafter  = (float)(h2*3600.0 + m2*60.0 + s2 + c2/100.0);
time[2] = timeafter - timebefore;
cls (0,0,24,79);

gettime (&h1,&m1,&s1,&c1);           /* Direct video string writes.     */
for (s=1;s<=10;++s)                  /* Write 10 screens of 'x' in blue. */
    for (r=0;r<=24;++r)              /* Write 25 lines.                 */
        printv ("xxxxxxxxxxxxxxxxxxxxxxxxxxxxxxxxxxxxxxxxxxxxxxxxxxxx"
                "xxxxxxxxxxxxxxxxxxxxxxxxxxxxxx",01,r,0);
gettime (&h2,&m2,&s2,&c2);
timebefore = (float)(h1*3600.0 + m1*60.0 + s1 + c1/100.0);
timeafter  = (float)(h2*3600.0 + m2*60.0 + s2 + c2/100.0);
time[3] = timeafter - timebefore;
cls (0,0,24,79);

gettime (&h1,&m1,&s1,&c1);           /* Direct video string writes      */
                                     /* using "no-snow" version.        */
for (s=1;s<=10;++s)                  /* Write 10 screens of 'x' in cyan. */
    for (r=0;r<=24;++r)              /* Write 25 lines.                 */
        printvcga ("xxxxxxxxxxxxxxxxxxxxxxxxxxxxxxxxxxxxxxxxxxxxxxxxxxxx"
                   "xxxxxxxxxxxxxxxxxxxxxxxxxxxxxx",03,r,0);
gettime (&h2,&m2,&s2,&c2);
timebefore = (float)(h1*3600.0 + m1*60.0 + s1 + c1/100.0);
timeafter  = (float)(h2*3600.0 + m2*60.0 + s2 + c2/100.0);
time[4] = timeafter - timebefore;
```

Figure 8.8: *A C benchmark program testing methods for generating video output (continued)*

```
        cls (0,0,24,79);

        gettime (&h1,&m1,&s1,&c1);              /* Direct video block move.       */
        for (s=1;s<=10;++s)                     /* Write 10 complete test screens. */
             printw (scr,0,0,24,79,0,0);
        gettime (&h2,&m2,&s2,&c2);
        timebefore = (float)(h1*3600.0 + m1*60.0 + s1 + c1/100.0);
        timeafter  = (float)(h2*3600.0 + m2*60.0 + s2 + c2/100.0);
        time[5] = timeafter - timebefore;
        cls (0,0,24,79);

        gettime (&h1,&m1,&s1,&c1);              /* Direct video block move using  */
                                                /* "no-snow" version.             */
        for (s=1;s<=10;++s)                     /* Write 10 complete test screens. */
             printwcga (scr,0,0,24,79,0,0);
        gettime (&h2,&m2,&s2,&c2);
        timebefore = (float)(h1*3600.0 + m1*60.0 + s1 + c1/100.0);
        timeafter  = (float)(h2*3600.0 + m2*60.0 + s2 + c2/100.0);
        time[6] = timeafter - timebefore;
        cls (0,0,24,79);

        printf (" Results of Benchmark\n");          /* Display final results. */
        printf ("------- -- ---------\n");
        printf ( "method                       time (seconds)\n");
        printf ( "------                       --------------\n");
        for (s=0;s<=6;++s)
             printf ("%s%8.2f\n", mess[s],time[s]);

        } /* end main */

#include <dos.h>

void gettime (h,m,s,c)                          /* This function uses MS-DOS to */
int *h,*m,*s,*c;                                /* obtain the system time.      */
/*
     h : hours
     m : minutes
     s : seconds
     c : hundredths ("centi-seconds")
*/
     {
     union REGS reg;

     reg.h.ah = 0x2c;
     int86 (0x21,&reg,&reg);
     *h = reg.h.ch;
     *m = reg.h.cl;
     *s = reg.h.dh;
     *c = reg.h.dl;

     } /* end gettime */
```

Figure 8.8: *A C benchmark program testing methods for generating video output (continued)*

below; all necessary functions can be found in this book (the figure containing each function is given in the comment following the function declaration).

The table below shows the results printed out when this program was run on a standard IBM-PC running at 4.77 MHz, with an EGA display:

Method	Function	Time (seconds)
DOS/ANSI.SYS, cooked	printf	52.95
DOS/ANSI.SYS, raw	printf	34.49
BIOS	printa	35.15
Direct video	printv	0.38
Direct video, CGA	printvcga	2.53
Block move	printw	0.22
Block move, CGA	printwcga	2.19

A number of observations may be based on these data. First, there is a significant improvement in the speed of DOS function calls when the console device is set to the raw mode rather than the default cooked mode; see Chapter 4 for an explanation of these modes. The second observation is that the function **printa**, which uses the BIOS services, made a rather dismal showing. The comparison is somewhat unfair, however, since this function is written in C, while the direct video functions are written in assembler. Generating interrupts through the C function **int86** is not as fast as direct interrupt invocation from assembler, and therefore this function is a good candidate for being rewritten in assembly language. Also, an inherent problem with using the BIOS to generate controlled video output is the need to invoke two separate interrupt functions for each character displayed. Third, the CGA methods are significantly slower than those that do not need to synchronize output with retrace periods. Fourth, among the functions that write directly to video memory, the block transfer methods are only slightly faster than the string write methods. However, the block methods are more convenient for designing and displaying entire screens or windows of data. The fifth and most significant observation is that the direct video methods are orders of magnitude faster than methods that use the operating system or BIOS, and yet direct video transfer is quite flexible and simple to implement.

▣ A Screen Generator

Figure 8.9 contains the complete assembly language source code for an interactive screen designing utility. The listing serves as an example of a fairly large assembler program that uses systems level resources, and is also a good starting point for a very useful utility. This section describes what the program does, how it works, and suggests some possible enhancements.

▤ What the Program Does

The program opens with a blank screen. You may now type any sequence of ASCII characters directly onto the screen. Most of the basic operations of the program are triggered through function keys; the following is a summary of these operations.

The F1 function key displays a window that lists all 253 visible characters in the extended IBM set. Select a character by moving the highlight with the arrow keys. When the desired character is chosen, press Escape to exit from the window, and the original screen will be restored. Subsequently, when any of the four arrow keys is pressed, the selected character is repeatedly duplicated in the corresponding direction (allowing the character to be "drawn" across the screen in any direction). This feature facilitates drawing lines, boxes, and textures, and enhances access to non-keyboard characters (for example, the characters with codes above 126). If, however, the shift key is pressed or Num Lock is on, then the arrow keys will only move the cursor, without replicating the selected character; this is the "pen up" state.

The F2 function key allows the selection of colors if a color system is present, or of monochrome attributes if a monochrome system is present. Select the desired attribute using the arrow keys as instructed, and exit from the screen with Escape. The + key (the grey one on the right side of the IBM keyboard) toggles the blinking attribute on and off. All subsequent characters entered will be displayed with the chosen attribute.

The F3 function key reads and displays an existing file of screen data (to allow additional editing to be performed on a file that was previously saved). Note that any existing screen data, not previously saved, are lost at this point. Pressing Escape aborts this operation.

The F4 function key writes the current contents of the screen to a 4000-byte data file (2000 characters and 2000 attributes—an exact dumping of video memory). Pressing Escape aborts this operation.

```
          page 50,130


          ;File:      SM.ASM

          ;An .EXE format for an interactive screen designing utility
          ;
          ;     To generate .EXE file from SM.ASM:
          ;         MASM SM;
          ;         LINK SM;

          INITATTR   equu    0fh                    ;Initial attribute.

          codeseg    segment 'CODE'
          codeseg    ends

          stackseg   segment stack 'STACK'
                     db      128 dup ('stack   ')
          stackseg   ends

          dataseg    segment 'DATA'

          sw_rec     record  color:1=0              ;Global flags.
          switches   sw_rec  <>
                                                    ;Messages.
          f2_1       db      'foreground',0
          f2_2       db      '+  toggle blinking',0
          f2_3       db      'SELECT COLOR ATTRIBUTE',0
          f2_4       db      27,26,' select foreground',0
          f2_5       db      24,25,' select background',0
          f2_6       db      'SELECT MONOCHROME ATTRIBUTE',0
          f2_7       db      27,26,' select attribute',0
          f3_1       db      'name of file to read:',0
          f3_2       db      49 dup (' '),0
          f3_3       db      'file not found, press a key to continue ...',0
          f4_1       db      'name of file to write:',0
          f4_2       db      'cannot write file, press a key to continue ...',0
          f10_1      db      'terminate program? (y/n): ',0


                                                    ;Table of monochrome attributes
                                                    ;used by 'f2'.
          attrtab    db      07h                    ;Normal.
                     db      0Fh                    ;High intensity.
                     db      01h                    ;Underlined.
                     db      09h                    ;High intensity and underlined.
                     db      70h                    ;Reverse video.
                     db      7fh                    ;White background/intense foreground
                                                    ;(visible only on some systems).
          TABLEN     equu    $-attrtab

          filename   db      50 dup (?)             ;Used by 'f3' & 'f4'.
          handle     dw      ?

          oldcur     dw      ?                      ;Used by 'hidecur' & 'showcur'.

          curpos     dw      ?                      ;Used by 'savecur' & 'restcur'.

                                                    ;Data for 'pushscr' & 'popscr'.
          stkptr     dw      offset scrstack        ;Pointer for screen stack.
          scrstack   label   byte                   ;Stack space for saving screens --
                                                    ;must be LAST in data segment to avoid
                                                    ;reserving space and bloating .EXE file.
          dataseg    ends

                     assume  cs:codeseg
                     assume  ds:dataseg
                     assume  es:dataseg
                     assume  ss:stackseg

          codeseg    segment 'CODE'
                                                    ;** Macros **
          cursor     macro                          ;Positions cursor at row/col
                     push    ax                     ;in DH/DL -- uses BIOS.
                     push    bx
                     mov     ah,02h
                     mov     bh,00h
                     int     10h
                     pop     bx
```

Figure 8.9: *An interactive screen-designing program in assembler*

```
                 pop     ax
                 endm

putchar    macro                          ;Writes character & attribute
                                           ;directly to video memory.
                 push    ax
                 push    bx                ;Entry:
                                           ;    CX = attribute/character
                 xor     ah, ah            ;    DX = row/column
                 mov     al, dh            ;    ES = segment address of
                 xor     bh, bh            ;         video memory
                 mov     bl, dh
                 push    cx                ;Calculates offset in video memory =
                 mov     cl, 7             ;    (row * 160) + (2 * column)
                 shl     ax, cl            ;Places result in BX.
                 mov     cl, 5
                 shl     bx, cl
                 pop     cx
                 add     ax, bx
                 xor     bh, bh
                 mov     bl, dl
                 shl     bx, 1
                 add     bx, ax
                 mov     word ptr es:[bx], cx      ;Write character & attribute.

                 pop     bx
                 pop     ax
                 endm

putattr    macro                          ;Writes attribute only directly
                                           ;to video memory.
                 push    ax

                 push    bx                ;Entry:
                                           ;    CH = attribute
                 xor     ah, ah            ;    DX = row/column
                 mov     al, dh            ;    ES = segment address of
                 xor     bh, bh            ;         video memory
                 mov     bl, dh
                 push    cx                ;Calculates offset in video memory =
                 mov     cl, 7             ;    (row * 160) + (2 * column)
                 shl     ax, cl            ;Places result in BX.
                 mov     cl, 5
                 shl     bx, cl
                 pop     cx
                 add     ax, bx
                 xor     bh, bh
                 mov     bl, dl
                 shl     bx, 1
                 add     bx, ax
                 mov     byte ptr es:[bx+1], ch    ;Write attribute to video memory.

                 pop     bx
                 pop     ax
                 endm

getchar    macro                          ;Gets character & attribute.
                                           ;Directly from video memory.
                 push    ax                ;Alters register: CX.
                 push    bx                ;Entry:
                                           ;    DX = row/column
                 xor     ah, ah            ;    ES = segment address of
                 mov     al, dh            ;         video memory
                 xor     bh, bh            ;Returns:
                 mov     bl, dh            ;    CX = attribute/character
                 mov     cl, 7             ;         at row/col in DX.
                 shl     ax, cl
                 mov     cl, 5             ;Calculates offset in video memory =
                 shl     bx, cl            ;    (row * 160) + (2 * column).
                 add     ax, bx            ;Places result in BX.
                 xor     bh, bh
                 mov     bl, dl
                 shl     bx, 1
                 add     bx, ax
                 mov     cx, word ptr es:[bx]      ;Read character and attribute.
```

Figure 8.9: *An interactive screen-designing program in assembler (continued)*

```
                pop     bx
                pop     ax
                endm

cls             macro   ulr, ulc, lrr, lrc  ;Clears the screen within the specified
                                            ;dimensions -- uses BIOS.
                push    ax
                push    bx
                push    cx
                push    dx
                mov     ah, 6               ;Scroll window up function.
                xor     al, al              ;0 => clear entire window.

                mov     ch, ulr             ;Specify the window.
                mov     cl, ulc
                mov     dh, lrr
                mov     dl, lrc
                mov     bh, 0fh             ;Attribute to use for blanked area
                int     10h                 ;(= white on black/high intensity).
                pop     dx
                pop     cx
                pop     bx
                pop     ax
                endm


main            proc    far                 ;** Main program. **                a

                mov     ax, dataseg         ;Initialize data segment.
                mov     ds, ax

                                            ;** Initialization. **
                xor     ax, ax              ;Set ES to correct video buffer segment.
                mov     es, ax
                cmp     byte ptr es:[449h], 7    ;Test video mode.
                je      a01
                mov     ax, 0b800h          ;Color buffer.
                or      switches, mask color     ;Set color flag.
                jmp     a02
a01:            mov     ax, 0b000h          ;Monochrome buffer.
a02:            mov     es, ax
                cls     0,0,24,79           ;Macro: clear entire screen.
                xor     dx, dx              ;Initialize cursor at 0,0.
                cursor                      ;Macro.
                mov     ch, INITATTR        ;Initialize attribute.
                mov     cl, 254             ;Initialize character to '~'.

                                            ;** Begin keyboard read loop. **
a03:            mov     ah, 0               ;Invoke BIOS keyboard read service.
                int     16h

                cmp     ah, 01              ;Test for escape.
                je      a03                 ;Return to top of loop.

                cmp     ah, 3bh             ;Test F1: select character.
                jne     a04
                push    cx
                push    dx
                call    f1
                pop     dx
                pop     cx
                mov     cl, al              ;Character returned in AL.
                jmp     a03                 ;Return to top of loop.

a04:            cmp     ah, 3ch             ;Test F2: select attribute.
                jne     a05
                push    cx
                push    dx

                call    f2
                pop     dx
                pop     cx
                mov     ch, ah              ;Attribute returned in AH.
                jmp     a03                 ;Return to top of loop.
```

Figure 8.9: *An interactive screen-designing program in assembler (continued)*

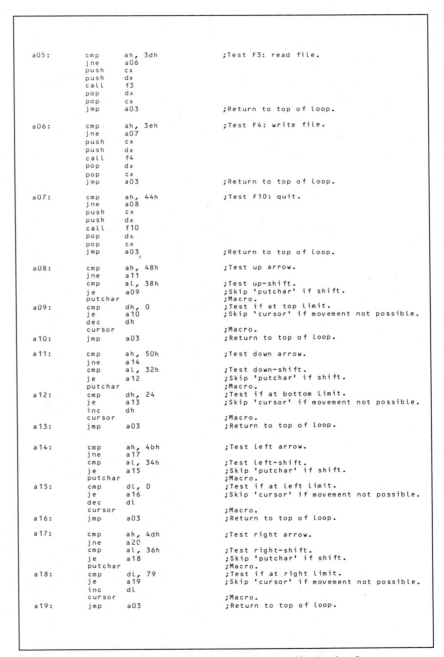

```
a05:      cmp      ah, 3dh          ;Test F3: read file.
          jne      a06
          push     cx
          push     dx
          call     f3
          pop      dx
          pop      cx
          jmp      a03              ;Return to top of loop.

a06:      cmp      ah, 3eh          ;Test F4: write file.
          jne      a07
          push     cx
          push     dx
          call     f4
          pop      dx
          pop      cx
          jmp      a03              ;Return to top of loop.

a07:      cmp      ah, 44h          ;Test F10: quit.
          jne      a08
          push     cx
          push     dx
          call     f10
          pop      dx
          pop      cx
          jmp      a03              ;Return to top of loop.

a08:      cmp      ah, 48h          ;Test up arrow.
          jne      a11
          cmp      al, 38h          ;Test up-shift.
          je       a09              ;Skip 'putchar' if shift.
          putchar                   ;Macro.
a09:      cmp      dh, 0            ;Test if at top limit.
          je       a10              ;Skip 'cursor' if movement not possible.
          dec      dh
          cursor                    ;Macro.
a10:      jmp      a03              ;Return to top of loop.

a11:      cmp      ah, 50h          ;Test down arrow.
          jne      a14
          cmp      al, 32h          ;Test down-shift.
          je       a12              ;Skip 'putchar' if shift.
          putchar                   ;Macro.
a12:      cmp      dh, 24           ;Test if at bottom limit.
          je       a13              ;Skip 'cursor' if movement not possible.
          inc      dh
          cursor                    ;Macro.
a13:      jmp      a03              ;Return to top of loop.

a14:      cmp      ah, 4bh          ;Test left arrow.
          jne      a17
          cmp      al, 34h          ;Test left-shift.
          je       a15              ;Skip 'putchar' if shift.
          putchar                   ;Macro.
a15:      cmp      dl, 0            ;Test if at left limit.
          je       a16              ;Skip 'cursor' if movement not possible.
          dec      dl
          cursor                    ;Macro.
a16:      jmp      a03              ;Return to top of loop.

a17:      cmp      ah, 4dh          ;Test right arrow.
          jne      a20
          cmp      al, 36h          ;Test right-shift.
          je       a18              ;Skip 'putchar' if shift.
          putchar                   ;Macro.
a18:      cmp      dl, 79           ;Test if at right limit.
          je       a19              ;Skip 'cursor' if movement not possible.
          inc      dl
          cursor                    ;Macro.
a19:      jmp      a03              ;Return to top of loop.
```

Figure 8.9: *An interactive screen-designing program in assembler (continued)*

```
a20:        cmp     ah, 0eh              ;Test backspace.
            jne     a22
            cmp     dl, 0                ;Move cursor back if possible.
            je      a21
            dec     dl
            cursor                       ;Macro.
            push    cx                   ;Write a space.
            mov     cl, 32
            putchar                      ;Macro.
            pop     cx
a21:        jmp     a03                  ;Return to top of loop.

a22:        cmp     al, 0                ;Test for no ASCII value.
            je      a23                  ;Go back if no ASCII value.
            jmp     a24
a23:        jmp     a03                  ;Return to top of loop.

a24:        push    cx                   ;Write out ASCII character.
            mov     cl, al
            putchar                      ;Macro.
            pop     cx
            cmp     dl, 79               ;Move cursor right if possible.
            je      a25
            inc     dl
            cursor                       ;Macro.
a25:        jmp     a03                  ;** End keyboard read loop. **

main        endp

                                         ;** Begin subroutines. **

frame       equ     [bp]


f1          proc    near                 ;** F1: select character. **          b
                                         ;Selected character returned in AL.

            push    cx                   ;Save current attribute/character.

            call    pushscr              ;Save old screen.
            call    hidecur              ;Hide the cursor.

            mov     ax, 36               ;Draw box 0,0 to 24,36.
            push    ax
            mov     ax, 24
            push    ax
            xor     ax, ax
            push    ax
            push    ax
            call    box
            add     sp, 8

            cls     1,1,23,35            ;Macro: clear inside of box.

            mov     ch, INITATTR         ;Write characters.
            mov     cl, 1                ;Start with ASCII 1.
            mov     dh, 1                ;Start w/ row 1.
            mov     dl, 3                ;Start w/ column 3.

            pop     ax                   ;Restore current att/char in AX.

                                         ;Start of loop.
b01:        putchar                      ;Macro.
            cmp     cl, al               ;Test for current character.
            jne     b02
            mov     bx, dx               ;Save row/col of current char. in BX.
b02:        inc     cl                   ;Step through all ASCII characters.
            cmp     cl, 32               ;Skip space.
            jne     b03
            inc     cl
```

Figure 8.9: *An interactive screen-designing program in assembler (continued)*

```
b03:        cmp     cl, 255         ;Test for last character.
            je      b05
            inc     dh              ;Go to next row.
            cmp     dh, 24          ;Test for last row.
            je      b04
            jmp     b01

b04:        inc     dl              ;Increment column.
            inc     dl
            inc     dl
            mov     dh, 1           ;Start over with row 1.
            jmp     b01             ;Return to top of loop.

b05:        mov     dx, bx          ;Start by highlighting current char.
            mov     ch, 112         ;Reverse video attribute.
            putattr                 ;Macro.

b06:        mov     ah, 0           ;Begin main read loop.
            int     16h
            cmp     ah, 48h         ;Test up arrow.
            jne     b07
            cmp     dh, 1           ;See if movement up is possible.
            je      b06             ;Return to top of loop if not possible.
            mov     ch, INITATTR    ;Restore attribute.
            putattr                 ;Macro.
            dec     dh              ;Move row counter up.
            mov     ch, 112         ;Display highlight at new position.
            putattr                 ;Macro.
            jmp     b06             ;Return to top of loop.

b07:        cmp     ah, 50h         ;Test down arrow.
            jne     b09
            cmp     dh, 23          ;See if movement down is possible.
            je      b08             ;Return to top of loop if not possible.
            mov     ch, INITATTR    ;Restore attribute.
            putattr                 ;Macro.
            inc     dh              ;Move row counter down.
            mov     ch, 112         ;Display highlight at new position.
            putattr                 ;Macro.
b08:        jmp     b06             ;Return to top of loop.

b09:        cmp     ah, 4bh         ;Test left arrow.
            jne     b11
            cmp     dl, 3           ;See if movement left is possible.
            je      b10             ;Return to top of loop if not possible.
            mov     ch, INITATTR    ;Restore attribute.
            putattr                 ;Macro.
            sub     dl, 3           ;Move column counter left.
            mov     ch, 112         ;Display highlight at new position.
            putattr                 ;Macro.
b10:        jmp     b06             ;Return to top of loop.

b11:        cmp     ah, 4dh         ;Right arrow.
            jne     b13
            cmp     dl, 33          ;Test if movement right is possible.
            je      b12             ;Return to top of loop if not possible.
            mov     ch, INITATTR    ;Restore attribute.
            putattr                 ;Macro.
            add     dl, 3           ;Move column counter right.
            mov     ch, 112         ;Display highlight at new position.
            putattr                 ;Macro.
b12:        jmp     b06             ;Return to top of loop.

b13:        cmp     ah, 01          ;Test for escape.
            jne     b14
            getchar                 ;Macro.
            push    cx              ;Save returned attribute/character.
            call    popscr          ;Restore screen.
            call    showcur         ;Restore cursor.
            pop     ax              ;Retrieve attribute/character into AX.
            ret

b14:        jmp     b06             ;End of main keyboard loop.
```

Figure 8.9: *An interactive screen-designing program in assembler (continued)*

```
f1          endp

f2          proc    near            ,       ;** F2: Select attribute. **        c
                                            ;Selected attribute returned in AH.

                                            ;Template for attribute byte.
attr_rec    record  blink:1, bckgnd:3, forgnd:4
            push    cx                      ;Save current attribute.
            call    pushscr                 ;Save old screen.
            call    hidecur                 ;Hide the cursor.

            mov     ax, 39                  ;Draw outer box:  0,0 to 14,39.
            push    ax
            mov     ax, 14
            push    ax
            xor     ax, ax
            push    ax
            push    ax
            call    box
            add     sp, 8

            cls     1,1,13,38               ;Macro: clear inside of box.

            mov     ax, 30                  ;Draw inner box:  4,9 to 6,30.
            push    ax
            mov     ax, 6
            push    ax
            mov     ax, 9
            push    ax
            mov     ax, 4
            push    ax
            call    box
            add     sp, 8
                                            ;Message 1.
            mov     ax, 15                  ;Column.
            push    ax
            mov     ax, 5                   ;Row.
            push    ax
            mov     ax, 0fh                 ;Attribute =
            push    ax                      ;white on black/high intensity.
            mov     ax, offset f2_1
            push    ax
            call    printv
            add     sp, 8                   ;Restore stack.

                                            ;Message 2.
            mov     ax, 10                  ;Column.
            push    ax
            mov     ax, 11                  ;Row.
            push    ax
            mov     ax, 0fh                 ;Attribute =
            push    ax                      ;white on black/high intensity.
            mov     ax, offset f2_2
            push    ax
            call    printv
            add     sp, 8                   ;Restore stack.

                                            ;Color and mono differ from this point.
            test    switches, mask color
            jnz     c01
            jmp     c11
                                            ;** Beginning of color routine. **

                                            ;Message 3.
c01:        mov     ax, 9                   ;Column.
            push    ax
            mov     ax, 2                   ;Row.
            push    ax
            mov     ax, 70h                 ;Attribute =
            push    ax                      ;black on white.
```

Figure 8.9: *An interactive screen-designing program in assembler (continued)*

```
                mov     ax, offset f2_3
                push    ax
                call    printv
                add     sp, 8                   ;Restore stack.

                                                ;Message 4.
                mov     ax, 10                  ;Column.
                push    ax
                mov     ax, 9                   ;Row.
                push    ax
                mov     ax, 0fh                 ;Attribute =
                push    ax                      ;white on black.
                mov     ax, offset f2_4
                push    ax
                call    printv
                add     sp, 8                   ;Restore stack.

                                                ;Message 5.
                mov     ax, 10                  ;Column.
                push    ax
                mov     ax, 10                  ;Row.
                push    ax
                mov     ax, 0fh                 ;Attribute =
                push    ax                      ;white on black.
                mov     ax, offset f2_5
                push    ax
                call    printv
                add     sp, 8                   ;Restore stack.

                pop     cx                      ;Restore current attribute.

c02:                                            ;Begin display/read/modify attr. loop.

                mov     dh, 5                   ;Display the current attribute in the
                mov     dl, 10                  ;inner box.
c03:            putattr
                inc     dl
                cmp     dl, 30
                je      c04
                jmp     c03

c04:            mov     ah, 0                   ;Read keyboard.
                int     16h

                cmp     ah, 48h                 ;Test for up arrow.
                jne     c05
                mov     bh, ch                  ;Increment background attribute.
                and     bh, mask bckgnd
                mov     cl, bckgnd
                shr     bh, cl
                inc     bh
                shl     bh, cl
                and     bh, mask bckgnd
                and     ch, not mask bckgnd
                or      ch, bh
                jmp     c02                     ;Return to top of loop.

c05:            cmp     ah, 50h                 ;Test down arrow.
                jne     c06
                mov     bh, ch                  ;Decrement background attribute.
                and     bh, mask bckgnd
                mov     cl, bckgnd
                shr     bh, cl
                dec     bh
                shl     bh, cl
                and     bh, mask bckgnd
                and     ch, not mask bckgnd
                or      ch, bh
                jmp     c02                     ;Return to top of loop.

c06:            cmp     ah, 4bh                 ;Test left arrow.
                jne     c07
                mov     bh, ch                  ;Decrement foreground attribute.
                and     bh, mask forgnd
                dec     bh
```

Figure 8.9: *An interactive screen-designing program in assembler (continued)*

```
              and      bh, mask forgnd
              and      ch, not mask forgnd
              or       ch, bh
              jmp      c02                    ;Return to top of loop.

      c07:    cmp      ah, 4dh                ;Test right arrow.
              jne      c08
              mov      bh, ch                 ;Increment foreground attribute.
              and      bh, mask forgnd
              inc      bh
              and      bh, mask forgnd
              and      ch, not mask forgnd
              or       ch, bh
              jmp      c02                    ;Return to top of loop.

      c08:    cmp      ah, 4eh                ;Test grey +.
              jne      c09
              xor      ch, mask blink         ;Toggle blink bit.
              jmp      c02                    ;Return to top of loop.

      c09:    cmp      ah, 1                  ;Test for escape.
              jne      c10
              jmp      c23                    ;Go to quit on escape.

      c10:    jmp      c02                    ;Return to start of loop.
                                              ;End of main loop.

                                              ;** Beginning of monochrome routine. **

      c11:                                    ;Message 6.
              mov      ax, 6                  ;Column.
              push     ax
              mov      ax, 2                  ;Row.
              push     ax
              mov      ax, 70h                ;Attribute =
              push     ax                     ;reverse video.
              mov      ax, offset f2_6
              push     ax
              call     printv
              add      sp, 8                  ;Restore stack.

                                              ;Message 7.
              mov      ax, 10                 ;Column.
              push     ax
              mov      ax, 10                 ;Row.
              push     ax
              mov      ax, 0fh                ;Attribute =
              push     ax                     ;white on black.
              mov      ax, offset f2_7
              push     ax
              call     printv
              add      sp, 8                  ;Restore stack.

              pop      cx                     ;Restore current attribute.
              mov      bx, offset attrtab + 1    ;Initialize attribute table ptr.

      c12:                                    ;Begin display/read/modify attr. loop.

              mov      dh, 5                  ;Display the current attribute in the
              mov      dl, 10                 ;inner box.
      c13:    putattr
              inc      dl
              cmp      dl, 30
              je       c14
              jmp      c13

      c14:    mov      ah, 0                  ;Read keyboard.
              int      16h

              cmp      ah, 4bh                ;Test left arrow.
              jne      c17
      c15:    dec      bx
              cmp      bx, offset attrtab     ;If gone below bottom of table, wrap
              jae      c16                    ;around to the top.
              add      bx, TABLEN
```

Figure 8.9: *An interactive screen-designing program in assembler (continued)*

```
c16:      cmp     ch, [bx]            ;Prevent repeat of same attribute on
          je      c15                 ;first time thru loop.
          mov     ch, [bx]            ;Assign CH the attribute from table.
          jmp     c12                 ;Return to top of loop.

c17:      cmp     ah, 4dh             ;Test right arrow.
          jne     c20
c18:      inc     bx
          cmp     bx, offset attrtab + TABLEN - 1
          jbe     c19                 ;If gone past end of table, go to start.
          mov     bx, offset attrtab
c19:      cmp     ch, [bx]            ;Prevent repeat of same attribute on
          je      c18                 ;first time thru loop.
          mov     ch, [bx]            ;Assign CH the attribute from the table.
          jmp     c12                 ;Return to top of loop.

c20:      cmp     ah, 4eh             ;Test grey +.
          jne     c21
          xor     ch, mask blink      ;Toggle blink bit.
          jmp     c12                 ;Return to top of loop.

c21:      cmp     ah, 1               ;Test escape.
          jne     c22
          jmp     c23                 ;Go to quit on escape.

c22:      jmp     c12                 ;Return to start of loop.
                                      ;End of loop.

                                      ;** Quit routine. **
c23:      push    cx                  ;Save selected attribute.
          call    popscr              ;Restore screen.
          call    showcur             ;Restore cursor.
          pop     ax                  ;Restore selected attribute into AX.
          ret

f2        endp


f3        proc    near                ;** F3: read file. **                  d

          call    pushscr             ;Save old screen.
          call    savecur             ;Save old cursor position.

          mov     ax, 79              ;Draw box:  0,0 to 4,79.
          push    ax
          mov     ax, 4
          push    ax
          xor     ax, ax
          push    ax
          push    ax
          call    box
          add     sp, 8

d00:      cls     1,1,3,78            ;Macro: clear inside of box.

                                      ;Message 1.
          mov     ax, 3               ;Column.
          push    ax
          mov     ax, 2               ;Row.
          push    ax
          mov     ax, 0fh             ;Attribute =
          push    ax                  ;white on black.
          mov     ax, offset f3_1
          push    ax
          call    printv
          add     sp, 8               ;Restore stack.

                                      ;Message 2: reverse video blanks.
          mov     ax, 26              ;Column.
          push    ax
          mov     ax, 2               ;Row.
          push    ax
          mov     ax, 70h             ;Attribute: black on white/reverse video.
```

Figure 8.9: *An interactive screen-designing program in assembler (continued)*

```
              push    ax
              mov     ax, offset f3_2
              push    ax
              call    printv
              add     sp, 8                    ;Restore stack.

                                               ;Read file name.
              mov     ax, 50                   ;Buffer size.
              push    ax
              mov     ax, 26                   ;Column.
              push    ax
              mov     ax, 2       .            ;Row.
              push    ax
              mov     ax, 70h                  ;Attribute: black on white/reverse video.
              push    ax
              mov     ax, offset filename ;Buffer address.
              push    ax
              call    getstr
              add     sp, 10
              cmp     ah, 0                    ;Test if operation completed.
              je      d01
              call    popscr
              jmp     d04                      ;Operation aborted by user: go to quit.

d01:          mov     ah, 3dh                  ;Open file.
              mov     dx, offset filename ;ASCIIZ file name.
              mov     al, 0                    ;Read only.
              int     21h
              jc      d02
              mov     handle, ax               ;Save file handle.
              jmp     d03
d02:                                           ;Begin error routine.
              cls     1,1,3,78                 ;Macro: clear inside of box.

                                               ;Message 3.
              mov     ax, 3                    ;Column.
              push    ax
              mov     ax, 2                    ;Row.
              push    ax
              mov     ax, 8fh                  ;Attribute =
              push    ax                       ;blinking white on black.
              mov     ax, offset f3_3
              push    ax
              call    printv
              add     sp, 8                    ;Restore stack.

              mov     dh, 2                    ;Pause until user enters key.
              mov     dl, 46
              cursor                           ;Macro.
              mov     ah, 0
              int     16h

              jmp     d00                      ;Go back and try again.

                                               ;Read file right into video memory!
d03:          call    popscr
              mov     ah, 3fh                  ;DOS read file function.
              mov     bx, handle
              mov     cx, 4000                 ;Number of bytes to read.
              push    ds                       ;Place ES into DS.
              push    es
              pop     ds
              mov     dx, 0
              int     21h
              pop     ds                       ;Restore DS.

              mov     ah, 3eh                  ;Close file.
              mov     bx, handle
              int     21h

d04:          call    restcur                  ;Restore the cursor.
              ret
```

Figure 8.9: *An interactive screen-designing program in assembler (continued)*

```
f3         endp

f4         proc    near                    ;** F4: write file. **           e

           call    pushscr                 ;Save old screen.
           call    savecur                 ;Save old cursor position.

           mov     ax, 79                  ;Draw box:  0,0 to 4,79.
           push    ax
           mov     ax, 4
           push    ax
           xor     ax, ax
           push    ax
           push    ax
           call    box
           add     sp, 8

e00:       cls     1,1,3,78                ;Macro: clear inside of box.

                                           ;Message f4_1.
           mov     ax, 3                   ;Column.
           push    ax
           mov     ax, 2                   ;Row.
           push    ax
           mov     ax, 0fh                 ;Attribute =
           push    ax                      ;white on black.
           mov     ax, offset f4_1
           push    ax
           call    printv
           add     sp, 8                   ;Restore stack.

                                           ;Message f3_2: reverse video blanks.
           mov     ax, 26                  ;Column.
           push    ax
           mov     ax, 2                   ;Row.
           push    ax
           mov     ax, 70h                 ;Attribute:black on white/reverse video.
           push    ax
           mov     ax, offset f3_2
           push    ax
           call    printv
           add     sp, 8                   ;Restore stack.

                                           ;Read file name.
           mov     ax, 50                  ;Buffer size.
           push    ax
           mov     ax, 26                  ;Column.
           push    ax
           mov     ax, 2                   ;Row.
           push    ax
           mov     ax, 70h                 ;Attribute:black on white/reverse video.
           push    ax
           mov     ax, offset filename     ;Buffer address.
           push    ax
           call    getstr
           add     sp, 10
           cmp     ah, 0                   ;Test if operation completed.
           je      e01
           call    popscr
           jmp     e04                     ;Operation aborted by user: go to quit.

e01:       mov     ah, 3ch                 ;"CREAT" file.
           mov     dx, offset filename     ;ASCIIZ file name.
           mov     cx, 0                   ;No special attributes.
           int     21h
           jc      e02
           mov     handle, ax              ;Save file handle.
           jmp     e03
e02:                                       ;Begin error routine.
           cls     1,1,3,78                ;Macro: clear inside of box.
```

Figure 8.9: *An interactive screen-designing program in assembler (continued)*

```
               mov      ax, 3             ;Message f4_2.
               push     ax                ;Column.
               mov      ax, 2             ;Row.
               push     ax
               mov      ax, 8fh           ;Attribute =
               push     ax                ;blinking white on black.
               mov      ax, offset f4_2
               push     ax
               call     printv
               add      sp, 8             ;Restore stack.

               mov      dh, 2             ;Pause until user enters key.
               mov      dl, 49
               cursor                     ;Macro.
               mov      ah, 0
               int      16h

               jmp      e00               ;Go back and try again.

e03:           call     popscr            ;Write file right from video memory!
               mov      ah, 40h           ;DOS write file function.
               mov      bx, handle
               mov      cx, 4000          ;Number of bytes to write.
               push     ds
               push     es
               pop      ds
               mov      dx, 0
               int      21h
               pop      ds

               mov      ah, 3eh           ;Close file.
               mov      bx, handle
               int      21h

e04:           call     restcur           ;Restore cursor.
               ret

f4             endp


f10            proc     near              ;** F10: quit. **

               call     pushscr           ;Save the screen.
               call     savecur           ;Save old cursor position.

               mov      ax, 49            ;Draw box:  4,10 to 8,49.
               push     ax
               mov      ax, 8
               push     ax
               mov      ax, 10
               push     ax
               mov      ax, 4
               push     ax
               call     box
               add      sp, 8

               cls      5,11,7,48         ;Clear inside of box.

                                          ;Display message 1.
               mov      ax, 16            ;Column.
               push     ax
               mov      ax, 6             ;Row.
               push     ax
               mov      ax, 8fh           ;Attribute =
               push     ax                ;intense blinking.
               mov      ax, offset f10_1
               push     ax
               call     printv
               add      sp, 8             ;Restore stack.
```

Figure 8.9: *An interactive screen-designing program in assembler (continued)*

```
                    mov     dh, 6                   ;Position cursor.
                    mov     dl, 43
                    cursor                          ;Macro.

                    mov     ah, 0                   ;Read user response.
                    int     16h
                    cmp     al, 'y'
                    je      f01
                    cmp     al, 'Y'
                    je      f01
                    call    restcur                 ;If "yes", restore cursor and screen
                    call    popscr                  ;before returning.
                    ret
                                                    ;** Terminate program routine. **
f01:                xor     dx, dx                  ;Home cursor and clear screen.
                    cursor                          ;Macro.
                    cls     0,0,24,79

                    mov     ah, 4ch                 ;Exit w/ errorlevel 0.
                    mov     al, 0
                    int     21h

f10                 endp


getstr              proc    near                    ;** Reads a string from keyboard. **   g
comment             /*
                    Reads characters until CR or until one less than the specified
                    number of characters has been read.  Terminates the string with
                    a null.  Returns AH = 0 if operation completed, AH = 1 if operation
                    aborted by user entering <ESC>.

                    Alters registers:  AX, BX, CX, DX, SI
                    */
gframe              struc                           ;Stack frame template.
gbptr               dw      ?
gret_ad             dw      ?

gbuf_ad             dw      ?                       ;Buffer address.
gatt                dw      ?                       ;Display attribute.
grow                dw      ?                       ;Starting row.
gcol                dw      ?                       ;Starting column.
gnum                dw      ?                       ;Number of characters to read (+ 1 for
                                                    ;null at end).

gframe              ends

                    push    bp
                    mov     bp, sp

                    mov     bx, frame.gbuf_ad       ;BX is buffer pointer.
                    mov     si, bx                  ;SI points to last buffer position.
                    add     si, frame.gnum
                    dec     si
                    mov     ch, byte ptr frame.gatt ;Initialize attribute.
                    mov     dh, byte ptr frame.grow ;Initialize row/column.
                    mov     dl, byte ptr frame.gcol
                    cursor                          ;Place cursor at first position.

g01:                mov     ah, 0                   ;Start keyboard read loop.
                    int     16h

                    cmp     ah, 1                   ;Test for escape => abort operation.
                    jne     g02
                    jmp     g08                     ;Go to quit routine.

g02:                cmp     al, 13                  ;Test for CR.
                    jne     g03
                    jmp     g07                     ;Go to end of loop on CR.

g03:                cmp     al, 8                   ;Test for backspace.
                    jne     g04
                    cmp     dl, byte ptr frame.gcol ;Test if backspace possible.
```

Figure 8.9: *An interactive screen-designing program in assembler (continued)*

```
                je      g01             ;Return to top of loop if not possible.
                dec     dl              ;Decrement column & move cursor back.
                cursor                  ;Macro.
                mov     cl, 32          ;Write space.
                putchar                 ;Macro.
                dec     bx              ;Decrement buffer pointer.
                jmp     g01             ;Read another character.

g04:            cmp     bx, si          ;Test to see if at end of buffer.
                jne     g05
                jmp     g01             ;Return to top of loop if at end (can
                                        ;act on BS or CR only).

g05:            cmp     al, 0           ;Test for non-ASCII key.
                jne     g06             ;Don't move cursor on non-ASCII value.
                jmp     g01             ;Return to top of loop.

g06:            mov     cl, al          ;Write the entered character.
                putchar                 ;Macro.
                inc     dl              ;Move to next column.
                cursor                  ;Macro.
                mov     [bx], al        ;Write the character to the buffer.
                inc     bx              ;Increment buffer pointer.
                jmp     g01             ;Return to top of loop.
                                        ;End of loop.

g07:            mov     byte ptr [bx], 0 ;Null termination.
                mov     ah, 0           ;Indicates operation completed.

g08:            pop     bp              ;Branch directly to this point if
                ret                     ;operation aborted.

getstr          endp


printv          proc    near            ;** Displays a string on screen. **    h
comment /*
                This procedure writes a null terminated string directly to video
                memory, and should be used only with IBM-compatible systems with
                controllers that do not produce "snow."

                Alters registers:  AX, CX, DX, SI, DI
*/

hframe          struc                   ;Stack frame template.
hbptr           dw      ?
hret_ad         dw      ?
hstr_ad         dw      ?               ;String address.
hatt            dw      ?               ;Display attribute.
hrow            dw      ?               ;Starting row.
hcol            dw      ?               ;Starting column.
hframe          ends

                push    bp
                mov     bp, sp

                mov     si, frame.hstr_ad ;DS:SI point to start of source string.

                                        ;Starting offset in video memory =
                                        ;   (row * 160) + (col * 2)
                mov     di, frame.hrow  ;Place row in DI and multiply by 160.
                mov     ax, di
                mov     cl, 7
                shl     di, cl
                mov     cl, 5
                shl     ax, cl
                add     di, ax

                mov     ax, frame.hcol  ;Multiply col by 2.
                shl     ax, 1
                add     di, ax          ;Add (col * 2) to DI.
```

Figure 8.9: *An interactive screen-designing program in assembler (continued)*

```
                                              ;Attribute in AH.
                   mov     ah, byte ptr frame.hatt
                   cld
h01:               cmp     byte ptr [si], 0     ;Test for null termination.

                   je      h02
                   lodsb                        ;Load a single character from source.
                   stosw                        ;Write a char AND attribute to dest.
                   jmp     h01                  ;Return for another character.

h02:               pop     bp
                   ret

printv     endp

pushscr    proc    near                         ;** Push current video display. **    i
                                                ;Alters registers: CX, SI, DI.

                   push    es                   ;Exchange ES and DS.
                   push    ds
                   pop     es
                   pop     ds

                   xor     si, si               ;Initialize SI, DI, CX.
                   mov     di, es:stkptr
                   mov     cx, 4000             ;Number of bytes to transfer.
                   cld
                   rep     movsb                ;Move entire screen.

                   push    es                   ;Restore ES and DS.
                   push    ds
                   pop     es
                   pop     ds

                   add     stkptr, 4000         ;Increment screen stack pointer.

                   ret

pushscr    endp

popscr     proc    near                         ;** Pop a pushed video display. **    j
                                                ;Alters registers: CX, SI, DI.

                                                ;Decrement stack pointer if not
                                                ;already at bottom.
                   cmp     stkptr, offset scrstack
                   jbe     j01
                   sub     stkptr, 4000         ;Decrement screen stack pointer.
j01:               mov     si, stkptr           ;Initialize SI, DI, CX.
                   xor     di, di
                   mov     cx, 4000             ;Number of bytes to transfer.
                   cld
                   rep     movsb                ;Move entire screen.

                   ret

popscr     endp

box        proc    near                         ;** Display box on screen. **        k
                                                ;Alters registers: AX, BX, CX, DX.

kframe     struc                                ;Stack frame template.
kbptr      dw      ?
kret_ad    dw      ?
kulr       dw      ?                            ;Upper left row.
kulc       dw      ?                            ;Upper left column.
klrr       dw      ?                            ;Lower right row.
klrc       dw      ?                            ;Lower right column.
kframe     ends

                   push    bp
```

Figure 8.9: *An interactive screen-designing program in assembler (continued)*

```
          mov     bp, sp

          mov     ah, byte ptr frame.kulr    ;Store upper/lower rows in AH/AL.
          mov     al, byte ptr frame.klrr

          mov     ch, INITATTR      ;Use default attribute.
          mov     cl, 201           ;Print upper left corner.
          mov     dh, ah
          mov     dl, byte ptr frame.kulc
          putchar                   ;Macro.

          mov     cl, 200           ;Print lower left corner.
          mov     dh, al
          putchar                   ;Macro.
                                    ;Calculate number of horizontal
                                    ;line characters:  store in BL.
          mov     bl, byte ptr frame.klrc
          sub     bl, dl            ;Subtract ulc.
          dec     bl

          mov     cl, 205           ;Print top and bottom lines.
k01:      inc     dl                ;Loop for printing all horizontal lines.
          mov     dh, ah            ;An upper line.
          putchar                   ;Macro.
          mov     dh, al            ;A lower line.
          putchar                   ;Macro.
          dec     bl
          jz      k02
          jmp     k01

k02:      mov     cl, 188           ;Print lower right corner.
          inc     dl
          putchar                   ;Macro.

          mov     cl, 187           ;Print upper right corner.
          mov     dh, ah
          putchar                   ;Macro.

          mov     bl, al            ;Calculate number of vertical line
          sub     bl, ah            ;characters: store in BL.
          dec     bl
          mov     ah, byte ptr frame.kulc    ;Store left/right cols in AH/AL.
          mov     al, dl

          mov     cl, 186           ;Print vertical lines.
k03:      inc     dh                ;Loop for printing all vertical lines.
          mov     dl, ah            ;A left line.
          putchar                   ;Macro.
          mov     dl, al            ;A right line.
          putchar                   ;Macro.
          dec     bl
          jz      k04
          jmp     k03

k04:      pop     bp
          ret

box       endp


hidecur   proc    near              ;** Makes the cursor disappear. **   l
                                    ;Alters registers: AX, BX, CX, DX.

          mov     ah, 3             ;BIOS read cursor function.
          mov     bh, 0
          int     10h               ;BIOS video services.
          mov     oldcur, cx        ;Save the old cursor style.

          mov     ah, 1
          mov     ch, 32            ;1 in bit 5 makes the cursor disappear.
          mov     cl, 0
          int     10h
```

Figure 8.9: *An interactive screen-designing program in assembler (continued)*

```
            ret

hidecur     endp

showcur     proc    near            ;** Restores the cursor. **        m
                                    ;Alters registers: AX, CX.

            mov     ah, 1           ;BIOS set cursor type function.
            mov     cx, oldcur
            int     10h             ;BIOS video services.

            ret

showcur     endp

savecur     proc    near            ;** Saves current cursor position. ** n
                                    ;Alters registers: AX, BX, CX, DX.

            mov     ah, 3           ;BIOS read cursor position function.
            mov     bh, 0

            int     10h             ;BIOS video services.
            mov     curpos, dx

            ret

savecur     endp

restcur     proc    near            ;** Restores saved cursor position. **o
                                    ;Alters registers: AX, BX, DX.

            mov     ah, 2           ;BIOS set cursor position function.
            mov     bh, 0
            mov     dx, curpos
            int     10h             ;BIOS video services.

            ret

restcur     endp

codeseg     ends

            end     main
```

Figure 8.9: *An interactive screen-designing program in assembler (continued)*

The F10 function key terminates the program.

Once a file containing data for an entire screen has been generated and saved to disk, there are two ways that it may be used. First, the file may be placed on the runtime disk together with the application program, which can then read the data directly into an internal buffer, and display it using a function such as **printw**. This method minimizes program size but slows execution speed.

Alternatively, the raw screen data may be used to generate the source code needed to initialize a program array at compile time. This method is preferred if the number of screens is small because it provides the fastest possible display time and obviates the need for supplementary data files on the runtime disk. How can the raw screen data be translated into the appropriate source code? Figure 8.10 lists a simple C utility that translates a 4000-byte screen data file into either C or assembler source code for initializing an array of bytes. This program does not generate the variable name or declaration, but only a list of 4000 ASCII values in decimal format, separated by commas (and for assembler, a **db** at the beginning of each line). Thus, in a C program the screen array **scr** would be declared as follows:

```
char scr [4000] =
    {
    #include "SCR.DAT" /* Contains 4000 decimal numbers. */
    };
```

As mentioned above, place this data definition in a separate file from the main application to avoid slowing compile time. Also, if you are using the **/W2** compiler switch, eliminate it while compiling this file to prevent the display of 4000 warning messages as each integer is converted to a character!

How the Screen Designer Works

The source code in Figure 8.9 is liberally commented and fairly straightforward. However, a few salient features deserve mention here. The program uses the standard .EXE format described in Chapter 1. The entry procedure **main** begins by setting the ES register to point to the correct segment address of video memory, and by setting a global flag to indicate whether the active display is color or monochrome. Performance is enhanced by storing the most repeatedly used values in registers. The following registers are used to store important values throughout the program (except in certain subroutines when they are temporarily saved and used for other purposes):

ES	Segment address of video memory
CH	Current selected display attribute
CL	Current selected character
DH	Current row
DL	Current column

Performance is also enhanced by using macros rather than subroutine calls in areas of the code where speed is important (such as the main loop, which reads the keyboard and writes characters to video memory).

```
        File:     CODER.C

        A C utility that converts a screen data file into C or assembler source

        This program reads a 4000 byte file which is an image of video memory,
        such as generated by SM.ASM (Figure 8.9), and converts it to the source
        code required to initialize a C or Assembler array.
*/

#include "stdio.h"
#include "conio.h"

FILE *infile,*outfile;

void main ()
        {
        char infilename[128];
        char outfilename[128];
        int  ok = 1;
        int  ch;
        int  col;
        int  asm;
                                                /* Select C or Assembler format. */
        printf ("language for include file:\n");
        printf ("   (1) C\n");
        printf ("   (2) assembler\n");
        printf ("enter 1 or 2: ");
        do
                {
                asm = getch () - 49;
                }
        while (asm < 0 || asm > 1);

        do                                      /* Input file: get name and open. */
                {
                ok = 1;
                printf ("\n\nenter name of screen data file: ");
                scanf ("%s",infilename);                 /* Read file name. */
                if ((infile = fopen (infilename,"rb")) == NULL)
                        {
                        printf ("can't open %s\n",infilename);
                        ok = 0;
                        }
                }
        while (!ok);

        do                                      /* Output file: get name and open. */
                {
                ok = 1;
                printf ("enter name of include file to create: ");
                scanf ("%s",outfilename);                /* Read file name. */
                if ((outfile = fopen (outfilename,"w")) == NULL)
                        {
                        printf ("can't open %s\n",outfilename);
                        ok = 0;
                        }
                }
        while (!ok);

        if (asm)
                fprintf (outfile,"db ");

        col = asm?3:0;                          /* Initialize starting column. */

        while ((ch = fgetc (infile)) != EOF)    /* Read and translate file.    */
                {
                if ((col > 3) | (col > 0 && !asm))
                        if (col <= 75)
                                fprintf (outfile,",");
```

Figure 8.10: *A C utility for translating a screen data file into C or assembler source code*

```
        else
            {
            fprintf (outfile,asm?"\ndb ":",\n");
            col = asm?3:0;
            }
        fprintf (outfile,"%1d",ch);
        if (ch < 10)
            col += 2;
        else if (ch < 100)
            col += 3;
        else
            col += 4;
        } /* end while */

fclose (infile);
fclose (outfile);

} /* end main */
```

Figure 8.10: *A C utility for translating a screen data file into C or assembler source code (continued)*

The procedure **main** consists of a loop that performs the following sequence of steps:

1. It reads the keyboard using BIOS interrupt 16h.

2. It returns immediately if Escape is pressed. (This key is used to exit a subroutine, and should be ignored by the main program.)

3. It tests for the function keys F1, F2, F3, F4, and F10. If one is pressed, it calls the appropriate subroutine.

4. It tests for arrow keys. If one is pressed, it moves the cursor and replicates the selected character if the shift state is not active.

5. It tests for a backspace. If it is detected, it moves the cursor back and erases the character to the left (unless the current column is 0).

6. It returns to the top of the loop if any control keys are entered other than those listed above (as evidenced by a 0 ASCII value). Thus, keys such as F6 are ignored and do not cause the cursor to advance.

7. If one of the above keys is detected, the program performs the required service and then returns to the beginning of the loop. Therefore, if the bottom of the loop is reached, the character must have a normal ASCII value, and it is written directly to video memory together with the selected display attribute, and the cursor position is updated.

Each of the five subroutines selected through function keys displays a window on top of the current screen. In order to preserve the current display, these functions call the procedures **pushscr** and **popscr**. Both **pushscr** and **popscr** use a standard stack data structure to store screens, and operate in a manner analogous to the machine instructions **push** and **pop** so that an entire series of screens may be saved and restored in a last-in-first-out order. (The stack pointer **stkptr** is incremented by 4000 with each call.) Rather than reserving a fixed amount of memory for the screen stack with a **db** instruction (the exact amount needed might not be known in advance, and reserved memory increases the size of the .EXE file on disk), the program performs a little trick:

The segments are declared so that the data segment is the highest in memory, and the stack (**scrstack**) is declared as a label at the end of the data segment. Therefore, the stack is located beyond the end of the program, in the area of memory that is automatically allocated to the process at load time. (By default, the .EXE header will request all of user memory; note, however, that if insufficient memory is available beyond the application, no warning message will ensue. A safer method would be to use one of the methods discussed in Chapter 6 for determining the actual amount of free memory available. Also, Chapter 10 discusses using expanded memory for this purpose.)

Possible Enhancements

Although the source file is almost 50K long, this screen designer is still quite rudimentary. However, it is a good framework upon which additional features can be implemented. The reader will doubtlessly think of many improvements; among the more obvious program enhancements are the following:

Use of window routines   The program does not use its own product: screens are generated character-by-character rather than by simple and rapid transfers from initialized data using **printw**. The reason **printw** is not used is to avoid typing in thousands of numbers to manually initialize arrays. Once the program is running, however, it can be used to efficiently create its own screens.

A help utility   One of the first additional screens should be some sort of help utility that displays a window explaining the operation of the program.

Cursor status   The program should optionally display the current row and column position of the cursor. Once a screen is designed, it can be printed (using Shift-PrtSc) and the row and column coordinates of important points on the screen jotted down for later reference when coding the program.

Snow prevention   The program should use "no snow" versions of the routines for writing to video memory if a CGA card is detected or specified by the user (with a command line flag, for example).

Video mode   On color systems, the current video mode should be preserved and restored, and the mode explicitly switched into 80 × 25 color text (number 3). The current version will not operate correctly if a graphics or 40-column mode is active when the program begins.

Warning for data loss   No provision is currently made to warn the user about loss of data. A flag should be set when the screen is modified, and reset when the screen is saved. The user should then be warned if changes are about to be lost when a new screen is read in, or the program is terminated.

Warning before overwriting file   The user should be warned when an existing file is about to be overwritten. The F4 function simply **creats** a new file (function 3Ch, which automatically truncates any existing file to 0 length).

Erasing   There should be a more convenient method for erasing data from the screen; for example, the space character could be added to the list of selectable characters, or some other means employed to cause the cursor to erase characters as it is moved in any direction.

Box drawing mode   More convenient access to the box drawing characters is needed. For example, there could be a box drawing mode in which a box style is selected, and then the cursor used to draw the lines, with corners and intersections automatically generated at the appropriate points.

Additional editing functions   More editing functions are needed; for example, block move and copy, filling a specified area with a character and attribute, and automatic centering.

Direct code generation   C or assembler code could be generated directly from the program to avoid the need to run a separate utility.

Note that these features, as well as a number of others, have been implemented in the enhanced version of this program included with the companion disk described at the end of this book.

■ The Use of Video Routines in a C Program

A wide variety of video functions and utilities have been presented in this book in various contexts. This concluding section demonstrates how a C programmer can use these functions as an integrated set of tools for designing attractive video screens, for rapidly displaying these screens, and for collecting user input. When developing a C program, you can use the functions in this book to perform the following basic video operations:

- Design screen displays interactively and store the resulting data within the C data segment

- Save and restore the current display using a data stack so that windows can be displayed on top of an existing screen, overlap other windows, and be moved on the screen

- Display any portion of a screen data array at any position on the physical screen

- Write strings at any position on the screen, using any display attribute, so that dynamic messages can be integrated with the constant elements of a screen design

- Read data from any position on the screen, echoing characters with any display attribute, and confining echoed output to a specific region consistent with the screen design

Figure 8.11 lists this set of functions and demonstrates their use within a C program. It is assumed that a screen has been designed using the screen utility in Figure 8.9 and that the data have been converted to C source code for initializing the external array **scr**. This array is defined in a separate file that is linked to the application. The program also needs to be linked with object modules containing all of the external functions called—see the declarations in the listing for the locations of these functions.

The demonstration begins by clearing the screen and homing the cursor. It then creates some standard teletype style screen output using **printf**. The current screen is now **pushed** and window 1 is displayed on top of it. Two more overlapping windows are then similarly displayed,

```
/*
       File:       WINTEST.C

       A C Program Demonstrating the use of Window Management Functions.

       This program uses a set of routines to manage the display of windows.
       The window data is contained in an initialized array, as produced by
       a screen designing utility (such as SM.ASM in Figure 8.9).  Note that
       the program must be linked with:
              ~  The C file containing the definition and initial data for the
                 array 'scr'.
              ~  Assembler and C modules containing the external functions called
                 (the sources are given in the declarations below).

       For example,

              cl /c WINTEST.C          This file.
              cl /c SCREEN.C           Contains screen data ('scr') and 'cls ()'.
              masm WINDOW;             Contains assembler functions listed below.
              link WINTEST+SCREEN+WINPROC;
*/

#include <stdio.h>
#include <conio.h>

extern char scr[4000];  /* Initialized array containing screen data;       */
                        /* located in a separate file to save compile time. */

                                                /* Assembler functions.*/
void printv (char *,int,int,int);               /* Figure 8.4          */
void printw (char *,int,int,int,int,int,int);   /* Figure 8.5          */
void pushscr (void);                            /* Figure 8.12         */
void popscr (void);                             /* Figure 8.12         */
void getstr (char *,int,int,int,int);           /* Figure 8.12         */

                                                /* External C function.*/
void cls (int,int,int,int);                     /* Figure 6.6          */

void cursor (unsigned char,unsigned char);      /* Internal function.  */

void main ()
   {
   char buf [15];                               /* Buffer to read in string.  */

   cls (0,0,24,79);                             /* Start with a clear screen. */
   cursor (0,0);                                /* Home the cursor.           */

   printf ("this is normal teletype display\n");
   printf ("press any key for window demo ... ");
   getch ();                                    /* Create a pause.            */

   pushscr ();                                  /* Save program screen. */
   printw (scr,0,0,11,39,0,0);                  /* Display window 1.    */
                                /* Substitute 'printwcga' for CGA adapter. */
```

Figure 8.11: *A demonstration of the use of functions for managing windows from a C program*

```
        printv ("please enter your name:",0x0f,5,7);
                                    /* Display dynamic message; substitute */
                                    /* printvcga for CGA adapter.          */


        printv ("                ",0x70,6,7);
                                    /* Display reverse video area for input. */


        getstr (buf,0x70,6,7,15);            /* Input string in reverse video. */


        pushscr ();                          /* Save screen with window 1. */
        printw (scr,0,40,11,79,4,12);        /* Display window 2.          */
        printv (buf,0x70,8,18);              /* Display dynamic messages.  */
        printv ("press any key for next window ...",0x0f,10,14);
        cursor (10,48);                      /* Pause for input.           */
        getch ();

        pushscr ();                          /* Save screen with window 2.*/
        printw (scr,12,0,23,39,8,25);        /* Display window 3.          */
        printv ("press any key to remove window ...",0x0f,13,27);
        cursor (13,62);
        getch ();

        popscr();                            /* Remove window 3, expose window 2. */
        printv ("press any key to remove window ...",0x0f,10,14);
        cursor (10,49);
        getch ();

        popscr ();                           /* Remove window 2, expose window 1. */
        printv ("press any key to remove final window",0x0f,5,2);
        printv ("...             ",0x0f,6,2);
        cursor (6,6);
        getch ();

        popscr ();                           /* remove window 1, expose original screen */
        cursor (10,0);
        printf ("back to teletype output ...\n");
        printf ("demonstration complete\n");

        } /* end main */


#include <dos.h>

void cursor (row, col)                /* Positions cursor at specified row/column. */
unsigned char row, col;
        {
        union REGS reg;

        reg.h.ah = 2;                         /* BIOS set cursor position function. */
        reg.h.dh = row;
        reg.h.dl = col;
        reg.h.bh = 0;                                              /* Page 0. */
        int86 (0x10,&reg,&reg);               /* BIOS video services interrupt. */

        } /* end cursor */
```

Figure 8.11: *A demonstration of the use of functions for managing windows from a C program (continued)*

pausing for user input before each new window is generated. Finally, the windows are removed one at a time by **popping** the previous screens off the stack until the original display is restored.

The program also demonstrates printing dynamic messages within a window using **printv**, and reading data from a window using **getstr**.

Figure 8.12 contains three of the assembler functions called by the C demonstration program. These functions are versions of similarly named functions appearing in the screen designer of Figure 8.9, modified to allow them to be called from a C program.

Note that among the changes necessary to allow these procedures to be called from C is the need to allocate a specific amount memory for the screen stack **scrstack**. In this case, 12,000 bytes are reserved, exactly enough to save up to three screens at any time. (Alternatively, a C dynamic memory allocation function such as **malloc** could be used to allocate a variable amount of memory.) It is also necessary to reinitialize the ES register to the correct segment address of video memory each time the function is called.

Note also that unlike a normal stack mechanism, in which it is an error to continue to **pop** after the last item has been removed, **popscr** will continue to restore the first window pushed, even after the stack is empty. This feature would be useful, for example, to repeatedly restore an underlying screen when moving a window across the screen.

Getstr is a useful general purpose function for reading data from the user in a windowed environment, with several advantages over the C library functions **scanf** and **gets**. First, it positions the cursor at a specific point on the screen, and echoes characters with a specific attribute consistent with the screen design. Second, it allows only a fixed number of characters to be entered, and confines the echoed output to a specified region so that the user cannot mess up the screen (which is quite easy with **scanf** and other functions that use DOS for string input). This function is ideal for entering all types of data because string data are best converted to integer or floating point types within the program, using C library functions such as **atoi** and **atof**.

The function **getstr** reads characters until one of three conditions occurs:

- A carriage return is pressed.

- One less than the maximum number of characters in the receiving buffer has been entered. Once this stage has been reached, the function does not automatically exit, but waits for either a carriage return or a backspace key.

- The user enters Escape. In this case, the function terminates immediately and returns 1 to the calling program, indicating that the input

```
page 50,130

;Figure:   8.12
;File:     WINDOW.ASM

;This file contains functions for saving and restoring screens on a stack,
;and a function for inputting data from the screen.  Note that these are
;versions of procedures contained in the screen designer (SM.ASM, Figure 8.9),
;modified to be callable from a C program.

public     stkptr, scrstack
public     _pushscr
public     _popscr
public     _getstr

_data      segment word public 'DATA'

stkptr     dw      offset dgroup:scrstack     ;Points to beginning of next
                                              ;free block of 4,000 bytes on stack.

scrstack   db      12000 dup (?)              ;Reserve data area for 3 screens.

_data      ends

dgroup     group   _data

_text      segment byte public 'CODE'

assume     cs:_text, ds:dgroup

include    window.mac                         ;Contains the macros:
                                              ;     'cursor'
                                              ;     'putchar'
                                              ;These macros are listed in Figure 8.9.

frame      equ     [bp]

_pushscr   proc    near                       ;** Push current video display. **     a
                                              ;     void pushscr ();
assume     cs:_text, ds:dgroup

           push    si
           push    di
           push    es
           push    ds

           xor     ax, ax                     ;Set AX to current video memory segment.
           mov     es, ax
           cmp     byte ptr es:[449h], 7      ;Test video mode.
           je      a01
           mov     ax, 0b800h                 ;Color buffer.
           jmp     a02
a01:       mov     ax, 0b000h                 ;Monochrome buffer.

a02:       push    ds
           pop     es                         ;ES now points to C data segment.

           xor     si, si                     ;Initialize SI, DI, CX.
           mov     di, stkptr
           mov     cx, 4000                   ;Number of bytes to transfer.
           cld
           mov     ds, ax                     ;Move AX into DS (segment of video mem).
           rep     movsb                      ;Move entire screen.

           pop     ds
           pop     es
           pop     di
           pop     si

           add     stkptr, 4000               ;Increment screen stack pointer.

           ret

_pushscr   endp
```

Figure 8.12: *Assembler functions for managing windows from a C program*

```
_popscr     proc      near                   ;** Pop a pushed video display. **    b
                                             ;     void popscr ();
assume      cs:_text, ds:dgroup

            push      si
            push      di
            push      es

            xor       ax, ax                 ;Set ES to current video memory segment.
            mov       es, ax
            cmp       byte ptr es:[449h], 7
            je        b01
            mov       ax, 0b800h
            jmp       b02
b01:        mov       ax, 0b000h
b02:        mov       es, ax

                                             ;Decrement screen stack pointer if not
                                             ;already at bottom.
            cmp       stkptr, offset dgroup:scrstack
            jbe       b03
            sub       stkptr, 4000           ;Decrement screen stack pointer.
b03:        mov       si, stkptr             ;Initialize SI, DI, CX.
            xor       di, di
            mov       cx, 4000               ;Number of bytes to transfer.
            cld
            rep       movsb                  ;Move entire screen.

            pop       es
            pop       di
            pop       si

            ret

_popscr     endp


_getstr     proc      near                   ;** Reads a string from keyboard. **   c
comment     /*
            Reads characters until <CR>, or until number read is one less than
            the specified buffer size.  Terminates the string with a null.
            Returns AX = 0 if operation completed, AX = 1 if operation aborted
            by user entering <ESC>.  Terminating <CR> is not placed in the
            buffer.

            void getstr (buf, att, row, col, num);
            char *buf;
            int att;
            int row;
            int col;
            int num;
            */

assume      cs:_text, ds:dgroup

cframe      struc                            ;Stack frame template.
cbptr       dw        ?
cret_ad     dw        ?
cbuf_ad     dw        ?                      ;Buffer address.
catt        dw        ?                      ;Display attribute.
crow        dw        ?                      ;Starting row.
ccol        dw        ?                      ;Starting column.
cnum        dw        ?                      ;Number of bytes in receiving buffer.

cframe      ends

            push      bp
            mov       bp, sp

            push      si
            push      di
            push      es
```

Figure 8.12: *Assembler functions for managing windows from a C program (continued)*

```
                xor       ax, ax                    ;Set ES to current video memory segment.
                mov       es, ax
                cmp       byte ptr es:[449h], 7
                je        c01
                mov       ax, 0b800h
                jmp       c02
c01:            mov       ax, 0b000h
c02:            mov       es, ax

                mov       bx, frame.cbuf_ad         ;BX is buffer pointer.
                mov       si, bx                    ;SI points to last buffer position.
                add       si, frame.cnum
                dec       si
                mov       ch, byte ptr frame.catt   ;Initialize attribute.
                mov       dh, byte ptr frame.crow   ;Initialize row/column.
                mov       dl, byte ptr frame.ccol
                cursor                              ;Place cursor at first position.

c03:            mov       ah, 0                     ;Start keyboard read loop.
                int       16h

                cmp       ah, 1                     ;Test for escape => abort operation.
                jne       c04
                mov       ax, 1                     ;1 => abort.
                jmp       c10                       ;Go to quit routine.

c04:            cmp       al, 13                    ;Test for CR.
                jne       c05
                jmp       c09                       ;Go to end of loop on CR.

c05:            cmp       al, 8                     ;Test for backspace.
                jne       c06
                cmp       dl, byte ptr frame.ccol   ;Test if backspace possible.
                je        c03                       ;Return to top of loop if not possible.
                dec       dl                        ;Decrement column & move cursor back.
                cursor                              ;Macro.
                mov       cl, 32                    ;Write space.
                putchar                             ;Macro.
                dec       bx                        ;Decrement buffer pointer.
                jmp       c03                       ;Read another character.

c06:            cmp       bx, si                    ;Test to see if at end of buffer.
                jne       c07
                jmp       c03                       ;Return to top of loop if at end (can
                                                    ;act on BS or CR only).

c07:            cmp       al, 0                     ;Test for non-ASCII key.
                jne       c08                       ;Don't move cursor on non-ASCII value.
                jmp       c03                       ;Return to top of loop.

c08:            mov       cl, al                    ;Write the entered character.
                putchar                             ;Macro.
                inc       dl                        ;Move to next column.
                cursor                              ;Macro.
                mov       [bx], al                  ;Write the character to the buffer.
                inc       bx                        ;Increment buffer pointer.
                jmp       c03                       ;Return to top of loop.
                                                    ;End of loop.

c09:            mov       ax, 0                     ;Indicates operation completed.

c10:            mov       byte ptr [bx],0           ;Null termination -- branch directly
                pop       es                        ;to this point if operation aborted.
                pop       di
                pop       si
                pop       bp
                ret

_getstr         endp

_text           ends
                end
```

Figure 8.12: *Assembler functions for managing windows from a C program (continued)*

operation was aborted (a return value of 0 indicates that the operation was completed normally).

The terminating carriage return is not placed into the buffer, and the buffer is always terminated with a null character.

The only editing function currently provided by **getstr** is a destructive backspace. It would be simple, however, to provide the following additional editing features:

- Cursor movement using the arrow keys
- Insert and overwrite modes
- Home and End to move the cursor to the beginning or end of the line

The function could also be modified to provide a number of other useful options, that would be activated by passing special parameters, such as:

- Allowing only numeric characters
- Automatic conversion to upper case
- Special formats, specifying the location of digits, decimal points, date separators, etc.
- Automatic field exit when the maximum number of characters has been entered

CHAPTER 9

THE ANATOMY OF A DEVICE DRIVER

A high-performance program should not only take advantage of internal hardware and software resources, but should also fully exploit the wide variety of peripheral devices available for MS-DOS machines. This chapter explores a unique and important resource provided by MS-DOS for creating interfaces to peripheral equipment: the installable device driver.

One of the primary functions of an operating system is to convert a collection of diverse and intractable physical devices into a set of consistent and easily managed logical devices. Typical peripherals such as disk drives, printers, serial ports, keyboards, and monitors require wildly divergent sets of control commands. Yet, under MS-DOS, all of these devices are accessed through a common set of standard input/output functions.

This uniform and easily handled logical interface is created through the mechanism of device drivers. For example, consider two very dissimilar devices: a disk drive and a printer. When an application program wants to access either device, it first calls an open function, passing DOS an identifying name: a path name for a disk file, or the name PRN for the printer. Once opened, I/O for either of these devices can be handled through the same set of DOS read and write functions (with some obvious limitations, such as that the printer is write-only). The DOS functions, however, do not directly control the device, but rather pass all I/O requests to the device driver that is associated with the particular device. The device driver provides a standard set of functions for the operating system, and contains all of the low-level, machine-specific code that controls the actual physical device. A device driver thus hides the code that is specific to the physical device, and allows DOS to provide a standard logical device for the application program.

The operating system contains a set of built-in device drivers, corresponding to the most common peripheral equipment found on an MS-DOS system. For example, this set might include the drivers listed in Table 9.1.

Although the collection of built-in device drivers might be quite comprehensive, optimal software performance may require additional drivers to

Device driver	Device
NUL	No device (the "bit bucket")
CON	Keyboard and monitor
AUX	Default serial port
PRN	Default printer
CLOCK$	Realtime clock
02	A block device for drives A and B
COM1	Primary serial port
LPT1	First printer
LPT2	Second printer
LPT3	Third printer
COM2	Secondary serial port

Table 9.1: *Built-in device drivers*

take advantage of nonsupported devices, and may also require the replacement of existing drivers to provide additional features or greater efficiency.

Before the release of MS-DOS 2.0, one of two approaches was required to access peripheral equipment not supported by the system. First, highly machine specific code could be included directly within the application to create device interfaces that would bypass the entire operating system and device driver mechanism. A second approach was to patch or replace portions of the operating system or BIOS code.

MS-DOS 2.0, however, added an important new resource: the user-installable device driver. Just as the open architecture of IBM-compatible systems facilitates the addition of new physical devices, the installable device driver facilitates the addition of new logical devices. New device drivers may be added or existing ones replaced. It is thus possible for applications to fully exploit peripheral equipment without building device dependence into the code or modifying the operating system. An additional advantage of the installable device driver is that a single set of device routines can be shared by multiple applications, eliminating redundant coding. Furthermore, by replacing a standard device driver, you can globally modify the behavior of all programs that are subsequently run.

The most familiar example of an installable device driver that replaces one of the built-in drivers is ANSI.SYS, which supplants the standard console driver CON (see Chapter 8). Examples of device drivers that are added to the standard set include RAM disks, mouse drivers, and expanded memory managers (see Chapter 10). (PC-DOS provides an assembly language listing for a device driver that creates a RAM disk, called VDISK.SYS.)

Note that when an application program performs I/O using the BIOS or lower level methods, the entire device driver mechanism is bypassed. This fact explains why installing ANSI.SYS has no effect on many programs. Although the advantages offered by the device driver mechanism are significant, it is a multilayered approach and tends to be slow; therefore, the programmer of a high-performance application may opt to include low-level device controlling code directly within the program and eliminate the use of DOS device drivers.

Before discussing the manner in which device drivers can be replaced or new ones added to the system, it is important to understand the differences between the two fundamental types of device drivers: character and block.

■□ Difference between a Block
■□ and a Character Device Driver

The names of these categories are not very descriptive. Both types of drivers may actually transfer blocks of data, and both may perform either sequential or random data access. The fundamental distinction between these two classifications is that a block device driver controls a real or virtual disk drive, and a character device driver controls all other types of devices. This primary distinction has several practical implications for the device-naming conventions, the number of units that may be managed, and the functions that must be made available.

□■ Naming Conventions

Each character device driver is identified by a name (such as *NUL* and *CON* in Table 9.1), selected by the operating system for built-in drivers or by the programmer for installed drivers. These names may be used exactly as file names; for example,

```
        C:>copy CON PRN                /* DOS shell        */
```
or
```
        fopen ("PRN","w");             /* C program        */
```

Block device drivers, however, are always assigned one or more letters by the operating system, the first unit on the list receiving the letter *A*, the second *B*, and so on. These letters are not equivalent to file names, but rather are logical disk drive designations that can be used within a path specification. For example, if one of the units managed by a disk device driver is assigned the letter *D*, then this letter is used to specify the associated logical drive within a file path as follows:

C:>type D:\myfile

Note that the maximum number of block device units is 26, corresponding to the number of available letters.

Number of Units

A character device driver can have only one assigned name (e.g., PRN), and manages only one physical device. A block device driver, however, can manage more than one unit; for each unit, DOS assigns a unique logical device letter. For example, a particular driver that manages two units might be assigned the two letters *C* and *D*. Each unit may refer to a distinct physical device, or two or more units may refer to the same physical device. Therefore, in this example, drive letters C and D could both refer to the same actual disk drive.

Function Differences

A disk drive is unique among devices in several ways:

- It manages I/O on storage media that can vary in format; therefore, block device drivers must provide current format information (normally obtained from the BIOS parameter block in the boot sector of the disk).

- The storage media of a disk drive is sometimes removable; for example, floppy disk drives or Bernoulli systems. Therefore, the driver should be able to inform the operating system when the media has changed.

- A disk drive always transfers data in full sector length blocks, and therefore block device I/O functions differ from those provided by character devices, which are able to transfer single bytes.

Due to these unique characteristics of block devices, there are a variety of differences between block and character device drivers with respect to both the functions that they must provide, and the nature of the information that is exchanged between the device driver and the operating system. Note that all of the drivers listed in Table 9.1, except 02, are of the character type. Specific differences are noted in the following descriptions.

▐▝ The Installation Process

At system initialization, MS-DOS first installs its set of built-in device drivers. These drivers are placed in memory as a linked list: the header of each driver contains the address of the next driver on the list, and the header of the last driver contains a −1. The original linked list of device drivers is as shown in Figure 9.1.

After installing the built-in device drivers, DOS opens the basic character devices (CON, AUX, and PRN). Subsequently, it processes the CONFIG.SYS file and installs any user-requested device drivers, which are specified by a line with the following format:

DEVICE = [d:][path]filename[.ext] [parameters]

Each character device driver is inserted in the linked list immediately after NUL. Each block device driver, however, is added to the end of the list, and is assigned the next free letter (or letters if there are multiple units). This placement has a very important implication: when DOS later receives an I/O request and searches for a specific device driver (as identified by a name for a character type, or by a letter for a block type), it starts at the beginning of the list and moves toward the end. Therefore, if a user installs a device driver with the same name as a built-in driver, the user's driver will be found first, and will replace the built-in driver. For example, if the user requests DOS to install a device driver with the name *CON*, this driver will replace the standard console driver.

However, since block devices are placed at the end of the list, and are given unique letter designations, it is not possible to replace a standard disk device driver. Note also that since all devices are added after the NUL device, it is likewise not possible to replace the NUL device.

Once a device driver has been installed in memory, DOS calls the driver's initialization routine (function 0, which will be described later). Since the basic character devices have already been opened, the initialization code may use DOS functions 01h through 0Ch for basic I/O (it may also call function 30h to get the current DOS version, but should not use other functions, since DOS has not completed its own initialization at this point). The initialization function is called only once, and therefore the

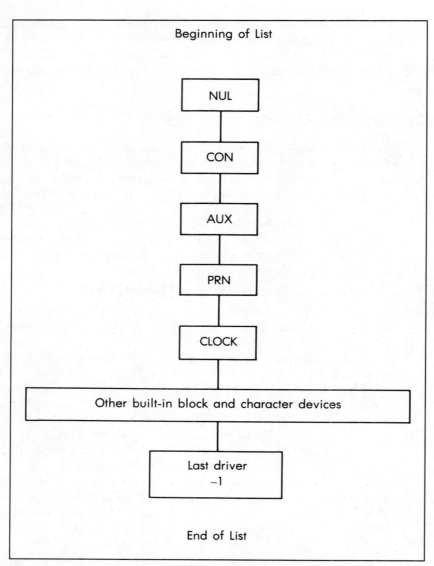

Figure 9.1: *The original linked list of built-in device drivers*

code need not be retained in memory. After all user-specified device drivers are installed, the basic character devices are closed and then reopened
in case any of them has been superseded by newly installed drivers.

In order to understand how DOS calls a device driver, it is necessary to understand something of the structure of the driver, which must follow the exact format specified in the DOS technical reference.

The Anatomy

The structure of a device driver will be described in terms of a specific example: the generic device driver template of Figure 9.2. This program is a mere skeleton of an actual functional driver, and has two purposes. First, it is designed to demonstrate the basic format and global features of a device driver without the clutter of device-specific code. Secondly, it can serve as a starting framework for generating a fully functional device driver, either block or character.

Although only a shell, the executable file that this listing generates can actually be installed under MS-DOS if the following line is included in CONFIG.SYS at boot time:

DEVICE = DRIVER.SYS

The initialization function performs the minimal number of required tasks. All other functions simply print a message, clear the **error** flag, set the **done** flag, and return summarily to DOS. This program creates a character device driver, which is given the name SAMPLE. However, all functions and data structures required for block devices are also included.

Once the driver is installed, it may be tested by typing such commands as

COPY CON SAMPLE
HELLO ˆZ

The driver will print out a series of internal messages and, since it returns without flagging an error, DOS will report that the file was successfully copied.

Unlike the standard .COM file format, a device driver does not use an **org 100h** statement (it is not loaded after a program segment prefix). Either there should be no **org** statement, or **org 0** should be placed at the beginning of the code segment. Note also that the code must not make any assumptions regarding its loading location in memory, which is unpredictable.

The device driver of Figure 9.2 has the following basic structure:

1. The device header

2. Data area

3. The strategy routine

```
 1:    page 50,130
 2:
 3:
 4:    ;File:    DRIVER.ASM
 5:
 6:    ;A Generic Device Driver.
 7:    ;
 8:    ;    This file is a template for constructing either a character or block
 9:    ;    device driver.  The executable file is capable of being installed (as
10:    ;    a character device) but performs only initialization;  all other
11:    ;    functions simply print a message and return.
12:    ;
13:    ;    To generate the installable device driver from DRIVER.ASM:
14:    ;        MASM DRIVER;
15:    ;        LINK DRIVER;
16:    ;        EXE2BIN DRIVER.EXE DRIVER.SYS
17:
18:    include    \MASM\DISPLAY.MAC            ;Contains 'printb' and 'printh'.  See
19:                                            ;text for 'printb' and Figure 4.4 for 'printh'.
20:
21:    stackseg   segment stack                ;This segment is to placate the linker
22:    stackseg   ends                         ;and must remain empty.
23:
24:    codeseg    segment 'CODE'
25:               assume  cs:codeseg
26:
27:               org     0                    ;Device driver is loaded at offset 0.
28:
29:    ;include   DRIVTEST.ASM                 To use testing routine of Figure 9.3
30:
31:                                            ;** DEVICE HEADER **
32:               dd      -1                   ;Double word pointer to next device
33:                                            ;header.  Set to -1 to indicate end of
34:                                            ;chain if only one header in file.
35:
36:               dw      0C000h               ;Attribute word, here indicating a character
37:                                            ;device capable of handling IOCTL requests.
38:                                            ;Bit 15 => character device (else block).
39:                                            ;Bit 14 => supports IOCTL (functions 3 & 12).
40:                                            ;Bit 13 => character: supports o/p until busy
41:                                            ;                       (function 16).
42:                                            ;          => block: non-IBM format.
43:                                            ;Bit 11 => supports open/close/removable media
44:                                            ;                       (functions 13,14,& 15).
45:                                            ;Bit  6 => supports get/set logical device
46:                                            ;                       (functions 23 & 24).
47:                                            ;Bit  3 => current clock device.
48:                                            ;Bit  2 => current NUL device.
49:                                            ;Bit  1 => current standard output device.
50:                                            ;Bit  0 => character: standard input device.
51:                                            ;          => block: supports "generic IOCTL"
52:                                            ;                       (function 19).
53:                                            ;All other bits must be 0.
54:
55:               dw      strategy             ;Offset of strategy routine.
56:
57:               dw      interrupt            ;Offset of interrupt routine.
58:
59:               db      'SAMPLE  '           ;Character: 8 byte device name.
60:                                            ;Block: first byte contains number of
61:                                            ;units, followed by 7 bytes of anything.
62:
63:                                            ;** CALL TABLE **
64:                                            ;Used by Interrupt routine to call
65:                                            ;appropriate service procedure.
66:
67:                                            ;Num: Function:
68:                                            ;---- ---------
69:    calltable  dw      init                 ;0    Initialization.
70:               dw      media_check          ;1    Media check (block only).
71:               dw      build_bpb            ;2    Build BIOS Parameter Block
72:                                            ;         (block only).
73:               dw      ioctl_in             ;3    Input IOCTL control string.
74:               dw      input                ;4    Input.
75:               dw      nondes_in            ;5    Non-destructive input (char. only).
```

Figure 9.2: *A generic device driver*

```
76:              dw      input_stat      ;6    Input Status (char. only).
77:              dw      input_flush     ;7    Input Flush (char. only).
78:              dw      output          ;8    Output.
79:              dw      output_ver      ;9    Output with verify.
80:              dw      out_status      ;10   Output status (char. only).
81:              dw      out_flush       ;11   Output flush (char. only).
82:              dw      ioctl_out       ;12   Output IOCTL control string.
83:              dw      dev_open        ;13   Device open (DOS 3.x).
84:              dw      dev_close       ;14   Device close (DOS 3.x).
85:              dw      rem_media       ;15   Removable media (DOS 3.x).
86:              dw      out_busy        ;16   Output until busy (DOS 3.x).
87:              dw      illegal         ;17   Illegal.
88:              dw      illegal         ;18   Illegal.
89:              dw      gen_ioctl       ;19   Generic IOCTL request (DOS 3.2).
90:              dw      illegal         ;20   Illegal.
91:              dw      illegal         ;21   Illegal.
92:              dw      illegal         ;22   Illegal.
93:              dw      get_log         ;23   Get logical device (DOS 3.2).
94:              dw      set_log         ;24   Set logical device (DOS 3.2).
95:
96:                                      ;Address of request header.
97:   rh_off     dw      ?               ;Offset.
98:   rh_seg     dw      ?               ;Segment.
99:
100:  strategy   proc    far             ;** STRATEGY ROUTINE **
101:  comment    /*
102:              When requesting a device driver service, MS-DOS always calls
103:              the strategy routine first, and passes it a pointer to the Request
104:              Header in ES:BX.  The strategy routine need only save this
105:              pointer and issue a far return.
106:              */
107:
108:              mov     cs:rh_off, bx   ;Must use code segment to access
109:              mov     cs:rh_seg, es   ;memory.
110:              ret
111:
112:  strategy   endp
113:
114:                                      ;** REQUEST HEADER DEFINITIONS **
115:
116:                                      ;Request Header Structures.
117:
118:  rhstruc    struc                    ;Common 13 Byte Request Header.
119:  length     db      ?               ;Length of the Request Header.
120:  unit       db      ?               ;Unit number: 0, 1, ... (block only).
121:  command    db      ?               ;Command code.
122:  status     dw      ?               ;Status.
123:             db      8 dup (?)       ;Reserved by DOS.
124:  rhstruc    ends
125:
126:  instruc    struc                    ;INIT (= 0).
127:             db      13 dup (?)      ;Common request header.
128:  num_unit   db      ?               ;Number of units (block only).
129:  end_addr   dd      ?               ;Ending address of resident code.
130:  bpba_ptr   dd      ?               ;Pointer to BPB ARRAY (block).  Initially
131:                                      ;contains pointer to arguments.
132:  dr_num     db      ?               ;Drive number (DOS 3.1+ only).
133:  instruc    ends
134:
135:  mcstruc    struc                    ;MEDIA CHECK (= 1).
136:             db      13 dup (?)      ;Common request header.
137:  media      db      ?               ;Media Descriptor Byte from DOS.
138:  return     db      ?               ;Return code.
139:                                      ;    -1   media changed.
140:                                      ;     0   don't know.
141:                                      ;     1   media not changed.
142:  mc_volid   dd      ?               ;Pointer to previous volumn ID (DOS 3.x).
143:  mcstruc    ends
144:
145:  bpstruc    struc                    ;BUILD BIOS PARAMETER BLOCK (= 2).
146:             db      13 dup (?)      ;Common request header.
147:  bp_media   db      ?               ;Media Descriptor Byte from DOS.
148:  bp_buf     dd      ?               ;Address of buffer (contains boot sector).
149:  bpb_ptr    dd      ?               ;Pointer to BPB.
150:  bpstruc    ends
151:
```

Figure 9.2: *A generic device driver (continued)*

```
152:   iostruc    struc                          ;INPUT/OUTPUT (= 3,4,8,9,12).
153:              db       13 dup (?)             ;Common request header.
154:   io_media   db       ?                      ;Media Descriptor Byte from DOS.
155:   io_buf     dd       ?                      ;Address of transfer buffer.
156:   count      dw       ?                      ;Count of bytes/sectors transfered.
157:   sector     dw       ?                      ;Starting sector number (block only).
158:   io_volid   dd       ?                      ;Pointer to volume ID (DOS 3.x on error 0Fh).
159:   iostruc    ends
160:
161:   ndstruc    struc                          ;NONDESTRUCTIVE INPUT (= 5).
162:              db       13 dup (?)             ;Common request header.
163:   read       db       ?                      ;Byte read.
164:   ndstruc    ends
165:
166:   gestruc    struc                          ;GENERIC IOCTL REQUEST (= 19, DOS 3.2).
167:              db       13 dup (?)             ;Common request header.
168:   major      db       ?                      ;Major function.
169:   minor      db       ?                      ;Minor function.
170:   rsi        dw       ?                      ;Contents of register SI.
171:   rdi        dw       ?                      ;Contents of register DI.
172:   req_ptr    dd       ?                      ;Pointer to request packet.
173:   gestruc    ends
174:
175:
176:   rheader    equ      es:[di]                ;Used to access fields of Request Header.
177:
178:   LASTCOMM   equ      24                     ;Last Legal Command.
179:
180:                                              ;Template for status field.
181:   statrec    record   error:1, res:5, busy:1, done:1, ecode:8
182:              ;error => error occurred.
183:              ;res: reserved.
184:              ;busy => device busy.
185:              ;done => process complete.
186:              ;ecode: error code
187:
188:
189:   interrupt  proc     far                    ;** INTERRUPT ROUTINE **
190:
191:              push     ax                     ;Save machine state.
192:              push     bx
193:              push     cx
194:              push     dx
195:              push     bp
196:              push     si
197:              push     di
198:              push     ds
199:              push     es
200:              pushf
201:
202:              les      di, dword ptr cs:rh_off  ;ES:SI now point to request header.
203:                                              ;Now 'rheader' (defined above)
204:                                              ;can be used to access the fields.
205:              mov      al, rheader.command    ;Get command code.
206:              cbw
207:              cmp      ax, LASTCOMM           ;Check for command within range.
208:              jbe      a01                    ;Command within range.
209:              call     illegal                ;Command out of range.
210:              jmp      a02                    ;Skip the call.
211:   a01:       shl      ax, 1                  ;Calculate offset in call table.
212:              mov      bx, ax                 ;Load into address register.
213:              call     cs:calltable [bx]      ;Call appropriate routine.
214:
215:   a02:       or       ax, mask done          ;Turn on "done" bit.
216:              mov      rheader.status, ax     ;Return status.
217:
218:              popf                            ;Restore machine state.
219:              pop      es
220:              pop      ds
221:              pop      di
222:              pop      si
223:              pop      bp
224:              pop      dx
225:              pop      cx
226:              pop      bx
227:              pop      ax
```

Figure 9.2: *A generic device driver (continued)*

```
228:
229:            ret                         ;Far return to DOS.
230:
231:    interrupt  endp
232:
233:                                        ;** DEVICE DRIVER FUNCTIONS **
234:
235:    media_check proc    near            ;Media Check (= 1)
236:
237:            printb <"media_check called (= 1)",13,10>
238:            xor     ax, ax
239:            ret
240:
241:    media_check endp
242:
243:
244:    build_bpb  proc     near            ;Build BIOS Parameter Block (= 2).
245:
246:            printb <"build_bpb called (= 2)",13,10>
247:            xor     ax, ax
248:            ret
249:
250:    build_bpb  endp
251:
252:
253:    ioctl_in   proc     near            ;Input IOCTL control string (= 3).
254:
255:            printb <"ioctl_in called (= 3)",13,10>
256:            xor     ax, ax
257:            ret
258:
259:    ioctl_in   endp
260:
261:
262:    input      proc     near            ;Input (= 4).
263:
264:            printb <"input called (= 4)",13,10>
265:            xor     ax, ax
266:            ret
267:
268:    input      endp
269:
270:
271:    nondes_in  proc     near            ;Non-destructive input (= 5).
272:
273:            printb <"nondes_in called (= 5)",13,10>
274:            xor     ax, ax
275:            ret
276:
277:    nondes_in  endp
278:
279:
280:    input_stat proc     near            ;Input Status (= 6).
281:
282:            printb <"input_stat called (= 6)",13,10>
283:            xor     ax, ax
284:            ret
285:
286:    input_stat endp
287:
288:
289:    input_flush proc    near            ;Input Flush (= 7).
290:
291:            printb <"input_flush called (= 7)",13,10>
292:            xor     ax, ax
293:            ret
294:
295:    input_flush endp
296:
297:
298:    output     proc     near            ;Output (= 8).
299:
300:            printb <"output called (= 8)",13,10>
301:            xor     ax, ax
302:            ret
303:
```

Figure 9.2: *A generic device driver (continued)*

```
304:   output      endp
305:
306:
307:   output_ver proc     near                    ;Output with verify (= 9).
308:
309:              printb <"output_ver called (= 9)",13,10>
310:              xor     ax, ax
311:              ret
312:
313:   output_ver endp
314:
315:
316:   out_status proc     near                    ;Output status (= 10).
317:
318:              printb <"out_status called (= 10)",13,10>
319:              xor     ax, ax
320:              ret
321:
322:   out_status endp
323:
324:
325:   out_flush  proc     near                    ;Output flush (= 11).
326:
327:              printb <"out_flush called (= 11)",13,10>
328:              xor     ax, ax
329:              ret
330:
331:   out_flush  endp
332:
333:
334:   ioctl_out  proc     near                    ;Output IOCTL control string (= 12).
335:
336:              printb <"ioctl_out called (= 12)",13,10>
337:              xor     ax, ax
338:              ret
339:
340:   ioctl_out  endp
341:
342:
343:   dev_open   proc     near                    ;Device open (= 13).
344:
345:              printb <"device open called (= 13)",13,10>
346:              xor     ax, ax
347:              ret
348:
349:   dev_open   endp
350:
351:
352:   dev_close  proc     near                    ;Device close (= 14).
353:
354:              printb <"dev_close called (= 14)",13,10>
355:              xor     ax, ax
356:              ret
357:
358:   dev_close  endp
359:
360:
361:   rem_media  proc     near                    ;Removable media (= 15).
362:
363:              printb <"rem_media called (= 15)",13,10>
364:              xor     ax, ax
365:              ret
366:
367:   rem_media  endp
368:
369:
370:   out_busy   proc     near                    ;Output until busy (= 16).
371:
372:              printb <"out busy called (= 16)",13,10>
373:              xor     ax, ax
374:              ret
375:
376:   out_busy   endp
377:
378:
379:   gen_ioctl  proc     near                    ;Generic IOCTL request (= 19).
```

Figure 9.2: *A generic device driver (continued)*

```
380:
381:               printb <"gen_ioctl called (= 19)",13,10>
382:               xor     ax, ax
383:               ret
384:
385:   gen_ioctl   endp
386:
387:
388:   get_log     proc    near                ;Get logical device (= 23).
389:
390:               printb <"get_log called (= 23)",13,10>
391:               xor     ax, ax
392:               ret
393:
394:   get_log     endp
395:
396:
397:   set_log     proc    near                ;Set logical device (= 24).
398:
399:               printb <"set_log called (= 24)",13,10>
400:               xor     ax, ax
401:               ret
402:
403:   set_log     endp
404:
405:
406:   illegal     proc    near                ;Illegal command.
407:
408:               mov     ax, 03              ;Error code for unknown command.
409:               or      ax, mask error      ;Switch on error bit.
410:               ret
411:
412:   illegal     endp
413:
414:
415:   init        proc    near                ;Initialization (= 0).
416:   comment     /*
417:           Function 0, the initialization routine, is called only once by
418:           DOS, and therefore the code need not remain resident in memory.
419:           It must perform any necessary device initializations, and return
420:           to DOS the first address beyond the portion of code to be kept
421:           resident.  Block device drivers must also:
422:           ~  Set the number of units ('num_unit').
423:           ~  Set the pointer to the BIOS parameter block array ('ppba_ptr').
424:           The field 'ppba_ptr' is initially set by DOS to point to the
425:           command line from CONFIG.SYS immediately following the '='.
426:               */
427:
428:                                           ;Print loading address.
429:               printb <13,10,"device driver installed at ">
430:               printh  cs                  ;Dump CS in hex.
431:               printb <":0000",13,10>
432:
433:                                           ;Return break address to DOS.
434:                                           ;Note that all code starting with
435:                                           ;'init' is discarded.
436:               mov     word ptr rheader.end_addr, offset init
437:               mov     word ptr rheader.end_addr+2, cs
438:
439:               xor     ax, ax
440:               ret
441:
442:   init        endp
443:
444:   codeseg     ends
445:
446:               end
447:
448:
449:
450:
451:
452:
453:
454:
```

Figure 9.2: *A generic device driver (continued)*

4. The interrupt routine

    a. Main dispatch and termination routine

    b. Driver service procedures

    c. Initialization procedure

All of the above sections are contained in a single code segment, **codeseg**. The device header must begin at offset 0; otherwise, these sections need not be in the exact order shown. If more than one device driver is contained in the same file, the above set of elements is repeated for each subsequent driver.

The Device Header

The device header begins on line 32 of the program in Figure 9.2, and provides basic information needed by DOS. It has the structure shown in Table 9.2.

Data Area

The next section of the program in Figure 9.2 is a convenient area for storing data to be used by the driver routines. It begins on line 69, and includes two major items:

- **calltable**, which contains the offsets of all service functions. This table is used by the interrupt routine to simplify calling the appropriate procedure.

- **rh_off** and **rh_seg** (line 97), which are used to store the double word pointer to the *request header* (see below) that DOS passes to the strategy routine.

The Strategy Routine

The strategy routine begins on line 100 of Figure 9.2. When MS-DOS requires the services of the device driver, it first calls the strategy routine, passing it a double word pointer to a request header, and then immediately calls the interrupt routine. The only task that the strategy routine must perform, therefore, is to store the pointer to the request header and return immediately to DOS. When the interrupt routine is subsequently called, it uses this pointer to access the request header, and performs the actual required service.

Field length (bytes)	Meaning
2	Offset of next header in file, or −1 if there are no subsequent headers
2	Segment of next header in file, or −1 if there are no subsequent headers
2	The attribute word. The bits in this word indicate to DOS the type of device driver and functions supported. The bits have the following meanings when they are turned on:

15	Driver is for a character device (if bit 15 = 0, then the driver is for a block device).
14	The IOCTL functions (3 & 12) are supported (see below)
13	Character drivers: output until busy (function 16) is supported. Block drivers: non-IBM format.
11	Supports open/close/removable media (functions 13, 14, and 15), and returns volume ID with function 1 (see below)
6	Supports get/set logical device (functions 23 and 24)
3	Current clock device
2	Current NUL device
1	Device is the standard output device
0	Character drivers: standard input device. Block drivers: supports generic IOCTL (function 19)

All other bits must be off.

2	The offset of the strategy routine
2	The offset of the interrupt routine

Table 9.2: *The device header*

8	Character drivers: eight byte device name (padded with blanks on the right, and *not* including a colon).
	Block drivers: The first of these eight bytes may be assigned the number of units managed by the driver; this assignment is optional since the field is set by DOS according to the value returned in the request header from the initialization procedure (see below). The remaining seven bytes can contain anything.

Table 9.2: *The device header (continued)*

Having two separate entry points—the strategy and the interrupt routines—certainly serves no useful purpose under current versions of MS-DOS. This feature does, however, conform to the classical two-level structure of device drivers designed for multitasking systems. In these systems, the upper level of the device driver (equivalent to the DOS strategy routine) is responsible for placing I/O requests in a queue, and either allows the calling process to return immediately (typically for a write request) or temporarily suspends the process (usually on a read request). The lower level of the device driver (corresponding to the DOS interrupt routine) is activated by hardware interrupts that occur when the associated device is ready to transfer data, and services I/O requests in order from the queue (and wakes up upper-level processes when necessary). Thus, in the multitasking versions of MS-DOS that should be available in the near future, these two routines may both have important functions and will be more than a mere facade.

Note also that in a multitasking version of the operating system, it would be necessary to copy the entire request header to a safe area of memory and not just keep a pointer to it because subsequent requests may overwrite the original request header before the interrupt routine has an opportunity to process it.

The Interrupt Routine

Placed immediately before the interrupt routine is a set of related definitions (beginning on line 118). The first of a series of structure definitions that correspond to the layouts of the request headers passed by DOS to the device driver is **rhstruc**, which represents the layout of the first 13 bytes of the request header used in common by *all* functions. Some functions employ a request header with only these 13 bytes; many others, however, require additional fields that follow the common part of the header. Separate structures are defined for all functions that use additional fields.

The common part of the request header, defined as **rhstruc**, contains the fields shown in Table 9.3.

The equate on line 176 provides a convenient mnemonic (**rheader**) for accessing the fields of the above structures (the registers ES and DI are to be loaded with the segment and offset addresses of the request header). The record **statrec** is defined on line 181 to be used as a template for accessing the above status word.

The actual interrupt routine begins on line 189. Its first job is to save all registers, which are simply pushed on the default stack provided by DOS; you should assume, however, that DOS provides stack space for only 20 pushes, and if greater depth is required, the interrupt routine must set up a local stack. The routine then uses the pointer to the request header to obtain the command code. If the value of this field is beyond the greatest legitimate value (**LASTCOMM**, equal to 24 for DOS 3.2), the routine **illegal** is called, which turns on the error bit of the status field and sets the error code to 3 to indicate an invalid command. If the command code is within the valid range, it is used as an index into the call table, and in line 213 the requested routine is called. (Note that there are several unused command numbers less than the value of **LASTCOMM**, which are handled by placing the offset of **illegal** in the call table at the corresponding positions). After the service routine returns, the **done** bit of the status word is turned on, the machine state is restored, and the strategy routine returns to DOS.

Beginning on line 235 are the individual service functions, each of which prints a message, sets the status bit to 0 (which is temporarily stored in AX) to indicate that no error has occurred, and returns to the strategy routine. These functions are listed in numerical order, except for the initialization routine (function 0), which is purposely placed last in the file so that its code may be discarded (it is called only once). The initialization procedure (beginning on line 415) first prints the loading address of the device driver. It then sets the **break** address fields in the request header (i.e., the first address beyond the portion of code that is to remain resident in memory). Note that the initialization routine performs an act of suicide by specifying that its own code be discarded. Finally, it clears the status word and returns to DOS.

One important limitation to bear in mind when designing the service routines of a device driver is the notorious fact that MS-DOS is *non-reentrant*. This means that routines that are executed inside of DOS, such

Field length (bytes)	Meaning
1	Length of the request header in bytes. This field is necessary because the structure of the request header varies past the first 13 bytes.
1	Unit number. This field has meaning only for block devices, and specifies the particular unit for drivers that manage multiple devices.
1	Command code. This field specifies the desired function; the meanings of these codes are defined in the following section.
2	Status word. This field is used by the driver to return the results of the function request to DOS. The meanings of the individual bits (when they are turned on) is as follows:

15	Error. If this bit is on, it signals DOS that an error has occurred; DOS will then look to bits 0–7 for an error code.
14–10	Reserved (for DOS)
9	Busy. This bit is used to return status information to DOS for functions 6, 10, and 15.
8	Done. This bit is turned on immediately before the strategy routine returns to DOS to indicate that the process is complete. (Again, this feature has no real significance under a nonmultitasking system, since the function would presumably not return if it were not done.)
7–0	Error code. These bits are used to pass DOS an error code when bit 15 is on.

Table 9.3: *Common Fields of the Request Header*

Note that the first 12 of these codes are the same as those that DOS reports to a critical-error handler (see Chapter 6). The error codes are as follows:

00	Attempt to write on write-protected diskette
01	Unit unknown
02	Device is not ready
03	Invalid command
04	CRC error
05	Length of request structure invalid
06	Seek error
07	Media unknown
08	Sector not found
09	Printer out of paper
10	Write fault
11	Read fault
12	General failure
13	Reserved
14	Reserved
16	Invalid disk change (DOS 3.x only)

Table 9.3: *Common Fields of the Request Header (continued)*

as device drivers or hardware interrupt handlers, are in general not free to invoke DOS services. MS-DOS maintains only one set of internal storage locations (such as the request header mentioned above), and a recursive call of DOS code can corrupt these locations and result in a system failure. One exception was mentioned earlier: the initialization routine can call DOS functions 01h–0Ch and 30h. Other areas of the device driver might also get away with certain DOS calls; however, as a general rule, it is safest to avoid DOS calls altogether and to rely on the BIOS or lower level methods. Following this dictum, the service routines in the example device driver display their messages using the macro

printb, which is functionally equivalent to **prints**, but uses the BIOS instead of DOS. The content of this macro is as follows:

```
printb  macro
        s                       ;;Displays string 's' at current
        local  a01, a02, a03, str  ;;cursor position. Similar to
                                ;;'PRINTS'
        jmp    a01              ;;except that it uses BIOS
                                ;;rather than
str     db     s                ;;DOS.
        db     0                ;;Sample usage:
a01:    push   ax               ;; printb "hello world"
        push   bx               ;;Saves all registers.
        xor    bx, bx
a02:    mov    al, cs:str [bx]
        cmp    al, 0
        je     a03
        mov    ah, 14
        int    10h
        inc    bx
        jmp    a02
a03:    pop    bx
        pop    ax
        endm
```

The Functions

The following is a brief summary of the service functions that DOS may request of a device driver. Note that DOS can require a function under one of two circumstances. First, DOS requests whatever device driver functions are necessary to complete basic I/O requests made by the application, such as opening files, and reading or writing data. Second, application programs have a more direct access to the device driver through DOS interrupt 21h, function 44h, "I/O control for devices" (IOCTL). Many of the services of this function communicate directly with the device driver so that a program can obtain information about the device or modify the behavior of the driver. A number of the device driver services described below are initiated by corresponding function 44h services. See Chapter 6 for an example of using function 44h to switch the mode of a character driver between the cooked and raw modes. See also the description of function 44h in the *IBM DOS Technical Reference*, Chapter 6.

The function numbers correspond to the values that are placed by DOS in the command code field (**command**, at offset 2) of the request header. The summaries are divided into three parts: the information DOS passes to the strategy routine (Passed), the tasks the routine must perform (Tasks), and the values the routine must return to DOS (Returned).

Note that in the following summaries, **rheader** represents offset 0 of the request header. Also, some block device drivers may manage more than one device unit; the **unit** field of the request header (offset 1) identifies the particular unit the request is for, where 0 refers to the first unit, 1 to the second, etc.

00: INIT

Passed

Request header field	Length and contents of field
rheader + 2 (**command**)	Byte command code
rheader + 18 (**bpba_ptr**)	Double word pointer to the command line from CONFIG.SYS. Points to first character following the " = ". This string is terminated with an ASCII 0, 0Dh, and 0Ah sequence; it may be read but must not be altered.
rheader + 22 (**dr_num**)	Byte letter designation for the first unit of a block driver, where 0 = A, 1 = B, etc. (DOS 3.*x*, block devices only).

Tasks

This function must perform any required device initializations and interrupt vector assignments. It may access the command line from CONFIG.SYS through **bpba_ptr**, and may use DOS functions 01h through 0Ch for basic I/O, and function 30h to obtain the current DOS version. If the initialization routine wants to bail out and not install the device for some reason, it should set the ending address to CS:0000 and (for a block driver) set the number of units to 0. This function is requested only once.

Returned

Request header field	Length and contents of field
rheader + 3 (**status**)	Word return status (**done** bit on)
rheader + 13 (**num_unit**)	Byte; number of units (block devices only). If, for example, a block device driver requests two units and the last assigned drive letter was *B*, then this driver will be assigned the drive letters *C* and *D*.
rheader + 14 (**end_addr**)	Double word break address (the first byte of free memory after the code to be kept memory-resident).
rheader + 18 (**bpba_ptr**)	Double word pointer to a BIOS parameter block (BPB) array (block devices only). The BPB array is a sequence of word offsets of BPBs, one for each unit managed by the block device driver; if there is only one BPB, all pointers can point to the same location. The BPB itself is a set of disk parameters normally found within the first sector of a floppy disk, or the first sector of the DOS partition on a hard disk. The offsets of the BPB within this sector are normally 11 through 23; see the DOS technical reference for details.

01: MEDIA CHECK (block devices only)

Passed

Request header field	Length and contents of field
rheader + 1 (**unit**)	Byte unit number
rheader + 2 (**command**)	Byte command code

rheader + 13 (**media**)   Media descriptor byte. This byte is coded as follows:

Bit	Meaning
0	1 means 2-sided; 0 means not 2-sided
1	1 means 8 sector; 0 means not 8 sector
2	1 means removable; 0 means not removable
3–7	Always set to 1

Tasks

This function should determine, if possible, whether removable media has been changed. Use the following clues:

- A changed disk volume ID or media byte (in the boot sector of the disk) would indicate that the media had changed; however, the same volume ID and media byte does not indicate that the media is unchanged because these values may be the same for two separate disks.

- The DOS technical reference recommends that if less than 2 seconds have elapsed since the last disk access, not even the fastest "power user" could have changed disks.

- A hardware line indicating that the drive door has been opened, if available.

This function allows DOS to avoid having to obtain a new BPB with each disk access if it can determine that the media has not changed. If this function reports that the media has *not* changed, then DOS proceeds with the disk I/O operation. If this function reports that the media has changed, then DOS calls function 02 (**Build BPB**), discarding all internal data buffers (even those containing new, unwritten data). If, however, this function reports an uncertain condition, then DOS will act as if the media had changed unless there are new, unwritten data in its buffers. If there are unwritten data, then DOS will write the data to the disk, assuming that the media is unchanged, and risking possible disk corruption if in fact the media has changed.

Returned

Request header field	Length and contents of field
rheader + 3 (**status**)	Word return status (**done** bit on)
rheader + 14 (**return**)	Byte return code:

Value	Meaning
– 1	Media has been changed
0	Uncertain whether media has been changed
1	Media has not been changed

Request header field	Length and contents of field
rheader + 15 (**mc_volid**)	Double word pointer to previous volume ID (or if not available, then a double word pointer to the string NO NAME, 0) if the media has changed, bit 11 of attribute word is set to 1, and DOS version is 3.0 or higher.

02: BUILD BIOS PARAMETER BLOCK (block devices only)

Passed

Request header field	Length and contents of field
rheader + 1 (**unit**)	Byte unit number
rheader + 2 (**command**)	Byte command code
rheader + 13 (**media**)	Media descriptor byte (see above)
rheader + 14 (**bp_buf**)	Double word address of a buffer that contains the boot sector of the disk

Tasks

This function is called when function 01 indicates that the media has been changed, or when function 01 returns an "uncertain" response, and there are no buffers that have been modified but not yet written to the disk. The invocation of this function thus indicates that the media has been legally changed, and that it is a good time for a driver under DOS 3.x to read and save the new volume ID from the disk. The function must return a pointer to a valid BIOS parameter block (BPB) for the current media.

Returned

Request header field	Length and contents of field
rheader + 3 (**status**)	Word return status (**done** bit on)
rheader + 18 (**bpb_ptr**)	Double word pointer to valid BPB for current media

03, 04, 08, 09, 12: INPUT/OUTPUT

Note that since the parameters passed by these functions are the same, they will be treated as a group.

Passed

Request header field	Length and contents of field
rheader + 1 (**unit**)	Byte unit number (block devices only)
rheader + 2 (**command**)	Byte command code
rheader + 13 (**media**)	Media descriptor style (block devices only, see above)
rheader + 14 (**io_buf**)	Double word address of transfer buffer (i.e., source for write requests, destination for read requests)
rheader + 18 (**count**)	Word count of bytes (character drivers) or sectors (block drivers) to be transferred
rheader + 20 (**sector**)	Word starting sector number for transfer (block devices only)

Tasks

Function 03, I/O CONTROL READ   The device driver passes control information to the application program (which has called DOS interrupt 21h, function 44h, subfunctions 02 or 04). Note that device driver functions 03 and 12 are for exchanging control or configuration information between the driver and the application (such as baud rates) and are not used for exchanging normal data with the device. This and function 12 will be called only if bit 14 of the device attribute word equals 1. DOS performs no error checking; however, the function must return the number of sectors/bytes actually transferred (see "Returned," below).

Function 04, READ   The routine must read the specified number of bytes/sectors from the device into the transfer buffer.

Function 08, WRITE   The routine must write the specified number of bytes/sectors from the transfer buffer to the device.

Function 09, WRITE WITH VERIFY   This is the same as 08 with the additional requirement that, if possible, data written to the device should be read back to verify its accuracy.

Function 12, I/O CONTROL WRITE   This is the same as function 03, except that control information is passed *from* the application program *to* the device driver. The application program has called DOS interrupt 21h, function 44h, subfunctions 03 or 05.

Returns

Request header field	Length and contents of field
rheader + 3 (**status**)	Word return status (**done** bit on). Note that if an error occurs, only functions 04, 08, and 09 need set the error information because there is no error checking for functions 03 and 12. *All* functions, however, must set the following count field when there is an error.
rheader + 18 (**count**)	Word; number of sectors or bytes actually transferred. This field must be set whether or not an error occurs.

rheader + 22 (**io_volid**)	Double word pointer to volume ID. Applies to functions 04, 08, and 09 only. If an illicit disk change is detected under DOS 3.*x* (open file counts maintained through the OPEN/CLOSE functions 13 and 14 can help detect this condition), error code 16 should be returned and this field assigned.

05: NON-DESTRUCTIVE INPUT (character devices only)

Passed

Request header field	Length and contents of field
rheader + 2 (**command**)	Byte command code

Tasks

This function does *not* wait for input from the device. If a character is ready to be read, it sets the busy bit in the status word to 0 and returns the next available character without removing it from the input buffer. If a character is *not* available, it sets the busy bit to 1 and returns immediately. This function thus allows DOS to look ahead one character, and permits it to determine the availability of a character without suspending the calling process.

Returned

Request header field	Length and contents of field
rheader + 3 (**status**)	Word return status (**done** bit on). **Busy** bit 0 means character is ready. **Busy** bit 1 means character not ready.
rheader + 13 (**read**)	Byte; the next character that would be read, if available (i.e., busy bit = 0).

06: INPUT STATUS (character devices only)

Passed

Request header field	Length and contents of field
rheader + 2 (**command**)	Byte command code

Tasks

This function reports to DOS whether or not one or more characters are available in the input buffer.

Returned

Request header field	Length and contents of field
rheader + 3 (**status**)	Word return status (**done** bit on). **Busy** bit 0 means characters are ready in the input buffer. **Busy** bit 1 means characters are not ready in the input buffer, and the driver would have to request input from the device. If there is no input buffer, the driver should set the **busy** bit to 0 to prevent DOS from waiting indefinitely.

7, 11: FLUSH INPUT/OUTPUT BUFFERS (character devices only)

Passed

Request header field	Length and contents of field
rheader + 2 (**command**)	Byte command code

Tasks

Function 7, FLUSH INPUT BUFFERS   This function should empty the input buffer if one is present.

Function 11, FLUSH OUTPUT BUFFERS   This function should empty the output buffer if one is present.

Returned

Request header field	Length and contents of field
rheader + 3 (**status**)	Word return status (**done** bit on)

10: OUTPUT STATUS (character devices only)

Passed

Request header field	Length and contents of field
rheader + 2 (**command**)	Byte command code.

Tasks

Returns current output status.

Returned

Request header field	Length and contents of field
rheader + 3 (**status**)	Word return status (**done** bit on). **Busy** bit = 0 means that a write request could be executed immediately. **Busy** bit = 1 means that the driver must wait for the completion of a current request before servicing a new request.

13, 14: OPEN/CLOSE (DOS 3.0 or later)

Passed

Request header field	Length and contents of field
rheader + 1 (**unit**)	Byte unit number for block devices only
rheader + 2 (**command**)	Byte command code

Tasks

These functions are called only if bit 11 of the attribute word equals 1. Each time DOS opens a file it calls function 13, and each time it closes a file it calls function 14. For block devices, these functions allow the driver to maintain a count of the number of open files on a particular drive, and to flush all buffers when the last file is closed in order to prepare for a possible media change. On character devices, these functions provide the driver the opportunity to send an initialization command to a device when it is opened (such as a reset code to a printer), and a post command when it is closed (such as a form feed to a printer). The standard devices CON, PRN, and AUX, however, are never closed.

Returned

Request header field	Length and contents of field
rheader + 3 (**status**)	Word return status (**done** bit on)

15: REMOVABLE MEDIA
(DOS 3.0 or later, block devices only)

Passed

Request header field	Length and contents of field
rheader + 1 (**unit**)	Byte unit code
rheader + 2 (**command**)	Byte command code

Tasks

This function simply informs DOS whether or not the media is removable. It is called only if bit 11 of the attribute word equals 1. This function is requested only when an application program invokes DOS interrupt 21h, function 44h, subfunction 08. No error checking is performed.

Returned

Request header field	Length and contents of field

rheader + 3 (**status**)   Word return status (**done** bit on). Since no error checking is performed, the function should not bother to set the error bits.

⊞ 16: OUTPUT UNTIL BUSY (DOS 3.0 or later, character devices only)

Passed

Request header field	Length and contents of field
rheader + 2 (**command**)	Byte command code
rheader + 14 (**io_buf**)	Double word address of transfer buffer
rheader + 18 (**count**)	Byte; number of characters to transfer

Tasks

The driver transfers data to the device until a busy state is reached (i.e., attempting to transfer additional characters would require the driver to wait for the device). This function is ideal for servicing a print spooler running in the background, which should print the maximum number of characters possible without waiting. It is called only if bit 13 of the attribute word equals 1.

Returned

Request header field	Length and contents of field
rheader + 3 (**status**)	Word return status (**done** bit on)
rheader + 18 (**count**)	Word; number of sectors or bytes actually transferred. This field must be set whether or not an error occurs. Note that it is not an error if the number of bytes actually transferred is less than the number requested. If, however, the device is not ready, and no characters can be sent, then it should return immediately with an error code.

19: GENERIC IOCTL REQUEST
(DOS 3.2 or later, block devices only)

Passed

Request header field	Length and contents of field
rheader + 1 (**unit**)	Byte unit code
rheader + 2 (**command**)	Byte command code
rheader + 13 (**major**)	Byte; the major function category, which is currently set to 08 for all generic function requests
rheader + 14 (**minor**)	Byte; the minor function code, the specific generic function requested
rheader + 15 (**rsi**)	Word contents of register SI
rheader + 17 (**rdi**)	Word contents of register DI
rheader + 19 (**req_ptr**)	Double word pointer to generic request packet. The layout of this request packet depends upon the specific generic function selected.

Tasks

On a generic IOCTL request, the device driver must execute one of six services, which are specified by the value passed in the request header at offset 14 (**minor**). These services perform sector level I/O for a wide variety of nonstandard media, and are requested by an application program through DOS interrupt 21h, function 44h, subfunction 0Dh. Please consult the *IBM DOS Technical Reference* documentation on IOCTL function 44h (Chapter 6) for a description of the individual services and the layout of the request packet for each service.

Note that this function is called only if bit 0 of the attribute word is set to 1.

Returned

Request header field	Length and contents of field
rheader + 3 (**status**)	Word return status (**done** bit on).

rheader + 19 (**req_ptr**)	Double word pointer to generic request packet. For this suite of services, most of the information is returned through the fields of the packet pointed to by this address.

23: GET LOGICAL DEVICE (DOS 3.2 or later, block devices only)

Passed

Request header field	Length and contents of field
rheader + 1 (**unit**)	Byte unit code
rheader + 2 (**command**)	Byte command code

Tasks

This function is requested by an application program through DOS interrupt 21h, function 44h, subfunction 0Eh. Its purpose is to inform the calling program whether more than one logical drive letter is assigned to a block device, and if so, to return the identity of the last drive letter that was used to reference the device. This function is called only if bit 6 of the attribute word is set to 1.

Returned

Request header field	Length and contents of field
rheader + 1 (**unit**)	Byte code for last drive letter that was used to reference the device, where 1 = *A*, 2 = *B*, etc. If the device has only one drive letter assigned to it, this field should be set to 0. (Note that under DOS 3.*x*, the device may determine its beginning drive letter at initialization from the one-byte request header field at offset 22, **dr_num**.)
rheader + 3 (**status**)	Word return status (**done** bit on)

24: SET LOGICAL DEVICE
(DOS 3.2 or later, block devices only)

Passed

Request header field	Length and contents of field
rheader + 1 (**unit**)	Byte unit code (0 = first unit, 1 = second unit, etc.) corresponding to the next logical drive letter that will be used to reference the block device. For example, if a device driver manages a single physical device but is assigned two drive letters, *C* and *D*, then if a 1 is passed in this field, *D* will be the next logical drive letter used to reference the device.
rheader + 2 (**command**)	Byte command code

Tasks

This function is requested by an application program through DOS interrupt 21h, function 44h, subfunction 0Fh. It is meaningful only for drivers that are assigned multiple logical drive letters referring to a single physical device. Normally, each time such a driver receives an I/O request for a different logical drive letter, it prompts the user to change the media. The purpose of this function is to inform the device driver which logical drive will next be used to reference the device, and to prevent it from issuing the prompt. For example, a DOS driver that manages a disk device referenced by drive letters *A* and *B* may issue the prompt

Insert diskette for drive B: and strike any key when ready.

when performing a copy operation and the single drive changes from source to target. Notifying the driver in advance of the change of letter can eliminate this prompt.

See Chapter 6, function 44h, of the *DOS Technical Reference*. This function is called only if bit 6 of the attribute word is set to 1.

Returned

Request header field	Length and contents of field
rheader + 3 (**status**)	Word return status (**done** bit on)

rheader + 1 (**unit**)   Byte code for last drive letter that was used to reference the device, where 1 = *A*, 2 = *B*, etc. If the device has only one drive letter assigned to it, this field should be set to 0. (Note that under DOS 3.*x*, the device may determine its beginning drive letter at initialization from the one-byte request header field at offset 22, **dr_num**.)

Debugging a Device Driver

Debugging a device driver can be difficult. One problem is that certain errors in the driver code may prevent the computer from booting, thus blocking further diagnostic efforts. Another difficulty is that a device driver is called by DOS. Most debuggers, including CodeView, will not debug code within DOS because the debugger itself makes DOS function calls and DOS is not reentrant. A specific problem with device drivers is that an I/O request from the debugger can overwrite the request header belonging to the driver that is being analyzed.

There are several techniques for debugging a device driver that can help overcome these difficulties:

- Use the macros in Figure 3.1 to display diagnostic clues. These macros are best suited for single character messages; they do not use DOS function calls and thus may be safely called from any part of the device driver. The macros of Figure 4.4 are suitable for more verbose messages, and since they use DOS calls only within the range 01h–0Ch, they may be called from the initialization code.

- Use a debugger that avoids DOS function calls and employs the BIOS or lower level methods whenever possible. An example is Periscope (see Chapter 3).

- Rather than installing the device driver and calling it through DOS, add a routine to the program that calls the driver in the same manner as DOS. Such a program would run outside of the DOS environment and would thus allow the driver code to be analyzed with a standard debugger.

The listing in Figure 9.3 is an example of a routine that simulates DOS device driver requests and can be used to test a device driver outside the

```
;File:     DRIVTEST.ASM

;A "Front End" to test the generic device driver of Figure 9.2.
;
;    To use this testing routine, "uncomment" line 29 of DRIVER.ASM
;    (Figure 9.2) in order to include this file at the appropriate point
;    in the device driver.
;
;    Assemble and link as indicated in Figure 9.2, but do NOT convert to .COM
;    file, since the resulting file is designed to be run as a freestanding
;    .EXE program, and not as an installable device driver.  This routine
;    calls all of the device driver functions in a manner similar to DOS,
;    passing them a request header, and reporting whether an error code
;    was returned by the function.

public      rh, comm, stat          ;Public declarations for CodeView.
public      z01, z02, z03, z04, z05
public      calltable, rh_off, rh_seg
public      strategy, interrupt, a01, a02
public      media_check, build_bpb, ioctl_in, input, nondes_in, input_stat
public      input_flush, output, output_ver, out_status, out_flush, ioctl_out
public      dev_open, dev_close, rem_media, out_busy, illegal, gen_ioctl
public      get_log, set_log, init


            jmp       z01               ;Skip over data.

                                        ;Request header.
rh          db        ?                 ;Length.
            db        ?                 ;Unit.
comm        db        ?                 ;Command.
stat        dw        ?                 ;Status.

z01:        mov       ax, codeseg       ;Initialize DS and ES for .EXE file.
            mov       ds, ax
            mov       es, ax

            mov       bx, offset rh     ;BX must point to offset of request header.

                                        ;Initial message.
            prints    "testing device driver;  press a key to continue ... "
            mov       ah, 0             ;Pause.
            int       16h
            prints    <" ",13,10>       ;What it takes to get DOS to simply
                                        ;make a newline.

                                        ;Call all commands in sequence.
            xor       cx, cx            ;Initialize command count to 0.
z02:        prints    <13,10,"calling function ">
            printn    cx                ;Macro: decimal dump of function number
            prints    " "               ;in CX.
            mov       comm, cl          ;Set command field.
            call      far ptr strategy  ;Far calls to both driver routines
            call      far ptr interrupt ;in sequence.

            test      stat, mask error  ;Test if error code returned.
            jnz       z03
            prints    "no error reported;  press key to continue ..."
            jmp       z04
z03:        prints    "error reported;   press key to continue ..."
z04:        mov       ah, 0             ;Pause.
            int       16h
            prints    <" ",13,10>
            inc       cx                ;Increment to next command.
            cmp       cx, LASTCOMM      ;Check if last command reached.
            ja        z05
            jmp       z02

z05:        mov       ax, 4c00h         ;Exit w/ errorlevel 0.
            int       21h
```

Figure 9.3: *A testing module for a device driver*

DOS environment. Both the calling routine and the driver itself can be programmed to print diagnostic messages, or the entire program can be pulled into a debugger such as CodeView.

In order to use this routine, simply include Figure 9.3 in the device driver by "uncommenting" line 29 of Figure 9.2. (This assumes that Figure 9.3 is contained in a file named DRIVTEST.ASM.) Now assemble and link the program, but do *not* convert it with EXE2BIN, since it is now designed to be run as a freestanding .EXE file, and not as an installable device driver.

When the resulting .EXE file is run, the testing routine calls each device driver service in a manner similar to DOS. The steps performed for each service are as follows:

1. A request header is set up (in this case only the command code field is assigned a value).

2. The address of the request header is passed in registers ES:BX.

3. Far calls are made to the strategy and interrupt routines in immediate succession.

4. After the driver service routine returns, the error bit in the status field of the request header is tested, and an appropriate message is displayed.

This testing routine would obviously have to be greatly modified for the specific device driver being tested, but it illustrates an effective general method.

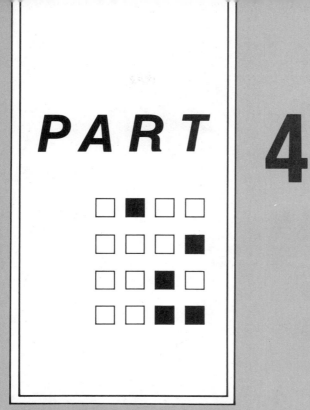

PART 4

MEMORY MANAGEMENT

CHAPTER 10

Expanded Memory: A C Interface

When designing a high-performance application, it is often necessary to weigh considerations of execution speed against code size; the cost of a fast program is often an increased memory demand. For example, the C compiler can be directed to concentrate its optimization on code speed, but only at the cost of larger code size. Also, loading a large application entirely into memory greatly increases efficiency, but consumes more memory than using a program that stores code overlays on disk. Finally, storing full screens of video data in initialized arrays produces blazingly fast displays, but uses significantly more memory than a program that reads screen data on demand from disk files.

It is obvious, therefore, that there is a direct correlation between the amount of memory available to an application and its potential for high performance. The 640 kilobytes of memory available under DOS versions through 3.3, although once seemingly vast, is now a major limitation for large applications, especially considering the penchant for loading memory with resident utilities and the popularity of large operating environments such as Microsoft Windows.

One of the most successful strategies for circumventing the DOS memory limit is the Expanded Memory Specification, developed jointly by Lotus, Intel, and Microsoft ("LIM-EMS"). Expanded memory cards conforming to this standard allow applications to access up to eight megabytes of memory above the DOS limit through use of a paging mechanism.

Note that "expanded" memory is distinct from "extended" memory, which refers specifically to the upper 15 of the 16 megabytes that are addressable by the 80286 processor. (This memory is addressable only in the *protected mode;* DOS, however, runs in the *real mode,* which emulates the 8086 address space, and therefore standard DOS applications are not able to directly access extended memory.)

All the functions in this chapter are compatible with the expanded memory specification version 3.2, released in September 1985. The most recent version of the specification is 4.0, published in August 1987. Version 4.0 increased the upper limit of expanded memory from 8 Mb to 32 Mb, and also added many sophisticated features useful for writing multitasking operating systems and environments. For example, under version

4.0, the page frame can be larger than 64 K, and it is also possible to map expanded memory into areas of memory below 640 K, to provide fast context switching when simultaneously running multiple conventional MS-DOS applications. Although the functions presented here do not *depend* on any of the features of the latest version, they can certainly take advantage of the additional memory capacity. For information on the advanced features of version 4.0, see the handbook *Lotus/Intel/Microsoft Expanded Memory Specification, Version 4.0*, cited in the Bibliography.

This chapter does not duplicate the information contained in the official document and in other MS-DOS reference books and articles. Rather, it serves two primary purposes: (1) to describe the general features of expanded memory, and (2) to present a set of functions that can be called from a C program and that constitute an integrated, high-level interface to expanded memory. These functions illustrate general methods for writing a high-level interface to a low-level resource; they are also a convenient addition to the library of ready-to-use C functions listed in this book.

An Overview of EMS

MS-DOS was designed to work within the context of the one megabyte of *conventional* memory addressable by the 8086/88 processors. The first 640K of this address space is designated as *user* memory; it is physically located on the motherboard and memory cards, and is used by the operating system and by resident and transient application programs. Memory above 640K is reserved for a variety of special purposes such as video adapters, disk controllers, network controllers, and the system ROM BIOS. (See the memory map in Appendix E.)

It is a simple matter to place memory chips on an adapter card but how is it possible to address memory above 640K without either conflicting with areas reserved by the operating system or exceeding the one-megabyte limit inherent in the 8086/88 processors and more advanced processors in their 8086 emulation modes? The answer lies in the fact that not *all* of the memory above 640K is actually used in a given computer system. It is almost always possible to find at least 64K of contiguous unused memory above the 640K mark. (The actual location of this unused memory depends on the other options that are present, and must be specified by setting switches when installing an expanded memory card.) This 64K of contiguous memory is known as a *page frame* and is used as a window to access up to eight megabytes of expanded memory. All accesses to expanded memory are achieved through standard reads and writes to addresses within the page frame. However, the actual location within expanded memory that is accessed through a given address depends on the current *mapping* that has been requested by the program. Read/write requests addressed to memory within the page frame are automatically rerouted by the hardware to the area of expanded memory specified by the current mapping. The basic method is as follows:

- The application program reserves a number of 16K *logical pages* of expanded memory; the maximum number of pages that may be allocated depends upon how much expanded memory is installed and how many pages have previously been reserved.

- The 64K page frame is divided into four contiguous 16K *physical pages* of directly addressable memory. The program can specify which four logical pages of expanded memory are to be mapped onto the four physical pages within the page frame. Thus, the application has direct read/write access to only 64K of expanded memory at a given time.

- In order to access other areas of expanded memory, the program must request another mapping, conceptually swapping other logical pages of expanded memory into the 64K page frame window. This process is known as *bank switching,* or *paging.* The contents of the logical pages that are currently switched out of the page frame are, of course, preserved.

The current page frame mapping is determined by the settings of hardware page registers (also known as *bank switches*) on the expanded memory card. The application program, however, should not directly address these registers, but rather should control expanded memory through a software utility known as the Expanded Memory Manager (EMM) that is supplied with the adapter. Using the EMM according to the specification, rather than direct hardware control, will prevent possible compatibility problems. The EMM is installed as a character device driver in order to render it memory resident (see Chapter 9). Any further resemblance to a typical device driver, however, is merely coincidental, since the EMM is not accessed through the DOS file system, but rather directly through interrupt 67h. (Note that other programs must not use interrupt 67h because the EMM does not "chain" to other interrupt handlers; see Chapters 6 and 11 for more on the topic of interrupt handlers.)

To install the EMM, you must include a **DEVICE =** statement in the CONFIG.SYS configuration file, specifying the name of the EMM driver together with appropriate parameters. A driver is generally supplied with the expanded memory board; for example, EMM.SYS is the name of the driver provided with the Intel Above Board. Note also that PC-DOS 4.0

furnishes both an EMM driver (XMA2EMS.SYS) and a driver to emulate expanded memory in an 80386 machine (XMAEM.SYS). This version of DOS provides options to use expanded memory for the BUFFERS and FASTOPEN operating system commands, and the PC-DOS 4.0 DEBUG utility includes commands for allocating and managing expanded memory pages.

The EMM provides all services necessary for an application to make full use of expanded memory. The services are requested by invoking interrupt 67h, in a manner exactly analogous to the mechanism for requesting MS-DOS and BIOS functions. All values are exchanged through registers. The exact register use depends upon the specific function; however, in all cases register AH is used by the program to pass a code specifying the desired funciton, and by the EMM to return a status code. The following are the basic EMM functions, arranged by category (this is a subset of the functions available under the Expanded Memory Specification, version 4.0):

Function	Purpose
Used by typical transient application programs:	
1	Get EMS status
2	Get segment address of page frame
3	Get unallocated logical page count
4	Allocate logical pages
5	Map logical page onto physical page
6	Deallocate logical pages
7	Get EMM version number
Used by memory-resident software:	
8	Save current page mapping
9	Restore saved page mapping
Reserved:	
10	
11	
Used by low-level memory managers:	
12	Get EMM handle count
13	Get number of pages allocated to a specific handle

14   Get number of pages allocated to all handles

Used by multitasking systems:

15   Get/set page mapping to/from a program array

Examples of the use of the most important of these services are included in the C interface described in the next section. For programmers desiring detailed information on all of the functions, the Expanded Memory Specification pamphlet available from Intel provides complete documentation, including the parameters passed, an example invocation, the registers that are modified, and the status codes and function results that are returned.

A C Interface to EMS

Figure 10.1 lists a set of assembler functions that may be called from a C program, and that constitute a high-level interface to expanded memory. These functions form a complete and integrated set: data are shared among the individual procedures, and the module has its own set of error messages. Therefore, the entire file should be linked to the C program, and it should not be used in conjunction with other functions that directly access the EMM.

The functions were written with the following goals in mind:

- To provide a comprehensive set of functions to manage expanded memory that can easily be called from C, and that are sufficient for most general purpose applications.

- To use as few functions as possible and to make them similar to the standard memory allocation functions in the C library.

- To hide low-level details from the calling C program, such as determining the presence of expanded memory or managing EMM *handles*. (The EMM returns a handle when a block of expanded memory is allocated, to be used as an identifier in subsequent function calls. However, the C program never has to see an EMM handle.)

- To provide a simple set of error messages and eliminate some of the possible sources of error, such as passing invalid function or subfunction numbers, or using invalid EMM handles.

One simplification made by the C interface is the elimination of multiple memory allocations. The EMM allows a single process to call the allocation function (04) more than once, obtaining several blocks of

```
 1:    page 50,130
 2:
 3:    ;Figure:    10
 4:    ;File:      EMS.ASM
 5:
 6:    ;A C Interface to LIM-EMS Expanded Memory.
 7:
 8:    public      emm_name, emm_alloc, emm_handle
 9:    public      _ememavail, a01, a02, a03, a04
10:    public      _ealloc, b00, b01, b02, b03
11:    public      _efree, c01, c02, c03
12:    public      _emap, d01, d02, d03, d04, d05
13:    public      _esave, e01, e02, e03
14:    public      _erestore, f01, f02, f03
15:
16:    _data       segment word public 'DATA'
17:
18:    extrn       _ems_err:word            ;Global error code.
19:
20:    emm_name    db      'EMMXXXX0'        ;Expected device name.
21:    emm_alloc   db      0                 ;Flag => EMS memory allocated/handle valid.
22:    emm_handle  dw      ?                 ;Handle for EMM.
23:
24:    _data       ends
25:
26:    dgroup      group   _data
27:    assume      cs:_text, ds:dgroup
28:
29:    _text       segment byte public 'CODE'
30:
31:    frame       equ     [bp]
32:
33:
34:    _ememavail  proc    near             ;Returns number of free EMS pages.
35:
36:    comment     /*
37:                This function returns the number of free 16K pages of LIM-EMS
38:                expanded memory.  If 0 is returned, 'ems_err' contains one of the
39:                following error codes:
40:
41:                01      Expanded memory not installed.
42:                02      No free expanded memory pages available.
43:                03      Software malfunction.
44:                04      Hardware malfunction.
45:
46:                int ememavail ();
47:
48:                */
49:
50:                push    di
51:                push    si
52:                push    es
53:                                         ;Test for presence of expanded memory.
54:                mov     ah, 35h          ;Get vector to EMM.
55:                mov     al, 67h
56:                int     21h
57:                                         ;Test for correct device name.
58:                mov     di, 000Ah        ;Offset of device name in header.
59:                                         ;Compare with expected name:
60:                mov     si, offset dgroup:emm_name
61:                mov     cx, 8            ;Compare 8 bytes.
62:                cld
63:                repe    cmpsb
64:                je      a01              ;EMM present.
65:                xor     ax, ax           ;EMM not present, therefore 0 pages.
66:                mov     _ems_err, 01     ;Set error code.
67:                jmp     a04              ;Go to end.
68:    a01:                                 ;Call EMM for number of free pages.
69:                mov     ah, 42h
70:                int     67h              ;EMM service interrupt.
71:                cmp     ah, 0            ;Test for EMM error.
```

Figure 10.1: *An interface to expanded memory for C programs*

```
72:                je       a02              ;No error.
73:                call     err_rtn          ;Set EMM error code.
74:                xor      ax, ax           ;EMM error, therefore 0 pages.
75:                jmp      a04              ;Go to end.
76:        a02:
77:                mov      ax, bx           ;BX contains free pages.
78:                cmp      bx, 0            ;Test for 0 pages free.
79:                jne      a03
80:                mov      _ems_err, 02     ;Set error code.
81:                jmp      a04              ;Go to end.
82:        a03:    mov      _ems_err, 00     ;Set error code: no errors.
83:        a04:
84:                pop      es
85:                pop      si
86:                pop      di
87:                ret                       ;Return to C program
88:
89:        _ememavail endp
90:
91:
92:        _ealloc  proc     near            ;Allocates LIM-EMS expanded memory.
93:
94:        comment  /*
95:                 This function allocates the requested number of 16K pages of
96:                 expanded memory.  It returns a far pointer to the beginning of
97:                 the page frame where memory will be mapped.  If NULL (= 0) is
98:                 returned, then 'ems_err' contains one of the following error codes:
99:
100:               03       Software malfunction.
101:               04       Hardware malfunction.
102:               05       EMS memory already allocated by this process.
103:               06       No EMM handles free.
104:               07       Insufficient EMS pages to fill request.
105:               08       Attempt to allocate 0 pages.
106:
107:               char far * ealloc (pages);
108:               int pages;                       Requested number of EMS pages.
109:
110:               */
111:
112:               assume cs:_text
113:
114:       bframe    struc                   ;Stack frame template.
115:       bbptr     dw       ?              ;Base pointer.
116:       bret_ad   dw       ?              ;Return address.
117:       bnum      dw       ?              ;Number of pages requested.
118:       bframe    ends
119:
120:               push     bp
121:               mov      bp, sp
122:
123:               cmp      emm_alloc, 0     ;Test if memory already allocated.
124:               je       b00
125:               xor      dx, dx           ;Already allocated, return NULL.
126:               mov      _ems_err, 05     ;Set error code.
127:               jmp      b03              ;Go to end.
128:       b00:
129:               mov      ah, 43h          ;Call EMM to allocate pages.
130:               mov      bx, frame.bnum   ;Load requested number of pages.
131:               int      67h
132:               cmp      ah, 0            ;Test for EMM error.
133:               je       b01              ;No error.
134:               call     err_rtn          ;Set EMM error code.
135:               xor      dx, dx           ;EMM error, return NULL.
136:               jmp      b03              ;Go to end.
137:       b01:                              ;Allocation successful.
138:               mov      emm_alloc, 1     ;Set flag => mem.allocated/valid handle.
139:               mov      emm_handle, dx   ;Save EMM handle.
140:
141:               mov      ah, 41h          ;Call EMM to get frame address.
142:               int      67h
```

Figure 10.1: *An interface to expanded memory for C programs (continued)*

```
143:            cmp     ah, 0           ;Test for EMM error.
144:            je      b02             ;No error.
145:            call    err_rtn         ;Set EMM error code.
146:            xor     dx, dx          ;Error, return NULL.
147:            jmp     b03             ;Go to end.
148:    b02:    mov     dx, bx          ;Return segment in DX.
149:            mov     _ems_err, 00    ;Set error code: no errors.
150:    b03:
151:            xor     ax, ax          ;AX returns offset, always 0.
152:            pop     bp
153:            ret                     ;Return to C program.
154:
155:    _ealloc endp
156:
157:
158:    _efree  proc    near            ;Frees expanded memory.
159:
160:    comment /*
161:            This function frees all LIM-EMS memory allocated to the current
162:            process.  It returns 0 if no error occurred, otherwise -1 is
163:            returned and 'ems_err' contains one of the following error codes:
164:
165:            03      Software malfunction.
166:            04      Hardware malfunction.
167:            09      EMS memory not allocated.
168:            10      'esave' called without subsequent 'erestore'.
169:
170:            int efree ();
171:
172:            */
173:
174:            cmp     emm_alloc, 0    ;Test if memory has been allocated.
175:            jne     c01
176:            mov     ax, -1          ;Error: no memory to deallocate!
177:            mov     _ems_err, 09    ;Set error code.
178:            jmp     c03             ;Go to end.
179:    c01:
180:            mov     ah, 45h         ;Call EMM to deallocate pages.
181:            mov     dx, emm_handle
182:            int     67h
183:            cmp     ah, 0           ;Test for EMM error.
184:            je      c02
185:            call    err_rtn         ;Set EMM error code.
186:            mov     ax, -1          ;Error on deallocation.
187:            jmp     c03             ;Go to end.
188:    c02:
189:            mov     emm_alloc, 0    ;Reset allocation flag.
190:            xor     ax, ax          ;Return value for no errors.
191:            mov     _ems_err, 00    ;Set error code: no errors.
192:    c03:
193:            ret                     ;Return to C program.
194:
195:    _efree  endp
196:
197:
198:    _emap   proc    near            ;Maps EMS pages.
199:
200:    comment /*
201:            This function maps logical EMS pages onto the four physical pages
202:            of the EMS page frame.  It returns 0 if no error occurred.
203:            If -1 is returned, 'ems_err' contains one of the following error
204:            codes:
205:
206:            03      Software malfunction.
207:            04      Hardware malfunction.
208:            09      EMS memory not allocated.
209:            11      Logical page out of range allocated to process.
210:
211:            int emap (p0, p1, p2, p3);
212:            int p0;                         logical page for physical page 0
```

Figure 10.1: *An interface to expanded memory for C programs (continued)*

```
213:              int p1;                           logical page for physical page 1
214:              int p2;                           logical page for physical page 2
215:              int p3;                           logical page for physical page 3
216:
217:              Note: p0 through p3 contain the logical page numbers to be mapped
218:              onto physical pages 0 through 3.  If any parameter = -1, then NO
219:              mapping is done to that physical page.
220:
221:              */
222:
223:    d frame   struc                             ;Stack frame template.
224:    dbptr     dw        ?                       ;Base pointer.
225:    dret_ad   dw        ?                       ;Return address.
226:    log0      dw        ?                       ;Logical page -> physical page 0.
227:    log1      dw        ?                       ;Logical page -> physical page 1.
228:    log2      dw        ?                       ;Logical page -> physical page 2.
229:    log3      dw        ?                       ;Logical page -> physical page 3.
230:    d frame   ends
231:
232:              push      bp
233:              mov       bp, sp
234:
235:              push      si
236:
237:              cmp       emm_alloc, 0            ;Test if memory has been allocated.
238:              jne       d01
239:              mov       ax, -1                  ;Error, no memory allocated!
240:              mov       _ems_err, 09            ;Set error code.
241:              jmp       d05
242:    d01:                                        ;Map 4 logical pages -> 4 physical pages.
243:              xor       cl, cl                  ;Physical page counter.
244:              mov       si, 0                   ;Index for accessing all 4 parameters.
245:    d02:
246:              mov       ah, 44h                 ;Call EMM to map page.
247:              mov       al, cl                  ;Physical page -> AL.
248:              mov       bx, ss:[bp+log0+si]     ;Logical page -> BX.
249:              cmp       bx, -1                  ;Test for dummy parameter.
250:              je        d03                     ;If parm = -1, go on to next one.
251:              mov       dx, emm_handle
252:              int       67h
253:              cmp       ah, 0                   ;Test for EMM error.
254:              je        d03
255:              call      err_rtn                 ;Set EMM error code.
256:              mov       ax, -1                  ;EMM error.
257:              jmp       d05                     ;Bail out.
258:    d03:
259:              inc       si                      ;Move to next parameter.
260:              inc       si
261:              inc       cl                      ;Next physical page.
262:              cmp       cl, 4                   ;Test for last physical page.
263:              jge       d04                     ;Last physical page, quit loop.
264:              jmp       d02                     ;Back for more mappings.
265:    d04:
266:              xor       ax, ax                  ;No error.
267:              mov       _ems_err, 00            ;Set error code: no errors.
268:    d05:
269:              pop       si
270:              pop       bp
271:              ret                               ;Return to C program.
272:
273:    _emap     endp
274:
275:
276:    _esave    proc      near                    ;Save page map.
277:
278:    comment   /*
279:              This function saves the current EMS state -- the values of
280:              registers on all EMS boards.  It returns 0 if successful.  If an
281:              error occurred, -1 is returned and 'ems_err' is set to one of the
282:              following values:
283:
284:              03        Software malfunction.
```

Figure 10.1: *An interface to expanded memory for C programs (continued)*

```
285:              04      Hardware malfunction.
286:              09      EMS memory not allocated.
287:              12      No room in save area.
288:              13      'Save' already called by this process.
289:
290:              int esave ();
291:
292:              */
293:
294:              cmp     emm_alloc, 0        ;Test if memory has been allocated.
295:              jne     e01
296:              mov     ax, -1              ;Error, no memory allocated!
297:              mov     _ems_err, 09        ;Set error code.
298:              jmp     e03                 ;Go to end.
299:     e01:                                 ;Call EMM to save page map.
300:              mov     ah, 47h
301:              mov     dx, emm_handle
302:              int     67h
303:              cmp     ah, 0               ;Test for EMM error.
304:              je      e02
305:              call    err_rtn             ;Set EMM error code.
306:              mov     ax, -1              ;EMM error.
307:              jmp     e03                 ;Go to end.
308:     e02:
309:              xor     ax, ax              ;No error.
310:              mov     _ems_err, 00        ;Set error code: no errors.
311:     e03:     ret                         ;Return to C program.
312:
313:     _esave   endp
314:
315:
316:     _erestore proc   near                ;Restores page map saved by 'esave'.
317:
318:     comment  /*
319:              This function restores the EMS state -- the values of registers
320:              on all EMS boards -- which was previously saved by 'esave.'  It
321:              returns 0 if successful.  If an error occurred, -1 is returned
322:              and 'ems_err' is set to one of the following values:
323:
324:              03      Software malfunction.
325:              04      Hardware malfunction.
326:              09      EMS memory not allocated.
327:              14      'erestore' called without prior 'esave'.
328:
329:              int erestore ();
330:
331:              */
332:
333:              cmp     emm_alloc, 0        ;Test if memory has been allocated.
334:              jne     f01
335:              mov     ax, -1              ;Error, no memory allocated!
336:              mov     _ems_err, 09        ;Set error code.
337:              jmp     f03                 ;Go to end.
338:     f01:                                 ;Call EEM to restore page map.
339:              mov     ah, 48h
340:              mov     dx, emm_handle
341:              int     67h
342:              cmp     ah, 0               ;Test for EMM error.
343:              je      f02
344:              call    err_rtn             ;Set EMM error code.
345:              mov     ax, -1              ;EMM error.
346:              jmp     f03                 ;Go to end.
347:     f02:
348:              xor     ax, ax              ;No error.
349:              mov     _ems_err, 00        ;Set error code: no errors.
350:     f03:     ret
351:
352:     _erestore endp
353:
354:
355:     err_table db      03                 ;80h  Software malfunction.
```

Figure 10.1: *An interface to expanded memory for C programs (continued)*

```
356:              db       04              ;81h  Hardware malfunction.
357:              db       15              ;82h  Unidentified error.
358:              db       15              ;83h  Unidentified error.
359:              db       15              ;84h  Unidentified error.
360:              db       06              ;85h  No free handles.
361:              db       10              ;86h  'Esave', no 'Erestore'.
362:              db       07              ;87h  Insufficient EMS pages.
363:              db       07              ;88h  Insufficient EMS pages.
364:              db       08              ;89h  0 page request.
365:              db       11              ;8Ah  Log. page out of range.
366:              db       15              ;8Bh  Unidentified error.
367:              db       12              ;8Ch  No save room.
368:              db       13              ;8Dh  'Save' already called.
369:              db       14              ;8Eh  'Erestore' w/out 'esave'.
370:
371:   MAX_ERR    equ      $ - err_table   ;Largest error number.
372:
373:
374:   err_rtn    proc     near            ;Sets 'ems_err' to current EMM error.
375:
376:   comment    /*
377:              This function translates an EMM error into the appropriate error
378:              code for the C Interface, and assigns the value to the global error
379:              variable 'ems_err'.  It is for internal use only and is not to be
380:              called from C.
381:
382:              */
383:
384:              push     ax
385:              push     bx
386:
387:              cmp      ah, 0           ;Test for "no error."
388:              jne      g00
389:              mov      _ems_err, 0     ;Assign code for "no error."
390:              jmp      g02             ;Go to exit.
391:
392:   g00:       xor      bh, bh          ;0 upper order byte of BX.
393:              mov      bl, ah          ;Place error code in BL.
394:              and      bl, 7fh         ;Mask off upper bit of error code.
395:              cmp      bl, MAX_ERR     ;Test if error code within defined range.
396:              jle      g01             ;Range OK.
397:              mov      _ems_err, 15    ;Unidentified error.
398:              jmp      g02             ;Go to end.
399:   g01:                                ;Use BX as index to error table.
400:              mov      al, cs:err_table [bx]
401:              cbw                      ;'ems_err' is a word.
402:              mov      _ems_err, ax    ;Assign 'ems_err'.
403:   g02:
404:              pop      bx
405:              pop      ax
406:              ret
407:
408:   err_rtn    endp
409:
410:
411:   _text      ends
412:              end
413:
414:
```

Figure 10.1: *An interface to expanded memory for C programs (continued)*

expanded memory, each having its own identifying handle. Generally, however, a program simply allocates a single block of expanded memory at the beginning of the code, and deallocates it at the end. For the sake of simplicity, the interface stores only a single handle, and returns an error code (05, "EMS memory already allocated by this process") if the application attempts to allocate memory a second time with **ealloc** (unless it has been deallocated in the meanwhile with **efree**).

Translation of Error Codes

The EMM functions all return a status code in register AH. The interface of Figure 10.1, however, provides its own set of error codes for two reasons. First, the interface supplies a number of error codes not provided by the EMM, such as "Expanded memory not installed." Also, a correctly written interface will prevent some of the possible EMM errors and can therefore dispense with the corresponding error codes; for example, "Invalid EMM handle" (83h) and "Invalid function code" (84h).

All of the assembler functions in Figure 10.1 return special values to the C program when an error occurs (such as 0, NULL, or – 1). The assembler functions also assign an error code to the external variable **ems_err**, which is defined in the C program. Therefore, when the C program detects that an error has occurred, it may test this global variable to determine the exact error. The comments at the beginning of each assembler function specify the possible error codes that may be returned by that function. The complete set of interface error codes and the corresponding EMM errors (if present) is given in Table 10.1.

The errors fall into two categories:

1. Those that are detected by the interface itself; for example, "Expanded memory not installed" or "EMS memory already allocated by this process." In this case, the function simply assigns the appropriate error code to **ems_err**.

2. Errors detected by the EMM, which are indicated by a nonzero value returned in register AH by an EMM function call. In this case, the interface function calls **err_rtn** (line 374), which translates the EMM error code into the appropriate interface error code and then assigns the value to **ems_err**. The translation is accomplished through use of the mapping **error_table** beginning on line 355. Note that all EMM status codes returned in AH have the high-order bit set (except the code for "no error," which is 00); therefore, **err_rtn** must mask off the high bit before using the value as an index into the error table.

"Unidentified" error is a catchall for errors that should theoretically not occur.

Interface Error Codes:		Corresponding EMM Errors:
00	No error	
01	Expanded memory not installed	
02	No free expanded memory pages	
03	Software malfunction	80h
04	Hardware malfunction	81h
05	EMS memory already allocated by this process	
06	No EMM handles free	85h
07	Insufficient EMS pages to fill request	87h/88h
08	Attempt to allocate 0 pages	89h
09	EMS memory not allocated	
10	**esave** called without subsequent **erestore**	86h
11	Logical page out of range allocated to process	8Ah
12	No room in save area	8Ch
13	**save** already called by process	8Dh
14	**erestore** called without prior **esave**	8Eh
15	Unidentified error	

Table 10.1: *Error Codes Used by the C Interface*

The Interface Functions

This section summarizes each of the functions provided by the C interface.

ememavail (lines 34–89)

The function **ememavail** returns the number of EMM logical pages that are available for allocation to the program. The possible error codes assigned to **emm_err** are 00, 01, 02, 03, and 04. It will return 0 for a variety of reasons, namely:

- EMM is not installed (**emm_err** = 01).

- All pages of expanded memory have already been allocated (**emm_err** = 01).

- A software or hardware error occurred (**emm_err** = 03 or 04).

The function **ememavail** consists of two main parts. First is a test to determine whether expanded memory is installed (lines 54 to 67). The official specification recommends two possible methods. One technique is to attempt to open the EMM as a device (remember that it has been installed as a character device driver). This method, however, cannot be employed by memory-resident code such as device drivers that are not free to call DOS. The second method is to use interrupt vector 67h; if the EMM has been installed, the segment portion of this vector will contain the segment address of the EMM device header, and the device name EMMXXXX0 will be found at offset 0Ah. This method can be used by any program, and is the simpler of the two. Therefore, **ememavail** uses the second technique.

Second, if it is determined that expanded memory is installed, EMM function 3 is called to determine the number of free logical pages. EMM function 3 uses the following calling conventions:

EMM Function 3: Get unallocated logical page count

Entry:

AH   42h

Return:

AH   Error code

BX   Number of free pages

DX   Total number of pages of expanded memory

ealloc (lines 92–155)

The function **ealloc** allocates expanded memory to the calling process. It takes a single integer parameter containing the requested number of logical pages, and returns a far (i.e., 32-bit) pointer to the first byte of the expanded memory page frame. It returns the value NULL (= 0) to indicate an error; possible error values assigned to **ems_err** are 00, 03, 04, 05, 06, 07, and 08.

The function **ealloc** performs four steps. First, it tests the flag **emm_alloc** to see if expanded memory is currently allocated to the calling program. Once expanded memory has been allocated to a program, it may not be allocated again unless **efree** is subsequently called (which resets **emm_alloc**).

Second, lines 129–136 call EMM function 4 to perform the actual allocation:

EMM Function 4: Allocate logical pages

Entry:

AH   43h

BX   Number of logical pages to allocate

Return:

AH   Error code

DX   EMM handle

Third, once expanded memory has been successfully allocated, the flag **emm_alloc** is set to 1 and the handle is saved in the variable **emm_handle** (lines 138 and 139). When **emm_alloc** is equal to 1, other interface functions know that **emm_handle** currently contains a valid handle, which may be safely passed to the EMM.

The fourth and final step is that lines 141–147 call EMM function 2 to obtain the segment address of the expanded memory page frame:

EMM Function 2: Get segment address of page frame

Entry:

AH   41h

Return:

AH   Error code

BX   Segment address of page frame

Note that a function interfacing with C returns a far pointer by placing the segment:offset values in registers DX:AX. In this case, the segment is obtained from the EMM, and the offset is 0. To return a NULL pointer value, both DX and AX are assigned 0.

efree (lines 158–195)

The function **efree** frees all expanded memory pages previously allocated to the process by **ealloc**. It returns 0 if no error occurred, and a

−1 to indicate an error. The possible error codes that may be assigned to **ems_err** are 00, 03, 04, 09, and 10. See the following descriptions of **esave** and **erestore** for an explanation of error code 10, "**esave** without subsequent **erestore**."

The function **efree** performs three major tasks. First, lines 174–178 test the global flag **emm_alloc** to make sure that **alloc** has been called, and a valid handle obtained.

Second, lines 180–187 call EMM function 6 to perform the memory deallocation:

EMM Function 6: Deallocate logical pages

Entry:

AH   45h

DX   EMM handle

Return:

AH   Error code

Third, on line 189, the flag **ems_alloc** is assigned 0. This value will signal **ealloc** that memory can now be allocated again, but will warn other functions (such as **emap**) that **emm_handle** does not contain a valid handle.

emap (lines 198–273)

emap is the only interface function that is typically called more than once during the execution of a program, and is used to map logical pages of expanded memory onto the four physical pages of the page frame. It accepts four integer parameters, which contain the logical page numbers to be mapped onto physical pages 0 through 3. If any of the parameters contains −1, then the mapping for the corresponding physical page is left unaltered. For example,

emap (3, −1, 4, 5);

would map logical page 3 onto physical page 0, logical page 4 onto physical page 2, logical page 5 onto physical page 3, and would leave the mapping for physical page 1 unaltered.

The function returns 0 if no error occurred, and a −1 to indicate an error. The possible error codes that may be assigned to **ems_err** are 00, 03, 04, 09, and 11.

emap performs two tasks. First, lines 237–241 test the flag **emm_alloc** to make sure that expanded memory has been successfully allocated to the program. The remainder of the program contains a loop that calls

EMM function 5 once for each parameter that does not equal −1. Function 5 uses the following calling conventions:

EMM Function 5: Map logical page onto physical page

Entry:

AH   44h

AL   The physical page onto which the logical page is to be mapped (0 ... 3)

BX   Logical page number

DX   The EMM handle

Return:

AH   Error code

esave (lines 276–313)

The function **esave** causes the EMM to save the current mapping (the values of all EMS registers) in an internal area associated with the handle that is passed. When **erestore** (described next) is subsequently called with the same handle, the saved values are restored to the registers. This pair of functions is thus useful for memory-resident code that may interrupt another program that is using expanded memory. Before the mapping is altered, the existing state should be saved with **esave**; it is later restored with **erestore** prior to returning to the interrupted program.

Note that when **efree** is called (after which the file handle is no longer valid), if **esave** has been called but not **erestore**, error code 10 is returned because **erestore** must be called before **efree** (while the EMM handle is still valid).

The function returns 0 if successful and −1 if an error occurred. The possible error codes that may be assigned to **ems_err** are 00, 03, 04, 09, 12, and 13.

esave performs two primary tasks. First, on lines 294–298, it checks **emm_alloc** to verify that expanded memory has been successfully allocated and that **emm_handle** therefore contains a valid handle. The remainder of the procedure simply calls EMM function 8 to cause the EMM to save the page mapping.

EMM Function 8: Save current page mapping

Entry:

AH   47h

DX   The EMM handle

Return:

AH   Error code

erestore (lines 316–352)

The function **erestore** is the restoration counterpart to **esave**; it restores the mapping saved by **esave** for a specified EMM handle. Its use was described under **esave**. This function also returns 0 if successful and −1 if an error occurred. The possible codes that may be assigned to **emm_err** are 00, 03, 04, 09, and 14.

Like **esave**, **erestore** also executes two primary tasks. On lines 333–337, it checks **emm_alloc** to verify that expanded memory has been successfully allocated and that **emm_handle** therefore contains a valid handle. Second, it calls EMM function 9 to restore the page mapping:

> **EMM Function 9: Restore saved page mapping**
>
> **Entry:**
>
> AH   48h
>
> DX   The EMM handle. This should be the same handle that was passed when the mapping was saved.
>
> **Return:**
>
> AH   Error code

A Possible Enhancement

An additional function might be added to the C interface: one that returns the version number of the EMM that is installed. This capability would be important for applications that are not compatible with certain versions of the EMM. The function could be easily implemented using EMM function 7:

> **EMM Function 7: Get EMM version number**
>
> **Entry:**
>
> AH   46h
>
> **Return:**
>
> AH   Error code

AL   Version number: the high-order four bits containing the digit before the decimal point, and the low-order four bits containing the digit after the decimal point.

Using Expanded Memory from a C Program

This section discusses using expanded memory from both transient and memory-resident C programs.

Transient Applications

The C program in Figure 10.2 demonstrates the basic sequence of steps required to use expanded memory from a typical *transient application,* a program that relinquishes the memory it occupies after it finishes running. The tasks should be performed in the order that follows.

First, use the function **ememavail** to determine whether expanded memory is installed, and if it is installed, to determine the number of free pages that can be allocated. The demo program simply quits if insufficient expanded memory is available; most real applications, however, use expanded memory if it is available, or carry on without it if it is unavailable (for whatever reason).

The second step is to allocate the required number of pages of expanded memory by calling **ealloc**. Unlike the standard C memory allocation functions (such as **malloc**), which can be called repeatedly during the course of a program, the recommended strategy for expanded memory is to allocate all required pages with a single request and then to deallocate all expanded memory with a single function call at the end of the program.

Third, access expanded memory by first calling **emap** to map logical pages onto the page frame, and then perform normal (**far**) read and write operations on addresses within the page frame, using the pointer returned by **ealloc**, plus the required offset. **emap** is the only expanded memory function that should be called repeatedly during the program. Typical access to expanded memory consists of a cycle of mapping, reading/writing, and remapping.

Note that expanded memory can be used to store both data and code; the only object that should not be located in expanded memory is the program stack. The DOS EXEC function 4Bh will not, however, load a program or overlay into the area of memory occupied by the page frame;

```
/*
        File:      EMSTEST.C

        A C Program demonstrating the use of the LIM-EMS C interface

        This program must be compiled using the COMPACT memory model, and must
        be linked with the assembler EMS interface EMS.ASM (Figure 10.1).
        To generate program from EMSTEST.C and EMS.ASM:

            cl /c /AC EMSTEST.C          use COMPACT memory model
            masm EMS;
            link EMSTEST+EMS;
*/

#include <stdio.h>
#include <string.h>

                                    /* Assembler EMS Interface functions   */
int ememavail (void);               /* (listed in Figure 10.1).            */
char far * ealloc (int);
int efree (void);
int emap (int, int, int, int);
int esave (void);
int erestore (void);

void exit (int);                    /* Other functions.                    */
char *err_desc (int);

int ems_err = 0;                    /* Global EMS error code.              */


#define PAGE0 0                     /* Offsets of physical pages in EMS    */
#define PAGE1 0x4000                /* page frame.                         */
#define PAGE2 0x8000
#define PAGE3 0xC000

void main ()
    {
    char *emsbase;                  /* Pointer to base of page frame.     */

    /**************************************************************************
        (1) Test if sufficient EMS memory is available to run program.
    **************************************************************************/

    if (ememavail () < 4)
        {
        if (ems_err == 0)           /* No error, but memory insufficient. */
            printf ("insufficient EMS memory to run demo\n");
        else                        /* 0 pages available, or error.       */
            printf ("%s\n", err_desc (ems_err));
        exit (1);                   /* Bail out with errorlevel 1.        */
        }

    /**************************************************************************
        (2) Allocate EMS memory.
    **************************************************************************/
```

Figure 10.2: *A C program demonstrating the use of the expanded memory interface*

```
                                    /* Allocate 4 logical pages of EMS    */
                                    /* memory and assign pointer to base of */
                                    /* page frame.                        */
        if ((emsbase = ealloc (4)) == NULL)
            {
            printf ("%s\n", err_desc (ems_err));
            exit (1);               /* Bail out with errorlevel 1.        */
            }

        /***********************************************************************
            (3)   Access EMS memory.
        ***********************************************************************/

                                    /* Map logical pages to physical pages. */
                                    /* Maps first 4 logical pages to first  */
                                    /* 4 physical pages.                  */
        if (emap (0, 1, 2, 3) == -1)
            {
            printf ("%s\n", err_desc (ems_err));
            exit (1);               /* Bail out with errorlevel 1.        */
            }

                                    /* Write a string to each page.       */
        strcpy (emsbase+PAGE0, "logical page zero");
        strcpy (emsbase+PAGE1, "logical page one");
        strcpy (emsbase+PAGE2, "logical page two");
        strcpy (emsbase+PAGE3, "logical page three");

                                    /* Remap logical pages to physical pages.*/
        if (emap (3, 2, 1, 0) == -1)
            {
            printf ("%s\n", err_desc (ems_err));
            exit (1);               /* Bail out with errorlevel 1.        */
            }

                                    /* Print contents of 4 physical pages. */
        printf ("%s\n",emsbase+PAGE0);
        printf ("%s\n",emsbase+PAGE1);
        printf ("%s\n",emsbase+PAGE2);
        printf ("%s\n",emsbase+PAGE3);

        /***********************************************************************
            (4)   Deallocate EMS memory.
        ***********************************************************************/

        if (efree () == -1)
            {
            printf ("%s\n", err_desc (ems_err));
            exit (1);               /* Bail out with errorlevel 1.        */
            }

        } /* end main */

char *err_desc (code)           /* Returns a pointer to string containing the */
int code;                       /* description of error corresponding to 'code'. */
```

Figure 10.2: *A C program demonstrating the use of the expanded memory interface (continued)*

```
{
static char *err_list [] =
    {
    "No error.",
    "Expanded memory not installed.",
    "No free expanded memory pages.",
    "Software malfunction.",
    "Hardware malfunction.",
    "EMS memory already allocated by this process.",
    "No EMM handles free.",
    "Insufficient EMS pages to fill request.",
    "Attempt to allocate 0 pages.",
    "EMS memory not allocated.",
    "'esave' called without subsequent 'erestore'.",
    "Logical page out of range allocated to process.",
    "No room in save area.",
    "'Save' already called by process.",
    "'erestore' called without prior 'esave.'",
    "Unidentified error."
    };

return (err_list [code]);

} /* end print_err */
```

Figure 10.2: *A C program demonstrating the use of the expanded memory interface (continued)*

therefore, the program itself must perform all loading of code into expanded memory.

The demo program performs a trivial task in order to illustrate the mapping, reading/writing, and remapping cycle. It first maps logical pages 0–3 onto physical pages 0–3. It then writes identifying strings to the beginning of each logical page. The demo then calls **emap** again to remap logical pages 0–3 onto the four physical pages, this time in reverse order. Finally, it prints out the identifying strings from the beginning of each physical page, demonstrating that the logical pages have been reversed in memory and are now in the order 3, 2, 1, 0.

The fourth and final step is to deallocate expanded memory by calling **efree**. Note that EMS memory is *not* automatically released when the program terminates; in order to make expanded memory available for other applications, **efree** *must* be called before the end of the program.

The C demo program handles errors by printing the corresponding error message, using the global error code **ems_err** as an index into a table of error messages maintained by the function **err_desc**; the program then simply terminates with the error level set to 1. Normally, a program would test for the specific error and handle it appropriately, typically using a **switch** construct with a branch for each possible error (the list of possible errors for each function is documented above and in the source listings of Figure 10.1).

Note that the demo program is compiled using the *compact* memory model, which employs near addresses (16 bit) for code items, but far addresses (32 bit) for data items. The advantage of using the compact memory model is that **ealloc** returns a far pointer to the page frame, and addressing data within expanded memory requires far pointers. In the compact model, all pointers (such as **emsbase** on line 39) are automatically far, and library functions (such as **strcpy**) accept far pointer parameters.

It would also be possible to compile the program using the small memory model without making modifications to the assembler interface routines (these routines would have to be modified only for the medium, large, and huge models). The C program, however, would have to be changed in three ways.

First the pointer **emsbase**, which is assigned the starting address of the page frame returned by **ealloc** and is subsequently used to access expanded memory, would have to be explicitly declared as a far pointer as follows:

```
char far *emsbase;
```

Second, **strcpy**, **printf**, and other C library functions that expect near data pointer parameters could not be used to directly access expanded memory. Alternate routines would have to be substituted, or data would have to be first copied into a near buffer. For example, to copy a string to the beginning of expanded memory:

```
char *source;            /* Near source,        */
char far *destination;   /* but far destination. */
...
source = "string to copy to expanded memory";
destination = emsbase;
while (*destination++ = *source++)
    ;
```

Third, note that certain C library functions in the small memory model can be used to access expanded memory because they accept both segment and offset address values. An example is **movedata**, which would be an excellent function for transferring large amounts of data to or from expanded memory (use **memcpy** for the compact model).

Memory-Resident Applications

A memory-resident utility or device driver can also use expanded memory to great advantage; however, the sequence of steps is slightly different than that employed by a transient application such as that illustrated in the demonstration program of Figure 10.2. A memory-resident application should manage expanded memory through the following series of steps:

1. The initialization code (which is typically called only once when the application is loaded into memory) should invoke **ememavail** to determine the availability of expanded memory, and then call **ealloc** to reserve the required number of pages. The program should allocate expanded memory at this time, before it gets snatched away by other applications.

2. Each time the memory-resident code is activated, it must first save the current EMM mapping state by calling **esave**. This is a vital procedure because the application that was interrupted by the memory-resident program may have been using expanded memory.

3. Once the current mapping has been saved, the memory-resident code may now access expanded memory using the standard cycle of mapping (**emap**), reading/writing, and remapping (**emap** again), as described earlier.

4. After the memory-resident code has completed its use of expanded memory, but before it terminates, it must restore the saved EMM mapping by calling **erestore**.

5. If the memory-resident application provides a mechanism for de-installation, which releases the conventional memory occupied by the program, at this time it should also free its allocation of expanded memory by calling **efree**.

See Chapter 11 for detailed information on memory-resident applications.

CHAPTER 11

MEMORY RESIDENCY

One of the major limitations of MS-DOS versions through 3.3 is the lack of support for multitasking. The terminate and stay-resident utility (TSR) is an ingenious device for at least partially overcoming this inherent limitation. A TSR is a program that loads itself into memory and returns control to DOS, but remains dormant in the background. When the user presses a designated key combination (the hotkey), the TSR comes to life, immediately interrupting whatever application is currently running, and allowing instant access to the services it offers. The TSR mechanism is currently extremely popular, and is used to implement a wide variety of programs including macro processors, desktop utilities, spelling checkers, thesauruses, and outliners. There are several paramount advantages to using TSRs instead of conventional programs that are loaded from the DOS command line (*transient applications*):

- Speed. Utilities such as notepads, calculators, spelling checkers, and outliners can be rapidly accessed without having to quit the current application, type a DOS command, and then restart the program. The speed savings is especially significant when a large and complex application is being run in the foreground.

- Data exchange. Many TSRs, especially notepad editors, macro processors, and outliners, allow the importing and exporting of data between the utility and the foreground application. These programs thus provide convenient channels for textual and graphic data exchange between dissimilar programs and files of heterogeneous format.

- Modularity. Loading a selected set of resident utilities, rather than running a single integrated package, allows the user to design an optimal computing environment. For example, a favorite word processor or program editor can be run in the foreground, and combined with a favorite memory-resident thesaurus, spelling checker, outliner, notepad, etc.

Multitasking environments such as Microsoft Windows offer an alternative to the TSR mechanism. Currently, however, these systems are less practical due to the limited supply of compatible utility software and because of their extreme slowness on an ordinary IBM PC/XT. At present, memory-resident utilities offer more flexibility and significantly greater performance.

MS-DOS machines have certain features that facilitate the development of TSRs, and other features that create problems for TSRs. One helpful resource is the DOS interrupt service that allows a program to terminate and remain resident in memory (number 31h). Another important feature is the channeling of hardware and software interrupts through a publicly available vector table, so that by replacing interrupt routines, a resident program can monitor both hardware events and software service requests.

The primary problematic aspect of MS-DOS for developing TSRs is the notorious and often cited fact that the DOS code is *nonreentrant*, meaning that the operating system kernel cannot be interrupted at an arbitrary point and have its code reused by another process. MS-DOS is not an operating system designed to handle simultaneous processes.

The first section of this chapter discusses the problems of implementing memory-resident programs under MS-DOS and some of the guidelines that can help overcome them. The second section describes the actual step-by-step methods for implementing a TSR by presenting a collection of assembler procedures that allow a C program to be made memory-resident. These procedures illustrate in detail a particular set of strategies for handling the problems of memory residency, especially that of allowing the memory-resident code to freely call MS-DOS functions. When this assembler module is linked to a C program, a single function call can convert a conventional C program into a TSR.

The Challenge of Writing a TSR

Developing a TSR is an adventure. The primary challenge is to write a memory-resident program that can peacefully coexist with other TSRs, with the operating system, with the interrupted foreground application, with BIOS disk activity, and with interrupt handlers. This section deals with these issues as well as the question of reentrancy, and presents the highlights of a proposed standard for writing TSRs.

Coexisting with Other TSRs

One of the principal advantages of the memory-resident mechanism is that several independent TSRs can be combined and used together. However, in their attempts to survive a hostile environment, these programs often resort to antisocial behavior, and one of the major problems of designing a new TSR is the possibility of conflicts with other memory-resident utilities that are present at runtime.

The occurrence of conflicts is not surprising since memory-resident programs must share hardware and software resources and interact intimately, and yet there has been no standard protocol or uniform set of guidelines for their development. The guidelines offered in this section will increase the chances that your TSR will operate successfully and will also make life easier for other TSRs; they cannot, however, guarantee that there will not be difficulties arising from other programs that do not follow the same set of rules. Among the specific areas of conflict are hotkey duplication, competition for available memory, and TSRs that do not properly chain to the other memory-resident programs that are currently installed.

Avoiding Hotkey Conflicts

Another TSR may be activated by the same key that you choose for your TSR, or the hotkey you select may be a control key used by some transient program. Which TSR is activated by a conflicting hotkey will usually depend on the loading order of the two programs. To avoid this difficulty, choose an uncommon default key combination, and also allow the user to change the hotkey to another value.

Conserving Memory

As the size and complexity of applications increases and the use of multiple TSRs becomes more common, memory is becoming an increasingly scarce resource. Within limitations, a transient program can use all available memory; however, because a TSR permanently reserves the memory it occupies, it should use as little memory as possible. The following measures can help reduce competition for available memory.

Whenever possible, allow the user to select the amount of memory reserved by the TSR when it is loaded.   For example, for a notepad or outliner, the user can choose the buffer size that is allocated for data (thereby setting the maximum file size that can be accommodated). Also, if a TSR contains more than one functional module, such as a desk accessory program that has a notepad, calendar, and dialer, let the user select any combination of modules to be loaded into memory.

Minimize memory demand by using disk files both for code overlays and as temporary holding areas for swapping data.   Note, however, that accessing the disk significantly decreases performance, and

□□■□

imposes a hardship particularly on the floppy disk user who must repeatedly insert the program disk when it is required. It might be best to restrict overlays and disk swapping to hard disk systems only.

If memory constraints are severe, consider writing the code entirely in assembly language.   Assembler not only can produce more compact code, but also allows the memory occupied by the initialization routine to be released after it has performed its function. Writing a TSR in C, using the assembler module described in the next section, makes it very easy to quickly develop a program; however, the C compiler normally generates larger code than a hand-written assembler program, especially if C library routines are called. Also, for reasons to be explained below, a TSR in C cannot release its initialization code.

Use expanded memory if it is available.   Expanded memory is ideal for TSRs, which can use it to store the bulk of their code and data, thus freeing conventional RAM for transient applications and other TSRs. The following sequence of steps illustrate an approach that might be taken to make optimal use of expanded memory for a resident program (see Chapter 10 for a general description of the use of expanded memory, and for a detailed description of the techniques).

1. The user loads the TSR from the DOS prompt. The initialization code then allocates all expanded memory required for both code and data.

2. The initialization code stores almost all of the program code and data within expanded memory pages. The actual interrupt handler, however, must remain in conventional memory because an interrupt vector should not point to an address within the expanded memory page frame (the contents of which are continually changing as various programs remap the pages).

3. When the TSR interrupt handler is activated, it saves the current page mapping (as explained in Chapter 10) and maps its own pages into the page frame. The program then has two options. First, it may simply transfer control to the code within the page frame and execute entirely within expanded memory (the stack, however, should be left in conventional RAM). Since the page frame is only 64K bytes, the program may need to use a carefully designed overlay system in order to swap in other pages of code and data as they are needed. Secondly, as an alternative approach, all code and data stored in expanded memory may be swapped into conventional memory (saving the current contents of

this memory back in expanded memory). The program may then execute normally, without the need for overlays. It would be best to use the high end of conventional RAM for this purpose, since this area is less likely to contain other TSRs. (Imagine what would happen if your code temporarily replaces another TSR in memory and the hotkey for that program is then pressed!)

4. When the TSR terminates, it restores the page mapping.

5. If the TSR is uninstalled, it frees all allocated expanded memory.

Chaining to Other TSRs

By not properly directing control, a miscreant TSR can totally disable its fellow memory-resident programs. Ideally, as multiple TSRs are loaded into memory, they are linked into a chain in which control is passed from program to program and none of the modules is bypassed. For example, consider a series of TSRs that replace the existing interrupt 16h vector (BIOS keyboard services). This interrupt is invoked by almost all programs to read a key from the keyboard, and is often intercepted by TSRs in order to detect when their hotkey has been pressed or to process characters coming from the keyboard. The first TSR that is loaded replaces the vector to the original BIOS code with a vector pointing to itself. It saves the original vector, and when it is activated it first calls the original routine and then performs its own tasks after the original routine has returned. Subsequently loaded routines insert themselves into the chain in a similar manner. The resulting structure is shown in Figure 11.1.

In this example, a transient application (or a TSR itself) has requested a keyboard read through BIOS interrupt 16h. The request is passed down the chain, eventually arriving at the BIOS code. The returned character is passed back up through the chain of TSRs, each of which may test for its hotkey or perform some other processing (e.g., a keyboard macro utility may translate characters). Note that if all TSRs observe the calling protocol indicated by this diagram, the returned character is passed from program to program in the order that the programs were installed. Therefore, if there is a conflict in hotkeys between two TSRs, the one that was installed first will receive the key, and the second one will be effectively disabled. Also, programs such as keyboard macro processors are considered *producers* and should normally be installed first (ending up at the BIOS end of the chain) so that they can properly translate the keystrokes that are then passed to the other TSRs.

To avoid breaking this chain, and to allow multiple TSRs to function together without disabling each other, two important rules should be

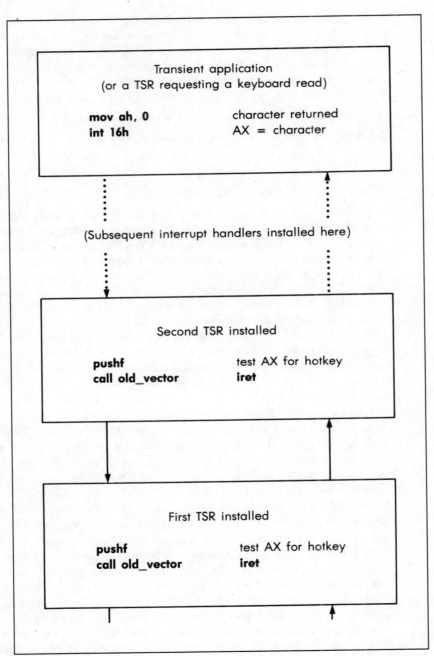

Figure 11.1: *Chain of TSRs on interrupt 16h*

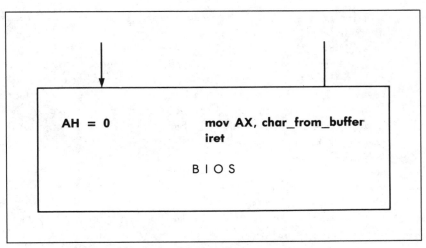

Figure 11.1: *Chain of TSRs on interrupt 16h (continued)*

observed. First, when a resident program replaces an interrupt service routine, it should always save the address of the former routine, and then call this routine at the onset of each activation. Thus, additional code may always be added to the sequence of events triggered by an interrupt, but an existing service routine is never eliminated. This rule prevents bypassing TSRs that were installed *before* the currently active one.

The second rule is that when a resident program itself requires an interrupt service, it should invoke the interrupt by number rather than simply calling the next routine on the chain. For example, if the routine labeled "First TSR installed" in Figure 11.1 wants to read the keyboard, it could simply call **old_vector** as a shortcut, immediately obtaining the desired character from the routine below it. Note, however, that this tactic totally bypasses "Second TSR installed" as well as any other subsequently installed TSRs, which would then not have an opportunity to monitor keyboard output and respond to appropriate keystrokes. If, however, the original interrupt 16h is invoked, both the request and the returned characters pass through *all* TSRs on the chain. This rule prevents bypassing TSRs that were installed *after* the currently active one.

The situation is actually more complex than implied by this illustration. One complication is the fact that some TSRs do not use interrupt 16h to watch for their hotkey, but rather intercept hardware interrupt number 09h, which is generated directly by keyboard activity (this method is used by the TSR shell described later). A TSR might also intercept a number of other interrupt vectors. SideKick, for example, replaces no less than 13 different vectors. However, no matter which interrupt vectors are used, the two rules above should be followed.

Note that if it is critical for a memory-resident program to receive early access to system resources, and avoid competition with other TSRs that are loaded from the command line, you can write the code as a device driver so that it will be installed by MS-DOS during booting. An example of a program that uses this strategy is the Expanded Memory Manager discussed in Chapter 10. See Chapter 9 for a complete description of installable device drivers.

Note also that under PC-DOS version 4.0 you can load a terminate and stay resident utility during system startup using the INSTALL command. This command is placed in the CONFIG.SYS file; you must supply the name of the program and any parameters that are passed. Loading a TSR from the configuration file results in a more efficient use of memory than loading it from the command line or from a batch file.

Coexisting with MS-DOS

The next and perhaps greatest challenge in designing a TSR is to make it compatible with the MS-DOS operating system so that the memory-resident program can freely use DOS interrupt services. The source of the problem with using MS-DOS services from within a TSR is twofold: the activation of a TSR is an asynchronous event, and the MS-DOS code is not reentrant.

Asynchronous activation   An asynchronous event is one that can occur at almost any time, regardless of the current state of the machine or the present active process. The very purpose of a TSR demands that it be able to interrupt any program and jump into the foreground at any moment the hotkey is pressed. The activation of a TSR through the hardware keyboard interrupt (09h) can occur at any time the interrupts are enabled, and is therefore clearly asynchronous. Some TSRs are activated through the software keyboard interrupt (16h), and can thus be triggered only when a program is reading the keyboard. Interrupt 16h is issued so frequently, however, that this event can also be considered virtually asynchronous.

Nonreentrant DOS code   As an asynchronous event, the triggering of a TSR can occur while MS-DOS is executing as well as during the execution of any other process (the MS-DOS code generally leaves interrupts enabled, and frequently reads the keyboard). This event can create a problem for the following reason. When an MS-DOS routine begins execution, it normally switches to an internal stack by first saving the current SS:SP values in memory variables, and then resetting SS:SP to point to the *top* of an internal DOS stack. As execution proceeds, the stack is of course used for the temporary storage of data. Consider the following scenario: the user now presses a hotkey and a TSR interrupts DOS and takes control. The TSR itself then calls a DOS service routine; the DOS routine will again switch to the *top* of an internal stack, quite possibly the same stack that is already being used to contain temporary data (DOS functions use one of only three internal stacks). The DOS function operates normally, and returns control to the TSR. When, however, the TSR returns control to the original invocation of DOS, the internal stack is now corrupted, and the subsequent behavior of the system is totally unpredictable (and usually results in a system failure).

What is the solution to the problem of using DOS from within a TSR? There are two possible approaches.

The first tactic would be to totally eliminate the use of DOS functions from within the memory-resident code. You would have to write all routines using BIOS services and lower-level techniques. This approach, however, is quite limiting, and the greatest loss would be that of the DOS file services. It would also be very difficult to write the program in C (as in the TSR shell presented below) because many important C library functions use MS-DOS routines.

A more felicitous approach would be to somehow postpone the activation of the TSR until MS-DOS is inactive. Once it is known that DOS is not executing, the TSR can be activated and can make free use of all DOS function calls with impunity. How is it possible to determine whether DOS is currently executing? MS-DOS itself provides a solution through the undocumented but well-known interrupt 21h, function number 34h. This interrupt returns a pointer to a flag maintained by DOS, which indicates whether the DOS code is currently active. This **indos** flag is actually a counter, indicating the number of recursive entries that have been made into the DOS code (DOS can call *itself* under controlled conditions without the difficulties discussed above). If **indos** is 0, then DOS is not active, and if it is greater than 0, DOS is active and its code has been entered one or more times. The calling protocol for function 34h is as follows:

Entry:

AH = 34h

Return:

ES   Segment of **indos**

BX   Offset of **indos**

This function should be called in the initialization code that installs the TSR, and the double word pointer to the **indos** flag saved where it may subsequently be accessed by the interrupt handler. The interrupt handler can easily test **indos** by means of the saved pointer, and does not have to call the interrupt again (in fact, since this is a DOS function, it may not be safe to call it at this time).

Consider the following simplified sequence of events: the interrupt handler (either interrupt 09h or 16h, as explained below) detects that the hotkey has been depressed. It now tests the **indos** flag through the double word pointer that has been saved in the code segment. If this flag equals 0, the interrupt handler activates the main body of the TSR code (which is now free to call DOS). If, however, the flag is greater than 0, the TSR is *not* activated and the interrupt handler has several choices.

First, it can simply ignore the hotkey and return; this is a simple approach, but one that may leave the user wondering what happened to the TSR (this method is chosen by the program listed later in the chapter in Figure 11.3 because of its simplicity).

Second, it can notify the user in some way that the TSR cannot currently be activated. One well-known desktop utility signals this situation by chirping like a wounded bird.

Third, it can set an internal flag (the **activate** flag) to indicate that the TSR is to be activated as soon as it is safe. If this flag is turned on, each time the interrupt handler is invoked, it will check whether DOS is free. If DOS is free, it will activate the TSR. The programmer might also install a handler for an interrupt that is frequently and regularly invoked, such as the clock tick interrupt (08h), which would likewise activate the TSR if the activate flag is on and DOS is not busy. One troubling aspect to this technique is that there can be a significant delay between the time the user presses the hotkey and the time the TSR finally activates, and the TSR can spring to life rather unexpectedly.

Thus far it may seem a rather trivial task to protect a TSR from interrupting MS-DOS. However, there is another serious problem: when COMMAND.COM displays its prompt and waits for user input, the **indos** flag is set to 1 (COMMAND.COM is using a DOS service to read the keyboard!). Therefore, the protection scheme described above, although it would be quite safe, would also prevent the TSR from being triggered from the DOS prompt. It is relatively safe, however, to interrupt DOS at this time, and therefore this is an unacceptable limitation.

What is needed is a method for allowing the TSR to be activated when **indos** is greater than 0, but only if DOS is sitting at its prompt waiting for user input.

Again, MS-DOS itself provides a solution. Whenever DOS is in an idle state, waiting for user input at the prompt, it continually invokes interrupt 28h; this interrupt is used to activate such background processes as print spooling. For the TSR programmer, it is an indication that it is relatively safe to interrupt DOS. By installing an interrupt 28h handler, the overall strategy would now be as follows: When the main TSR interrupt handler (which can be invoked at almost any time) detects the hotkey, it activates the TSR only if **indos** is 0. When the interrupt 28h handler (which is invoked only when DOS is idle) detects the hotkey, it activates the TSR regardless of the state of the **indos** flag.

There is one further precaution that must now be taken. As mentioned earlier, interrupting DOS through interrupt 28h is only relatively safe. It is still dangerous for the TSR to call DOS functions 01h to 0Ch because these functions use the same stack that DOS was using when interrupted at the prompt. This group of services, however, is employed by C library functions such as **getch** and **getche**. In order to allow the use of these routines, the TSR preparation code needs to take one last and rather drastic measure: it must save the current DOS stack on the TSR's local stack, and then restore it on termination. See the TSR shell program in Figure 11.3 for a rather shotgun approach to preserving the DOS stack. (At this point, it has probably occurred to the astute reader that if the entire DOS stack is always saved, it would be safe to interrupt DOS at any time, and it is not even necessary to check **indos**. However, it is safest to interrupt DOS only when it is idle; during a disk operation, for example, DOS is especially vulnerable.)

The peaceful coexistence of a TSR with MS-DOS requires a few final measures. When DOS loads a program, it assumes that it will continue to run until it is called once again to terminate the program. While the program is running, DOS maintains certain internal information regarding this process. If a TSR asynchronously interrupts the current program, DOS is uninformed of the change and some of its internal information thus becomes incorrect. Two of the values maintained by DOS are the program segment prefix (PSP) and the disk transfer area (DTA).

The PSP   DOS maintains an internal record of the segment address of the program segment prefix of the currently executing process. As described in Chapter 6, the PSP is used to maintain information regarding the associated process. When a TSR interrupts a program, DOS will continue to use the PSP belonging to the interrupted program instead of that belonging to the TSR. Ideally, the TSR should temporarily change DOS's internal record of the PSP. There is a documented function available only under DOS 3.0 and later to *get* the value of the PSP (62h) (see the DOS technical reference). There are also undocumented functions available under DOS 2.0 and later to get the PSP (51h) and to set the PSP (50h). The function 51h is called as follows:

Function 51h: Get current PSP (undocumented)

Entry:

AH   51h

Return:

BX   Segment address of current PSP

An example of this function is:

```
mov     ah, 51h
int     21h
mov     cs:old_psp, bx
```

Function 50h: Set PSP (undocumented)

Entry:

AH   50h
BX   Segment address of new PSP

Return:

Nothing

As an example,

```
mov     ah, 50h
mov     bx, __psp ;
        This would set up the PSP for a C program.
int     21h
```

The TSR shell program in Figure 11.3 does not attempt to change DOS's record of the PSP; remember, however, that if this approach is taken, your TSR is borrowing the PSP belonging to some other unknown process. Specifically, if files are opened, DOS will use the file handle table belonging to the other process, which might not contain a sufficient number of free file handles. Therefore, the TSR should open as few files as possible and *close them all before termination;* ideally, it should open only one file at a time, and then immediately close it.

The DTA   As discussed in Chapter 6, the disk transfer area is the memory buffer used by DOS for transferring file data with the file control block functions, and also for the find matching file functions 4Eh and 4Fh. DOS maintains an internal record of the segment:offset address of the current DTA, which should be temporarily changed if the TSR uses a DTA for any operation (the former value should be saved and restored). Obtaining and setting the DTA can be accomplished through DOS functions 2Fh and 1Ah (see the DOS technical reference).

A final point concerning harmony with MS-DOS: Remember that these routines are not compatible with version 1.*x*. It is therefore a good idea for the initialization routine to check the operating system version (through function 30h, explained in Chapter 7); if the version is pre-2.*x*, then the program should print an error message and quit.

Note that the issues discussed above relate only to compatibility with MS-DOS. There are other factors, discussed in the following section, that should be tested before it can be deemed safe to activate the main body of TSR code. The TSR shell program presented in Figure 11.3 demonstrates the use of a complete set of tests within a working program.

The guidelines presented so far have focused on the peaceful coexistence of the TSR with other memory-resident programs installed on the interrupt chain and with the operating system. The TSR, however, must also interact smoothly with several other elements in the system, including the foreground program that is interrupted, BIOS disk activity, and interrupt handlers.

🔳 Coexisting with the Foreground Program

As mentioned before, the activation of a TSR is an asynchronous event. Since the TSR can interrupt the foreground program at any moment, it must be extremely thorough in saving the existing machine state. There are three parts to the machine state that must be preserved: the registers, the video display, and the DOS parameters.

Preserving the Registers

It is imperative that *all* registers be saved and restored by the TSR. The only registers that do not need to be explicitly saved in the TSR activation code are the instruction pointer (IP), the code segment (CS), and the flags, since these registers are automatically saved and restored by the **int** and **iret** machine instructions.

Preserving the Video Display

If the TSR writes to the screen, it must save the complete existing video state, set the display to the appropriate video mode, and then restore the complete video state before exit. There are three distinct elements of the video state that must be preserved: the video mode, the cursor parameters, and the screen data.

Preserving the video mode and display page   The current video mode and display page can be found through BIOS interrupt 10h, function 15. This task is performed by the C function **getmode** in Figure 5.1. Before the TSR terminates, interrupt 10h function 0 can be used to restore the video mode, and function 5 can be used to restore the display page. The C function **setmode** in Figure 5.1 restores both of these values.

Preserving the cursor parameters   A TSR must preserve both the cursor position and the cursor "style" (i.e., the start and stop lines used to generate the cursor). BIOS interrupt 10h function 3 gets both of these values, function 2 sets the cursor position, and function 1 sets the cursor style. Both sets of parameters can be saved and restored using the functions **getcur** and **setcur** in Figure 5.1. Note that the cursor parameters are obtained for a specific video page; therefore, it is necessary to first obtain the current active display page, as just described.

Preserving screen data   The method for preserving screen data depends on whether the current video mode of the interrupted program is a text or graphics mode.

If the video mode of the interrupted program is found to be one of the standard text modes (modes 0, 1, 2, 3, or 7), saving and restoring the screen data is no great trick. It is possible to preserve only the portion of the screen actually overwritten by the TSR, but if the area is more than a few lines, it is generally easier to save the entire screen. There are two methods for reading data directly off the screen, and then restoring it back to the screen.

The first method is to use BIOS interrupt 10h function 8, which reads the character and attribute at the current cursor position. Move the cursor to each position that is to be saved, reading and storing each character and attribute. Similarly, restore the display before program termination using function 9, which writes a character and attribute at the current cursor position. This method is suitable for preserving small areas of the display, but it is hideously slow for moving entire screens.

The second method for preserving the screen is to use direct writes from and to video memory. This approach is blazingly fast, and is discussed at great length in Chapter 8. A simple way to save and restore the entire screen is to call the assembler functions **pushscr** and **popscr**, which can be invoked from a C or assembler program, and appear in Figure 8.12.

If the video mode is found to be one of the graphics modes (4, 5, 6, 8, 9, 10, 13, 14, 15, and 16), preserving screen data is not so simple. Text modes use an area of video memory consisting of only 4000 bytes. The memory mapping for graphics modes on a CGA card, however, has a size of 16K bytes, and an EGA adapter has up to 256K bytes of video memory. Therefore, to save the data for the entire screen when switching out of a graphics mode can require a tremendous amount of memory (and memory use should be minimized in a TSR).

If the TSR uses only text output, it might seem that it would be necessary to save and restore only the 4000-byte area of video RAM actually overwritten by the TSR. The problem, however, is that when the standard CGA BIOS is called to switch the display into a text mode, it erases the current screen data. The following are three possible solutions to the problem of displaying a TSR over a program in a graphics mode.

The first solution is to sacrifice the underlying display whenever the TSR is popped up over a program in a graphics mode. Simply save the current graphics mode, switch into text mode at the beginning of the TSR, and then restore the graphics mode before exiting, using the BIOS functions mentioned earlier. This option would mean that when the user activates the TSR, the existing screen is erased, and must somehow be regenerated after returning to the main application.

A second solution is as follows. Save only the area of video memory that is actually going to be overwritten by the TSR; assuming that the display uses text mode, this would be within the 4000 bytes beginning at segment address B800h. Use the BIOS to determine the current mode as described above, but when switching into a text mode, write a routine that bypasses the BIOS and directly programs the mode on the video controller chip (for the CGA, this is the 6845). Such a routine should include all of the tasks performed by the BIOS mode setting procedure, except for erasing the screen data. This routine must:

- Program the Color-Select register for the appropriate mode (for the CGA, this port is at I/O address 3D8h)

- Set all other register values according to the parameters found in the BIOS video initialization table (the address of this table is pointed to by interrupt vector 1Dh, as explained in Chapter 6)

- Update all BIOS video parameters (these parameters begin at address 0400h:0049h, and are described in Chapter 6)

The procedure will vary depending on the specific mode switch that must be made. Before attempting to write such a routine, consult the BIOS source listing (in the PC, the mode changing procedure is labeled **SET_MODE** and begins at offset F0FCh). This listing can be found in the PC/AT technical references. Also consult the register information in the CGA section of the *Options and Adapters Technical Reference, Volume 2.* (These manuals are cited in Appendix H.)

A third method of preserving the current contents of video memory is available only with the EGA BIOS. Again, save the 4000 bytes of video memory that will be overwritten by the TSR in text mode. Then, when invoking interrupt 10h function 0 to change the mode, set the high-order bit of register AL; this will cause the EGA routine to save the current video memory data.

The situation becomes even more complex in the presence of alternative graphics modes. A Hercules graphics mode, for example, is not indicated by the standard BIOS video parameters, nor is it reported by the BIOS function to get the current video mode (function 15). In order to maintain compatibility with such graphics standards, it is necessary to use proprietary tests to detect the mode, and to program specific ports to switch modes. TSRs often fail miserably when activated over nonstandard graphics modes, especially in the presence of "clones" of the original adapter cards, which typically contain subtle differences. See Chapter 7 for information on detecting the video adapter type, and consult the documentation for the specific graphics adapter.

Following is a summary of the basic steps required to save and restore the complete video state:

1. Save the current video mode and active display page.

2. Save the current cursor position and style for the active display page.

3. Save the screen data (note that this must be performed before switching modes).

4. Switch into the appropriate video mode, if necessary. The application may now freely write to the screen and modify the cursor position and style.

5. Before exit, restore the former video mode.

6. Restore the cursor position and style.

7. Restore the screen data.

Preserving DOS Parameters

The final basic elements of the machine state that must be saved and restored are the two DOS variables that are maintained for the current process: the segment address of the program segment prefix (PSP) and the segment:offset address of the disk transfer address (DTA). These variables are discussed in the section "Coexisting with MS-DOS."

Coexisting with BIOS Disk Activity

A disk drive is a nonsharable resource—only one process can use it at a given time. Also, its operations are timing sensitive. Therefore, a TSR should never be activated when the BIOS is engaged in a disk service. All BIOS disk services are accessed through interrupt 13h. Normally, the application program communicates with the disk through MS-DOS, and DOS then calls the low-level BIOS routines. If this procedure is followed, the techniques outlined above for avoiding interrupting DOS would be sufficient to prevent the disruption of disk activity. However, some applications directly access the BIOS disk services through interrupt 13h. Therefore, the TSR needs a separate mechanism to prevent activation while interrupt 13h is in progress. The sample program in Figure 11.3 traps this interrupt, and sets a flag while the BIOS is busy. See the explanation of the program listing.

Coexisting with Interrupt Handlers

The events signaled by hardware interrupts typically need to be serviced promptly; for example, the tick of the system clock or the arrival of a character at the serial port. A TSR, however, is capable of blocking hardware interrupts for arbitrary periods of time. You should therefore use the following two guidelines to minimize the amount of time that a TSR delays the handling of these interrupts.

First, issue the **sti** machine instruction as soon as possible. When an interrupt routine receives control, hardware interrupts are disabled, and must be explicitly enabled through the **sti** instruction. (They may be disabled again through the **cli** instruction.) Remember, however, that as soon as hardware interrupts are enabled, the TSR can be asynchronously suspended by other interrupt handlers. Therefore, make sure interrupts remain disabled within critical sections of code, where branching to another process at an unpredictable point in time can cause data corruption or other problems. (See Figure 11.3 and the following description for examples of disabling interrupts within critical sections of code.)

Second, send an end-of-interrupt signal to the 8259A interrupt controller if necessary. This guideline applies only to TSRs that are activated through hardware interrupts (typically the keyboard interrupt number 09h). See the comments in Chapter 6 in the section "General Guidelines for Hardware Interrupt Handlers."

Reentrancy

Designing a TSR goes beyond the issues of simple sequential programming. Because of the presence of the hardware interrupt mechanism, it is almost always possible for your memory-resident code to be entered recursively. To illustrate how this is possible, consider the two common methods for triggering a TSR: through the hardware keyboard interrupt (09h) and through the software keyboard interrupt (16h).

When triggering through the hardware keyboard interrupt, and the user presses the hotkey, interrupt 09 is generated and causes branching to your interrupt handler, which detects the hotkey and activates the main body of the TSR. When the TSR is active, the user may again press the hotkey, suspending the current execution of the TSR (if interrupts are enabled), and causing a second execution of the TSR code from the beginning.

When using the software keyboard interrupt, your TSR is installed on the chain of interrupt 16h handlers. While the TSR is active, there are two possible ways that it can be recursively reentered. First, your program itself may issue an interrupt 16h in order to read the keyboard, and if the user presses the hotkey again, the TSR may be reentered from the beginning. Secondly, even if your program never issues an interrupt 16h, if the interrupts are currently enabled, a hardware interrupt may occur (such as the clock tick, number 08h), which causes branching to a routine that subsequently reads the keyboard through interrupt 16h. Again, your code may be recursively reentered.

Code that is designed to properly handle possible recursive calls is classified as reentrant. Unless your code is reentrant, serious problems can result, which are generally due to the storage of data in fixed memory locations. For example, if your program stores temporary values in memory variables, a recursive call can corrupt these values. Also, if your program switches to a fixed location in a local stack, a recursive call can corrupt the values stored by the original invocation. Note that MS-DOS itself is *not* reentrant, resulting in the multitude of problems described above.

There are two basic methods for making memory-resident code reentrant. The first and simplest method is to set a **busy** flag whenever the code is active. The interrupt handler that activates the TSR must first check this flag. If the flag is set, the routine returns immediately, preventing a recursive activation; if the flag is not set, then it proceeds with its other tests and possibly activates the TSR. The TSR shell in Figure 11.3 uses this simple method.

The other method for producing reentrant code is to allow the code to be entered recursively, but avoid storing temporary local values in fixed memory locations. There are two primary precautions that will prevent the corruption of local data. First, store local values in registers rather than in memory variables, and save and restore the original contents of all registers. Secondly, prevent data corruption in a local stack using one of the following methods:

- Eliminate the use of a local stack. This practice prevents the TSR from corrupting its own stack, but unfortunately makes use of the stack belonging to the interrupted process, which may not be sufficiently large. Only a very small TSR, which makes minimal use of the stack, might be able to get by without a local stack and employ this technique.

- Use a series of local stacks, and maintain a pointer to the top of the next available stack area. At the beginning of the code, switch to the next free stack (rather than always switching to the top of a single stack).

- Temporarily switch to a fixed local stack only during portions of the code where the interrupts are disabled, or areas that are protected by a flag from reentry by an interrupting process.

⊞ The Microsoft Standard

In an attempt to bring order to the chaotic realm of memory residency, Microsoft, in conjunction with other software developers, is working on a set of standard guidelines for writing TSRs. The guidelines that have been released so far are preliminary and far from complete. Many of the potential benefits of the specification cannot be realized until it has been drafted in its final form and becomes generally accepted by the community of software developers. In the meanwhile, however, a number of the suggested rules are useful for producing reliable TSRs. The preliminary specification is contained in a document printed by Microsoft and entitled "Programming Guidelines for MS-DOS Terminate and Stay Resident Programs" (issue number 1, 2/1/86). The guidelines to date fall into two major categories: rules of good conduct and the definition of a standard interface.

Rules of Good Conduct

These optional guidelines are helpful for producing reliable TSRs. They have immediate benefit, even before the general adoption of the standard. A number of the rules have already been mentioned above and will not be repeated here; some of the other rules that are included in the specification are listed below. Keep in mind that a TSR can normally be interrupted at any time by another memory-resident program; this fact is the rationale behind several of the following guidelines.

First, a memory-resident program should replace interrupt vectors only once, at the time that it is installed. Some TSRs set a timer to reappropriate interrupt vectors after subsequent TSRs have been installed; this tactic is a defense mechanism against possible miscreant programs, but is considered antisocial behavior. Rather, a TSR should assume that there is an unbroken chain of control (as illustrated above), and should politely assume its position in line.

The second guideline is to use the BIOS whenever possible to change video modes or cursor parameters. If for some reason it is necessary to directly change port settings on the video controller, the TSR should update the BIOS data maintained in low memory in order to keep the system and other applications apprised of the modifications. These parameters are maintained in segment 0040h at offsets 0049h–0066h, and for the EGA, at the additional offsets 0084h–00ABh. Note specifically that any change to the mode control register (3B8h for monochrome, or 3D8h for CGA) should be reflected by a corresponding change to the **CRT_MODE_SET** field at address 0040h:0065h. Also, if the program maintains its own software cursor rather than using the hardware cursor, it should continually update the cursor position maintained in the **CURSOR_POSN** field at address 0040h:0050 (this would allow an interrupting TSR such as a thesaurus to identify the current cursor position). See the BIOS listings in the PC/AT technical references and the EGA manual (cited in Appendix H) for the definition of these fields.

Third, use a critical-error handler (interrupt 24h; see the discussion of this topic in Chapter 6) to perform the following action on a hard error: save the error code returned by DOS in a global flag that can subsequently be examined by the program, assign 0 to AL to signal DOS to ignore the error, and issue an interrupt return. Do not jump directly back to the program, which would not allow DOS to clean up its stacks.

A Standard Interface

This part of the specification goes beyond the goal of mere peaceful coexistence, and defines an official set of data records and calling protocols so that both the operating characteristics of the TSR and a standard set of service routines become globally available to other programs. The developer can safely postpone implementing this interface until the final format is defined and accepted by a critical mass of software writers. Its essential features, however, are worth mentioning; there are two basic parts: a program identification record and a standard set of functions.

A *program identification record* is quite analogous to the device header of a device driver (see Chapter 9), and is a standard record contained in the TSR to provide basic information to other programs. Ideally, if every TSR in the system included such a record, it would be possible for any program to determine the identity and operating characteristics of all TSRs installed in the current runtime environment, and then modify its own behavior if necessary or detect possible conflicts. Among the fields in this record are an ID that indicates a valid program identification record, a version number, a pointer to data on all interrupts that are taken over, pointers to all hotkeys used by the TSR, and a program ID sting.

The data on each interrupt is contained in an *interrupt information record*. One of the fields of this record is a pointer to the former interrupt routine, so that the entire chain of routines servicing a given interrupt can be traced. The interrupt information record also contains a priority field, which specifies the desired position of the service routine in the interrupt chain. For example, in Figure 11.1, the highest priority TSRs would be the closest to the BIOS end of the chain. It would thus be possible for a TSR to scan the sequence of handlers already installed on a given interrupt, and install itself at the appropriate position in the chain (ideally, this list would be ordered according the values of the priority fields). This feature realizes a important goal of the specification: all TSRs should function properly regardless of the loading order.

How is it possible to locate the interrupt information record and the program identification record for a given interrupt number? Another proposal of the specification is that each interrupt procedure (i.e., the code pointed to by the interrupt vector) be preceded by a record containing a pointer to the corresponding interrupt information record. The interrupt information record in turn contains a pointer to the program identification record. You can see that the record linking is rather complex. See the Microsoft programming guidelines for details.

The second part of the interface is a set of standard service routines that are provided by the TSR, and can be accessed by any other program through interrupt 15h (this vector is chosen since it is seldom used). Currently, most TSRs are activated only when the user presses a hotkey. This proposed enhancement would allow another program to activate features of a TSR, just as it is presently possible for a program to invoke operating system services or load transient applications. Included in the prospective standard are functions to obtain information on a specific TSR, to activate or deactivate particular TSR features, and to enable or disable the entire TSR. For example, a program might be able to run the editor of a desktop accessory TSR or trigger a macro of a keyboard enhancement utility. Note that this arrangement also provides a uniform channel for the transient parts of a program to communicate with the resident parts. See the Microsoft programming guidelines for details.

Future goals, which are not included in the current draft of the standard, include a standard mechanism for deinstalling a TSR, which would deactivate the code and release the memory, and a standard mechanism for TSRs to use expanded memory.

A Memory-Resident Shell for C

Figure 11.2 is a demonstration C program that is converted to a TSR by calling the assembler routine **tsr**. The assembler procedures that initialize and activate the TSR are listed in Figure 11.3. The purpose of these programs is to illustrate the important features of a memory-resident program, to demonstrate specific strategies for solving some of the problems inherent in TSR design, and to provide a simple and rapid means for generating a TSR using the C language.

Developing a truly bullet-proof TSR that can handle almost any situation and function in a wide variety of hardware and software environments can require a very large and messy body of code. One of the major design goals of the TSR procedures presented in this chapter was to simplify the coding as much as possible in order to emphasize the major elements and to provide a tractable starting point for adding necessary enhancements. This section begins with an explanation of the use of the assembler module for generating a TSR from a C program. It then describes the assembler implementation, emphasizing design alternatives where appropriate. The chapter concludes with a discussion of possible enhancements to the assembler routines.

Use of the tsr Function by a C Program

Using the **tsr** function to convert a normal C program into a TSR is quite simple; most of the low-level implementation details are encapsulated in the separate assembler module. As illustrated in Figure 11.2, the C program first prints appropriate messages to the user and performs any

```
/*
      Figure:    11.2
      File:      TSR.C

      A demonstration C program that terminates, stays resident, and is
      activated by a hotkey

      This program must be linked with the assembler module TSRA.ASM
      (Figure 11.3) and the object module(s) containing the other external
      routines listed below:
*/

#include <stdio.h>

/******** External Routines that must be linked with this program. ********/

int tsr (void (*)(), int);                      /* Figure 11.3               */
void pushscr (void);                            /* Figure 8.12               */
void printv (char *, int, int, int);            /* Figure 8.4                */
void popscr (void);                             /* Figure 8.12               */

/******************** Internal Routine Declarations ********************/

void demo (void);
int getkey (void);

/*************************** Main Program ****************************/

void main ()
    {
    int error;                        /* Error code.                          */

                                      /* Print message -- also perform any    */
                                      /* initializations at this point.       */
    printf ("Installing TSR Demo ... \n");
    printf ("Press <alt>-<left shift> to activate.\n");


    error = tsr (demo, 0x000A);       /* Install program as TSR, with hotkey  */
                                      /* <alt>-<left-shift> activating 'demo', */
                                      /* and terminate program.               */


    printf ("Error %d installing TSR.\n", error);
                                      /* If code reaches this point, an error  */
                                      /* has occurred.                         */

    } /* end main */

/******************** Routine Activated by Hotkey ********************/

void demo ()                          /* C entry point when hotkey is pressed. */
    {
    int row = 3;
    int col = 10;

    pushscr ();                       /* Save screen of interrupted program.  */

    printv ("------------------------------------------------",15,row++,col);
    printv ("|                                              |",15,row++,col);
    printv ("|         T   S   R      D  E  M  O            |",15,row++,col);
    printv ("|                                              |",15,row++,col);
    printv ("|                                              |",15,row++,col);
    printv ("|                                              |",15,row++,col);
    printv ("|         press any key to continue ...        |",15,row++,col);
    printv ("|                                              |",15,row++,col);
    printv ("|                                              |",15,row++,col);
    printv ("------------------------------------------------",15,row++,col);

    getkey ();
```

Figure 11.2: *A model TSR program in C*

```
        popscr ();                      /* Restore screen of interrupted program.*/

        } /* end demo */

#include <dos.h>

int getkey ()                           /* Reads a key using BIOS interrupt 16h. */
                                        /* See Figure 5.3.                        */
        {
        union REGS reg;

        reg.h.ah = 0;
        int86 (0x16, &reg, &reg);
        return (reg.x.ax);

        } /* end getkey */
```

Figure 11.2: *A model TSR program in C (continued)*

necessary initializations; this is the last opportunity to perform initialization because the next time the program will receive control is when activated through the hotkey. The program now calls the **tsr** function, passing it two parameters. The first parameter is the address of the C function that is to be activated through the hotkey. Thus, **main** is the C entry point when the program is run from the command line to load and initialize the TSR, and the function whose address is passed to **tsr** is the C entry point when the hotkey is pressed. The second parameter is the hotkey to be used to activate the program. The hotkey is not an ASCII or special character (such as a function key), but rather the mask used by the BIOS to represent a particular combination of "shift keys." The example uses the mask 000Ah, which indicates both the Alt and Left-Shift keys. Therefore, the TSR will be activated whenever the user simultaneously holds down both these keys. The following are the BIOS codes for the shift keys:

Bit	Shift key
0	Right-Shift depressed
1	Left-Shift depressed
2	Ctrl depressed
3	Alt depressed
4	ScrollLock active
5	NumLock active
6	CapsLock active
7	Ins active
8-10	Not used

```
 1:    page 50,130
 2:
 3:
 4:    ;File:     TSRA.ASM
 5:
 6:    ;Routines for generating a terminate and stay-resident C program
 7:
 8:    public    _tsr                          ;Procedure called by C program.
 9:
10:    extrn     __psp:word                    ;C global variable containing the
11:                                            ;segment address of the PSP.
12:
13:    HEAPSIZE  equ    64                      ;Size of heap in 16 byte paragraphs;
14:                                            ;must increase this value on a DOS
15:                                            ;Allocation Error.
16:
17:    _data     segment word public 'DATA'
18:    _data     ends
19:
20:    dgroup    group    _data
21:
22:    _text     segment byte public 'CODE'
23:
24:    extrn     _sbrk:near                    ;C library function which returns
25:                                            ;offset (w.r.t. DS) of break address.
26:
27:    assume    cs:_text, ds:dgroup
28:
29:    ;*********************** Code segment data. ****************************
30:
31:    c_ss      dw     ?                       ;C Stack Segment.
32:    c_sp      dw     ?                       ;C Stack Pointer.
33:    c_ds      dw     ?                       ;C Data Segment.
34:    c_es      dw     ?                       ;C Extra Segment.
35:
36:    fun_ptr   dw     ?                       ;Address of main TSR C function.
37:
38:    hot_key   dw     ?                       ;Hotkey keyboard shift-status mask.
39:
40:    c_dta_off dw     ?                       ;C Disk Transfer Address.
41:    c_dta_seg dw     ?
42:    d_dta_off dw     ?                       ;Disk Transfer Address of interrupted
43:    d_dta_seg dw     ?                       ;program.
44:
45:    indos_ptr label  dword                   ;Pointer to DOS "indos" flag.
46:    indos_off dw     ?
47:    indos_seg dw     ?
48:
49:    int28_vec label  dword                   ;Old interrupt 28h vector.
50:    int28_off dw     ?
51:    int28_seg dw     ?
52:
53:    int13_vec label  dword                   ;Old interrupt 13h vector.
54:    int13_off dw     ?
55:    int13_seg dw     ?
56:
57:    int09_vec label  dword                   ;Old interrupt 09h vector.
58:    int09_off dw     ?
59:    int09_seg dw     ?
60:
61:    break_off dw     ?                       ;Save heap break offset.
62:
63:    busy      db     0                       ;Flag to prevent recursive TSR calls.
64:    in_bios   db     0                       ;Flag to indicate int 13h activity.
65:
66:    dos_ss    dw     ?                       ;Saves SS of interrupted program.
67:    dos_sp    dw     ?                       ;Saves SP of interrupted program.
68:
69:    ;*********************** Installation procedure ***********************
70:
```

Figure 11.3: *An assembler module that converts a C program to a TSR*

```
71:     _tsr       proc    near                ;Makes program resident, installs
72:                                            ;hotkey, & terminates.
73:     comment    /*
74:                This function terminates a C program, leaving the code resident in
75:                memory.  After the program terminates, the specified C function
76:                will be activated by the selected hotkey.  Normally, this routine
77:                never returns to the C program;  if it does return, an error
78:                occurred and one of the following codes is passed back:
79:
80:                Error Codes:
81:
82:                1       insufficient memory
83:                2       pre DOS 2.0 version
84:                3       TSR already installed     (not currently implemented)
85:
86:                int tsr (funptr, hotkey);
87:                void (*funptr)();               Pointer to function to activate.
88:                int hotkey;                     Mask for hotkey which activates function.
89:
90:                */
91:
92:     aframe     struc                       ;Stack frame template.
93:     abptr      dw      ?
94:     aret_ad    dw      ?
95:     afun_ptr   dw      ?                   ;Pointer to C TSR function to activate.
96:     ahot_key   dw      ?                   ;Hotkey keyboard status mask.
97:     aframe     ends
98:
99:                push    bp
100:               mov     bp, sp
101:               push    es
102:
103:               mov     ah, 30h             ;Test DOS version.
104:               int     21h
105:               cmp     al, 0               ;Major version returned in AL.
106:               jg      a00                 ;2.x or greater.
107:               mov     ax, 2               ;Version 1.x, set error code.
108:               jmp     a02                 ;Quit.
109:    a00:
110:               mov     cs:c_ss, ss         ;Save C SS.
111:               mov     cs:c_sp, sp         ;Save C SP.
112:               add     cs:c_sp, 10         ;Adjust saved C stack pointer to its
113:                                           ;value before 'tsr_init' was called.
114:               mov     cs:c_ds, ds         ;Save C DS.
115:               mov     cs:c_es, es         ;Save C ES.
116:
117:               mov     ax, [bp].afun_ptr   ;Save pointer to C TSR function.
118:               mov     cs:fun_ptr, ax
119:               mov     ax, [bp].ahot_key   ;Save hotkey mask.
120:               mov     cs:hot_key, ax
121:
122:               mov     ah, 2fh             ;Get C Disk Transfer Address.
123:               int     21h
124:               mov     cs:c_dta_off, bx    ;Save it.
125:               mov     cs:c_dta_seg, es
126:
127:               mov     ah, 34h             ;Call DOS to retrieve pointer to
128:               int     21h                 ;"indos" flag.
129:               mov     cs:indos_off, bx    ;Save dword pointer to "indos" flag.
130:               mov     cs:indos_seg, es
131:
132:               mov     ah, 35h             ;Get old interrupt 28h vector.
133:               mov     al, 28h
134:               int     21h
135:               mov     cs:int28_off, bx    ;Save old vector.
136:               mov     cs:int28_seg, es
137:
138:               mov     ah, 35h             ;Get old interrupt 13h vector.
139:               mov     al, 13h
140:               int     21h
```

Figure 11.3: *An assembler module that converts a C program to a TSR (continued)*

```
141:            mov     cs:int13_off, bx    ;Save old vector.
142:            mov     cs:int13_seg, es
143:
144:            mov     ah, 35h             ;Get old interrupt 09h vector.
145:            mov     al, 09h
146:            int     21h
147:            mov     cs:int09_off, bx    ;Save old vector.
148:            mov     cs:int09_seg, es
149:
150:            push    ds
151:            mov     ax, cs              ;Set new interrupt 28h vector.
152:            mov     ds, ax
153:            mov     ah, 25h
154:            mov     al, 28h
155:            mov     dx, offset int28
156:            int     21h
157:
158:            mov     ax, cs              ;Set new interrupt 13h vector.
159:            mov     ds, ax
160:            mov     ah, 25h
161:            mov     al, 13h
162:            mov     dx, offset int13
163:            int     21h
164:
165:            mov     ax, cs              ;Set new interrupt 09h vector.
166:            mov     ds, ax
167:            mov     ah, 25h
168:            mov     al, 09h
169:            mov     dx, offset int09
170:            int     21h
171:            pop     ds
172:                                        ;Calculate number of paragraphs to
173:                                        ;retain in memory.
174:            mov     ax, HEAPSIZE        ;Size of heap in 16 byte paragraphs.
175:            mov     bl, 16              ;Convert to bytes.
176:            mul     bl
177:            push    ax                  ;Attempt to move break address.
178:            call    _sbrk               ;'Sbrk' returns offset (wrt DS) of
179:            add     sp, 2               ;former break address.
180:            mov     cs:break_off, ax    ;Save break offset address.
181:
182:            cmp     ax, -1              ;'Sbrk' returns -1 if insufficient
183:            jne     a01                 ;memory is available for heap.
184:            mov     ax, 1               ;Set error code.
185:            jmp     a02                 ;Return to C.
186:   a01:
187:            mov     ax, HEAPSIZE        ;Restore C heap.
188:            mov     bl, 16
189:            mul     bl
190:            neg     ax
191:            push    ax
192:            call    _sbrk
193:            add     sp, 2
194:
195:            mov     dx, cs:break_off    ;Convert offset of break address to
196:            add     dx, 15              ;absolute segment (paragraph) value.
197:            mov     cl, 4               ;Convert offset to paragraphs,
198:            shr     dx, cl              ;rounding up.
199:
200:            mov     ax, ds              ;Add DS.
201:            add     dx, ax              ;DX now has segment value of current
202:                                        ;break address.
203:
204:            mov     ax, __psp           ;AX now has segment address of PSP.
205:
206:            sub     dx, ax              ;DX now has number of paragraphs of C
207:                                        ;code and data.
208:
209:            add     dx, HEAPSIZE        ;Leave room for Heap.
210:
```

Figure 11.3: *An assembler module that converts a C program to a TSR (continued)*

```
211:                                  ;Call DOS Terminate and Stay Resident
212:            mov     ah, 31h       ;service.
213:            mov     al, 0         ;Set errorlevel to 0.
214:            int     21h
215:
216:    a02:    pop     es            ;Branch here if an error occurs.
217:            pop     bp
218:            ret                   ;Return to C program on error only.
219:
220:    _tsr    endp
221:
222:    ;************************  Interrupt Handlers ********************************
223:
224:    int28   proc    near          ;Patches into interrupt 28h.  Similar
225:                                  ;to 'int09' except the 'indos' flag
226:                                  ;is not tested.
227:
228:            pushf                 ;Chain to prior installed int 28 handler.
229:            call    cs:int28_vec
230:
231:            cli                   ;Make sure interrupts are disabled.
232:            cmp     cs:busy, 0    ;Test 'busy' flag to prevent recursive
233:            je      b01           ;calls.
234:            iret                  ;TSR busy.
235:    b01:                          ;TSR not busy.
236:            cmp     cs:in_bios, 0 ;Test for BIOS disk activity.
237:            je      b02
238:            iret                  ;BIOS disk services active.
239:    b02:                          ;BIOS disk services NOT active.
240:            push    ax            ;Test if hot key is pressed.
241:            push    es
242:            xor     ax, ax
243:            mov     es, ax        ;Read BIOS keyboard flag at 0000:0417h.
244:            mov     ax, word ptr es:[417h]
245:            and     ax, cs:hot_key ;Test if keyboard flag has all bits on
246:            cmp     ax, cs:hot_key ;that are on in 'hot_key'.
247:            pop     es
248:            pop     ax
249:            je      b03
250:            iret                  ;Hot key not pressed.
251:    b03:                          ;Hot key pressed.
252:            call    activate      ;Activate TSR.
253:            iret                  ;Return to interrupted process.
254:
255:    int28   endp
256:
257:
258:    int13   proc    far           ;Patches into interrupt 13h to set
259:                                  ;flag when disk services are active.
260:
261:            mov     cs:in_bios, 1 ;Turn on BIOS active flag.
262:
263:            pushf                 ;Invoke original interrupt.
264:            call    int13_vec
265:
266:            mov     cs:in_bios, 0 ;Turn off BIOS active flag.
267:
268:            ret     2             ;Return from interrupt, saving flags.
269:
270:    int13   endp
271:
272:
273:    int09   proc    near          ;Patches into interrupt 09h.
274:
275:            pushf                 ;Chain to prior installed int 09h handler.
276:            call    cs:int09_vec
277:
278:            cli                   ;Disable interrupts for tests.
279:            cmp     cs:busy, 0    ;Test 'busy' flag to prevent recursive
280:            je      c01           ;calls.
```

Figure 11.3: *An assembler module that converts a C program to a TSR (continued)*

```
281:            iret                            ;TSR busy.
282:    c01:                                    ;TSR not busy.
283:            cmp     cs:in_bios, 0           ;Test for BIOS disk activity.
284:            je      c02
285:            iret                            ;BIOS disk services active.
286:    c02:                                    ;BIOS disk services not active.
287:            push    ax                      ;Test if hot key is pressed.
288:            push    es
289:            xor     ax, ax
290:            mov     es, ax                  ;Read BIOS keyboard flag at 0000:0417h.
291:            mov     ax, word ptr es:[417h]
292:            and     ax, cs:hot_key          ;Test if keyboard flag has all bits on
293:            cmp     ax, cs:hot_key          ;which are on in 'hot_key'.
294:            pop     es
295:            pop     ax
296:            je      c03
297:            iret                            ;Hot key not pressed.
298:    c03:                                    ;Not busy & hot key pressed.
299:            push    ds                      ;Test if in DOS.
300:            push    bx
301:            lds     bx, cs:indos_ptr        ;Load pointer to 'indos' flag.
302:            cmp     byte ptr ds:[bx], 0     ;Test 'indos' flag.
303:            pop     bx
304:            pop     ds
305:            je      c04
306:            iret                            ;Are in DOS.
307:    c04:                                    ;Not busy, hot key pressed, & not in DOS.
308:            call    activate                ;Activate TSR.
309:            iret                            ;Return to interrupted process.
310:
311:    int09   endp
312:
313:
314:    activate proc   near                    ;Activates the C TSR function.
315:
316:    comment         /*
317:            This procedure performs a context switch which saves the current
318:            machine state, initializes the runtime environment for C, calls
319:            the C TSR function, and then restores the former state.  It is
320:            called by either 'int28' or 'int09' when the hotkey is pressed,
321:            and it is safe to interrupt the current program.
322:            */
323:
324:            mov     cs:busy, 1              ;Set busy flag to prevent recursive calls.
325:
326:                                            ;Switch to C stack.
327:            mov     cs:dos_ss, ss           ;Save current SS.
328:            mov     cs:dos_sp, sp           ;Save current SP.
329:
330:            mov     ss, cs:c_ss             ;Set up C stack segment.
331:            mov     sp, cs:c_sp             ;Set up C stack pointer.
332:
333:            push    ax                      ;Save machine state on C stack.
334:            push    bx
335:            push    cx
336:            push    dx
337:            push    bp
338:            push    si
339:            push    di
340:            push    ds
341:            push    es
342:
343:                                            ;Save the DOS stack.
344:            mov     cx, 64                  ;Set counter for 64 words.
345:            mov     es, cs:dos_ss           ;Point ES:SI to top of DOS stack.
346:            mov     si, cs:dos_sp
347:    d01:
348:            push    word ptr es:[si]        ;Loop to save 64 words of DOS stack.
349:            inc     si
350:            inc     si
```

Figure 11.3: *An assembler module that converts a C program to a TSR (continued)*

```
351:            Loop    d01
352:
353:            mov     ah, 2fh                 ;Save DTA for interrupted program.
354:            int     21h
355:            mov     cs:d_dta_off, bx
356:            mov     cs:d_dta_seg, es
357:
358:            mov     ah, 1ah                 ;Set up C DTA.
359:            mov     dx, cs:c_dta_off
360:            mov     ds, cs:c_dta_seg
361:            int     21h
362:
363:            mov     ds, cs:c_ds             ;Set up C segment registers.
364:            mov     es, cs:c_es
365:
366:            sti                             ;Set interrupts back on.
367:            call    cs:fun_ptr              ;Call the C TSR function.
368:            cli                             ;Turn interrupts back off.
369:
370:            mov     ah, 1ah                 ;Restore DTA of interrupted program.
371:            mov     dx, d_dta_off
372:            mov     ds, d_dta_seg
373:            int     21h
374:
375:                                            ;Restore DOS stack.
376:            mov     cx, 64                  ;Set counter for 64 words.
377:            mov     es, cs:dos_ss
378:            mov     si, cs:dos_sp
379:            add     si, 128
380:    d02:                                    ;Loop to restore 64 words of DOS stack.
381:            dec     si
382:            dec     si
383:            pop     word ptr es:[si]
384:            Loop    d02
385:
386:            pop     es                      ;Restore machine state.
387:            pop     ds
388:            pop     di
389:            pop     si
390:            pop     bp
391:            pop     dx
392:            pop     cx
393:            pop     bx
394:            pop     ax
395:
396:            mov     ss, cs:dos_ss           ;Restore stack of interrupted process.
397:            mov     sp, cs:dos_sp
398:
399:            mov     cs:busy, 0              ;Reset busy flag.
400:            ret                             ;Return to 'int28' or 'int09'.
401:
402:    activate    endp
403:
404:    _text       ends
405:            end
406:
407:
```

Figure 11.3: *An assembler module that converts a C program to a TSR (continued)*

11	Ctrl-NumLock active
12	ScrollLock depressed
13	NumLock depressed
14	CapsLock depressed
15	Insert depressed

Note that codes indicating that a key is *depressed* signify that the key is currently being held down by the user. Codes indicating that a key is *active* refer to keys that toggle particular states on and off (for example, Ins or CapsLock); if the bit is on, then the corresponding state is currently active (the key may or may not be actually depressed). Since the hotkey mask is passed as a parameter to **tsr**, it is a simple matter to allow the user to modify the selected hotkey (to avoid conflicts with other programs).

The **tsr** function stores data that will be needed by the assembler routine that activates the TSR; it then installs the interrupt handlers and terminates the program, leaving the code and data resident in memory. If all goes well, this routine never returns, and thus bypasses the normal C termination code. If, however, an error condition arises, **tsr** returns one of the following error codes:

1   Insufficient memory

2   Wrong DOS version (1.*x*)

3   TSR already installed (not currently implemented)

Since **tsr** does not check to see if the TSR has already been installed (this precaution is presented later as a possible enhancement), the third error code is never actually returned by this version of the routine. If an error occurs and **tsr** returns, **main** prints an error message and terminates normally (i.e., the code is not left in memory).

As mentioned above, the actual code executed when the hotkey is pressed is located in a function other than **main** (in Figure 11.2, this code is contained in **demo**). In most regards the TSR entry point is a normal C function that can call any number of other functions. However, there are a few special responsibilities and restrictions.

First, the C TSR entry function must save and restore the current video state (described earlier in the section "Interacting with the Foreground Program"). The example program merely saves and restores the screen data using **pushscr** and **popscr**; however, a more versatile implementation should also save the cursor parameters and video mode. The assembler function automatically preserves both the registers and the DOS disk transfer address.

In addition, a few C library functions do not work properly in a TSR environment, including **system**, **alloc**, and **exit**. The function **system** requires a large body of allocated memory immediately above the program and will return an "insufficient memory available" message when called from a TSR. The function **alloc** allocates memory from the heap space initially reserved by the C start-up code. Most of this memory, however, is returned to the system by **tsr**, and only the amount specified by the constant **HEAPSIZE** in Figure 11.3 is actually available; **alloc**, however, is unaware of the reduced heap size. If memory is used beyond that actually allocated to the process, a DOS memory allocation error will result. For a TSR it is better to use **alloca**, which allocates memory from the stack space (which remains safely resident in memory in the TSR). See the following discussion on the method for calculating the size of the memory-resident code. Do *not* use the **exit** call in any C function destined to become part of a TSR. The program must **return**, so that control goes back through the assembler module, which needs to properly restore the machine state. As you work with this system, you will undoubtedly discover other C library functions to add to this list.

The Assembler Implementation

This section describes the assembly language routines of Figure 11.3 that install and activate a C program as a TSR. Although the optimal method for writing a flexible and compact TSR would be to develop the entire code in assembly language, for programs where memory size is not critical, the convenience of programming in C outweighs the disadvantages. Interfacing with a C program, however, limits the programmer's control over the exact placement of code and data, and the establishment of the runtime environment. For example, a TSR written entirely in assembly language would normally place the initialization code at the *end* of the program so that the memory it occupies can be released. The C compiler, however, places all code *before* the data segment, thereby preventing the release of the initialization code. Other examples of the need to work around the C compiler will be evident in the following description of the assembler module. Note that the C program must be compiled using the small-memory model in order to be compatible with these assembler routines. This section describes the three major components of the assembler module: the initialization code, the interrupt handlers, and the activation procedure.

The Initialization Code

The beginning of the code segment **_text** (lines 31–67) is used to declare the variables that are accessed by the interrupt handlers. When an interrupt handler receives control, the DS register does *not* point to the C data segment, and therefore it is more convenient to place these data in the **_text** segment rather than in the **_data** segment. Note that all references to these variables use the **cs:** segment override.

Lines 103–108 test whether the DOS version is 2.0 or later, since earlier versions do not support some of the necessary functions. Lines 109–115 save important register values from the C runtime environment (SS, SP, DS, and ES), so that these values can later be restored immediately before the C TSR routine is activated. Next, **tsr** saves the two parameters that are passed: the address of the C TSR entry point, and the hotkey mask (lines 117–120), so that they will be available to the interrupt handlers. The next few lines (127–130) employ the undocumented DOS function 34h to retrieve a double word pointer to the **indos** flag, described above; the interrupt handlers can subsequently access **indos** directly through this pointer, and do not need to reissue the interrupt.

The next section of code initializes the handlers for interrupts 09h, 13h, and 28h. First, the old values are saved so that the handlers can chain to the prior routines (lines 132–148). Next, the vectors are set to point to the appropriate routines within the assembler module (lines 150–172). Note that once the keyboard interrupt handler (09h) is installed, it will be immediately activated by any keyboard activity. Therefore, make sure that all necessary initializations are performed *before* this vector is installed.

The final section of **tsr** (lines 174–214) calculates the number of 16-byte paragraphs to retain in memory and calls the DOS terminate and stay-resident function (31h). Calculating the appropriate number of paragraphs from within a C program is a bit tricky. To understand how the method works, consider the diagram in Figure 11.4, which shows the organization of memory used by a small-memory model C program.

Note that the data, stack, and heap are all contained within a single 64K block, and can all be addressed through the data segment register (the SS register has the same value as DS). The C startup routine frees all memory above the heap, but for even a very small program, the entire 64K block remains allocated (which results in a large heap area). A TSR, however, must minimize memory use; it therefore frees memory beginning at a point a short distance above the stack, leaving only a minimal amount of memory for the heap.

The technique begins by using the C library function **sbrk**. This function is normally employed as a low-level means for allocating memory from the heap. It is passed a parameter that indicates the number of bytes (plus or minus) that the current break address for the heap is to be moved (the break address is the offset with respect to the data segment register of the first former break address. Rather than arbitrarily reserving the entire byte of *unallocated* memory in the heap space); this function returns remainder of the 64K block for heap space as the C compiler does, **tsr** reserves only the amount of

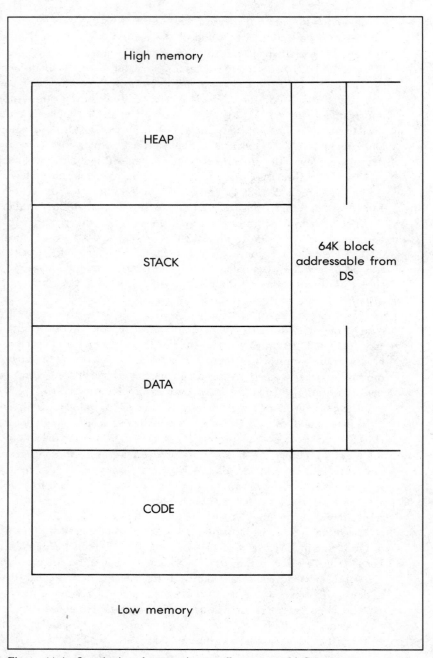

Figure 11.4: *Organization of memory in a small-memory model C program*

heap space indicated by the constant **HEAPSIZE**. In order to calculate the total number of paragraphs that must remain resident in memory, **tsr** performs the following series of steps.

First, it calls **_sbrk** to attempt to move the break address up in memory by the number of bytes desired for the heap (calculated by multiplying **HEAPSIZE** by 16). If insufficient free memory is available within the 64K block to accommodate the required heap, **_sbrk** returns a -1, and **tsr** returns an error message to the C program. **_sbrk** also returns the *former* break address, which is saved in the variable **break_off** (this address will normally be immediately above the stack, unless the prior C code has allocated heap memory). Note that this step is performed only to make sure that there is sufficient free memory available for the heap; the break value maintained by the C library code must be restored in the following step (lines 174–185).

tsr now reverses the effect of step 1 by calling **_sbrk** with a negative number. This restores the heap break address to its original value so that C allocation functions will begin allocating heap space at the offset contained in **break_off** (lines 187–193).

tsr next converts the break offset contained in **break_off** to 16-byte paragraphs and adds to this the value contained in the DS register. The resulting total is the segment address of the beginning of the heap (lines 195–201).

tsr now subtracts the segment address of the beginning of the program segment prefix (contained in the global C variable **__psp**) from the segment address of the beginning of the heap (lines 204–206).

Finally, **tsr** adds the number of paragraphs required for the runtime heap contained in the constant **HEAPSIZE**. The final result is the total number of paragraphs that must be kept memory-resident (line 209).

Once the total size of the resident code and data is calculated, **tsr** invokes DOS function 31h, which terminates the process, leaving the requested number of paragraphs resident in memory.

As mentioned above, the C program should avoid calling allocation functions such as **malloc** and **calloc**, which allocate memory from the heap, since heap space is now a scarce resource. However, some C library functions (such as **fprintf**) allocate memory from the heap and therefore a minimal amount of heap space must be provided. If the C program allocates heap memory beyond the memory block reserved by DOS for the TSR, the disconcerting message

Memory Allocation Error. System Halted

will soon ensue. The remedy is to simply increase the value assigned to **HEAPSIZE** until the message goes away.

The final lines of **tsr** (216–218) receive control only if an error that prevents the installation of the TSR occurred. These lines restore the registers and return in disgrace to the C program, bearing an appropriate error message.

The Interrupt Handlers

The assembler module contains three interrupt handlers: **int09** for the hardware keyboard interrupt (09h), **int28** for the DOS idle interrupt (28h), and **int13** for the BIOS disk services interrupt (13h). Alternative designs for writing TSRs may install handlers for other interrupts, such as the clock tick (08h) and the keyboard software interrupt (16h).

The hardware interrupt handler **int09** (lines 273–311) is used to detect when the hotkey is pressed. Interrupt 09h is generated any time a key is pressed or released. Other TSRs may detect the hotkey through the software keyboard interrupt (16h) instead, which is generated only when a program is reading the keyboard.

int09 first calls the previously installed interrupt handler. Upon return from the previous routine, it performs a series of tests to determine whether the TSR should be activated. If any of these tests fail, it immediately issues an **iret** instruction to return to the interrupted program. The following tests are performed on lines 279–306:

- The **busy** flag is tested to see whether the TSR is already active (the TSR code is not designed to be called recursively).

- If the **in_bios** flag equals 1, then the BIOS disk service interrupt 13h is currently active, and the interrupt handler returns.

- Next, the interrupt handler reads the memory word at address 0000h:0417h, which contains the BIOS shift key flag (the codes are listed above), to determine whether the hotkey combination is currently depressed.

- If the **indos** flag accessed through the double word pointer **indos_ptr** is greater than 0, then DOS should not be interrupted, and therefore the handler simply returns.

If all the above tests are passed, the procedure **activate** is called to trigger the main TSR code. Note that if the hotkey is pressed, but the tests indicate that it is not safe to call DOS, the program simply ignores the request and returns (to simplify the code); see the discussion in the section "Coexisting with MS-DOS" for more elegant ways to handle this situation.

Another simplifying feature of this implementation is the detection of the hotkey through reading the shift key flag rather than by reading a character. Although using shift keys rather than character keys allows fewer possible combinations, it eliminates the need to process all keystrokes. For example, if an interrupt 09h handler needed to detect an Alt-F10 hotkey, it would have to search through the keyboard buffer for this key, and carefully remove it if discovered, so that it would not be passed on to another program. To detect a shift key combination is a simple and fast matter of testing the status flag.

Note that the use of the shift status flag is not possible within an interrupt 16h handler. The BIOS interrupt 16h service does not return control unless an actual character is entered. When shift keys are pressed, the BIOS updates its status flag, but does not return control to the calling programs, and thus a TSR might never detect a changed shift status.

As mentioned earlier, the interrupt handler **int28** (lines 224–255) is installed to allow the TSR to be activated from the DOS prompt, even though the **indos** flag is nonzero. The rationale is that it is safe to interrupt DOS while it is issuing the idle interrupt, number 28h. Therefore, this interrupt handler performs the same series of tests as **int09** *except* testing the **indos** flag.

The interrupt 13h handler (lines 258–270) serves quite a different purpose. It simply traps the interrupt in order to set **in_bios** flag while the BIOS disk service routine is currently active. Note that the handler returns using **ret 2** rather than **iret**. Since the procedure is declared far, **ret 2** generates a far return and restores the stack from the original **int** instruction (which pushes the flags). This method, however, eliminates the popping of the flags and therefore preserves the current flag value, which is important since the BIOS signals an error by setting the carry flag (the BIOS code itself returns with **ret 2**).

The Activation Procedure

Both **int09** and **int28** call **activate** (lines 314–402) once they determine that the TSR should be activated. The purpose of this function is to save the current machine state, set up the runtime environment for C, call the C TSR function, and then restore the saved machine state.

The function **activate** first sets the busy flag to 1 to prevent recursive entries into the code (which would be possible once the interrupts are enabled). It then switches to a local stack by saving the current values of SS and SP and then setting SS and SP to the values saved by the initialization code. The program switches to the local stack before saving the current machine state to make sure that there is sufficient stack space. Lines 333–341 save all the current registers.

The program then saves 64 words from the top of the stack belonging to the interrupted program (lines 344–351). This precaution, as explained earlier, is taken to avoid stack corruption when interrupting MS-DOS while the **indos** flag is set (through interrupt 28h, while DOS is in an idle state). Note that the number 64 is rather arbitrary, but seems to be a sufficient value. You might experiment with this number; try reducing the amount, but if there are problems after using DOS functions 01h–0Ch and then returning to DOS, you must increase the value.

On lines 353–361 **activate** now saves the old disk transfer address and sets the DTA to the value from the C program that was saved by the initialization code. Before calling the C TSR entry point, **activate** sets DS and ES to the Ç values also saved by the initialization code, and enables the hardware interrupts. Line 367 finally transfers control to the C TSR function.

Upon return from the C function, **activate** disables the interrupts and restores the complete machine state belonging to the interrupted program in the following order:

- The DTA
- The 64 words that were saved from the top of the stack
- The registers
- SS and SP (thereby switching back to the original stack)

Immediately before returning, the busy flag is set back to 0 (remember, however, that the program is still not subject to recursive reentry since the interrupts are disabled until the end of the program).

Enhancements

In an effort to make the code as simple as possible, a number of useful features were left out. Among these features are Ctrl-Break and critical-error handlers, prevention of reinstallation, and provision for deinstallation.

Ctrl-Break and Critical-Error Handlers

One important feature that should be added to make the code more robust are interrupt handlers for Ctrl-Break (interrupt 23h) and critical error (interrupt 24h). If these handlers are not installed, and DOS summarily terminates the current process while a TSR is active, the ensuing possible sequence of events is not pleasant to contemplate. See Chapter 6 for a complete discussion of this topic and for source code listings of sample interrupt routines. Note that if these interrupt handlers are implemented, each time **activate** is called it must save the old values of the vectors and set the vectors to point to the new interrupt handlers, and then restore the original values before exit.

Prevention of Reinstallation

The current version of this TSR makes no provision for preventing the reinstallation of the code. It is not a trivial matter, however, for the installation routine to detect if the TSR has already been installed. It cannot simply look at the code pointed to by interrupt vectors used to activate the TSR because other TSRs may have subsequently replaced these vectors.

There are some complicated schemes that trace through the memory blocks allocated by DOS, searching for a specific identifying signature. A simpler method, however, is to employ one of the user interrupt vectors, in the range from 60h to 67h. The installation program searches for the first interrupt in this range that has a 0 value (and is therefore presumably not used by another program). It can then set this vector to an identifying code value, or it can assign it the address of a signature within the resident code. If no vectors are free, it should notify the user with a message. Whenever the initialization code is run, it scans vectors 60h to 67h for the identifying signature, and if found, it aborts the installation and returns an error code.

Provision for Deinstallation

An optional feature of a TSR is a mechanism for removing the code from memory and returning the memory to the DOS free list. If a TSR deinstalls itself, it should use DOS function 49h to release the block of memory beginning at the program segment prefix *and* the block containing the environment. See Chapter 6 for a description of obtaining the segment addresses of the PSP and the environment.

Allowing a TSR to release itself can be problematic, since the TSR must be the last one installed in memory. Otherwise, a large gap is left in the blocks of allocated memory maintained by DOS. Also, a subsequently installed TSR may have saved the interrupt vector pointing to the code that is now released; if this TSR uses the saved address to chain to the former routine, it will branch to memory that is now released and may contain anything.

The best general approach for releasing and reloading TSRs is to use an independent utility that manages multiple memory-resident programs from various vendors, and releases them from memory in the correct order. There is an excellent set of such utilities called **MARK** and **RELEASE** available as shareware from TurboPower Software.

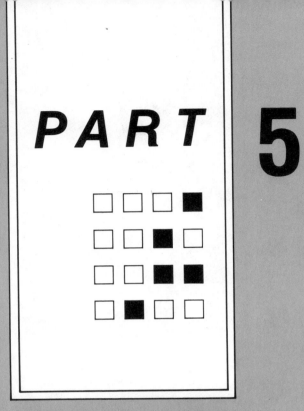

PART 5

OS/2 COMPATIBILITY

CHAPTER 12

Writing Programs for the OS/2 DOS-Compatibility Environment

OS/2 is a multitasking operating system designed to run on the IBM PC-AT, the IBM PS/2 (except Models 25 and 30), and other microcomputers based on the 80286 or 80386 processor. The user of OS/2 can run several concurrent program sessions, each of which maintains its own separate screen output and keyboard input; the user can switch among these sessions using a system hotkey, bringing one session at a time into the foreground. The current version of OS/2 allows up to 12 sessions. *One* of these sessions is designed to run standard MS-DOS programs. (Programs that run in any of the *other* sessions must be specially written to execute under the *protected mode* of the 80286/386 processor. The protected mode is a special processor state that allows programs to be executed concurrently and to access a memory space much larger than the 1 Mb limit imposed on MS-DOS programs. MS-DOS applications run in the *real mode*, which emulates the operation of the 8086/88 processors.)

The special program session that supports standard MS-DOS applications is known variously as the *real mode screen group*, the *DOS-compatibility environment*, or the *3.x box* of OS/2. The designers of OS/2 provided this environment so that the users of the system can continue to run their favorite MS-DOS applications while they gradually convert to the new operating system and begin acquiring specially written OS/2 software. Ideally, all MS-DOS programs should run in the compatibility environment exactly as they run under MS-DOS. In reality, however, MS-DOS applications must obey certain rules and follow a set of guidelines in order to run successfully in this environment. These guidelines form the topic of this chapter. Software developers should follow these caveats whenever possible. Not only is OS/2 becoming an increasingly important system, but also a program that violates these rules can sabotage the entire operating system, defeating the very purpose of a protected mode operating system. (The restrictions on DOS applications are primarily due to the fact that these programs are suspended while they are in the background, and due to the lack of hardware protection the 80286 processor provides for real mode programs.)

The techniques, limitations, and rules presented in this chapter are for developers who are writing or updating programs targeted primarily for the MS-DOS operating system, but would also like these programs to run in the compatibility mode of OS/2; the ability to run under OS/2 is thus a secondary purpose for these applications. If a program is targeted primarily for OS/2, it should be written to run in a protected mode screen group, using the techniques presented in *Programmer's Guide to OS/2* (see the Bibliography) and other books on OS/2 development.

A program that runs only in the compatibility environment cannot take advantage of any of the advanced features of OS/2. In fact, such programs often run faster and are subject to fewer limitations when executed under MS-DOS. The primary advantage of being able to run an MS-DOS application in the compatibility box is that an OS/2 user can load this program simultaneously with protected mode applications, and can run it in the foreground whenever desired.

The first section of this chapter briefly describes the basic structure of the compatibility environment. The next section presents the rules for developing compatibility mode applications, and describes the limitations OS/2 imposes on these applications. The last section focuses specifically on the rules for developing a standard MS-DOS device driver that can run under OS/2. See Chapter 9 for complete information on writing standard MS-DOS device drivers.

The Structure of the Compatibility Environment

This section briefly describes how the DOS-compatibility environment is implemented by OS/2. Note that the user of OS/2 can specify whether the compatibility environment is to be included in the system, and can indicate the amount of memory it will occupy, using the PROTECTONLY and RMSIZE OS/2 configuration commands (see an OS/2 user's guide for an explanation of the configuration commands). Note also that while the compatibility environment is in the foreground, the protected mode applications in the background continue to receive processor time slices; however, when a protected mode screen group is in the foreground, the compatibility environment is suspended—all programs in this environment stop running.

The primary goal of the compatibility environment is to emulate MS-DOS as closely as possible so that applications can run in this screen group exactly as they run under MS-DOS. As illustrated in Figure 12.1, MS-DOS programs access the underlying computer hardware in one of three general ways, all of which have been discussed in this book. First, they may invoke the services of the operating system, typically by placing appropriate parameters in machine registers and issuing software interrupt 21h. Second, to gain greater control over the system hardware and a higher level of efficiency, these programs may call the lower-level services of the ROM BIOS. Finally, MS-DOS programs can bypass both the operating system and the BIOS and directly control the hardware—by reading and writing to port addresses or specific locations in memory. To provide full MS-DOS compatibility, the OS/2 real mode environment must support all three of these channels.

Figure 12.2 illustrates the mechanisms used by OS/2 to provide support for MS-DOS programs in the compatibility environment. OS/2 must not only provide all requested services, but must also try to prevent real mode programs from interfering with protected mode programs that are sharing the same devices or memory locations. There is nothing OS/2 can do to control direct hardware access by real mode programs; accordingly, programs that directly access certain I/O addresses, to be described later in this chapter, cannot run under OS/2. OS/2, however, controls requests to the operating system and the ROM BIOS by intercepting the software interrupts used to access these services.

MS-DOS service requests, most of which are issued through interrupt 21h, are intercepted by an OS/2 router routine. The OS/2 router passes control to the appropriate code in the operating system kernel. To conserve memory and still provide a rapid response, the code for servicing real mode applications is divided into two portions. The most frequently requested routines are located within the section of the kernel in low memory. (One portion of the OS/2 kernel code is located in low memory,

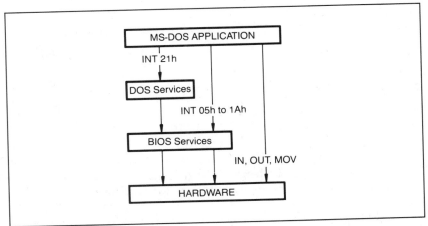

Figure 12.1: *The three ways MS-DOS applications access the underlying hardware*

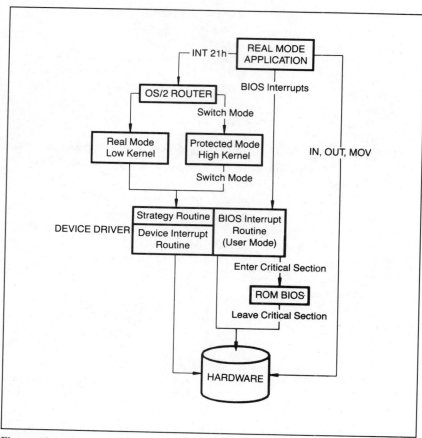

Figure 12.2: *OS/2 mechanisms for supporting real mode applications*

in the same general area as the operating system code under MS-DOS. The other portion of the OS/2 kernel code is placed above 1 Mb, in extended memory.) The router calls this code directly, since it can be executed in real mode. For less frequently invoked services, the OS/2 router transfers control to routines within the high section of the kernel (above 1 Mb), which are also used to service protected mode applications. The code for these routines, therefore, does not need to be duplicated in low memory. The operating system, however, must first switch into protected mode before calling the routine, and then switch back to real mode before returning control to the application, causing a lengthening of response time.

Once the kernel code has received control, if it needs to access a hardware device, it must call the strategy routine of the appropriate device driver. (The basic structure of an OS/2 device driver is similar to an MS-DOS device driver, although an OS/2 driver is much more complex.) Note that a single OS/2 device driver can be called by kernel code running in either real or protected mode, since these device drivers are designed to operate in either mode.

BIOS requests from real mode programs are typically intercepted by an interrupt routine belonging to the OS/2 device driver controlling the corresponding device. (For example, calls to the BIOS printer services using interrupt 17h would be intercepted by the printer device driver.) While handling such BIOS requests, the OS/2 device driver is said to be in *user mode*. There are two reasons for the device driver to intercept these requests rather than simply letting a real mode application access the ROM BIOS directly. First, since protected mode applications run concurrently with the real mode screen group, the device driver must prevent a real mode program from interfering with a device that is currently being used by a protected mode program. Therefore, it may have to use the semaphore mechanism (a form of interprocess synchronization) to serialize access to the device. Second, the device driver must prevent the user from switching into a protected mode screen group during a time-sensitive I/O operation, since the real mode process is totally suspended when placed in the background. The device driver can call a special operating system service to lock the real mode screen group temporarily in the foreground.

Once the device driver is ready to allow the real mode program access to the device, it has two choices. First, it may handle the low-level device operations itself, eliminating the need for the BIOS code. Second, it may simply invoke the original BIOS routine. Note that when intercepting a BIOS software interrupt, the device driver always receives control in real mode; therefore, unlike the strategy and hardware interrupt routines, it may safely call the ROM BIOS (which can run *only* in real mode).

▌ Guidelines for Real Mode Applications

The OS/2 compatibility environment closely emulates the environment of MS-DOS versions 3.0 and later with the SHARE program loaded (which supports network file sharing). Most standard MS-DOS applications will run without modification in the compatibility box, including many of those that perform "ill-behaved" actions such as writing directly to video memory or calling undocumented operating system functions. This section begins with a summary of some of the specific MS-DOS features that are supported by the OS/2 compatibility environment. Following this summary is a description of the features that are *not* supported, and then a discussion of some general differences between MS-DOS and the compatibility box.

Supported Features

Programs in the compatibility environment run in the real mode of the 80286 processor. Therefore, they may use all of the machine instructions available in the 8086/88 processors, plus several new instructions provided by the real mode of the 80286. In addition to the basic real mode instruction set, compatibility programs may access many of the system resources available to MS-DOS applications. The following is a description of some of the most important MS-DOS resources that are supported by the OS/2 DOS-compatibility environment. These resources are found at three levels within the system: the operating system level, the ROM BIOS level, and the hardware level.

The Operating System Level

Almost all of the MS-DOS services provided for application programs are available in the OS/2 compatibility environment. As described in Chapter 4, most of these services are accessed by placing the number of the desired function in register AH and invoking software interrupt number 21h. The available MS-DOS services are listed in Table 12.1. Note that the file sharing support normally provided by the MS-DOS 3.x SHARE command is automatically present in the OS/2 compatibility environment (consequently, there is no SHARE command in the OS/2 real mode).

MS-DOS Interrupt	Service Provided/Limitations
20h	Program terminate.
21h	Primary function dispatcher.
25h	Absolute disk read.
26h	Absolute disk write; supported only for diskettes.
27h	Terminate and stay resident.

Table 12.1: *MS-DOS Services Provided by the OS/2 DOS-Compatibility Environment*

In addition to this basic set of services, several undocumented DOS functions commonly used by memory resident utilities are also provided. For example, you may use interrupt 21h, function 34h, to obtain a pointer to a flag indicating when DOS (or in this case, OS/2) is active (see Chapter 11).

In addition to the providing MS-DOS application services, the OS/2 real mode also supports the following interrupt vectors in the same manner as MS-DOS:

Interrupt 22h	This interrupt vector stores the address of the program terminate routine. This address is used by the operating system, and the interrupt should *not* be invoked by your program.
Interrupt 23h	OS/2 invokes this interrupt when it detects a Ctrl-C or Ctrl-Break key. You can point this vector to your own Break-key handler (see Chapter 6).
Interrupt 24h	OS/2 invokes this interrupt when it encounters a critical error. You can point this vector to your own critical error handler (see Chapter 6).
Interrupt 28h	OS/2 repeatedly invokes this interrupt when in an idle state—for example, while waiting for keyboard input at the operating system prompt. This interrupt is provided for the benefit of background memory resident programs such as print spoolers (see Chapter 11).

The BIOS Level

Table 12.2 lists the ROM BIOS services that are supported by the OS/2 compatibility environment (see also Chapter 5 and Appendix C). Note that some of these vectors may actually point to routines belonging to OS/2 device drivers, so that the device drivers can control access to the devices they manage. Accordingly, you must invoke these services through the appropriate interrupt vectors and not through absolute memory addresses.

In addition to the basic BIOS services, OS/2 supports several other BIOS-level features present in MS-DOS machines. First, the following interrupts are invoked by the BIOS:

Interrupt 1Bh	The BIOS invokes this interrupt when it detects a Control-Break key. You can point this vector to your own Break-key handler (see Chapter 6).

BIOS Interrupt	Service Provided/Limitations
10h	Video services.
11h	List of installed equipment.
12h	Size of Memory (reports only the size of the compatibility environment).
13h	Disk/diskette services. For disk, only functions 01h, 02h, 0Ah, and 15h are supported (no writes). For diskettes, all functions are supported.
14h	Serial port services. If the OS/2 COM.SYS driver is installed, you must enable the serial port in real mode by running the SETCOM40 command.
15h	System servics. All these functions are supported except numbers 87h through 91h.
16h	Keyboard services.
17h	Printer services.
19h	Bootstrap loader.
1Ah	System-timer and real-time clock services. These functions are supported except for numbers 02h through 07h.

Table 12.2: *ROM BIOS Services Supported by the OS/2 DOS-Compatibility Environment*

Interrupt 1Ch   The BIOS invokes this interrupt with each clock tick hardware interrupt (approximately 18.2 times per second; see Chapter 6). You can point this vector to your own clock tick routine; note, however, that this routine will *not* be called when the real mode screen group is placed in the background.

Second, as with MS-DOS, the system consults the parameter tables that are pointed to by the following interrupt vectors (see Chapter 6):

Interrupt 1Dh   This vector points to a table of video initialization parameters.

| Interrupt 1Eh | This vector points to a table of diskette parameters used during system initialization. |
| Interrupt 1Fh | This vector points to a table of graphics characters for the upper 127 ASCII codes. |

Finally, the standard BIOS data area is maintained in low memory. This area begins at the address 0040h:0000h, and contains a large set of parameters including the following (see Chapter 6):

- Addresses of serial and parallel ports.
- A list of installed devices.
- The amount of memory installed.
- The keyboard buffer.
- Disk and diskette parameters.
- Video parameters.
- Time of day information.

The Hardware Level

A program that is to run in the OS/2 compatibility environment may take direct control over the hardware in several ways.

First, as with MS-DOS, you may write a hardware interrupt handler and redirect a hardware interrupt vector to point to your routine rather than to the original handler. This procedure is known as *hooking* an interrupt. Under OS/2, however, there are three important exceptions:

- You may not hook the CMOS real-time clock interrupt (interrupt number 70h).
- You may not hook an interrupt that is already owned by an OS/2 device driver. (An example of a hardware interrupt vector that is typically owned by a device driver is number 76h, which is invoked by the fixed disk controller.)
- You *may* hook the keyboard interrupt (number 09h), even if it is owned by an OS/2 device driver.

If your real mode program attempts to hook the real-time clock interrupt or an interrupt vector that is already owned, OS/2 immediately stops the program and displays the error message shown in Figure 12.3. The system gives you the choice of either terminating the program or continuing the program without changing the interrupt vector.

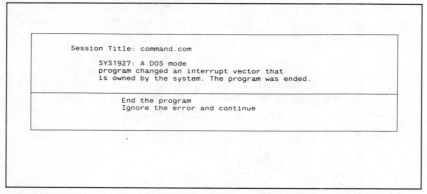

```
        Session Title: command.com

            SYS1927: A DOS mode
        program changed an interrupt vector that
        is owned by the system. The program was ended.

                End the program
                Ignore the error and continue
```

Figure 12.3: *The error message displayed if your program attempts to hook an interrupt vector owned by the system*

The following are examples of useful hardware interrupt vectors that your program may safely hook:

Interrupt 08h   This interrupt is invoked approximately 18.2 times per second by the 8253 timer chip.

Interrupt 09h   This interrupt is invoked each time a keyboard key is either pressed or released.

Just as with MS-DOS, you may set the appropriate interrupt vector to point to your routine; however, you should save the old address and call this address from your routine to avoid blocking interrupt handlers installed by other real mode programs. Note that there are two limitations that may affect timing-sensitive interrupt handlers in the real mode of OS/2:

- Remember that while the real mode screen group is in the foreground, background protected mode threads continue to receive processor time slices. If a hardware interrupt occurs while a protected mode thread is running, the system must switch thread contexts *and* switch into real mode in order to pass control to a real mode interrupt handler. The delay produced by this switching procedure could cause applications with strict timing requirements to loose interrupts.

- Remember also that real mode programs are suspended when the user switches this screen group to the background. Therefore, *no* interrupts are received when the real mode screen group is in the background. A handler for the clock tick interrupt (number 08h), for example, must not depend upon receiving an uninterrupted sequence of interrupts. Also, a real mode communications program that is interrupt driven will not receive characters when a protected mode screen group is in the foreground.

A real mode program may also control the hardware by directly reprogramming the following devices:

- The 8253 timer chip—For example, a program that generates sound can reprogram this chip to obtain various frequencies.

- The serial and parallel ports—A real mode program may reprogram these devices; however, doing so makes the devices associated with these ports unavailable to protected mode programs.

□■ Features Not Supported
□□

It is important to remember that programs within the OS/2 compatibility environment run in the *real mode*, and therefore may not use any of the unique protected mode features provided by OS/2, such as the OS/2 application program interface and the large virtual memory space. Furthermore, your program must not switch itself into protected mode by calling the BIOS or directly setting the protection enable bit of the machine status word. Also, a program running in the compatibility environment cannot use extended memory (that is, memory above 1 Mb, normally accessed through several BIOS services that will be described later in this section). Extended memory is reserved for the operating system and protected mode programs. Therefore, you cannot run print spoolers, RAM disks, disk caches, or other utilities that use extended memory. Note, however, that a real mode program may access expanded memory that follows the Lotus/Intel/Microsoft expanded memory specification, described in Chapter 10.

The following is a description of resources that exist in a typical MS-DOS machine and that are off-limits for a compatibility environment program. These resources are found at the levels of the operating system, the ROM BIOS, and the hardware.

The DOS Level

First, your program must not demand a specific MS-DOS version. Under the initial release of OS/2, the DOS "get version" service (function number 30h) returns a value of 10.0. Therefore, if your program requires the features of MS-DOS version 3.0 or later, for example, you should test that the major version number is equal to or greater than 3.

Also, under OS/2 you may not perform sector level writes to a fixed disk through DOS interrupt 26h. You may, however, use this function for direct writes to floppy disks. You should perform all writes to fixed disks through the DOS file system (for example, using function 40h, "write to a file or device"; see Chapter 4).

Another DOS service that has been eliminated from OS/2 is the direct access to the DOS PRINT queue that is provided by MS-DOS version 3.0 or later through interrupt 2Fh, function 01h. Under MS-DOS, the PRINT command installs itself as a memory resident utility so that it can continue to print files in the background while the user runs other programs. Interrupt 2Fh, function 01h, allows a program to access the services of the resident PRINT program. Under OS/2, however, the PRINT program no longer remains resident in memory, and therefore this interrupt function is not provided. Note that OS/2 provides background printing through the SPOOL utility, which services real mode as well as protected mode programs.

Finally, Microsoft offers several general suggestions for maintaining compatibility with present and future versions of MS-DOS and the OS/2 real mode environment; note, however, that these are not absolute rules. Among the guidelines are the following:

- Use the file handle functions rather than the older functions that employ file control blocks.

- Avoid the character device I/O functions in the range from 01h to 0Ch. Rather, perform I/O to character devices whenever possible through the file handle functions (for example, function number 40h, "write to a file or device").

- Allocate and deallocate memory through the DOS memory management services (numbers 48h, 49h, and 4Ah). Do not use areas of memory not allocated through the operating system.

- Use DOS function 4Bh ("load or execute a program") for loading programs and overlays, rather than the obsolete function 26h ("create new program segment"). Also, using function 4Bh is superior to writing a custom loading routine that may depend upon a specific .EXE header format (the .EXE format is subject to change).

- Use DOS function 31h to terminate a resident program rather that interrupt 27h. Function 31h supports larger programs and allows you to return a error level code to the parent process.

- Use functions 25h and 35h to modify interrupt vectors, rather than writing directly to the interrupt vector table in memory.

- Use the .EXE executable file format rather than the .COM format, which does not contain loading information and is being phased out.

The BIOS Level

A program that runs in the compatibility environment of OS/2 cannot use the following BIOS services (see Chapter 5 and Appendix C):

Interrupt 05h	Under MS-DOS, this interrupt generates a print screen as if the shift-PrtSc keys were pressed. Under OS/2, the interrupt is ignored.
Interrupt 13h	This interrupt provides access to the BIOS disk services. Under OS/2, for a fixed disk, you may not use any of the functions that *write* to the disk (such as function 03h, "write sectors", or 05h, "format cylinder"). For a removable disk, you may use any appropriate function.

Also, you may not use the following BIOS functions that are accessed through interrupt 15h and are provided on 80286 and 80386 machines for managing extended memory, switching into protected mode, and sharing devices in multitasking systems:

Function 87h	Move block to or from extended memory.
Function 89h	Switch processor to protected mode.
Function 90h	Device busy.
Function 91h	Interrupt complete.

Finally, under OS/2 you are not free to manage the CMOS real-time clock, since this device is the exclusive province of the operating system. The following functions, accessed through interrupt 1Ah, are therefore off-limits:

Function 02h	Read real-time clock.
Function 03h	Set real-time clock.
Function 04h	Read real-time clock date.
Function 05h	Set real-time clock date.
Function 06h	Set real-time clock alarm.
Function 07h	Reset real-time clock alarm.

The Hardware Level

As mentioned in the section in this chapter on supported features, you may not hook the CMOS real-time clock interrupt (number 70h); nor may you hook a hardware interrupt that belongs to an OS/2 device driver (other than the keyboard interrupt, number 09h). Also, under OS/2 you may not reprogram the following devices:

- The 8259 interrupt controller.

- The disk controller (sometimes remapped by copy protection schemes).

- The DMA controller (sometimes remapped by high speed communications programs).

General Differences

In addition to the specific limitations imposed on MS-DOS applications by the OS/2 compatibility box, there are several general differences in the behavior of a program running in each of these two environments.

First, the overall performance of a program may vary between MS-DOS and the OS/2 compatibility environment. Whether an application runs faster or slower in the compatibility environment depends upon the type of application and the current configuration of OS/2. Among the factors that tend to make a program run faster under OS/2 are the more efficient file-handling algorithms and the faster screen display methods used by this operating system. For example, the TYPE command runs approximately ten percent faster under OS/2 than under MS-DOS. Among the factors that tend to make an MS-DOS program run slower under OS/2 are the following:

- Protected mode tasks running in the background compete with the real mode program for processor cycles. Obviously, the more background protected mode programs are loaded (especially those assigned a high priority level), the slower the real mode program will run.

- As described in the section on the structure of the compatibility environment, some operating system services require mode switching, which lengthens response time.

- Hardware interrupt service routines in real mode programs may also necessitate mode switching (as well as switching thread contexts) if a protected mode thread is active when an interrupt occurs.

Most MS-DOS applications run in the OS/2 compatibility box with acceptable performance. The compatibility environment, however, is unsuitable for two general categories of programs. The first category consists of programs that cannot tolerate being temporarily suspended. One example is a program that relies on a steady stream of clock interrupts to time events; while such a program is suspended, no interrupts would be received and its timing information would become invalid. Another example is a real-time equipment control system, which would miss external events while suspended.

The second group of programs that cannot run in the OS/2 compatibility environment are those that must respond to hardware interrupts at a high rate. Because OS/2 intercepts hardware interrupts and may need to perform a context and processor mode switch before passing control to the real mode interrupt handler, an OS/2 program cannot respond to interrupts as rapidly as an MS-DOS program, which receives interrupts directly. The OS/2 interrupt response may be especially slow if there are many protected mode threads in the background. An example of a program that may fail under the real mode of OS/2 is a terminal emulator that operates at a high baud rate.

The OS/2 print spooler may also cause real mode programs to behave differently under OS/2 than under MS-DOS. If the spooler is installed, printer output will be quickly stored in a spool file, and the program will continue running without waiting for the output to print. The output will normally not begin printing until either the printer file is closed (for example, **fclose (stdprn)**), or the program terminates. Note, however, that the user can flush the print spooler and send the output immediately to the printer at any time by pressing the Control-Alt-PrtSc key combination.

∷ Rules for Device Drivers

Under the OS/2 model for device support, there is a single device driver for each physical device. A standard OS/2 device driver receives I/O requests from both protected mode and real mode programs. These device drivers must be written according to the guidelines given in the *OS/2 Device Driver Guide* (supplied with the Microsoft OS/2 Software Development Kit), and although they will support real mode applications in the compatibility environment of OS/2, they will *not* run under MS-DOS.

A limited number of MS-DOS device drivers, however, *can* be installed under OS/2. These drivers are designed to run only in real mode, and can support I/O requests only from programs in the compatibility environment. Since OS/2 allows a limit of one device driver per physical device, a device controlled by an MS-DOS driver remains unavailable to protected mode applications. The advantage of these device drivers, however, is that you can write a single driver for both MS-DOS and OS/2, and you can follow the relatively simple rules for writing a device driver under MS-DOS. For information on writing MS-DOS device drivers, see Chapter 9.

There are three major limitations placed on MS-DOS device drivers that are to run under OS/2. First, the device driver must be for a character device. MS-DOS block device drivers cannot be installed. Second, the character device driver cannot employ a hardware interrupt handler. Rather than being driven by interrupts, it must *poll* to determine if the device is ready. Note that for an MS-DOS device driver, the operating system itself calls the "interrupt routine" (which is therefore an interrupt routine only by name). Third, the supported character device cannot be either a mouse or a clock device. Driving either of these devices with an MS-DOS device driver would make them available exclusively to real mode programs; however, exclusive real mode access to these two devices is not permitted. Examples of MS-DOS device drivers that can be installed under OS/2 are old VDI (video display interface) and CON (console) drivers.

There is one more restriction to keep in mind when programming an MS-DOS device driver that is to run under OS/2. The initialization routine of an MS-DOS device driver may call DOS interrupt 21h functions 01h through 0Ch to perform I/O, and function 30h to obtain the operating system version. Under OS/2, however, the initialization code may not call any DOS interrupt 21h functions.

Note that a device driver following the MS-DOS model is installed in the same manner as an OS/2 device driver—by placing a DEVICE = command in the configuration file. OS/2, however, keeps MS-DOS and OS/2 device drivers in separate lists.

INTERRUPT VECTOR TABLE

The following table summarizes the entries of the interrupt vector table, as they are used in IBM-PC, AT, and PS/2 compatible machines. The *interrupt* is the hexadecimal interrupt number or *type*. The *address* is the hexadecimal offset within segment 0000h of the actual interrupt vector table entry; this value is obtained by multiplying the interrupt number by 4. The *class* is the classification of the interrupt: *H* for an external hardware interrupt, *I* for an internal hardware interrupt, *S* for a software interrupt, and *D* for a data interrupt (i.e., one that stores the address of a data table, not an executable routine). The *function* column describes the current conventional use for the vector table entry. See Chapter 4 for a general explanation of the interrupt mechanism and a description of internal, hardware, and software interrupts. See Chapter 6 for more information on the data interrupt vectors. There are a number of additional internal interrupts generated by the AT that are not supported by the BIOS and are not included in this table.

Interrupt	Address	Class	Function
00	0000	I	Generated by the CPU on attempted division by 0
01	0004	I	Generated by the CPU when the trap flag is set (for single stepping)
02	0008	H	The nonmaskable interrupt (see Chapter 6)
03	000C	S	Used to set break-points by debuggers (this is a *one-byte* interrupt instruction)
04	0010	I	Generated by the CPU on arithmetic overflow (overflow flag set on an **into** instruction)

Interrupt	Address	Class	Function
05	0014	S	BIOS print-screen routine
06	0018		Reserved by IBM
07	001C		Reserved by IBM
08	0020	H	Generated by clock tick (IRQ0)
09	0024	H	Generated by keyboard action (IRQ1)
0A	0028	H	Reserved by IBM (IRQ2)
0B	002C	H	Generated by COM2 (IRQ3)
0C	0030	H	Generated by COM1 (IRQ4)
0D	0034	H	XT: Generated by hard disk (IRQ5) AT: Generated by LPT2 (IRQ5)
0E	0038	H	Generated by diskette (IRQ6)
0F	003C	H	Generated by LPT1 (IRQ7)
10	0040	S	BIOS video services
11	0044	S	BIOS equipment list service
12	0048	S	BIOS memory size service
13	004C	S	BIOS disk/diskette services
14	0050	S	BIOS communications services
15	0054	S	BIOS cassette services AT, PS/2, PC Convertible, and certain models of the PC XT: Extended services

Interrupt	Address	Class	Function
16	0058	S	BIOS keyboard services
17	005C	S	BIOS printer services
18	0060	S	Activates ROM BASIC
19	0064	S	Reboots system
1A	0068	S	BIOS time-of-day services
1B	006C	S	Called by BIOS interrupt 09 handler on a Ctrl-Break (user can install a routine)
1C	0070	S	Called by BIOS interrupt 08 handler (user can install a routine)
1D	0074	D	Table of video initialization parameters
1E	0078	D	Table of disk parameters
1F	007C	D	Table of high graphics characters
20	0080	S	DOS program terminate service
21	0084	S	Main entry point for DOS services
22	0088	S	Terminate routine; the EXEC function transfers control to the routine at this address on program termination
23	008C	S	Interrupt issued by DOS when Ctrl-Break is detected
24	0090	S	Interrupt issued by DOS on critical error
25	0094	S	DOS absolute disk read
26	0098	S	DOS absolute disk write
27	009C	S	DOS terminate but stay-resident service

Interrupt	Address	Class	Function
28	00A0	S	DOS "idle" interrupt (see Chapter 11)
29–2E		S	Reserved for DOS
2A	00A8	S	Accesses MS-NET
2F	00BC	S	DOS print spooler and multiplex interrupt
30–3F		S	Reserved for DOS
40–5F			Reserved for BIOS
40	0100	S	New diskette interrupt vector if hard disk installed
41	0104	D	Fixed disk parameter vector for first fixed disk
42	0108	S	Used by EGA BIOS to redirect the video interrupt
43	010C	D	EGA initialization parameters
44	0110	D	EGA character table
46	0118	D	Fixed disk parameter vector for second fixed disk
4A	0128	S	AT: alarm called by interrupt 70
5A	0168	S	Cluster
5B	016C	S	Used by cluster program
60–67		S	Available for user programs
67	019C	S	Expanded Memory Manager services
68–7F			Not used in PC/XT
70	01C0	H	AT, XT 296, and PS/2 except Models 25 and 30: real-time clock (IRQ8)

Interrupt	Address	Class	Function
71	01C4	H	AT, XT 296, and PS/2 except Models 25 and 30: redirection to interrupt 0A (IRQ9)
75	01D4	H	AT, XT 296, and PS/2 except Models 25 and 30: redirection to NMI interrupt
80–85		S	Reserved for BASIC
86–F0		S	Used while BASIC interpreter is running
F1–FF			Not used; reserved for user program interrupts

APPENDIX B

THE MS-DOS FUNCTIONS

▪▫ MS-DOS Interrupts
▫▪

The following table lists the MS-DOS interrupt functions that provide services to programs. *Interrupt* is the interrupt number in hexadecimal. *Version* indicates the first version of the operating system that supports the function; the function would thus be available with this and all subsequent MS-DOS versions.

Interrupt	Version	Service performed
20	1.0	Terminate program
21	1.0	Main function dispatcher
25	1.0	Absolute disk read
26	1.0	Absolute disk write
27	1.0	Terminate program and stay resident
2F	3.0	Multiplex interrupt; currently provides access to the resident portions of the DOS PRINT spooler (function 01h), ASSIGN command (06h), SHARE utility (10h), and APPEND command (B7h)

▪▫ Interrupt 21h Functions
▫▪

The following table lists the functions available through the main MS-DOS function dispatcher, interrupt 21h. *Function* gives the function numbers in hexadecimal (i.e., the values loaded into register AH when invoking interrupt 21h). A function is available under the version given in the *version* column as well as all later versions.

Function	Version	Service Performed
00	1.0	Terminate program
01	1.0	Read character from standard input, with echo
02	1.0	Write character to standard output device
03	1.0	Read character from standard auxiliary device
04	1.0	Write character to standard auxiliary device
05	1.0	Write character to standard printer device
06	1.0	Read/write character from standard input/output device
07	1.0	Read character from standard input, without echo; no check for Ctrl-Break
08	1.0	Read character from standard input, without echo; checks Ctrl-Break
09	1.0	Write string to standard output device
0A	1.0	Read string from standard input device
0B	1.0	Check if character available from standard input
0C	1.0	Clear keyboard buffer and invoke I/O function
0D	1.0	Reset disk
0E	1.0	Select disk
0F	1.0	Open file
10	1.0	Close file
11	1.0	Find first matching file
12	1.0	Find next matching file
13	1.0	Delete file

Function	Version	Service Performed
14	1.0	Sequential read
15	1.0	Sequential write
16	1.0	Create file
17	1.0	Rename file
19	1.0	Get current default drive
1A	1.0	Set disk transfer address
1B	1.0	Get allocation table information for default drive
1C	1.0	Get allocation table information for specified drive
1D		Reserved for DOS
1E		Reserved for DOS
1F		Reserved for DOS
20		Reserved for DOS
21	1.0	Random read
22	1.0	Random write
23	1.0	Get file size
24	1.0	Set random record field
25	1.0	Set interrupt vector
26	1.0	Create new program segment
27	1.0	Random block read
28	1.0	Random block write
29	1.0	Parse filename
2A	1.0	Get system date
2B	1.0	Set system date
2C	1.0	Get system time
2D	1.0	Set system time
2E	1.0	Set or clear DOS verify switch
2F	2.0	Get disk transfer address
30	2.0	Get DOS version number
31	2.0	Terminate program and remain resident

Function	Version	Service Performed
32		Reserved for DOS
33	2.0	Get or set state of Ctrl-Break checking
34	2.0	Return **indos** flag (undocumented, see Chapter 11)
35	2.0	Get interrupt vector
36	2.0	Get disk free space
37		Reserved for DOS
38	2.1	Get/Set country dependent information
	3.0	Get or set country dependent information
39	2.0	Create subdirectory
3A	2.0	Remove subdirectory
3B	2.0	Change the current directory
3C	2.0	Create a file
3D	2.0	Open a file
3E	2.0	Close a file
3F	2.0	Read from a file or device
40	2.0	Write to a file or device
41	2.0	Delete a file from a specified directory
42	2.0	Move file read-write pointer
43	2.0	Change file mode
44	2.0	I/O control for devices
45	2.0	Duplicate a file handle (returns a *new* handle pointing to same file as passed handle)
46	2.0	Force a given file handle to refer to same file as another handle
47	2.0	Get current directory
48	2.0	Allocate memory
49	2.0	Free allocated memory

Function	Version	Service Performed
4A	2.0	Modify allocated memory block
4B	2.0	Load or execute a child program
4C	2.0	Terminate program, setting return status
4D	2.0	Get return status from a child process
4E	2.0	Find first matching file
4F	2.0	Find next matching file
50		Set program segment prefix (undocumented, see Chapter 11)
51		Get program segment prefix (undocumented, see Chapter 11)
52		Reserved for DOS
53		Reserved for DOS
54	2.0	Get current setting of DOS verify switch
55		Reserved for DOS
56	2.0	Rename a file
57	2.0	Get/set a file's date and time
58		Reserved for DOS
59	3.0	Get extended error information
5A	3.0	Create a unique file
5B	3.0	Create a new file (will fail if file exists)
5C	3.0	Lock/unlock file access
5D		Reserved for DOS
5E	3.1	Get machine name, set/get printer setup
5F	3.1	Get redirection list (nonlocal network assignments), redirect device/cancel redirection
60		Reserved for DOS
61		Reserved for DOS

Function	Version	Service Performed
62	3.0	Get program segment prefix (PSP) address
65	3.3	Get extended country information
66	3.3	Get/set global code page
67	3.3	Set file handle count
68	3.3	Flush file data and update directory entry (rather than using close/open sequence)
6Ch	4.0	Extended open/create. Combines the services offered by functions 3Dh (open), 3Ch (create file), and 5Bh (create new file).

The BIOS Functions

The following pages summarize the service routines available through the BIOS of IBM PC/AT compatible computers. See Chapter 5 for a general description of the BIOS services, strategies for selecting the optimal routine, and programming examples. The description of each interrupt function consists of two major parts: the entry, which describes the values that must be loaded into the registers before invoking the interrupt, and the return, which describes the values that are returned to the application by the interrupt function. Chapter 4 contains general information on the interrupt mechanism and the process of accessing interrupt functions from C and assembly language.

▣ Interrupt 05h: Print-Screen Service

Entry:

　None

Return:

　None

Note:　This is the same routine that is invoked by pressing the Shift-PrtSc keys, and is conveniently available to an application program through interrupt 05h.

Interrupt 10h: The Video Services

Function 00h: Set Video Mode

Entry:

AH   00h

AL   Video mode. The following are the possible values:

00h	40 × 25 B&W text
01h	40 × 25 color text
02h	80 × 25 B&W text
03h	80 × 25 color text
04h	320 × 200 4-color graphics, 2-color palettes
05h	320 × 200 B&W graphics
06h	640 × 200 B&W graphics
07h	80 × 25 monochrome
08h	160 × 200 16-color graphics (PCjr)
09h	320 × 200 16-color graphics (PCjr)
0Ah	640 × 200 4-color graphics (PCjr)
0Dh	320 × 200 16-color graphics (EGA)
0Eh	640 × 200 16-color graphics (EGA)
0Fh	640 × 350 monochrome graphics (EGA)
10h	640 × 350 4-color (EGA with 64K video RAM) or 16-color (EGA with 128K video RAM) graphics
11h	640 × 480 2-color graphics (MCGA and VGA)
12h	640 × 480 16-color graphics (VGA)
13h	320 × 200 256-color graphics (MCGA and VGA)

Return:

Nothing

Function 01h: Set Cursor Type

Entry:

AH	01h
CH	Bits 0–4: Starting line for cursor (other bits should be 0).
CL	Bits 0–4: Stopping line for cursor (other bits should be 0).

Note: The range for lines is 0–13 on a monochrome system, and 0–7 on a CGA system. Lines are numbered beginning from the top. The default for MDA is start = 12 and stop = 13, and for CGA it is start = 6 and stop = 7. Setting on bit 5 or 6 generally makes the cursor disappear. The cursor blinking is hardware controlled and cannot be disabled via a software routine.

Return:

Nothing

Function 02h: Set Cursor Position

Entry:

AH	02h
BH	Video page number (must be 0 for graphics modes)
DH	Cursor row (0–24)
DL	Cursor column

The permissible range of values for the cursor column is 0 to 39 in 40-column text modes or low-resolution graphics modes (04h and 05h). The range is 0 to 79 in 80-column text modes and medium-resolution graphics mode (06h).

Return:

Nothing

Function 03h: Read Cursor Position

Entry:

AH   03h

BH   Page number

Note: The monochrome adapter has only one page. In color modes, there is a separate cursor for each page.

Return:

CH   Current starting line for cursor

CL   Current stopping line for cursor

Note: The above two values are the same as those set by function 01h.

DH   Cursor row

DL   Cursor column

Function 04h: Read Light Pen Position

Entry:

AH   04h

Return:

AH   0 means light pen switch not down/not triggered

        1 means valid light pen value in registers

BX   Pixel column (0 to 319 or 639, depending on mode)

CH   Raster line (0–199)

DH   Row of character light pen position (0–24)

DL   Column of character light pen position (0–39 or 0–79)

⊟▪ Function 05h: Select Active Display Page (text modes only)

Entry:

AH	05h
AL	New display page. The ranges of possible values are as follows:

0–7 for video modes 00h and 01h

0–3 for video modes 02h and 03h

Return:

Nothing

Note: Monochrome adapters have only a single display page, and color adapters have multiple pages only in text modes. Data can be written to any page, and the cursor controlled, regardless of which page is currently displayed. Also, changing display pages does not alter the contents of any page.

⊟▪ Function 06h: Scroll Active Page Up

Entry:

AH	06h
AL	Number of lines to scroll
	Blank lines are inserted at the bottom; a value of 0 means to blank the entire window
BH	Video display attribute to be used on blank lines
CH	Row of upper-left corner of window to scroll
CL	Column of upper-left corner of window to scroll
DH	Row of lower-right corner of window to scroll
DL	Column of lower right corner of window to scroll

Return:

Nothing

Note: Functions 06h and 07h can be used for scrolling or clearing either windows or the entire screen. Only the currently displayed video page is scrolled. Old lines are lost off the screen, and the new lines are filled with blanks that have the attribute specified through BH.

Function 07h: Scroll Active Page Down

Entry:

AH	07h
AL	Number of lines to scroll
	Blank lines are inserted at the bottom; a value of 0 means to blank the entire window.
BH	Video display attribute to be used on blank lines
CH	Row of upper-left corner of window to scroll
CL	Column of upper-left corner of window to scroll
DH	Row of lower-right corner of window to scroll
DL	Column of lower-right corner of window to scroll

Return:

Nothing

Note: See comments for function 06h.

Function 08h: Read Character/Attribute at Current Cursor Position

Entry:

AH	08h
BH	Display page (valid for text modes only)

Return:

> AL   Character read
>
> AH   Attribute of character read (text modes only)

Note: This function reads characters in either text or graphics modes.

▛ Function 09h: Write Character/Attribute at Cursor Position

Entry:

> AH   09h
>
> AL   Character to write

Note: If in a CGA graphics mode, only the first 128 characters are available in the BIOS; the higher 128 characters must be contained in a table pointed to by interrupt vector 1Fh (see Chapter 6).

> BH   Display page (valid for text modes only)
>
> BL   If in a text mode: the display attribute
>
>   If in a graphics mode: the color
>
>   The valid range of colors for graphics mode 04h is 0–3 to choose a color from the current palette. If bit 7 is on, graphics character pixels are combined, using an exclusive **OR**, with underlying pixels to provide contrast, so that the characters are legible. The setting of BL has no effect on high-resolution graphics mode 06h.
>
> CX   Number of characters to write

Note: This factor causes a single character to be replicated, and in a graphics mode will produce valid results only for characters contained in the same row.

Return:

> Nothing

Note: This function does not update the cursor position; function 02h must be called to move the cursor. Control characters such as backspace and carriage return are not treated as special characters, but are simply displayed as symbols.

Function 0Ah: Write Character Only at Cursor Position

Entry:

AH	0Ah
AL	Character to write

Note: If in a CGA graphics mode, only the first 128 characters are available in the BIOS; the higher 128 characters must be contained in a table pointed to by interrupt vector 1Fh (see Chapter 6).

BH	Display page (valid for text modes only)
CX	Number of characters to write

Note: This factor causes a single character to be replicated, and in a graphics mode will produce valid results only for characters contained in the same row.

Return:

Nothing

Note: This function is the same as function 09h except that the display attribute is not modified (it uses the display attribute that already exists at the position where the character is written). Function 0Ah does not update the cursor position; function 02h must be called to move the cursor. Control characters such as backspace and carriage return are not treated as special characters, but are simply displayed as symbols.

Function 0Bh: Set Color Palette

Entry:

AH	0Bh

BH   Request ID:

0 means that the background/border color is to be set.

1 means that the color palette is to be selected.

BL   The color value

If BH is 0, then BL should contain a value from 0 to 31 (16 to 31 select high intensity) to indicate the color of the background and border in graphics modes, or of just the border in color text modes. If BH is 1, then BL selects the color palette. For the CGA, there are only two such palettes, and they pertain only to the low-resolution graphics mode, 04h, in which each pixel is encoded in video memory using two bits. The following table lists the colors available in each of the two palettes. Background refers to whatever color is currently selected for the background.

Palette	Two-bit pixel value	Color
0	0	Background
	1	Green
	2	Red
	3	Yellow
1	0	Background
	1	Cyan
	2	Magenta
	3	White

Return:

Nothing

Function 0Ch: Write Pixel

Entry:

AH   0Ch

AL   Color of pixel to be written

If the video mode is 04h, then AL should be given a value in the range 0–3 to select a color from the current palette. If the video mode is 06h, then AL should be 0 or 1 to select black or white. If bit 7 is on, the pixel is combined using an exclusive **OR** with the underlying pixel value to provide contrast.

CX   Column number

If the video mode is 04h or 05h, then the range of column values is 0–319. If the video mode is 06h, then the range is 0–639.

DX   Row number

If the video mode is 04h, 05h, or 06h, then the valid range of row numbers is 0–199.

Return:

Nothing

Function 0Dh: Read Pixel

Entry:

AH   0Dh

CX   Column number

If the video mode is 04h or 05h, then the range of column values is 0–319. If the video mode is 06h, then the range is 0–639.

DX   Row number

If the video mode is 04h, 05h, or 06h, then the valid range of row numbers is 0–199.

Return:

AL   The pixel value read

Function 0Eh: Teletype Style Write to Active Page

Entry:

AH	0Eh
AL	Character to write
BL	Foreground color in graphics modes only

Return:

Nothing

Note: Unlike functions 09h and 0Ah, this function automatically advances the cursor and recognizes carriage return, line feed, backspace, and bell as special characters. Also, it correctly handles line wrapping and screen scrolling. However, except for the foreground color in graphics modes, it does not allow specification of display attributes (it simply uses the current attribute found at the cursor position). Note also that the screen width is determined by the last mode set.

Function 0Fh: Get Current Video State

Entry:

AH	0Fh

Return:

AH	Current number of text columns
AL	Current video mode

The following are the possible video mode values:

00h	40 × 25 B&W text
01h	40 × 25 color text

02h	80 × 25 B&W text
03h	80 × 25 color text
04h	320 × 200 4-color graphics
05h	320 × 200 B&W graphics
06h	640 × 200 B&W graphics
07h	80 × 25 monochrome
08h	160 × 200 16-color graphics (PCjr)
09h	320 × 200 16-color graphics (PCjr)
0Ah	640 × 200 4-color graphics (PCjr)
0Dh	320 × 200 16-color graphics (EGA)
0Eh	640 × 200 16-color graphics (EGA)
0Fh	640 × 350 monochrome graphics (EGA)
10h	640 × 350 4-color (with 64K video RAM) or 16- color (with 128K video RAM) graphics
11h	640 × 480 2-color graphics (MCGA and VGA)
12h	640 × 480 16-color graphics (VGA)
13h	320 × 200 256-color graphics (MCGA and VGA)
BH	Current active display page

Function 10h: Set Palette Registers, Set Intensity/Blink Attribute (EGA, MCGA, and VGA)

Entry:

AH	10h
AL	This register contains a value from 0 to 3 to indicate the specific service requested. These values select the following services:

    0   Set individual palette register

If this service is requested, then BL must contain the number of the palette register to be set, and BH must contain the value that is to be assigned to the register.

1   Set overscan (border) register

If this service is selected, then BH must contain the value to be assigned the overscan register.

2   Set all palette registers and overscan

If this service is selected, then registers ES:BX must point to a 17-byte table of palette values, followed by the overscan register value.

3   Toggle intensity/blinking bit (bit 7 of the attribute code)

If this service is selected, then BL should be set to 0 to enable intensity, or to 1 to enable blinking.

Return:

Nothing

Note: Function 10h provides 12 additional services that are available only for VGA systems (some of these services are also supported by MCGA systems). See the BIOS interface technical reference cited in the Bibliography for further details.

▣ Function 11h: Character Generator Interface (EGA, MCGA, and VGA)

Entry:

AH   11h

AL   Specifies the desired service

Note: Function 11h provides 15 individual subfunctions. See the BIOS interface technical reference cited in the Bibliography for a description of these services.

Return:

See the BIOS interface reference.

Function 12h: Video Configuration/Alternate Select (EGA, MCGA, and VGA)

Entry:

AH   12h

BL   This register should be assigned one of the following values to select the desired service:

    10h   Return video configuration

    20h   Select alternate print screen routine

Note: Function 12h provides 7 additional services available only for MCGA and VGA systems. See the BIOS interface technical reference.

Return:

If BL was set to 10h, then the following information is returned:

BH   0 or 1 indicating whether the monochrome or color mode is in effect:

    0   Color mode is in effect

    1   Monochrome mode is in effect

BL   The amount of EGA memory installed, according to the following codes:

    00   064K

    01   128K

    10   192K

    11   256K

CH   Feature bits

CL   Switch setting

If BL is set to 20h, then nothing is returned.

Function 13h: Write String (AT, EGA, and PS/2)

Entry:

AH	13h
AL	Contains a value from 0 to 3 indicating one of the following modes for writing the string:

0	Writes the string with a single specified attribute, without moving the cursor. BL should contain the attribute and the string should have the format: (**char**, **char**, **char**, etc.).
1	Writes the string with a single specified attribute, and moves the cursor. BL should contain the attribute and the string should have the format: (**char**, **char**, **char**, etc.).
2	Writes a string that contains an attribute for each character, without moving the cursor. The string should have the format: (**char**, **attr**, **char**, **attr**, etc).
3	Writes a string that contains an attribute for each character, and moves the cursor. The string should have the format: (**char**, **attr**, **char**, **attr**, etc).

BH	Video page number
BL	Attribute if AL is 0 or 1
CX	Number of characters in string (do not include number of attributes)
DH	Starting row
DL	Starting column
ES:BP	Pointer to string to be written

Return:

Nothing

Note: This function is available only with the AT, PC Convertible, PS/2, EGA systems, and the XT BIOS dated 1/10/86 and after. It writes a complete string, allows specification of an attribute, and recognizes carriage return, line feed, backspace, and bell as commands rather than as printable characters.

Other Interrupt 10h Services

The following two functions are available only in the PC Convertible. See the BIOS interface technical reference cited in the Bibliography for details.

Function 14h	Load LCD character font/set LCD high-intensity substitute (PC Convertible only)
Function 15h	Return physical display parameters for active display

The BIOS supplied with PS/2 machines provides the following additional functions, designed to support the MCGA and VGA video adapters. See the BIOS interface technical reference cited in the Bibliography for details.

Function 1Ah	Read/write display combination code
Function 1Bh	Return functionality/state information
Function 1Ch	Save/restore video state

▖▝ Interrupt 11h: Equipment List Service

Entry:

None

Returns:

AX   In the PC, the bits of this register indicate the installed equipment as follows (coding in the AT is slightly different, so see the AT technical refernce):

Bit	Meaning
15,14	Number of attached printers
13	Not used
12	Game I/O attached (if bit = 1)
11,10,9	Number of RS-232 adapters
8	Not used
7,6	Number of diskette drives. The following codes specify the number of diskette drives, but *only if bit 0 is 1:*

Code	Number of drives
00	1
01	2
10	3
11	4

5,4   Initial video mode:

Value	Mode
00	Not used
01	40 × 25 CGA card
10	80 × 25 CGA card
11	80 × 24 monochrome card

3,2 RAM on motherboard:

Code	Amount of RAM
00	16K
01	32K
10	48K
11	64K

1 Not used

0 If bit = 1, one or more diskette drives are present (see bits 7,6 for the actual number).

Note: This function returns the equipment flag word stored at location 0000h:0410h, which the BIOS sets only once at system startup on the basis of its diagnostics.

◼ Interrupt 12h: Memory Size Service

Entry:

None

Returns:

AX   Number of contiguous 1K blocks of memory

Note: This function obtains the amount of memory in the XT from the switches on the motherboard. This is the same value as stored at memory location 0000h:0413h.

Interrupt 13h: Diskette/Hard Disk Services

Function 00h: Reset Diskette/Disk System

Entry:

AH   00h

DL   A code indicating whether to reset a diskette or a hard disk. If the value is less than 80h, then a diskette is indicated; if the value is equal to or greater than 80h, then a hard disk is indicated.

Return:

Nothing

Note: This function resets the diskette or hard disk system and prepares for I/O. The function should be called after an error is detected.

Function 01h: Read Diskette/Hard Disk Status

Entry:

AH   01h

DL   A code indicating whether to obtain the status of the diskette system or the hard disk system. A value less than 80h indicates a diskette; a value equal to or greater than 80h indicates a hard disk.

Return:

AL   Status of last diskette/hard disk operation. The following are the possible values:

FFh   Hard disk only; sense operation failed

BBh   Hard disk only; undefined error

80h   Time out

40h	Bad seek
20h	Controller has failed
11h	Hard disk only; ECC corrected a data error
	The data were corrected by the ECC algorithm and are probably valid; the program, however, should check the validity.
10h	For a diskette, bad CRC on read
	For a hard disk, bad ECC on read
0Bh	Hard disk only: bad track flag detected
09h	Attempt to DMA across 64K boundary
08h	Diskette only: DMA overrun on operation
07h	Hard disk only: drive parameter activity failed
05h	Hard disk only: bad reset
04h	Record not found
03h	Diskette only: write protect error
02h	Address mark not found
01h	Bad command passed to BIOS

Note: This function returns the status of the last diskette or floppy disk operation attempted.

Function 02h: Read Sectors into Memory

Entry:

AH	02h
AL	Number of sectors to read (value not checked). For a diskette, the valid range is 01h–09h; for a hard disk, the valid range is 01h–80h.
CH	For a diskette, CH contains the track number, 0–39. For a hard disk, CH contains the cylinder number, 0–1023 (this is a 10-bit value; the two

high-order bits are placed in the upper two bits of register CL). The value is not checked.

CL   Sector number (value not checked). For a diskette, the valid range is 1–9. For a hard disk, the valid range is 1–17, and the upper two bits of CL are used for the two high-order bits of the cylinder number.

DH   Head number (value not checked). For a diskette, the valid range is 0–1; for a hard disk, the range is 0–7.

DL   Drive number (value checked). For a diskette, the valid range is 00h to 03h; for a hard disk, the range is 80h to 87h.

ES:BX   Address of buffer to receive data read.

Return:

If the carry flag is clear, the following information is returned:

AH   0

AL   Number of disk sectors successfully read

If the carry flag is set, the following information is returned:

AH   Error code

See the list of these codes defined under interrupt 13h, function number 01h (the values returned in AL).

Note: If an error occurs when reading a diskette, the correct procedure is to reset the system (function 00h) and retry the operation three times. This is to make sure that the problem is not due to motor startup, since no delay is automatically taken to allow the diskette drive motor to come up to speed.

Function 03h: Write Sectors from Memory

Entry:

AH   03h

AL   Number of sectors to write (value not checked). For a diskette, the valid range is 01h–09h; for a hard disk, the valid range is 01h–80h.

CH   For a diskette, CH contains the track number, 0–39. For a hard disk, CH contains the cylinder number, 0–1023 (this is a 10-bit value; the two high-order bits are placed in the upper two bits of register CL). The value is not checked.

CL   Sector number (value not checked). For a diskette, the valid range is 1–9. For a hard disk, the valid range is 1–17, and the upper two bits of CL are used for the two high-order bits of the cylinder number.

DH   Head number (value not checked). For a diskette, the valid range is 0–1; for a hard disk, the range is 0–7.

DL   Drive number (value checked). For a diskette, the valid range is 00h–03h; for a hard disk, the range is 80h–87h.

ES:BX   Address of buffer to containing data to be written

Return:

If the carry flag is clear, the following information is returned:

AH   0

AL   Number of disk sectors successfully written

If the carry flag is set, the following information is returned:

AH   Error code

See the list of these codes defined under interrupt 13h, function number 01h (the values returned in AL).

Note: The correct response to a write error is to reset the system and retry the operation.

Function 04h: Verify Sectors

Entry:

AH   04h

AL   Number of sectors to verify (value not checked). For a diskette, the valid range is 01h–09h; for a hard disk, the valid range is 01h–80h.

CH   For a diskette, CH contains the track number, 0–39.

           For a hard disk, CH contains the cylinder number, 0–1023 (this is a 10-bit value; the two high-order bits are placed in the upper two bits of register CL). The value is not checked.

CL   Sector number (value not checked). For a diskette, the valid range is 1–9. For a hard disk, the valid range is 1–17, and the upper two bits of CL are used for the two high-order bits of the cylinder number.

DH   Head number (value not checked). For a diskette, the valid range is 0–1; for a hard disk, the range is 0–7.

DL   Drive number (value checked). For a diskette, the valid range is 00h–03h; for a hard disk, the range is 80h–87h.

Return:

If the carry flag is clear, the following information is returned:

AH   0

AL   Number of disk sectors successfully verified

If the carry flag is set, the following information is returned:

AH   Error code

           See the list of these codes defined under interrupt 13h, function number 01h (the values returned in AL).

Note: The correct response to an error is to reset the system and retry the operation.

Function 05h: Format Track

Entry:

AH   05h

AL   Hard disk only: Interleave factor, in the range 1–16.

CH   For a diskette, CH contains the track number, 0–39. For a hard disk, CH contains the cylinder number, 0–1023 (this is a 10-bit value; the two high-order bits are placed in the upper two bits of register CL). The value is not checked.

DH   Head number (value not checked). For a diskette, the valid range is 0–1; for a hard disk, the range is 0–7.

DL   Drive number (value checked). For a diskette, the valid range is 00h–03h; for a hard disk, the range is 80h–87h.

ES:BX   Pointer to list of 4-byte address fields for the track. There must be a field for each sector on the track; each field contains the following:

              Track number

              Head number

              Sector number

              Number of bytes per sector

            The number of bytes per sector is coded as follows: 00 = 128, 01 = 256, 02 = 512, 03 = 1024. These data are used for labeling sectors so that they may be located during read or write operations. Note that the format of these fields applies to diskette drives; consult the controller documentation when writing routines to format hard disks.

Return:

If the carry flag is clear, the following information is returned:

AH   0

If the carry flag is set, the following information is returned:

AH   Error code

       See the list of these codes defined under interrupt 13h, function number 01h (the values returned in AL).

Note: The correct response to an error is to reset the system and retry the operation.

Additional Interrupt 13h Functions

The BIOS in the XT, AT, and PS/2 machines provides a series of additional service routines. The use of these routines requires knowledge of many low-level details of diskette and hard disk controllers, and is beyond the scope of this book. Consult one of the IBM hardware technical references or the BIOS interface technical reference, both cited in the Bibliography, for information on these functions.

The following additional functions are provided for floppy disk support:

Function 08h	Read diskette drive parameters
Function 15h	Read DASD type
Function 16h	Obtain diskette change status
Function 17h	Set DASD type for format
Function 18h	Set media type for format

The following additional functions are provided for fixed disks:

Function 06h	Format cylinder and set bad sector flags
Function 07h	Format drive starting at a specified cylinder
Function 08h	Read fixed disk drive parameters
Function 09h	Initialize drive pair characteristics
Function 0Ch	Seek
Function 0Dh	Alternate disk reset
Function 10h	Test drive ready
Function 11h	Recalibrate
Function 15h	Read DASD type
Function 19h	Park heads
Function 1Ah	Format unit

▪▫ Interrupt 14h: Communications Services

▫▪ Function 00h: Initialize Communications Port

Entry:

AH   00h

AL   Specifies the communications parameters as follows:

Bits 7, 6, and 5 = baud rate:

Bit value	Baud rate
000	110
001	150
010	300
011	600
100	1200
101	2400
110	4800
111	9600

Bits 4 and 3 = parity:

Bit value	Parity
x0	none
01	odd
11	even

Bit 2 = number of stopbits:

Bit value	Number of stopbits
0	1
1	2

Bits 1 and 0 = word length:

Bit value	Word length
10	7 bits
11	8 bits

DX   Specifies the serial port number, where 0 = COM1 and 1 = COM2.

Return:

AX   Serial port status, where AH contains the line status and AL contains the modem status. The bits have the following meanings when they are turned on:

AH =	Line status:
Bit 7	Time out
Bit 6	Transmission shift register empty
Bit 5	Transmission hold register empty
Bit 4	Break detected
Bit 3	Framing error
Bit 2	Parity error
Bit 1	Overrun error
Bit 0	Data ready
AL =	Modem status:
Bit 7	Receive line signal detected
Bit 6	Ring indicator
Bit 5	Data set ready
Bit 4	Clear to send
Bit 3	Change in receive line signal detected
Bit 2	Trailing edge ring detected
Bit 1	Change in status of data set ready
Bit 0	Change in status of clear to send

⊞ Function 01h: Send Character to Communications Port

Entry:

AH	01h
AL	Character to send (this register is preserved)
DX	Serial port number (0 = COM1, 1 = COM2)

Return:

AH If bit 7 = 1, then the routine was unable to transmit the character (timeout error).

If bit 7 = 0, then the remainder of AH contains the current line status:

Bit 6	Transmission shift register empty
Bit 5	Transmission hold register empty
Bit 4	Break detected
Bit 3	Framing error
Bit 2	Parity error
Bit 1	Overrun error
Bit 0	Data ready

⊞ Function 02h: Receive Character from Communications Port

Entry:

AH	02h
DX	Serial port number (0 = COM1, 1 = COM2)

Return:

AH If bit 7 = 1, a timeout occurred and the remaining status bits in AH are unreliable.

If bit 7 = 0 (no timeout), then the other *error* bits in AH reliably indicate the occurrence of errors:

Bit 4   Break detected

Bit 3   Framing error

Bit 2   Parity error

Bit 1   Overrun error

Thus, AH will be 0 only if *no* error occurred.

AL   If no error occurred, contains the character read.

Function 03h: Return Communication Port Status

Entry:

AH   03h

DX   Serial port number (0 = COM1, 1 = COM2)

Return:

AX   Serial port status, where AH contains the line status and AL contains the modem status. The bits have the following meanings when they are turned on:

AH =   Line status:

Bit 7   Time out

Bit 6   Transmission shift register empty

Bit 5   Transmission hold register empty

Bit 4   Break detected

Bit 3   Framing error

Bit 2   Parity error

Bit 1   Overrun error

Bit 0   Data ready

AL =   Modem status:

Bit 7   Receive line signal detected

Bit 6	Ring indicator
Bit 5	Data set ready
Bit 4	Clear to send
Bit 3	Change in receive line signal detected
Bit 2	Trailing edge ring detected
Bit 1	Change in status of data set ready
Bit 0	Change in status of clear to send

Extended Communications Functions

The following two extended services are available only in PS/2 machines. See the BIOS interface technical reference cited in the Bibliography for details.

Function 04h	Extended communications port initialize
Function 05h	Extended communications port control

▪︎ Interrupt 15h: Cassette I/O and Extended Services for the AT

▪︎ Function 00h: Turn Cassette Motor On

Entry:

AH   00h

Return:

Nothing

▪︎ Function 01h: Turn Cassette Motor Off

Entry:

AH   01h

Return:

Nothing

▪︎ Function 02h: Read 256K Blocks from Cassette

Entry:

AH   02h
CX   Count of bytes to read
ES:BX Address of buffer to receive data

Return:

AH   If carry flag is set, an error occurred, and this register contains one of the following error codes:

01   CRC error

02	Data transitions lost
04	No data found

DX   Count of bytes actually read

ES:BX Address of last byte read + 1

◻■ Function 03h: Write 256K Blocks to Cassette
◻◻

Entry:

AH	03h
CX	Count of bytes to write
ES:BX	Address of buffer containing bytes to write

Return:

AH	If carry flag is set, an error occurred and AH contains an error code:
	80 Invalid command
CX	0
ES:BX	Address of last byte written + 1

◻■ Extended Services
◻◻

Also available under interrupt 15h is the following collection of
extended services for the AT, PS/2, PC Convertible, and certain
models of the XT; these services deal with special features of the
hardware. For a description of these services and a list of the
machines for which they are provided, see the BIOS interface technical reference cited in the Bibliography.

Function 0Fh	Format unit periodic interrupt
Function 21h	Power-on self-test error log
Function 40h	Read/modify profiles
Function 41h	Wait for external event
Function 42h	Request system power off
Function 43h	Read system status

Function 44h	Activate/deactivate internal modem power
Function 4Fh	Keyboard intercept
Function 80h	Device open
Function 81h	Device close
Function 82h	Program termination
Function 83h	Event wait
Function 84h	Joystick support
Function 85h	System request key pressed
Function 86h	Wait
Function 87h	Move block
Function 88h	Extended memory size determine
Function 89h	Switch processor to protected mode
Function 90h	Device busy
Function 91h	Interrupt complete
Function C0h	Return system configuration parameters
Function C1h	Return extended BIOS data area segment address
Function C2h	Pointing device BIOS interface
Function C3h	Enable/disable watchdog time-out
Function C4h	Programmable option select

■□ Interrupt 16h:
Keyboard Services

□■ Function 00h: Return Next Character Entered from Keyboard

Entry:

AH   00h

Return:

AH   Extended code

AL   ASCII code

Note: See Chapter 6 for an explanation of these codes and the use of this function.

■□ Function 01h: Test If Character Is Ready

Entry:

AH   01h

Return:

Zero Flag	If the zero flag = 1, then no character is ready. If the zero flag = 0, then a character is ready to be read. If a character is ready, it is placed in register AX (as Function 00h), but it is not removed from the keyboard buffer (therefore this character is read by the next invocation of Function 00h).

Function 02h: Return Current Shift Status

Entry:

AH   03h

Return:

AL   Current shift status:

Bit	Shift key
0	Right-Shift depressed
1	Left-Shift depressed
2	Ctrl-Shift depressed
3	Alt-Shift depressed
4	Scroll Lock active
5	Num Lock active
6	Caps Lock active
7	Ins active

Note: *Depressed* means that the key is currently being held down by the user. The active status refers to a state that is toggled on and off by a key such as Caps Lock (the key need not be currently pressed). These values are maintained by the BIOS at memory location 0000h:0417h.

Additional Functions

In addition to the basic keyboard functions described above, the following functions are available on certain machines. For a description of these services see the BIOS interface technical reference cited in the Bibliography.

Function 03h   PCjr, AT (11/15/85 and later), PC XT Model 286, and PS/2 only: Set typematic rate. Sets the initial delay and rate at which keys are automatically repeated by the keyboard.

Function 04h	PCjr and PC Convertible only: Keyboard click adjustment.
Function 05h	AT (11/15/85 and later), PC XT (1/10/86 and later), PC XT Model 286, and PS/2 only: Keyboard write. Places an extended-code/character-code combination in the keyboard buffer as if it came from the keyboard.
Function 10h	AT (11/15/85 and later), PC XT (1/10/86 and later), PC XT Model 286, and PS/2 only: Extended keyboard read. Similar to function 00h but returns codes unique to the 101/102 key keyboard.
Function 11h	AT (11/15/85 and later), PC XT (1/10/86 and later), PC XT Model 286, and PS/2 only: Extended keystroke status. Similar to function 01h but returns codes unique to the 101/102 key keyboard.
Function 12h	AT (11/15/85 and later), PC XT (1/10/86 and later), PC XT Model 286, and PS/2 only: Extended shift status. Similar to function 02h but returns shift states unique to the 101/102 key keyboard.

■□ Interrupt 17h: Printer Services

□■ Function 00h: Print Character

Entry:

AH   00h
AL   Character to be printed
DX   Printer to use (0, 1, or 2)

Return:

AH   Printer status
     The bits have the following meanings when they are
     turned on:

    Bit 7   Not busy
    Bit 6   Acknowledge
    Bit 5   Out of paper
    Bit 4   Selected
    Bit 3   I/O error
    Bit 2   Unused
    Bit 1   Unused
    Bit 0   Time out

□■ Function 01h: Initialize the Printer Port

Entry:

AH   02h
DX   Printer to use (0, 1, or 2)

Return:

AH   Printer status:

The bits have the following meanings when they are turned on:

Bit 7	Not busy
Bit 6	Acknowledge
Bit 5	Out of paper
Bit 4	Selected
Bit 3	I/O error
Bit 2	Unused
Bit 1	Unused
Bit 0	Time out

Note: A program should not call this function unless absolutely necessary, because it will mess up any printing jobs that are currently running in the background (for example, through the DOS PRINT command). A number of applications arbitrarily issue this command at the beginning of the code—a very thoughtless practice.

⊞ Function 02h: Read Printer Status

Entry:

AH   02h

DX   Printer to use (0, 1, or 2)

Return:

AH   Printer status:

Bit 7	Not busy
Bit 6	Acknowledge
Bit 5	Out of paper
Bit 4	Selected

Bit 3   I/O error

Bit 2   Unused

Bit 1   Unused

Bit 0   Time out

■· Interrupt 18h: Load ROM BASIC

Entry:

   None

Return:

   Nothing

Note: This routine activates the version of BASIC contained in ROM, and may be used to override disk BASIC or BASICA.

Interrupt 19h: Boot Strap Loader

Entry:

None

Return:

Nothing

Note: This routine causes rebooting of the system. However, it eliminates the lengthy diagnostics performed during a cold boot initiated by powering down the computer, and also eliminates the resetting of the system data stored in segment 0400h (see Chapter 6) that occurs when Ctrl-Alt-Del is pressed.

▪▫ Interrupt 1Ah: Time-of-Day Services

▫▪ Function 00h: Read Clock Count

Entry:

AH   00h

Return:

AL   Equals 1 if timer has passed 24 hours since the last time the service was invoked. AL = 0 otherwise.

CX   Upper word of count

DX   Lower word of count

Note: The BIOS time count is incremented with each clock tick interrupt (08h), and indicates the number of clock ticks since midnight. This interrupt occurs at the rate of 1193180/65536 (approximately 18.2) times per second; thus, the time elapsed since midnight can be calculated in terms of hours, minutes, and seconds. When midnight is reached (count = 1,573,040), the count begins over again and a flag is set. Since the flag is set, the next function 00h invocation will return 1 in AL to indicate a new day (the flag is then cleared so that subsequent invocations will return 0 in AH until the next midnight).

▫▪ Function 01h: Set Clock Count

Entry:

AH   01h

CX   Upper word of count

DX   Lower word of count

Return:

Nothing

Note: See notes for function 00h.

Function 02h: Read Realtime Clock (AT, XT Model 286, and PS/2)

Entry:

AH   02h

Return:

CH   Hours

CL   Minutes

DH   Seconds

DL   Daylight savings enable (00–01)

Note: The carry flag is set if the real-time clock is not operating. This function—available only in the AT, XT Model 286, and PS/2— provides a more convenient interface by automatically converting between clock tick counts and hours, minutes, and seconds. For this and the following AT functions, all values are specified in BCD format.

Function 03h: Set Realtime Clock (AT, XT Model 286, and PS/2)

Entry:

AH   03h

CH   Hours

CL   Minutes

DH   Seconds

DL   1 to enable automatic daylight savings time updates

0 to disable daylight savings time updates

Return:

Nothing

Function 04h: Read Date from Realtime Clock (AT, XT Model 286, and PS/2)

Entry:

AH   04h

Return:

CH   Century (19 or 20)
CL   Year
DH   Month
DL   Day

Note: The carry flag is set if the real-time clock is not functioning.

Function 05h: Set Date for Realtime Clock (AT, XT Model 286, and PS/2)

Entry:

AH   05h
CH   Century (19 or 20)
CL   Year
DH   Month
DL   Day

Return:

Nothing

Function 06h: Set Alarm (AT, XT Model 286, and PS/2)

Entry:

AH	06h
CH	Hours
CL	Minutes
DH	Seconds

Return:

Nothing

Note: The carry flag is set if the real-time clock is not functioning or the alarm is already enabled. When the elapsed time has passed, interrupt 4Ah is invoked. Therefore, you should set this vector to point to the routine you would like activated when the alarm goes off.

Function 07h: Reset Alarm (AT, XT Model 286, and PS/2)

Entry:

AH	07h

Return:

Nothing

Additional Functions

The BIOS of certain machines also provides the following time-related functions. For a description of these services, see the BIOS interface technical reference cited in the Bibliography.

Function 08h	PC Convertible only: Set real-time clock activated power-on mode

Function 09h	PC Convertible only: Read real-time clock alarm time and status
Function 0Ah	PC XT (1/10/86 and after) and PS/2: Read system-timer day counter
Function 80h	PCjr only: Set up sound multiplexer

APPENDIX D

THE PROGRAM SEGMENT PREFIX

Chapter 6 contains a general description of the program segment prefix (PSP) as an important resource for performance programming, emphasizing those fields that have practical uses. The following is a short summary of the overall structure of the PSP. *Offset* is the hexadecimal offset with respect to the segment address of the PSP, and *length* is the size of the field in bytes.

Offset	Length	Description
00h	2	**int 20h** instruction (terminates the program)
02h	2	Segment address of the top of allocated memory
04h	1	Reserved for DOS
05h	5	Long call instruction to the DOS function dispatcher
06h	2	Number of bytes in segment (note that this field serves a double purpose; it is also the offset address portion of the five-byte long call to DOS)
0Ah	4	Terminate address (value stored from vector 22h)
0Eh	4	Ctrl-Break address (value stored from vector 23h)
12h	4	Critical-error address (value stored from vector 24h)
16h	2	Reserved for DOS
18h	20	DOS file table (undocumented, see Chapter 6)
2Ch	2	Segment address of the environment
2Eh	34	Reserved for DOS

Offset	Length	Description
50h	3	**int 21h**, **retf** instructions (a nonrecommended method of invoking a DOS function)
53h	2	Reserved for DOS
55h	7	Area for FCB number 1 extension
5Ch	9	FCB number 1
65h	7	Area for FCB number 2 extension
6Ch	20	FCB number 2
80h	1	Length of command line. Also, beginning of the 128-byte default disk transfer area (DTA)
81h	127	Command line (beginning with first space after name of program)

MEMORY MAP

The following table is a brief outline of the conventional use of memory in a typical IBM-PC compatible system. The *segment* and *offset* values specify the starting address of each area described, and *size* gives the amount of memory occupied in bytes.

Segment	Offset	Size	Description
0000h	0000h	1024	Interrupt vector table
	0400h	172	BIOS communication area (see Chapter 6)
	04ACh	68	Reserved by IBM
	04F0h	16	User communication area (see Chapter 6)
	0500h	256	DOS communication area (see Chapter 6)
	0600h	Varies	Operating system (the following file names apply specifically to PC-DOS):
			IBMBIO.COM (DOS interface to the BIOS)
			IBMDOS.COM (DOS interrupt handlers, and interrupt 21h service routines)
			DOS buffers, control areas, and device drivers
			COMMAND.COM (resident portion), interrupt 22h, 23h, and 24h handlers, and routine to reload transient portion of COMMAND.COM

Segment	Offset	Size	Description
			Memory-resident utilities
			Transient applications
			Transient portion of COMMAND.COM
9000h	FFFFh		Highest address of user memory
A000h	0000h	128K	Reserved area of ROM (segments A000h and B000h)
	0000h		Beginning of area used by EGA and PS/2 video systems
B000h	0000h	4000	Monochrome video memory
	0800h	16K	Color graphics adapter video memory
C000h	0000h	192K	ROM expansion and control area (segments C000h, D000h, and E000h)
	8000h		ROM for hard disk
D000h			ROM expansion and control area
E000h			ROM expansion and control area
F000h	0000h	16K	Reserved ROM
	4000h	40K	Base system ROM, ROM BASIC
	E000h	8K	ROM BIOS

Port Map

The following table is a summary of the current port assignments in IBM-PC/AT compatible machines. IBM may use any of the unlisted I/O addresses in the future.

I/O address range	Usage
0000h–000Fh	PC: DMA Chip (8237A-5)
0000h–001Fh	AT: DMA Chip 1 (8237A-5)
0020h–0021h	PC: Interrupt controller (8259A)
0020h–003Fh	AT: Interrupt controller 1 (8259A)
0040h–0043h	PC: Programmable timer (8253-5)
0040h–005Fh	AT: Programmable timer (8254)
0060h–0063h	PC: Programmable peripheral interface (8255A-5)
0060h–006Fh	AT: Keyboard
0070h–007Fh	AT: Nonmaskable interrupt (NMI) mask register
0080h–0083h	PC: DMA page registers
0080h–009Fh	AT: DMA page registers
00A0h	PC: Nonmaskable interrupt (NMI) mask register
00A0h–00BFh	AT: Interrupt controller 2 (8259A)
00C0h–00DFh	AT: DMA chip 2 (8237A-5)
00F0h–00FFh	AT: Math coprocessor
01F0h–01F8h	AT: Hard disk controller
0200h–0207h	AT: Game control
0200h–020Fh	PC: Game control
0210h–0217h	PC: Expansion unit
0278h–027Fh	AT: Secondary parallel printer

I/O address range	Usage
02F8h–02FFh	Secondary serial port
0300h–031Fh	Prototype card
0320h–032Fh	PC: Hard disk controller
0378h–037Fh	Primary parallel printer
0380h–038Ch	SDLC communications
0380h–0389h	Secondary binary synchronous communications
0390h–0393h	Cluster
03A0h–03A9h	Primary binary synchronous communications
03B0h–03BFh	Monochrome display adapter/printer
03D0h–03DFh	Color graphics adapter (CGA)
03F0h–03F7h	Diskette controller
03F8h–03FFh	Primary serial port
0790h–2393h	Cluster adapter 1 through 4

APPENDIX

G

Summary of C Functions

This appendix summarizes all of the functions listed in the book that can be called from a C program. These functions are written in either C or assembler. The first section simply lists the functions by category, and the second section reviews them in alphabetical order. Note that these functions may also be called from an assembler program, provided that C calling conventions are used. (Functions written in C may be called by assembler programs only if these programs follow the special formats given in Figures 2.2 or 2.3.)

Functions by Category

Disk/File Management

curr_drv

Expanded Memory Management

ealloc

efree

emap

ememavail

erestore

esave

Interrupt Handlers

ce_init

init_kbrk

Keyboard

getkey

Memory Residency

tsr

Miscellaneous

gettime

Printer

prnready

Resource Determination

cur_cpu

cur_gameport

cur_mach

cur_memsiz

cur_ncp

cur_numdisk

cur_numprn

cur_numser

cur_video

dos_ver

Video Control

cookmode

cursor

getcur

getmode

getstr

popscr

printa

printv

printvcga

printw

printwcga

pushscr

rawmode

setcur

setmode

■□ Alphabetical Summary

The following descriptions briefly summarize the functions is this book that can be called from a C program. Included is a short statement of the purpose of the function, the function and parameter declarations, together with comments on each parameter, and the number of the figure containing the source code listing.

ce_init

Purpose

Initializes a critical error (interrupt 24h) handler.

Declaration

void ce_init (func);

void (*func)();   Address of C function to be called on critical error.

Source listing

Figure 6.5

cookmode

Purpose

Places standard input, output, and error in cooked (ASCII) mode.

Declaration

void cookmode ();

Source listing

Figure 4.8

cur_cpu

Purpose

Returns the current processor type. Return codes defined in Figure 7.2.

Declaration

```
unsigned char cur_cpu ();
```

Source listing

Figure 7.2

cur_gameport

Purpose

Returns true if a gameport is installed, false otherwise.

Declaration

```
unsigned char cur_gameport ();
```

Source listing

Figure 7.2

cur_mach

Purpose

Returns the make of the computer. Return codes defined in Figure 7.2.

Declaration

```
unsigned char cur_mach ();
```

Source listing

Figure 7.2

cur_memsiz

Purpose

Returns the total number of kilobytes of installed user memory.

Declaration

```
unsigned int cur_memsiz ();
```

Source listing

Figure 7.2

cur_ncp

Purpose

Returns true if a numeric coprocessor is installed, false otherwise.

Declaration

unsigned char cur_ncp ();

Source listing

Figure 7.2

cur_numdisk

Purpose

Returns the total number of floppy disk drives installed.

Declaration

unsigned char cur_numdisk ();

Source listing

Figure 7.2

cur_numprn

Purpose

Returns the total number of printers attached to ports on the system.

Declaration

unsigned char cur_numprn ();

Source listing

Figure 7.2

cur_numser

Purpose

Returns the total number of serial devices installed.

□□■□

Declaration

    unsigned char cur_numser ();

Source listing

    Figure 7.2

cursor

Purpose

    Positions the cursor at the specified row and column.

Declaration

    void cursor (row, col);
    int row;
    int col;

Source listing

    Figure 8.11

cur_video

Purpose

    Returns the features of the current video display system. Return codes defined in Figure 7.2.

Declaration

    unsigned char cur_video ();

Source listing

    Figure 7.2

curr_drv

Purpose

    Returns a string containing the current drive specification.

Declaration

    char *curr_drv ();

Source listing

Figure 4.5

dos_ver

Purpose

Supplies the major and minor DOS version numbers.

Declaration

void dos_ver (dosptr);

struct dos *dosptr;   Structure defined in Figure 7.2

Source listing

Figure 7.2

ealloc

Purpose

Allocates the requested number of expanded memory logical pages and returns a far pointer to the beginning of the page frame.

Declaration

char far *ealloc (pages);

int pages;   Number of pages requested

Source listing

Figure 10.1

efree

Purpose

Deallocates expanded memory assigned to a process by **ealloc**. It returns 0 if no error occurred, or − 1 if there was an error (the global flag **ems_err** is set to the code for the error).

Declaration

int efree ();

Source listing

Figure 10.1

emap

Purpose

Maps the specified logical pages of expanded memory onto the four physical pages of the page frame. It returns 0 if no error occurred, or −1 if there was an error (the global flag **ems_err** is set to the code for the error).

Declaration

```
int emap (p0, p1, p2, p3);
int p0;
int p1;
int p2;
int p3;
```

The four logical pages to be mapped to the four physical pages 0 ... 3. A logical page value of −1 leaves the current mapping for the corresponding physical page.

Source listing

Figure 10.1

ememavail

Purpose

Returns the number of free pages of expanded memory.

Declaration

```
int ememavail ();
```

Source listing

Figure 10.1

erestore

Purpose

Restores the expanded memory page mapping saved by **esave**. It returns 0 if no error occurred, or −1 if there was an error (the global flag **ems_err** is set to the code for the error).

Declaration

```
int erestore ();
```

Source listing

Figure 10.1

esave

Purpose

Saves the current expanded memory page mapping. It returns 0 if no error occurred, or −1 if there was an error (the global flag **ems_err** is set to the code for the error).

Declaration

int esave ();

Source listing

Figure 10.1

getcur

Purpose

Obtains the current cursor position and style (i.e., start and stop rows). Places the values into the structure whose address is passed to the function.

Declaration

void getcur (curptr, page);

struct cursor *curptr;　　　Defined in Figure 5.1.

int page;　　　Video page.

Source listing

Figure 5.1

getmode

Purpose

Gets the current video mode, number of display columns, and video page. Places the values into the structure whose address is passed to the function.

Declaration

void getmode (modeptr);

struct crtmode *modeptr;　　　Defined in Figure 5.1

Source listing

Figure 5.1

getkey

Purpose

Pauses for input from the keyboard and returns an integer containing both the ASCII value of the key (low-order byte) and the extended code of the key (high-order byte). Input is unbuffered (CR need not be entered).

Declaration

int getkey ();

Source listing

Figure 5.3

getstr

Purpose

Reads a string from the keyboard, echoing output to a specified position on the screen, with a specified display attribute. See the more complete description in Chapter 8 and Figure 8.12. Returns 0 if operation completed, 1 if aborted by user entering Escape.

Declaration

int getstr (buf, att, row, col, num);	
char *buf;	Buffer to receive string
int att;	Display attribute of echoed characters
int row;	Starting row of echo display
int col;	Starting column of echo display
int num;	Number of bytes in receiving buffer

Source listing

Figure 8.12

gettime

Purpose

Obtains the system time. Assigns values to the integer variable whose addresses are passed as parameters.

Declaration

void gettime (h, m, s, c);

int *h;	Pointer to hours (0–23)
int *m;	Pointer to minutes
int *s;	Pointer to seconds
int *c;	Pointer to 1/100 seconds

Source listing

Figure 8.8

init_kbrk

Purpose

Initializes a keyboard interrupt (09h) handler.

Declaration

void init_kbrk ();

Source listing

Figure 6.7

popscr

Purpose

Removes a saved screen from the screen stack, and restores its contents to video memory.

Declaration

void popscr ();

Source listing

Figure 8.12

printa

Purpose

Displays a null-terminated string at the specified position on the screen, with the specified display attribute. Uses the BIOS.

Declaration

void printa (s, a, r, c);

char *s;	String to be printed
int a;	Display attribute
int r;	Starting row
int c;	Starting column

Source listing

Figure 5.2

printv

Purpose

Displays a null-terminated string on the screen by writing directly to video memory. Designed for adapters that do not produce snow.

Declaration

void printv (str, att, row, col);

char *str;	The string to print
int att;	The display attribute
int row;	The starting row
int col;	The starting column

Source listing

Figure 8.4

printvcga

Purpose

Displays a null-terminated string on the screen by writing directly to video memory. Designed for adapters that produce snow, such as the standard CGA.

Declaration

void printvcga (str, att, row, col);

char *str;	The string to print
int att;	The display attribute
int row;	The starting row
int col;	The starting column

Source listing

Figure 8.4

printw

Purpose

Transfers a block of screen data from a program buffer directly to video memory. Designed for adapters that do not produce snow.

Declaration

void printw (buf,ulr_s,ulc_s,lrr_s,lrc_s,ulr_d,ulc_d);

char *buf;	Screen data buffer
int ulr_s;	Upper-left row in buffer
int ulc_s;	Upper-left column in buffer
int lrr_s;	Lower-right row in buffer
int lrc_s;	Lower-right column in buffer
int ulr_d;	Upper-left row in video memory
int ulc_d;	Upper-left column in video memory

Source listing

Figure 8.5

printwcga

Purpose

Transfers a block of screen data from a program buffer directly to video memory. Designed for adapters that produce snow, such as the standard CGA.

Declaration

void printwcga (buf,ulr_s,ulc_s,lrr_s,lrc_s,ulr_d,ulc_d);

char *buf;	Screen data buffer
int ulr_s;	Upper-left row in buffer
int ulc_s;	Upper-left column in buffer
int lrr_s;	Lower-right row in buffer
int lrc_s;	Lower-right column in buffer
int ulr_d;	Upper-left row in video memory
int ulc_d;	Upper-left column in video memory

Source listing

Figure 8.5

prnready

Purpose

Returns true if the printer is ready for output, and false if there is an I/O error associated with the printer.

Declaration

int prnready ();

Source listing

Figure 5.4

pushscr

Purpose

Saves the current video display on the screen stack.

Declaration

void pushscr ();

Source listing

Figure 8.12

rawmode

Purpose

Places standard input, output, and error in raw (or binary) mode.

Declaration

> **void rawmode ();**

Source listing

> Figure 4.8

setcur

Purpose

> Sets the cursor position and style (i.e., start and stop rows).

Declaration

> **void setcur (curptr, page);**
>
> **struct cursor *curptr;**   Defined in Figure 5.1
>
> **int page;**   Video page

Source listing

> Figure 5.1

setmode

Purpose

> Sets the video mode and display page.

Declaration

> **void setmode (modeptr);**
>
> **struct crtmode *modeptr;**   Defined in Figure 5.1

Source listing

> Figure 5.1

tsr

Purpose

> Makes a C program memory-resident, and terminates the program. This function normally does not return; if it returns, an error occurred, and one of the following error codes is passed back:

Error Code	Meaning
1	Insufficient memory
2	Pre DOS 2.0 version

| 3 | TSR already installed (not currently implemented). |

Declaration

int tsr (funptr, hotkey);

void (* funptr) ();   Pointer to function to activate

int hotkey;   Mask for hotkey

Source listing

Figure 11.3

BIBLIOGRAPHY

Among the many books available on C and assembly language programming, and the smaller number of books on programming under MS-DOS, I have found the following to be especially helpful. This is not an exhaustive list, and there are doubtlessly many other books of equal merit. These are simply the ones that I have discovered, and have used in my own programming efforts. Also included are a number of very useful and interesting programmer's magazines.

Angermeyer, J. and Jaeger, K. *MS-DOS Developer's Guide.* Indianapolis, IN: Howard W. Sams, 1986.

Byte (magazine). New York: McGraw-Hill.

Computer Language (magazine). San Francisco, CA: CL Publications Inc.

Dr. Dobb's Journal (magazine). Redwood City, CA: M & T Publishing.

Duncan, Ray. *Advanced MS-DOS.* Redmond, WA: Microsoft Press, 1986.

Durant, D. Carlson, G. and Yao, P. *Programmer's Guide to Windows.* Alameda, CA: SYBEX, 1987.

IBM. *AT Technical Reference,* part number 6280070. Boca Raton, Florida: IBM Corp, 1986.

IBM. *DOS Technical Reference,* part number 6024213. Boca Raton, Florida: IBM Corp, 1987.

IBM. *Enhanced Graphics Adapter (Options and Adapters supplement),* part number 6280131. Boca Raton, Florida: IBM Corp, 1984.

IBM. *IBM Personal System/2 and Personal Computer BIOS Interface Technical Reference*, part number 68X2260. Boca Raton, Florida: IBM Corp, 1987.

IBM. *IBM Personal System/2 Hardware System Technical Reference for the Model 30* (part number 68X2201), *Model 50 and 60* (part number 68X2224), or *Model 80* (part number 68X2256). Boca Raton, Florida: IBM Corp, 1987.

IBM. *Options and Adapters Technical Reference,* part number 6322509. Boca Raton, Florida: IBM Corp, 1984.

IBM. *PC Technical Reference,* part number 6322507. Boca Raton, Florida: IBM Corp, 1984.

IBM. *Personal Computer AT (Options and Adapters supplement),* part number 6280134. Boca Raton, Florida: IBM Corp, 1986.

IBM. *IBM Personal Computer Seminar Proceedings,* 1:3 (Nov. 1983): 22-26 (Available from IBM Entry Systems Division, P.O. Box 1328, Boca Raton, FL 33432).

IBM. *XT and Portable Technical Reference,* part number 6280089. Boca Raton, Florida: IBM Corp, 1985.

Intel. *iAPX 88 Book.* Santa Clara, CA: Intel Corp, 1983.

Kernighan, B. and Ritchie, D. *The C Programming Language.* Englewood Cliffs, NJ: Prentice-Hall, 1978.

King, Richard Allen. *The MS-DOS Handbook.* Alameda, CA: SYBEX, 1986.

Lafore, Robert, *Assembly Language Primer for the IBM PC & XT.* New York: Plume/Waite, 1984.

Lotus, Intel, Microsoft. *Lotus/Intel/Microsoft Expanded Memory Specification (Version 4.0).* Hillsboro, OR: Intel Corporation, 1987.

Microsoft C Compiler, version 5.1, documentation. Redmond, WA: Microsoft Corp, 1986.

Microsoft Macro Assembler, version 5.1, Documentation. Redmond, WA: Microsoft Corp, 1985.

Microsoft, *MS-DOS Technical Reference Encyclopedia.* Redmond, WA: Microsoft Press, 1986.

Miller, Alan R. *Assembly Language Techniques for the IBM PC.* Alameda, CA: SYBEX, 1986.

Norton, Peter. *Programmer's Guide to the IBM PC.* Redmond, WA: Microsoft Press, 1985.

PC Tech Journal (magazine). New York: Ziff-Davis.

Programmer's Journal (magazine). Eugene, OR: Oakley.

Systems Journal (magazine). Redmond, WA: Microsoft Corp.

Young, Michael J. *Programmer's Guide to OS/2.* Alameda, CA: SYBEX, 1988.

Young, Michael J. *Systems Programming in Turbo C.* Alameda, CA: SYBEX, 1988.

IBM technical publications may be ordered from the following address. A catalog, the *Technical Directory,* is also available.

IBM Technical Directory

P.O. Box 2009

Racine, WI 53404-3336

(800) 426-7282

Literature may be ordered from Intel through the following address; also available is a catalog, the *Literature Guide*.

Intel Literature Sales

P.O. Box 58130

Santa Clara, CA 95052-8130

(800) 548-4725

INDEX

Selections from The SYBEX Library

OPERATING SYSTEMS

The ABC's of DOS 4
Alan R. Miller
275pp. Ref. 583-2
This step-by-step introduction to using DOS 4 is written especially for beginners. Filled with simple examples, *The ABC's of DOS 4* covers the basics of hardware, software, disks, the system editor EDLIN, DOS commands, and more.

ABC's of MS-DOS (Second Edition)
Alan R. Miller
233pp. Ref. 493-3
This handy guide to MS-DOS is all many PC users need to manage their computer files, organize floppy and hard disks, use EDLIN, and keep their computers organized. Additional information is given about utilities like Sidekick, and there is a DOS command and program summary. The second edition is fully updated for Version 3.3.

DOS Instant Reference
SYBEX Prompter Series
Greg Harvey/Kay Yarborough Nelson
220pp. Ref. 477-1, 4 ¾" × 8"
A complete fingertip reference for fast, easy on-line help:command summaries, syntax, usage and error messages. Organized by function—system commands, file commands, disk management, directories, batch files, I/O, networking, programming, and more. Through Version 3.3.

DOS User's Desktop Companion
SYBEX Ready Reference Series
Judd Robbins
969pp. Ref. 505-0
This comprehensive reference covers DOS commands, batch files, memory enhancements, printing, communications and more information on optimizing each user's DOS environment. Written with step-by-step instructions and plenty of examples, this volume covers all versions through 3.3.

Essential OS/2 (Second Edition)
Judd Robbins
445pp. Ref. 609-X
Written by an OS/2 expert, this is the guide to the powerful new resources of the OS/2 operating system standard edition 1.1 with presentation manager. Robbins introduces the standard edition, and details multitasking under OS/2, and the range of commands for installing, starting up, configuring, and running applications. For Version 1.1 Standard Edition.

Essential PC-DOS (Second Edition)
Myril Clement Shaw
Susan Soltis Shaw
332pp. Ref. 413-5
An authoritative guide to PC-DOS, including version 3.2. Designed to make experts out of beginners, it explores everything from disk management to batch file programming. Includes an 85-page command summary. Through Version 3.2.

Graphics Programming Under Windows
Brian Myers/Chris Doner
646pp. Ref. 448-8
Straightforward discussion, abundant examples, and a concise reference guide to graphics commands make this book a must for Windows programmers. Topics

range from how Windows works to programming for business, animation, CAD, and desktop publishing. For Version 2.

Hard Disk Instant Reference
SYBEX Prompter Series
Judd Robbins
256pp. Ref. 587-5, 4 ¾" × 8"
Compact yet comprehensive, this pocket-sized reference presents the essential information on DOS commands used in managing directories and files, and in optimizing disk configuration. Includes a survey of third-party utility capabilities. Through DOS 4.0.

Mastering DOS
(Second Edition)
Judd Robbins
722pp. Ref. 555-7
"The most useful DOS book." This seven-part, in-depth tutorial addresses the needs of users at all levels. Topics range from running applications, to managing files and directories, configuring the system, batch file programming, and techniques for system developers. Through Version 4.

The IBM PC-DOS Handbook
(Third Edition)
Richard Allen King
359pp. Ref. 512-3
A guide to the inner workings of PC-DOS 3.2, for intermediate to advanced users and programmers of the IBM PC series. Topics include disk, screen and port control, batch files, networks, compatibility, and more. Through Version 3.3.

MS-DOS Advanced
Programming
Michael J. Young
490pp. Ref. 578-6
Practical techniques for maximizing performance in MS-DOS software by making best use of system resources. Topics include functions, interrupts, devices, multitasking, memory residency and more, with examples in C and assembler. Through Version 3.3.

MS-DOS Handbook
(Third Edition)
Richard Allen King
362pp. Ref. 492-5
This classic has been fully expanded and revised to include the latest features of MS-DOS Version 3.3. Two reference books in one, this title has separate sections for programmer and user. Multi-DOS partitons, 3 ½-inch disk format, batch file call and return feature, and comprehensive coverage of MS-DOS commands are included. Through Version 3.3.

MS-DOS Power User's Guide,
Volume I
(Second Edition)
Jonathan Kamin
482pp. Ref. 473-9
A fully revised, expanded edition of our best-selling guide to high-performance DOS techniques and utilities—with details on Version 3.3. Configuration, I/O, directory structures, hard disks, RAM disks, batch file programming, the ANSI.SYS device driver, more. Through Version 3.3.

Programmers Guide to
the OS/2 Presentation Manager
Michael J. Young
683pp. Ref. 569-7
This is the definitive tutorial guide to writing programs for the OS/2 Presentation Manager. Young starts with basic architecture, and explores every important feature including scroll bars, keyboard and mouse interface, menus and accelerators, dialogue boxes, clipboards, multitasking, and much more.

Programmer's Guide to
Windows
(Second Edition)
David Durant/Geta Carlson/Paul Yao
704pp. Ref. 496-8
The first edition of this programmer's guide was hailed as a classic. This new edition covers Windows 2 and Windows/386 in depth. Special emphasis is given to over fifty new routines to the Windows

interface, and to preparation for OS/2 Presentation Manager compatibility.

Understanding DOS 3.3
Judd Robbins

678pp. Ref. 648-0

This best selling, in-depth tutorial addresses the needs of users at all levels with many examples and hands-on exercises. Robbins discusses the fundamentals of DOS, then covers manipulating files and directories, using the DOS editor, printing, communicating, and finishes with a full section on batch files.

Understanding Hard Disk Management on the PC
Jonathan Kamin

500pp. Ref. 561-1

This title is a key productivity tool for all hard disk users who want efficient, error-free file management and organization. Includes details on the best ways to conserve hard disk space when using several memory-guzzling programs. Through DOS 4.

Up & Running with Your Hard Disk
Klaus M Rubsam

140pp. Ref. 666-9

A far-sighted, compact introduction to hard disk installation and basic DOS use. Perfect for PC users who want the practical essentials in the shortest possible time. In 20 basic steps, learn to choose your hard disk, work with accessories, back up data, use DOS utilities to save time, and more.

ASSEMBLY LANGUAGES

DOS Assembly Language Programming
Alan R. Miller

365pp. Ref. 487-9

This book covers PC-DOS through 3.3 and gives clear explanations of how to assemble, link, and debug 8086, 8088,

80286, and 80386 programs. The example assembly language routines are valuable for students and programmers alike.

Programming the 6502
Rodnay Zaks

408pp. Ref. 135-7

The best-selling, step-by-step course in assembly-language programming for the 6502 chip used in Apple, Atari and Commodore computers. From basic concepts to architecture, instruction set, addressing, I/O, sample applications and more.

Programming the 6809
Rodnay Zaks/William Labiak

362pp. Ref. 078-4

A step-by-step course in assembly-language programming for 6809-based home computers. Covers hardware organization, the instruction set, addressing, I/O, data structures, program development and complete sample applications.

Programming the 68000
Steve Williams

539pp. Ref. 133-0

This tutorial introduction to assembly-language programming covers the complete 68000 architecture and instruction set, as well as advanced topics such as interrupts, I/O programming, and interfacing with high-level languages.

Programming the 8086/8088
James W. Coffron

311pp. Ref. 120-9

A concise introduction to assembly-language programming for 8086/8088-based systems, including the IBM PC. Topics include architecture, memory organization, the complete instruction set, interrupts, I/O, and IBM PC BIOS routines.

Programming the 80286
C. Vieillefond

487pp. Ref. 277-9

In-depth treatment of assembly-level programming for the IBM PC/AT's 80286 processor. Topics include system architecture, memory management, address modes, multitasking and more; plus a complete reference guide to the instruction set.

Programming the 80386
**John H. Crawford/
Patrick P. Gelsinger**
775pp. Ref. 381-3
A detailed tour of the 80386 for assembly-language programmers. Topics include registers, data types and instruction classes, memory management, protection models, multitasking, interrupts, the numerics coprocessor, and more.

Programming the Z80
(Third Edition)
Rodnay Zaks
624pp. Ref. 069-5
A self-teaching guide to assembly-language programming for the wide range of Z80-based microcomputers. Includes the Z80 architecture and instruction set, addressing, I/O techniques and devices, data structures and sample programs.

Z80 Applications
James W. Coffron
295pp. Ref. 094-6
A handbook for assembly-language programmers on the principles of Z80 hardware operations. Topics include using ROM, static and dynamic RAM, I/O, interrupts, serial communication and several specific LSI peripheral devices.

LANGUAGES

The ABC's of Quick C
Douglas Hergert
309pp. Ref. 557-3
This is the most unintimidating C language tutorial, designed especially for readers who have had little or no computer programming experience. The reader will learn programming essentials with step-by-step instructions for working with numbers, strings, arrays, pointers, structures, decisions, and loops. For Version 2.0.

The ABC's of Turbo C
Douglas Hergert
310pp. Ref. 594-8
This unintimidating C language tutorial was written especially for those with little or no experience with computer programming. The ABC's teaches fundamental programming concepts and techniques with lots of program examples for working with numbers, strings, arrays, pointers, loops, decisions, and more. For Version 2.0.

Introduction to Pascal:
Including Turbo Pascal
(Second Edition)
Rodnay Zaks
464pp. Ref. 533-6
This best-selling tutorial builds complete mastery of Pascal—from basic structured programming concepts, to advanced I/O, data structures, file operations, sets, pointers and lists, and more. Both ISO Standard and Turbo Pascal.

Introduction to Turbo BASIC
Douglas Hergert
523pp. Ref. 441-0
A complete tutorial and guide to this now highly professional language: Turbo BASIC, including important Turbo extras such as parameter passing, structured loops, long integers, recursion, and 8087 compatibility for high-speed numerical operation.

Introduction to Turbo Prolog
(Second Edition)
Carl Townsend
325pp. Ref. 611-1
Written with beginning and intermediate users in mind, this thorough guide covers practical techniques for I/O, string and arithmetic operations, windows, graphics, sound, expert systems, natural language interfaces, and simulation systems. Includes exercises. For Version 2.0.

Mastering C
Craig Bolon
437pp. Ref. 326-0
This in-depth guide stresses planning, testing, efficiency and portability in C

applications. Topics include data types, storage classes, arrays, pointers, data structures, control statements, I/O and the C function library.

Mastering QuickBASIC
Rita Belserene
450pp. Ref. 589-1

Readers build professional programs with this extensive language tutorial. Fundamental commands are mixed with the author's tips and tricks so that users can create their own applications. Program templates are included for video displays, computer games, and working with databases and printers. For Version 4.5.

Mastering QuickC
Stan Kelly-Bootle
602pp. Ref. 550-6

This extensive tutorial covers C language programming and features the latest version of QuickC. Veteran author Kelly-Bootle uses many examples to explain language and style, covering data types, storage classes, file I/O, the Graphics Toolbox, and the window-oriented debugger. For Version 2.0.

Mastering Turbo C
(Second Edition)
Stan Kelly-Bootle
609pp. Ref. 595-6

With a foreword by Borland International President Philippe Kahn, this new edition has been expanded to include full details on Version 2.0. Learn theory and practical programming, with tutorials on data types, real numbers and characters, controlling program flow, file I/O, and producing color charts and graphs. Through Version 2.

Mastering Turbo Pascal 5
(Second Edition)
Douglas Hergert
628pp. Ref. 647-2

Explore the potential of the fast and efficient programming environment offered by Turbo Pascal 5 Version 5.5. Discover the powerful new advanced object-oriented programming, in addition to all the essential elements of a professional programming language; file-handling procedures; recursion; support for the 8087 numeric coprocessor chip; and user-defined units.

QuickC Instant Reference
SYBEX Prompter Series
J. Daniel Gifford
394pp. Ref. 586-7, 4 3/4" × 8"

This concise guide to QuickC key words and library functions should be on every programmer's desk. Organized alphabetically for quick and easy access, it covers all the essential information such as format, syntax, arguments, and usage.

Systems Programming in Microsoft C
Michael J. Young
604pp. Ref. 570-0

This sourcebook of advanced C programming techniques is for anyone who wants to make the most of their C compiler or Microsoft QuickC. It includes a comprehensive, annotated library of systems functions, ready to compile and call.

Systems Programming in Turbo C
Michael J. Young
365pp. Ref. 467-4

An introduction to advanced programming with Borland's Turbo C, and a goldmine of ready-made routines for the system programmer's library: DOS and BIOS interfacing, interrupt handling, windows, graphics, expanded memory, UNIX utilities, and more.

Turbo Pascal Toolbox
(Second Edition)
Frank Dutton
425pp. Ref. 602-2

This collection of tested, efficient Turbo Pascal building blocks gives a boost to intermediate-level programmers, while teaching effective programming by example. Topics include accessing DOS, menus, bit maps, screen handling, and much more.

UTILITIES

The ABC's of the IBM PC (Second Edition)
Joan Lasselle/Carol Ramsay
167pp. Ref. 370-8

Hands-on experience—without technical detail—for first-time users. Step-by-step tutorials show how to use essential commands, handle disks, use applications programs, and harness the PC's special capabilities.

Mastering the Norton Utilities
Peter Dyson
373pp. Ref. 575-1

In-depth descriptions of each Norton utility make this book invaluable for beginning and experienced users alike. Each utility is described clearly with examples and the text is organized so that readers can put Norton to work right away. Version 4.5.

Mastering PC Tools Deluxe
Peter Dyson
400pp. Ref. 654-5

A complete hands-on guide to the timesaving—and "lifesaving"—utility programs in Version 5.5 of PC Tools Deluxe. Contains concise tutorials and in-depth discussion of every aspect of using PC Tools—from high speed backups, to data recovery, to using Desktop applications.

Mastering SideKick Plus
Gene Weisskopf
394pp. Ref. 558-1

Employ all of Sidekick's powerful and expanded features with this hands-on guide to the popular utility. Features include comprehensive and detailed coverage of time management, note taking, outlining, auto dialing, DOS file management, math, and copy-and-paste functions.

Up & Running with Norton Utilities
Rainer Bartel
140pp. Ref. 659-6

Get up and running in the shortest possible time in just 20 lessons or "steps." Learn to restore disks and files, use UnErase, edit your floppy disks, retrieve lost data and more. Or use the book to evaluate the software before you purchase. Through Version 4.2.

COMMUNICATIONS

Mastering Crosstalk XVI (Second Edition)
Peter W. Gofton
225pp. Ref. 642-1

Introducing the communications program Crosstalk XVI for the IBM PC. As well as providing extensive examples of command and script files for programming Crosstalk, this book includes a detailed description of how to use the program's more advanced features, such as windows, talking to mini or mainframe, customizing the keyboard and answering calls and background mode.

Mastering PROCOMM PLUS
Bob Campbell
400pp. Ref. 657-X

Learn all about communications and information retrieval as you master and use PROCOMM PLUS. Topics include choosing and using a modem; automatic dialing; using on-line services (featuring Compu-Serve) and more. Through Version 1.1b; also covers PROCOMM, the "shareware" version.

Mastering Serial Communications
Peter W. Gofton
289pp. Ref. 180-2

The software side of communications, with details on the IBM PC's serial programming, the XMODEM and Kermit protocols, non-ASCII data transfer, interrupt-level programming and more. Sample programs in C, assembly language and BASIC.

HARDWARE

From Chips to Systems: An Introduction to Microcomputers (Second Edition)
Rodnay Zaks/Alexander Wolfe
580pp. Ref. 377-5

The best-selling introduction to microcomputer hardware—now fully updated, revised, and illustrated. Such recent advances as 32-bit processors and RISC architecture are introduced and explained for the first time in a beginning text.

Microprocessor Interfacing Techniques (Third Edition)
Austin Lesea/Rodnay Zaks
456pp. Ref. 029-6

This handbook is for engineers and hobbyists alike, covering every aspect of interfacing microprocessors with peripheral devices. Topics include assembling a CPU, basic I/O, analog circuitry, and bus standards.

The RS-232 Solution (Second Edition)
Joe Campbell
193pp. Ref. 488-7

For anyone wanting to use their computer's serial port, this complete how-to guide is updated and expanded for trouble-free RS-232-C interfacing from scratch. Solution shows you how to connect a variety of computers, printers, and modems, and it includes details for IBM PC AT, PS/2, and Macintosh.

NETWORKS

The ABC's of Novell Netware
Jeff Woodward
282pp. Ref. 614-6

For users who are new to PC's or networks, this entry-level tutorial outlines each basic element and operation of Novell. The ABC's introduces computer hardware and software, DOS, network organization and security, and printing and communicating over the netware system.

Mastering Novell Netware
Cheryl C. Currid/Craig A. Gillett
500pp. Ref. 630-8

This book is a thorough guide for System Administrators to installing and operating a microcomputer network using Novell Netware. Mastering covers actually setting up a network from start to finish, design, administration, maintenance, and troubleshooting.

Networking with TOPS
Steven William Rimmer
350pp. Ref. 565-4

A hands on guide to the most popular user friendly network available. This book will walk a user through setting up the hardware and software of a variety of TOPS configurations, from simple two station networks through whole offices. It explains the realities of sharing files between PC compatibles and Macintoshes, of sharing printers and other peripherals and, most important, of the real world performance one can expect when the network is running.

DATABASES

The ABC's of dBASE III PLUS
Robert Cowart
264pp. Ref. 379-1

The most efficient way to get beginners up and running with dBASE. Every 'how' and 'why' of database management is demonstrated through tutorials and practical dBASE III PLUS applications.

The ABC's of dBASE IV
Robert Cowart
338pp. Ref. 531-X

This superb tutorial introduces beginners to the concept of databases and practical dBASE IV applications featuring the new menu-driven interface, the new report writer, and Query by Example.

The ABC's of Paradox
Charles Siegel
300pp. Ref. 573-5
Easy to understand and use, this introduction is written so that the computer novice can create, edit, and manage complex Paradox databases. This primer is filled with examples of the Paradox 3.0 menu structure.

Advanced Techniques in dBASE III PLUS
Alan Simpson
454pp. Ref. 369-4
A full course in database design and structured programming, with routines for inventory control, accounts receivable, system management, and integrated databases.

dBASE Instant Reference
SYBEX Prompter Series
Alan Simpson
471pp. Ref. 484-4; 4 3/4" × 8"
Comprehensive information at a glance: a brief explanation of syntax and usage for every dBASE command, with step-by-step instructions and exact keystroke sequences. Commands are grouped by function in twenty precise categories.

dBASE IV Programmer's Instant Reference
SYBEX Prompter Series
Alan Simpson
544pp. Ref. 538-7, 4 3/4" × 8"
This comprehensive reference to every dBASE command and function has everything for the dBASE programmer in a compact, pocket-sized book. Fast and easy access to adding data, sorting, performing calculations, managing multiple databases, memory variables and arrays, windows and menus, networking, and much more. Version 1.1.

dBASE III PLUS Programmer's Reference Guide
SYBEX Ready Reference Series
Alan Simpson
1056pp. Ref. 508-5
Programmers will save untold hours and effort using this comprehensive, well-organized dBASE encyclopedia. Complete technical details on commands and functions, plus scores of often-needed algorithms.

dBASE IV User's Desktop Companion
SYBEX Ready Reference Series
Alan Simpson
950pp. Ref. 523-9
This easy-to-use reference provides an exhaustive resource guide to taking full advantage of the powerful non-programming features of the dBASE IV Control Center. This book discusses query by example, custom reports and data entry screens, macros, the application generator, and the dBASE command and programming language.

dBASE IV User's Instant Reference
SYBEX Prompter Series
Alan Simpson
349pp. Ref. 605-7, 4 3/4" × 8"
This handy pocket-sized reference book gives every new dBASE IV user fast and easy access to any dBASE command. Arranged alphabetically and by function, each entry includes a description, exact syntax, an example, and special tips from Alan Simpson.

Mastering dBASE III PLUS: A Structured Approach
Carl Townsend
342pp. Ref. 372-4
In-depth treatment of structured programming for custom dBASE solutions. An ideal study and reference guide for applications developers, new and experienced users with an interest in efficient programming.

Mastering dBASE IV Programming
Carl Townsend
496pp. Ref. 540-9
This task-oriented book introduces structured dBASE IV programming and commands by setting up a general ledger system, an invoice system, and a quotation management system. The author carefully explores the unique character of

dBASE IV based on his in-depth understanding of the program.

Mastering Q & A
(Second Edition)
Greg Harvey
540pp. Ref. 452-6

This hands-on tutorial explores the Q & A Write, File, and Report modules, and the Intelligent Assistant. English-language command processor, macro creation, interfacing with other software, and more, using practical business examples.

Mastering Paradox
(Fourth Edition)
Alan Simpson
636pp. Ref. 612-X

Best selling author Alan Simpson simplifies all aspects of Paradox for the beginning to intermediate user. The book starts with database basics, covers multiple tables, graphics, custom applications with PAL, and the Personal Programmer. For Version 3.0.

Power User's Guide to R:BASE
Alan Simpson/Cheryl Currid/Craig Gillett
446pp. Ref. 354-6

Supercharge your R:BASE applications with this straightforward tutorial that covers system design, structured programming, managing multiple data tables, and more. Sample applications include ready-to-run mailing, inventory and accounts receivable systems. Through Version 2.11.

Understanding dBASE IV
(Special Edition)
Alan Simpson
880pp. Ref. 509-3

This Special Edition is the best introduction to dBASE IV, written by 1 million-reader-strong dBASE expert Alan Simpson. First it gives basic skills for creating and manipulating efficient databases. Then the author explains how to make reports, manage multiple databases, and build applications. Includes Fast Track speed notes.

Quick Guide to dBASE:
The Visual Approach
David Kolodney
382pp. Ref. 596-4

This illustrated tutorial provides the beginner with a working knowledge of all the basic functions of dBASE IV. Images of each successive dBASE screen tell how to create and modify a database, add, edit, sort and select records, and print custom labels and reports.

Simpson's dBASE Tips and
Tricks (For dBASE III PLUS)
Alan Simpson
420pp. Ref. 383-X

A unique library of techniques and programs shows how creative use of built-in features can solve all your needs—without expensive add-on products or external languages. Spreadsheet functions, graphics, and much more.

Understanding dBASE III
Alan Simpson
300pp. Ref. 267-1

dBASE commands and concepts are illustrated throughout with practical, business oriented examples—for mailing list handling, accounts receivable, and inventory design. Contains scores of tips and techniques for maximizing efficiency and meeting special needs.

Understanding dBASE III PLUS
Alan Simpson
415pp. Ref. 349-X

A solid sourcebook of training and ongoing support. Everything from creating a first database to command file programming is presented in working examples, with tips and techniques you won't find anywhere else.

Understanding R:BASE
Alan Simpson/Karen Watterson
609pp. Ref. 503-4

This is the definitive R:BASE tutorial, for use with either OS/2 or DOS. Hands-on lessons cover every aspect of the software, from creating and using a database, to custom systems. Includes Fast Track speed notes.

Understanding Oracle
James T. Perry/Joseph G. Lateer
634pp. Ref. 534-4
A comprehensive guide to the Oracle database management system for administrators, users, and applications developers. Covers everything in Version 5 from database basics to multi-user systems, performance, and development tools including SQL*Forms, SQL*Report, and SQL*Calc. Includes Fast Track speed notes.

Understanding SQL
Martin Gruber
400pp. Ref. 644-8
This comprehensive tutorial in Structured Query Language (SQL) is suitable for beginners, and for SQL users wishing to increase their skills. From basic principles to complex SQL applications, the text builds fluency and confidence using concise hands-on lessons and easy-to-follow examples.

Up & Running with Q&A
Ranier Bartel
140pp. Ref. 645-6
Obtain practical results with Q&A in the shortest possible time. Learn to design and program forms, use macros, format text, use utilities, and more. Or use the book to help you decide whether to purchase the program.

SCIENCE AND ENGINEERING

1-2-3 for Scientists and Engineers
William J. Orvis
341pp. Ref. 407-0
Fast, elegant solutions to common problems in science and engineering, using Lotus 1-2-3. Tables and plotting, curve fitting, statistics, derivatives, integrals and differentials, solving systems of equations, and more.

BASIC Programs for Scientists and Engineers
Alan R. Miller
318pp. Ref. 073-3
The algorithms presented in this book are programmed in standard BASIC code which should be usable with almost any implementation of BASIC. Includes statistical calculations, matrix algebra, curve fitting, integration, and more.

FORTRAN Programs for Scientists and Engineers (Second Edition)
Alan R. Miller
280pp. Ref. 571-9
In this collection of widely used scientific algorithms—for statistics, vector and matrix operations, curve fitting, and more—the author stresses effective use of little-known and powerful features of FORTRAN.

Turbo BASIC Programs for Scientists and Engineers
Alan R. Miller
276pp. Ref. 429-1
This practical text develops commonly-needed algorithms for scientific and engineering applications, and programs them in Turbo BASIC. Simultaneous solution, curve fitting, nonlinear equations, numerical integration and more.

Turbo Pascal Programs for Scientists and Engineers
Alan R. Miller
332pp. Ref. 424-0
The author develops commonly-needed algorithms for science and engineering, then programs them in Turbo Pascal. Includes algorithms for statistics, simultaneous solutions, curve fitting, integration, and nonlinear equations.

PERFORMANCE PROGRAMMING TOOLKIT

A Companion Disk Set for *MS-DOS Advanced Programming*

For readers who would like to make immediate use of all the listings in this book, and who would like enhanced versions of many of the utilities and functions that have been presented, a companion diskette set is available. The two diskettes contain the following files:

- All source code listings as they are presented in the book, in ASCII format and ready to compile or assemble

- The executable versions of all programs in the book

- An enhanced version of the screen designer presented in Chapter 8, written entirely in C

- An enhanced set of screen and window management functions, callable from C

- Additional utilities and functions not included in the book

---

ORDER FORM

_____ copies of the Companion Diskette Set for *MS-DOS Advanced Programming* @ $29.50 each   _____

_____ California residents: add 6% sales tax   _____

_____ Shipping and Handling: add $2.50 ($5.00 foreign)   _____

Total Order _____

_____ I would like to receive information on other development tools for MS-DOS and OS/2 from Michael J. Young, Software Engineering.

Name _____

Address _____

City / State / Zip _____

All diskettes are in standard 5-¼'' IBM format. Please send a check for full payment payable to Michael J. Young (no purchase orders or bank cards; for foreign orders please send an international money order in U.S. dollars). Your diskettes will be shipped immediately. Send your order to:

Michael J. Young, Software Engineering
P.O. Box 5068
Mill Valley, CA 94942

SYBEX is not affiliated with Software Engineering and assumes no responsibility for any defect in the disk or program.

SYBEX Computer Books *are different.*

Here is why . . .

At SYBEX, each book is designed with you in mind. Every manuscript is carefully selected and supervised by our editors, who are themselves computer experts. We publish the best authors, whose technical expertise is matched by an ability to write clearly and to communicate effectively. Programs are thoroughly tested for accuracy by our technical staff. Our computerized production department goes to great lengths to make sure that each book is well-designed.

In the pursuit of timeliness, SYBEX has achieved many publishing firsts. SYBEX was among the first to integrate personal computers used by authors and staff into the publishing process. SYBEX was the first to publish books on the CP/M operating system, microprocessor interfacing techniques, word processing, and many more topics.

Expertise in computers and dedication to the highest quality product have made SYBEX a world leader in computer book publishing. Translated into fourteen languages, SYBEX books have helped millions of people around the world to get the most from their computers. We hope we have helped you, too.

For a complete catalog of our publications:

SYBEX, Inc. 2021 Challenger Drive, #100, Alameda, CA 94501
Tel: (415) 523-8233/(800) 227-2346   Telex: 336311
Fax: (415) 523-2373

■ FILE AND DEVICE I/O

TRADITIONAL FCB FUNCTIONS

Function Number	DOS Version	Description
14h	1.0	Sequential read.
15h	1.0	Sequential write.
24h	1.0	Set random record field.
21h	1.0	Random read, single record.
22h	1.0	Random write, single record.
27h	1.0	Random block read, multiple records.
28h	1.0	Random block write, multiple records.

HANDLE FUNCTIONS

Function Number	DOS Version	Description
3Fh	2.0	Read from a file or device.
40h	2.0	Write to a file or device.
42h	2.0	Move file read-write pointer.
44h	2.0	I/O control for devices.

■ NETWORK MANAGEMENT FUNCTIONS

Function Number	DOS Version	Description
5Ch	3.0	Lock/unlock file access.
5Eh	3.1	Get machine name, set/get printer setup.
5Fh	3.1	Get redirection list (nonlocal network assignments), redirect device/cancel redirection.

■ MEMORY AND PROCESS MANAGEMENT

Function Number	DOS Version	Description
26h	1.0	Create new program segment prefix.
48h	2.0	Allocate memory.
49h	2.0	Free allocated memory.
4Ah	2.0	Modify allocated memory block.
4Bh	2.0	Load or execute a child program.
4Dh	2.0	Get return status from a child process.